Writing Queer History

Writing History

The Writing History series publishes accessible overviews of particular fields in history, focusing on the practical application of theory in historical writing. Books in the series succinctly explain central concepts to demonstrate the ways in which they have informed effective historical writing. They analyse key historical texts and their producers within their institutional arrangement and as part of a wider social discourse. The series' holistic approach means students benefit from an enhanced understanding of how to negotiate the contours of successful historical writing.

Series editors: Stefan Berger (Ruhr University Bochum, Germany), Heiko Feldner (Cardiff University, UK) and Kevin Passmore (Cardiff University, UK)

Published:

Writing Medieval History, edited by Nancy F. Partner
Writing Early Modern History, edited by Garthine Walker
Writing Contemporary History, edited by Robert Gildea and Anne Simonin
Writing Gender History (second edition), Laura Lee Downs
Writing Postcolonial History, Rochona Majumdar
Writing the Holocaust, edited by Jean-Marc Dreyfus and Daniel Langton
Writing the History of Memory, edited by Stefan Berger and Bill Niven
Writing the History of Crime, Paul Knepper
Writing the History of Nationalism, edited by Stefan Berger and Eric Storm
Writing Transnational History, Fiona Paisley
Writing History (third edition), edited by Stefan Berger, Heiko Feldner and Kevin Passmore
Writing Visual Histories, edited by Florence Grant and Ludmilla Jordanova
Writing Material Culture History (second edition), edited by Anne Gerritsen and Giorgio Riello
Writing the History of Slavery, edited by David Doddington and Enrico del Lago
Writing the History of the Humanities, edited by Herman Paul

Forthcoming:

Writing Gender History (third edition), Laura Lee Downs
Writing Animal History, Timm Schönfelder
Writing Game Histories, Esther Wright, Nick Webber and Iain Donald
Writing the History of Disabilities: Agency, Intersections and Concepts, Monika Baár and Paul van Trigt

Writing Queer History

Matt Cook

BLOOMSBURY ACADEMIC
LONDON · NEW YORK · OXFORD · NEW DELHI · SYDNEY

BLOOMSBURY ACADEMIC
Bloomsbury Publishing Plc, 50 Bedford Square, London, WC1B 3DP, UK
Bloomsbury Publishing Inc, 1359 Broadway, New York, NY 10018, USA
Bloomsbury Publishing Ireland, 29 Earlsfort Terrace, Dublin 2, D02 AY28, Ireland

BLOOMSBURY, BLOOMSBURY ACADEMIC and the Diana logo are trademarks of
Bloomsbury Publishing Plc

First published in Great Britain 2026

A catalogue record for this book is available from the British Library.

A catalog record for this book is available from the Library of Congress.

ISBN: HB: 978-1-4742-4751-1
        PB: 978-1-4742-4752-8
        ePDF: 978-1-4742-4754-2
        eBook: 978-1-4742-4753-5

Series: Writing History

Typeset by RefineCatch Limited, Bungay, Suffolk
Printed and bound in Great Britain

To find out more about our authors and books visit www.bloomsbury.com
and sign up for our newsletters.

For Ben, Jaya, Chet and Harrison
In memory of Stephen Kenneth Tooke

Contents

Preface and Acknowledgements

My fiftieth birthday fell on 6 August, 2019, six months before the Covid-19 virus hit the United Kingdom. I celebrated in a way that would soon become unimaginable – with my large birth family, my family of friends, colleagues from Birkbeck College (University of London), fellow editors from *History Workshop Journal* (*HWJ*), and what law makers in my early adulthood would have described as my 'pretended family':[1] my then-teenage children, their mothers, their other dad (my ex), my current partner, and our newly adopted son. This cast of people, their coming together, speaks to social and cultural changes in Britain over a lifetime which coincides almost exactly with the period since the Stonewall riots in New York of late June and early July 1969.

After I came out to my mum in the late 1980s, she told me that she distantly remembered reading of some trouble in New York when she was heavily pregnant that summer. She may have remembered or she might have thought she did because those events became an activist, community, and campaigning touchstone and a pivot in queer collective memory as well as queer history making. Stonewall was commemorated annually with pride/Pride in New York from 1970, and then in London from 1972, Paris and Madrid from 1977, and Berlin from 1979. These were just some of the metropolitan celebrations in the Global North which indirectly served a particular historical progress narrative about identity, community, rights and equalities, but which shaded out other ways of thinking about the queer past.

The cultural significance heaped upon Stonewall meant that I was busy in my own fiftieth birthday year. I was involved in working up a feature on Stonewall in global perspective for *History Workshop Journal* and I spoke at conferences in Manchester and New York on Stonewall's multivalent, transnational and homonational legacies.[2] Conference events in New York included a walking tour in which our guide described the policing, topographical and countercultural contexts of the riots, including the too often forgotten involvement of trans people and people of colour. He also noted precedent protests in and around this part of the city and in San Francisco and Chicago which could each have become fabled starting points for a movement.[3] After the walk, I took in a commemorative exhibition in the New York Public Library: a visual history of the LGBTQ+ movement 'post-Stonewall', showcasing material collected and curated by the library in the years since the riots.[4] There were two parades in Manhattan in this commemoration year. The Gay Liberation March traced the original route in a riposte to the larger 'official' NYC Pride parade underpinned by corporate sponsorship. The former spoke of community roots, 'lost' history, and queer 'authenticity' and difference; the latter of 'distance travelled', of 'progress', and of the individualism, commercialization and neo-liberalism which had shifted the coordinates of LGBTQ+ lives in this city in the years since 1969.[5] Many people attended both; many more people who identified queerly in various ways or who do things considered queer went to neither.[6] Identifications, affiliations and commitments remain diverse, diffuse and contradictory – rather like the queer histories I describe in this book.

These events of 2019 turned me back across my own fifty years with a sense of vertigo – across the varied and tangled social, cultural, political, sexual and legal changes of that period; the layering up of new themes and approaches in history; and the intimately related twists and turns in rendering the queer past which I track in the pages to come. I wrote the first draft of this book in the midst of the pandemic and lockdown, doom scrolling news of Covid, of incompetent and malign governments, of police brutality and the Black Lives Matter movement, and of burgeoning environmental crisis. I felt acutely conscious of the power and privilege attendant to my middle-classness, whiteness, cis-maleness and middle age. In the pandemic I had financial security, I had the company of a partner and small son, and I had space. Writing in this context pushed me to think further about the play of power around desire, sexuality and gender, about disciplinary and institutional power, and about the way they related to my position, experience and history. Partly as a result, this book emerged as more personal than I had first envisaged. I wanted to give some account of myself as well as the genre of history I work with because the former has deeply affected my engagement with the latter. More broadly, gay and lesbian, LGBTQ+, queer and trans histories have emerged as especially personal and political projects, and *Writing Queer History* illustrates this in part by reflecting on the way these things have intersected for me. It is thus also about the privileges that are attendant to making queer history from within the academy, which in large part determine which histories get made, which are ignored and side-lined, which find a wide audience and which do not. These factors are not tangential or a footnote: they are a fundamental part of the story I tell.

Concerted work on that Covid draft had to wait. A three-year spell as Head of Department at Birkbeck, a job move, forfeited research leave, and some serious ill health delayed my proper re-engagement. When I did come back to it properly I found what I had written was already out of date. So much exciting new work had appeared; some of the growing number of doctoral students in the field had completed their PhDs, and LGBTQ+ public and community history had burgeoned. The political landscape had shifted again. In the United Kingdom there was increasingly vocal transphobia and backsliding in government promises and rhetoric. In the United States the re-election of Donald Trump as president presaged a full force assault on minoritized people via intersecting attacks on Equality, Diversity and Inclusion programmes, universities, and representation in museums and heritage sites. In accordance with Trump's order to restore 'biological truth' to federal government, for example, references to transgender people were removed from the National Park Service website for the Stonewall National Monument, erasing (again) their involvement in the riots and so also the grassroots allyship evident (in all its unease) at that moment. Such allyship has become visible again in activist and scholarly work in the face of this fresh assault: queer and trans history has become more entwined in the time since I left off that first draft. Uncertain of my way forward, I invited queer and trans historian colleagues to join me in a discussion of the catching up I needed to do. Their generosity – intellectually, in making the time, in coming together – speaks to a longstanding tradition of support and collaboration in LGBTQ+ historical work. Meanwhile, the very fact that there was catching up to do speaks to the contingency of a book like this dealing with a field that is so alive, productive and urgent. *Writing Queer History* is certainly not conclusive.

The period since I started writing the book in 2019 has been rich in such generosity. That I started writing at all is thanks to a fellowship from Leverhulme Trust which gave me the time to do the initial research. Support for research visits during that year and subsequently came from Birkbeck College, University of London. These trips gave me the opportunity to talk to innovative and dedicated archivists, museum and heritage professions, tour guides and film-makers who provided the detail and inspiration I needed for chapters 4 and 5 especially. I am particularly grateful to Runar Jordåen (Bergen's Skievt Archive), Linda Chernis (GALA in Johannesburg), Gerard Koskovich (GBLT Society, Museum and Archive in San Francisco), Ben Miller (Schwules Museum in Berlin), Stefan Dickers (Bishopsgate, London), Siobhan Fahey (Rebel Dykes) and E.-J. Scott (Museum of Transology in Brighton and nationwide).

I began trying the material out when I moved jobs to Oxford University in 2023: in a research seminar for the Women's, Gender and Queer History Centre, in the content of courses I taught on 'Approaches to Queer and Trans History' and on 'Queer Britain', and more gesturally in my inaugural lecture.[7] The serious and thoughtful way in which colleagues and students at all levels engaged in the ideas and material I presented in these various forums was touching and highly productive. My PhD students at Birkbeck and Oxford have inspired with their own work and in the conversations we have had in supervision. They, together with the doctoral students I have had the privilege to examine over these last several years, give me hope for the future of queer and trans history. Several of them appear in the book alongside scholars and scholar activists from earlier decades, and to whom I also owe a debt. Such intergenerational 'conversations' in texts and in-person are crucial to the field, and in this book I deliberately flag work by early career and more established historians.

I am very lucky to have known and worked with some queer history pioneers, and several have generously engaged with this project. And so my thanks go to Chris Waters who first encouraged me to take on this commission from Bloomsbury and fired my imagination for what the book could be. Alison Oram, Jeffrey Weeks, Heike Bauer and Fiona Candlin read drafts, as did Jennifer Evans, Tone Hellesund, Peter Edelberg, Jack Doyle and Glyn Davis for that reflective gathering I mentioned above. This came at a moment of some despair about my then precarious health and also about the book (I am used to working from the archives up; *Writing Queer History* demanded an overview I was struggling to deliver). Knowingly or not, these readers picked me up and set me back to work with their astute observation, commentary and critique, and also with their friendship. Jaya Rathbone helped with fact checking and referencing as I had my head down rewriting, and nine months later Mori Reithmayr applied their keen editorial eye to the reworked draft and offered invaluable suggestions for further reading. In the weeks before submission, my new colleague and friend, Sarah Knott, read and commented with what I am learning is her characteristic clear-sightedness, precision and care. Between them, Jaya, Mori and Sarah topped up my red pen and gave me the impetus I needed to finish up.

I am hugely grateful to all of these people. They bear no responsibility, though, for the way I acted (or failed to act) on their advice: the errors and missteps in what follows are entirely my own. I delivered this final manuscript to Bloomsbury with some embarrassment. It was delayed repeatedly and I am thankful for the patience of the editors at Bloomsbury (Emily Drewe,

Megan Harris and Maddie Smith), the series editors (Garthine Walker, Kevin Passmore, Heiko Feldner, and Stefan Berger), and the production team (Don Cleeter, Merv Honeywood, and Paige Harris). I am grateful also to the anonymous reviewers who agreed to read and comment (extremely helpfully) on an early uncooked draft.

The people I mentioned in the opening paragraph of this preface – my family of birth and of choice, my friends, and my colleagues at History Workshop, Birkbeck, and I add now Oxford – have provided care and support in ways that directly and indirectly allowed me to keep readings and writing. My husband, Ben Tooke, has seen me through these rocky years with his unerring empathy and sustaining commitment to kindness. My children – Jaya, Chetan and Harrison – inspire me daily and light my way. This book is dedicated to these wonderful people, and stands in memory of Stephen Tooke, my father-in-law, who died as I was finishing up. He understood fathering expansively, inclusively and with a deep ethic of care. I am privileged to have known him.

Introduction: Tendencies[1]

History is what we make of and do with the past. It can fix and normalize forms and structures of power and be a 'tool of organized forgetting'.[2] But it can also take certainty to task and trouble the status quo when it delivers alternate stories, signals unexpected connections and cross-overs, and shows how apparently intractable norms have shifted unevenly, incrementally and sometimes dramatically. This more exciting potential of history and of the historicity (that is, the historical dimensions and complexion) of the present, brings with it a sense of contingency and of ideas and ways of being changing with time and place.[3] It is this quality that has made history especially important to LGBTQ+ lives, communities and politics. Conjuring lives lived queerly and in divergent ways in the past can be sustaining and give a sense of possibility and hope in hostile and marginalizing contexts now. This makes history worth working at and fighting for, even as, indeed because, it has omitted and excluded so much.[4]

The specific marker 'queer history' has only been around since the mid 1990s – a response in part to the provocations of queer theory from the start of that decade. The account here begins earlier, though, because the methods and tendencies associated with queer history are clearly identifiable under other names, most obviously homosexual history of the 1950s and 1960s, lesbian and gay history from the 1970s, and a broader history of sexuality which was gaining some limited traction as an academic subdiscipline in the 1980s. Indeed the story this book tells is partly about the overlaps between these and other closely aligned historical genres.

Thinking about queer history in this broad and connective way means looking at a wide ranging and multidimensional practice. For the last fifty plus years it has been undertaken by activist, community and academic historians, within and well beyond university settings, across different disciplines and genres of writing, art and performance, and in relation to short and much longer periods of time – from a single year to several centuries. Some of this work has focused on individuals, streets and bars, and on activism and social movements. Some has looked at queer domesticities and queer lives lived far away from traditional sites of socializing and politics. Some has conjured the broader queer dimensions of particular cities, regions, or whole countries. And some has ranged across the globe, showing how transnational flows of people and ideas have shaped desires, lives, understandings and experiences. Historians working on queer themes have tried to account for how people acted and understood themselves and to discern what did and did not change, why, and with what consequences. They have approached and conceptualized history and its significance to the present in a variety of ways, sometimes, from the early 1990s, following those queer theoretical turns. Much work has been done in conversation with sociology, geography, anthropology, and literary, film and cultural studies, and in relation to other historical traditions and fields – from social and cultural history through to global, women's, gender and postcolonial history, the history of the emotions, and disability history. Historians who identify themselves first and foremost by period or place (as medievalists or modernists, Americanists and Africanists, for example) have brought further methods and sources to bear on queer historical work. The archive, heritage and museums sectors have meanwhile become increasingly involved in queer historical practice, frequently engaging creatively with activist and community history projects which have been the backbone of much queer history since the 1970s.

Writing Queer History is an introduction to this area of work. Across the five chapters is a consideration of queer history's own history and shifts in focus and approach. The book carries reflections on the challenges and rewards of working in this way and the sources, fragments, gaps and silences which historians navigate to assemble a sense of the queer past. Given the ephemeral nature of desire and its expression, and the compelling need felt by many to hide the illegal or 'immoral' sex they were having, this work has often been about supposition and chasing shadows rather than making decisive claims.[5] It has also often been about developing an understanding of context and the conditions in which desires were mobilized, sexual types gained definition, and forms of collective consciousness took shape. Queer history is a body of work which has struggled with knotty questions about agency, identification, emotion and the inexplicable and unknowable, and so about the relationship between the social and cultural on the one hand and the individual and subjective on the other. As a result, it has tended to be especially alert to the specificities and anomalies of place and time, and has highlighted fractures in synthesizing and grand narratives which can easily obscure those who do not fit straightforwardly within them or are purposely excluded. Such narratives rarely account for what historian Anna Clark describes as 'twilight moments', those times when (and places where) people behaved contrary to type, expectation, or 'law and custom', though usually without fundamentally 'threaten[ing] the continuity of class, religion and racist structures'.[6]

Such perspectives on the past encourage us to be open to a gamut of possibilities in terms of identification, bodily pleasures and pains, and allegiance, connection and community. Queer histories thus not only engage with the direct oppression of queerly-identified people (crucial as this is to grasp) but with dynamics and imbalances of power – associated, for example, with colonialism, race, gender and class – and with what these meant for understandings and experiences of desire, self, and intimate and social relationships.[7] There are glimpses in this of the entangled factors at stake in the way people experienced their bodies and themselves, and of the shifting ideas about what it has meant to be considered human or less than human. Queer historians tend to work from the premise that we do not and can not already know how people in the past understood themselves in relation to the desires they felt and the sex they were having. A core queer historical task is to locate the particular social, cultural, political and economic factors which shaped those understandings and experiences and which mobilized desire. Thinking queerly in relation to the past thus means trying to hold our presumptions back (when we can identify them) and being alert to other possibilities and configurations.[8] If we lay off the binary goggles we are more likely to notice that, for example, bisexuality (as lived practice rather than an identity) was often commonplace or that the gender split (on which the categories of gay and lesbian depend) was not always and everywhere so stark, with implications for the way desire and sexual acts were understood and experienced.[9] As a consequence, we perceive forms of sexual selfhood and behaviour in the past which do not straightforwardly trend towards – or map onto – contemporary Western understandings of sexuality and the identity categories attendant to them. In relation to those identity categories – like lesbian, gay, bisexual and trans – queer historians have meanwhile traced their distinct modern histories and the social/cultural contexts and power dynamics from which they emerged and in which they played out, most pressingly of colonialism, race science and shifts in norms, ideologies and hierarchies of gender.[10]

Writing Queer History shows that this work has been driven by the desire to uncover those 'hidden from history',[11] to find antecedents and 'touch[es] across time',[12] but also to discern the irreducible difference between queer past and present – to find particular dynamics, productions and experiences of desire in different times and places, without necessarily focusing on what gets carried forward into the story of 'what next'.[13] Fundamentally, queer history has sought in different ways to look askance and so trouble normative perspectives and the power of 'common sense'.[14] It has relatedly sought to complicate and question collective memories of progress and of the significance of particular events, turning points and heroes. Queer history has in this sense been myth-busting, even as it has also taken these myths seriously for the ways in which they have orientated and anchored identity and community at various moments. Myths and collective memories are in this manner very much part of the queer history project.[15]

The 'queer' in queer history gestures to a loosening of identity and looking beyond its bounds, but the usual focus remains same sex intimacy, sex and relationality and often the identities that have formed in association with these things. This is partly what connects queer history so closely to gay and lesbian history, which owns that focus, these objects of study, more explicitly or specifically. This is not antithetical to queer's related deployment as an approach to the past – an approach based on the attempt to withhold presentist presumptions about identity and configurations of desire in historical analysis (and which, as we will see in Chapter 1, owes much to pioneering gay and especially lesbian historians). But there is also tension between the two uses of queer in relation to history and historical practice. However much we avow a queer approach, the terminology alone can still compel our gaze and sense of what we will find. We land most often on queer subjects and can tend to look to them for the kind of radical alterity queer can suggest – at least theoretically – in the present. For these reasons historians have sometimes found, ironically, that other lenses and languages can be more queerly productive. Using notions of the twilight, of secrecy, or of kinship, for example, helps historians Anna Clark, Deborah Cohen and Jennifer Evans to reach more readily across the sexual and gender divisions that queer continues to imply (even as it seeks to undo them).[16] In so doing they suggest the limits of what queer can straightforwardly signal to the reader. It is not an easy catch all and the book's argument is that it often works best in dialogue with other approaches, terms and frames of reference – including those which came before. This means being sceptical about the familiar academic reflex of establishing critical distance from or dismissing precedent work. Better, perhaps, to think in terms of conversations started and ongoing with other ways of thinking about and making history, and holding the idea of queer history as an open, deft and promiscuous practice.

Seeking closely to determine its boundaries – and so what and who is in and out – runs counter to the queer historical project as I see it. I thus make no definitive claims for what queer history is or should ideally be. Instead the pages that follow survey work that has shaped this practice and that has been done either under its banner or in relation to it.

Working in this way might not allow for an encapsulation of queer history, but it does suggest certain 'tendencies', showing that it is (1) an intersectional practice which tends to be (2) deeply sceptical of received norms, common sense, generalization and transhistorical assumptions, and (3) acutely aware of historical gaps and silences (which practitioners have often sought to address creatively). It is (4) a patchwork of influences, historical traditions and turns (cultural, spatial and archival, for example), and (5) strongly associated with a cross-over of academic, community, activist, and public history. And then, relatedly, queer history is (6) especially reflexive about the contexts in which it is researched and written, and (7) deeply – in some ways problematically – connected to a sense of identity and community in the present. These seven tendencies trouble broader historical practices and conventions, encouraging historians working in other areas to rethink pat assumptions about their categories of analysis and frames of reference. It is also true, though, that these adjacent practices and conventions have been important to queer history making, and not least because they help make it legible to a wider audience. If queer history has been cutting edge and creative, it has also been entangled with other threads of historical work. This is very far from being a sequestered pursuit.

Language, perspectives, and context

The capaciousness of queer history comes in part from the multiple meanings of the word queer itself. It has its own history as a term of vile abuse; as a longstanding broad signifier of oddity (including perceived oddities of gender and sexual behaviour); as a self-deprecating and also activist identification; as a position radically opposed to prevailing norms, or, more problematically, to heterosexuality;[17] as a theoretical mode of deconstructive and radical questioning; and, more recently, as a jaunty synonym for gay and (less often) lesbian.[18] These divergent, clustering and shifting associations are part of what can complicate queer history but also allows it to function in an embracing way which is politically and epistemologically appealing and useful. In particular, though queer has been used to signal opposition to the norm in a way that echoes the gay/straight binary, historians have also used queer's more oblique sense of eccentricity to think about how sex and desire were configured within – and couched and sustained by – 'regimes of the normal' and were indivisible from them.[19] This includes contexts where same-sex affection and physical intimacy were themselves seen as ordinary or unremarkable. Literary scholar Eve Sedgwick captured this sense when she talked of queer's potential to refer to 'the open mesh of possibilities, gaps, overlaps, dissonances and resonances, lapses and excesses of meaning when the constituent elements of anyone's gender, of anyone's sexuality aren't made (or can't be made) to signify monolithically'.[20] This sense of queer is helpful when looking to the complexity of the past, and not least because it encourages us to think about desire and sex beyond the idea of a minority/majority (homosexual/heterosexual) model of sexuality which has had such a powerful hold in the Global North in the present and recent past.[21] How do we see the past differently when we withhold our contemporary classificatory systems? How, also, did we come to feel the truth of that system so decisively in the first place?

The past is meanwhile strewn with terms other than 'queer' to describe configurations of same-sex behaviour and desire: 'Sodomite', 'tribade', 'Molly', 'homosexual', 'fag', 'fairy', 'dyke', 'gay girl', to take just a handful in English. Each, like 'queer', has a different tenor and invokes different places and histories relating to class, race, gender and more besides. Some – like gay, lesbian, queer, trans and the collective LGBTQ+ and its variants (including the North American incorporation of two spirits in LGBTQ2S) – have been used in activism in ways which signal a particular contemporary political purpose in engaging with the past. These various terms are clearly not synonyms, and using queer as an umbrella, as I do here, is not to deny their particularity. This is especially important given the wider critique of queer as an elite white north American academic term and perspective and the related counter deployment of 'cuir' and 'queer of colour' as analytical positions which make more clearly visible the power imbalances associated with implicitly white 'queer' knowledge production, including in history.[22]

The dominance of English in the academic conference and publishing worlds has meant that some other terms, their histories, and their associations have been sidelined and obscured. There were, the feminist scholar and activist Manuela L. Picq reminds us, 'hundreds of languages across the Americas [which] had words referring to same-sex practices and non-binary, fluid understandings of gender long before the emergence of international sexual rights frameworks'.[23] In translation (and if translated), such terms can get pressed into the mould of queer or gay or trans, and so an English lexicon, logic, and history associated with sexology and a Western version of gay liberation.[24] And yet historians working in other languages have had to deploy these terms to get their work circulated. Partly as a result, non-English vocabulary can seem parochial even though placing it front and centre can be revelatory. Historian Howard Chiang notes that 'Renyao' in Mandarin translates as 'person demon' with the 'yao' signifying goblin, witch or devil, or the quality of being bewitching or enchanting. It has had, he notes, changing and slippery meanings, drawing together associations of 'gender dislocation, sex transformation, same-sex relations and male prostitution'.[25] This is a knot of meanings with colloquial and formal uses relating to a specific social and cultural context. But this gets lost in a simple translation to 'queer'. Chiang's analysis complicates taken-for-granted understandings of sex and desire in English, and also gestures to ways in which meanings have moved and morphed transnationally.[26] 'Queer' cannot adequately encompass all this (and more) but if held lightly and reflexively, alongside and in conjunction with other terms and frames, it can serve as a place holder of sorts for that 'open mesh of possibilities'. This is especially the case for historians – like me – working exclusively in English.

The historical environments we inhabit, including the languages we speak, shape the histories we write. Positionality matters, and there is no doubt that the narrow personal and broader social, political and cultural contexts in which I have lived underpin and steer what I know and the way I work – including on *Writing Queer History*. The book is fundamentally about what I have read and where I have been. I thus lean heavily into queer history making in and of Britain in the nineteenth and twentieth centuries and also into work from the United States which has had such an influence upon it and upon me. This is not to suggest the pre-eminence of output from these contexts, but it does help an argument about the significance of local, national, political, academic, and community contexts in what gets produced. I seek to localize queer history rather than making global claims from the context in which I happen to be most 'at home' intellectually and in my day-to-day. Reaching for other (and frequently 'othered') places, contexts and times alongside helps me to query and complicate the presumptions and tendencies attendant to this Anglo-American axis. The book remains necessarily partial; it is suggestive and invitational rather than definitive.

Lesbian, gay, trans and queer historians have routinely asked how our vision of the past is shaped by our personal histories and experiences, by political imperatives, by particular conceptions of time and memory, by disciplinary traditions and expectations, and by the force and direction of our own desires. Such reflexiveness is also observable in other minoritized fields which have struggled to gain legitimacy or an academic foothold. Our questioning and lines of inquiry have often arisen in relation to our individual and collective sense of living on the margins (socially, culturally, in the academy) and our various and uneven experiences of queer and trans hate; of love, desire and heartbreak; of connection, community and allyship; or of isolation and loneliness. These things energize queer historical work in particular ways and often get explicitly referenced and discussed within it. I do this too, and engage my own experience to summarize, exemplify and to be an actor in different pasts I otherwise report. I reach for the autobiographical in reflexive passages within the chapters that follow, and especially in the codas attached to each of them and in the book's preface and epilogue. I thus attempt to unpick the enmeshed threads of the personal, political and historical in my own work, and to model my claims about the significance of queer history in providing personal anchorage. There is a danger of this slipping into 'narcissism and ego history'.[27] But in a field that emerged from the strident mantra of the personal being political, there is mileage in exploring the investments and perspectives of those doing the writing.[28] It troubles the notion of historical objectivity and embeds the personal within the academic as 'a way to consider thoughts, responses and insights which would not traditionally be recognised as knowledge' (as literary scholar Jane Gallop has it).[29]

Writing Queer History, the title assigned by the series to which it belongs, suggests the need to be reflexive in these ways, and so to engage with the process and status of writing as an act and not just with what has been written. It directs us to the contexts in which that writing has taken place and to the materials that underpin it. More tacitly, it draws our attention to the way the written word is privileged in the pursuit of history, both in terms of the sources that get most consulted and what we think we need to produce by way of output. The book has been written in the context of an upsurge in community LGBTQ+ history work in the United Kingdom and elsewhere, with accompanying walks, websites, performances exhibitions, and more. History in these contexts is constituted through the sometimes careful, sometimes chaotic curation of art, objects, ephemera, performances, and voices. It can be in 'a gossipy grain' rather than 'the academic sublime' (as feminist literary scholar Nancy K. Miller puts it).[30] These public history genres are often enviably more direct and directly engaging than more academic histories. So whilst the onus in this book is on queer history as it has developed in the form of books and articles, it also holds close other ways of 'doing' queer history and the ways history might be metaphorically 'written' elsewhere – including on our bodies in the way we experience, understand and explain them.[31]

Running through the book, then, is a concern with positionality, context and process, and also with the question of why queer history matters. Queer history is distinct in part because of where and how it has felt crucial and because of the people who have made it. The quest for the queer past has been deeply significant – personally, communally and politically – and if we do not find a mirror image of ourselves there, we do see varied dances of desire which include some familiar steps and suggest the scope to re-choreograph.[32] There is a powerful urge to feel for resonances with the past, to trace lines of association, to find a queer 'family history' which a 'regular' family cannot or can only partially supply.[33] This personal passion and drive behind queer history is part of its joy, but can also be problematic. It can tip into the foregrounding of a proud lineage and history to help with an urgent politics and to comfort and sustain in the present.[34] We might see or assume identities and lines of connection in the past which fall apart when we think more carefully in relation to historical contexts and 'structures of feeling' then.[35] We might also hone in on people and communities in the past who seem best to meet a felt need for affirmation and hope now, rather than on others who do not speak so directly. There can be a related shying away from shameful or difficult pasts relating to violence, exploitation and abuse and to the dominant and reactionary exercise of power.[36] An appetite for queer radicalism in the present can meanwhile lead us to bypass mundane and 'normative' queer lives and cultures in the past in favour of the exceptional or astonishing.[37] Queer theory from the early 1990s onwards has perhaps nudged us in that direction. It importantly energized historians to question sexual and gender categories and certainty, to interrogate associated meaning, and, following queer and feminist theorist Sara Ahmed, to 'notice' that which has usually gone 'unnoticed'.[38] Once we have, we can not quite see history in the same way as before because 'what we pull apart we cannot put together in the same way'.[39] And yet queer history does not straightforwardly deliver on the radical aspirations of queer theory in terms, for example, of anti-normativity, alternate temporalities or the fluid subject.[40] We mostly find lives and dynamics in the past that are quite ordinary and unremarkable for their moment, and need to be aware of the temptation to land only on those which most fire a radical queer imaginary and meet the theoretical aspirations of the present. What we find in 'the flesh of [historical] practice' rarely accords to 'abstract, disembodied theory'.[41] Queer history might be radically coalitional with other anti-patriarchal and anti-racist strands of historical practice, and be radically questioning in its approach, but this does not mean that what we find in the past will be radical or radical on these terms.

Structure

The first three chapters focus on loosely successive influences, phases, or trends in queer historical work which make it some sort of a field, albeit an unfenced one. Chapter 1 ('Foundations') looks at literary and legally oriented homosexual histories which bolstered the pitch for reform in Britain in the 1960s, and examines the turn in the 1970s towards lesbian and gay history inflected by civil rights, women's and gay liberation, history from below, and social and then cultural history. It looks at the way literary and cultural studies, emergent queer theory and cultural history posed renewed questions about the forces operating on the production and representation of dissident desire and associated identities. This constituted a partial shift in emphasis from social to cultural history in queer historical work, and from work beyond to work within the academy. Chapter 2 ('Identifications and Intersections') opens out questions of identity and identification further via interventions in the 1990s and 2000s. It looks in particular at the ways in which theorizations of agency and identification, the history of the emotions, and postcolonial and gender history and theory provided additional frameworks for thinking about the 'mesh of [queer] possibilities' in the past.[42] Chapter 3 ('Space and Time') follows the spatial and temporal turns to look at the growing focus in the 2000s on the queer significance of different places (bars, homes, hospitals, prisons, workplaces), kinds of space (urban, suburban, rural), divisions of space (into region, nation, continent, empire and colony) and movements between spaces (proximate and distant). The chapter shows how these places, types of space, and spatial dynamics came with temporal associations – relating to stasis, degeneration and progress, for example. These, historians have shown, further inflected understandings and experiences of queerness in the past.

Chapters 4 ('Queer History/Public History') and 5 ('Archives and Sources') focus on queer history making for and in the present. Chapter 4 explores the especially close relationship between queer, public and community history. It looks at particular political, cultural and subcultural contexts and challenges for the mobilization of LGBTQ+ history in the streets, in regular and queer museums and archives, and via individual icons and the creative arts. It considers who these histories serve and, as importantly, who they do not. The final chapter (Chapter 5) takes the so-called archival turn and looks at problems and possibilities associated with some of the sources queer historians have drawn on – including legal and newspaper records, books, visual materials, material culture, ephemera, oral history and other kinds of testimony. It also looks, all too briefly, at the impact of the virtual world on queer history making. This chapter forms a conclusion of sorts about a practice of history undertaken by those who navigate these materials, push at the edges of historical convention, and exercise their creative historical imagination in the interests of the queer past – and present. The book's epilogue draws this consideration into the detritus of my own life.

These chapters track loose phases in queer history-making – with a period of activism and community history followed by social and then cultural historical work in the academy and an upsurge in public history – but they also show that there is no neat sequence. Individual, communal and academic interactions with the past roll on in conversation, with some approaches receding and others coming into focus at different times and in different places. Queer history as conceived from the mid 1990s did not displace lesbian and gay history or function apart from it. Activist and community history has not been and gone; historically-oriented performance, film, exhibitions, guided walks, graphic novels, literature and various online presentations of the past have instead burgeoned such that our broader historical environment in the United Kingdom now has a vibrant queer pulse running through it (albeit one which can sanitize the queer past by making it more consumable in a neo-liberal context).[43] Developments in trans history over the past twenty years have had a particular impact on queer history thematically and in terms of approach, expanding the queer field of vision to think beyond and between the cultural productions of masculinity and femininity and the way bodies might 'mean otherwise' (to cite pioneering trans historian Susan Stryker).[44] Indeed, since the first draft of this book, the 'kinship' between queer and trans history has become even closer.[45] We see this in the resonant calls to think beyond identity categories and presumptions of cis-normativity and heterosexuality, and so 'to queer' and 'to trans' the past.[46] And we see it, too, in closer examinations of the ways sex, desire, gender and experiences and understandings of the body are enmeshed in dynamics and hierarchies of power, relating to religion, class, race and colonialism.[47]

There have been tensions between different approaches and epistemologies, between the five+ identifications flagged in the LGBTQ+ formulation, between trained historians and historically-inclined literary and cultural theorists, and between historical work produced in the academy and beyond.[48] Community history makers have, for example, sometimes reproduced a familiar pantheon of queer heroes and timelines, rather than questioning their significance or exploring their affects (as academic historians have been more wont to do). Whilst queer is theoretically embracing, it has a male coding. Aside from being crucial in and of themselves, histories specifically of lesbianism have therefore been important as a corrective to – and reminder of – queer's androcentric tendencies. Trans historians have meanwhile faced resistance and have had to push hard to cleave space for their historical work. This is a key reason why trans history is not subsumed here; there are political and intellectual imperatives in retaining a visible sense of what distinguishes as well as what connects these fields. But looking across the years, there has probably been less rank division than in other historical subfields and in part because of the imperative to allyship in the period since lesbian and gay and LGBTQ+ and queer history became a thing. Researching this book reminded me that this has tended to be a mode of history in which connection and resonance have been valued – both in the history making itself and in the broader sense of community and solidarity history can engender. Collective endeavour amongst activist scholars was palpable in the 1970s and it is palpable again as we face a fresh mobilization of fear and hate in the overlapping culture wars on immigration, race, Islamophobia, gender identity and sexuality.

During periods of backlash, history has been a key tool for resisting the simplified narratives wielded by those with power for the consumption of those who have very little. This matters not because human rights should be reliant on history (they should not), but because documenting a history of rights denied, of racism and patriarchy, of marginalization, and of same-sex sex and intimacy across time has been such a well worked method of making and substantiating arguments for protection and change. Scholars have in addition increasingly tuned into intersectional histories which illustrate historical links between oppressions and complex understandings of personhood which counter reductive, simplifying contemporary rhetorics. Some of the most recent queer and queer-adjacent work has taken an avowedly connective approach in looking to the past. US literary scholar Simon Joyce in his *LGBT Victorians* (2022) reassesses the utility of the four-way alliance of his title in his re-examination of infamous cases and figures of the nineteenth century, for example.[49] If the identity denominations are new, the different labels and their conjunction help him – and might encourage us – to look at entangled past configurations of gender and sexuality. Historian Jennifer Evans makes a different though resonant plea for an ethic and lens of 'kinship' in our work on the past.[50] She shows how such an approach brings different allegiances into view, displacing a politics and mode of history which can tend to exclusion, especially of queer and trans people of colour and of refugee or migrant status. Historian Diarmuid Hester finds in bisexuality an expansive point of view rather than an identity. It suggests to him a way of thinking across normative assumptions about desire, and with a double rather than singular vision.[51] And, finally, in his 2024 inaugural professorial address, the historian of Britain and Ireland, Mo Moulton, described the 'latent commons' connecting human and more than human worlds, with the potential to find sustaining links in and with the past as we confront transphobia, transmisogyny and homophobia now.[52] Each of these works offers a manifesto for looking across and between rather than fiercely preserving distinction. I have taken heed of this in my approach to writing *Writing Queer History*.

1

Foundations

<hr>

> During the period I was writing [*Surpassing the Love of Men*] I was not only discovering past eras in which love between women was widely condoned, but I was observing what was happening between women in the feminist movement in the 1970s. . . . What I saw before me confirmed microcosmically what I had found through my historical research with regard to same-sex love: that 'any woman can'.[1]

Lillian Faderman's reflections on writing her pathbreaking 1981 study captures a sense of excitement and possibility that came with the Women's and Gay Liberation movements of the early 1970s. It was clear to Faderman, as it was to other pioneer scholar-activists, that the personal was political and that both had deep, anchoring historical dimensions which gave impetus and hope to contemporary life experiments. 'We believed profoundly that ideas mattered and that history could change lives, because it had changed ours', remembered fellow US literary scholar and historian Martha Vicinus. Their contemporary, Jonathan Ned Katz, echoed the sentiment: 'We experienced the present as history, ourselves as history makes', he wrote. 'In our lives and in our hearts, we experienced the change of one historical form of homosexuality to another. We experienced homosexuality as historical'.[2] Here were testimonies to the power of history in personal, social and political lives, and to the ways in which these cutting-edge historians saw themselves living through, documenting and contributing to changing ideas about sexual identity and community.

It is no coincidence that the drive to explore lesbian and gay history arrived most forcefully in places where those identities were being owned especially vocally and where, more broadly, voices 'from below' from the Civil Rights movement and youth and counter cultures were challenging established ways of knowing and being. There was hope that things could be different – and this included the sorts of history that could be made. If initially the quest for the homosexual, lesbian and gay past was seen as a marginal pursuit for marginalized people, its significance became clearer as Faderman, Vicinus, Katz and others showed how sexuality was modulated by wider social and cultural dynamics and by powerful discourses and institutions of the law, science and religion.[3] Lesbian and gay history in this vein, they suggested, could offer new perspectives on culture and society much more broadly. Another American gay history pioneer, John D'Emilio, thus noted that 'the movement of which our research and writings and forums and slide shows were a part was so evidently remaking the world around us that it seemed inevitable that we would strive to connect our [historical] work to broad themes and large social processes.[4]

The particular tenor and epistemological basis of this work becomes clearer when we look at it in relation to the homosexual histories of the 1950s and 1960s. This is where the chapter begins, couching the ensuing discussion of the emergence of lesbian and gay social history and history from below in the 1970s and 1980s. The second part explores theoretical and literary scholarship which turned the dial towards cultural history. This work was often seen to be in tension with that grounded in social history, but the approaches were also complimentary and together animated the history of sexuality. Though it ranged widely, this new subdiscipline, discussed in the chapter's final section, was most consistently concerned with queer lives and dynamics, etching out a somewhat more secure place for lesbian, gay and then queer history in the academy. Overall, the following pages encompass historical practices of recovery and attempts to understand how particular social and cultural contexts produced meanings around same-sex intimacies. Part of this involved tracing what it was about Western cultures, and in particular the US and UK, that fostered the emergence of distinct identity types and communities. Through this work it became clear that these types and communities were not ubiquitous – either globally or across time. They had a history.

1. Histories of homosexuality and the emergence of gay and lesbian history

Legal and literary histories

German sexologist Iwan Bloch's *The Sexual Life of England: Past and Present* appeared in German in 1908, part of the first wave of sexological writing.

Between chapters on 'Flagellomania' ('an evil peculiar to the English') and 'Sadism and Masochism' (to which the English were apparently 'predispos[ed]'), was the chapter on 'Homosexuality'. Here Bloch sketched (and tellingly collapsed together) accounts of 'Urning' monarchs, homosexual scandals, 'Tommies' and lesbians, cross-dressing, the 'man-woman', and (briefly) hermaphroditism, in the period from the English king, William Rufus (1087–1100) through to Bloch's present.[5] He does this to substantiate an argument about the aetiology of homosexuality and, tacitly, to suggest scope for different social and legal responses to it. This resonated with the approach taken by some of his sexologist contemporaries. Berliner Magnus Hirschfeld conjured a historical homosexual lineage in his pioneering work, whilst Havelock Ellis, in London, included in the first English edition of his *Sexual Inversion* (1897), an essay on homosexuality amongst the ancient Greeks by Classicist John Addington Symonds.[6] Though Bloch worked on the common sexological premise of an in-born tendency, he, like Ellis, identified something culturally and situationally specific in sexual cultures and attitudes. This meant England's sexual life could be distinguished from that of other places and times, gesturing to a contextually particular history of sexuality. According to Bloch the English had encouraged homosexuality via the 'unique institution of gentlemen's clubs' and 'avid cultivation' of 'gymnastic sport' (rather, he noted, as the ancient Greeks had done). But they had also provided 'a very strong deterrent to the development of homosexuality' because 'no other people has looked upon this act with so much disgust or judged those participating so harshly'.[7]

The Sexual Life of England appeared in English in 1934 and was re-issued by trade publisher Corgi twice in the decade between the Wolfenden Committee recommendations that sex between men be (partially) decriminalized and those recommendations passing into law in 1967.[8] The book joined other new fictional and scholarly works addressing 'the homosexual problem' (as it was dubbed in this period and just prior), and which frequently also marshalled history to make a tacit or explicit case for reform.[9] These works came alongside, and contributed to, the growing cultural currency of sexology and psychoanalysis in Britain and America.[10] Alfred Kinsey's famous reports on *Sexual Behavior in the Human Male* (1948) and *Sexual Behavior in the Human Female* (1953) were widely discussed, including in relation to the continuum of sexuality Kinsey observed and which resonated through some subsequent historical work calling the supposed binary of sexuality into question.[11] The German-American philosopher Herbert Marcuse had in the meantime widened the significance of the play of desire in his influential exploration of the relationship between *Eros and Civilization* (1955). Sex was not, to Marcuse, individual and private but a fundamental component of social order and disorder.[12] His ideas can be found weaving through subsequent radical (including radical historical) work which suggested the potential for entwined sexual and social revolution.[13] The re-issue of *The Sexual Life of England* in these years exemplifies the evocation of history to frame a putative movement from the darkness of history into the promise of light in the present and future. In this and other work history was used to suggest that homosexuals were uniquely creative and talented, with a historically proven ability to enrich society, but also to show that they had often suffered terribly, and especially in places like England.

Most of this early historical work was authored not by professional historians but by lawyers, literary scholars, biographers, sexologists and medics. No real space was afforded within academic history to a topic seemingly of interest only to those with some personal axe to grind. Literary scholar Phyllis Grosskurth's sympathetic biography of John Addington Symonds (1964) and Brian Read's and Timothy D'Arch Smith's historically-framed literary anthologies (both 1970) brought together work from the later nineteenth and early twentieth centuries which showcased artistic elite men who were often inspired by, and harked nostalgically back to, classical civilizations.[14] Barrister H. Montgomery Hyde's *The Other Love* (1970) was anchored in legal cases across the centuries, though mainly focused on the scandals of the late nineteenth, which he elaborated further in his subsequent studies of the 1895 Oscar Wilde and 1889/90 Cleveland Street scandals (published in 1973 and 1976 respectively).[15] These three works gestured to a close relationship between sex and the state and the way in which strategic homophobia became a tool in statecraft. It was important, for example, in Henry VIII's campaign against the Catholic church: allegations of sexual dissipation in monasteries and the introduction of anti-sodomy legislation to the secular statute books were a means of exposure, coercion and control.[16]

Historical work on lesbians appearing around the same time did not have the same legal focus. There was, however, a related attempt to demonstrate – and create – a long tradition of lesbianism to anchor relationships and desires which were gaining some legibility in the present. American librarian, poet and literary scholar Jeannette Foster's *Sex Variant Women in Literature: A Historical and Quantitative Study* (1952) surveyed work from Sappho in the sixth century BCE (who was re-popularized by an 1885 translation of her work) through to Foster's present.[17] Walter Braun, the German historian, extended that reach to the 1960s in his *Lesbian Love: Old and New* (1966).

(Though he took the same serious tone as Hyde, Foster and others, when the book was reissued in 1967, Luxor Press chose a titillating cover, repackaging history as lesbian pulp and erotica.)[18] *Arena Three*, the British lesbian magazine, carried pieces on historic female couples from its first issue in 1964 through to the last in 1971. Biographies appeared detailing the same-sex relationships of Vita Sackville West (1892–1962) and of the Ladies of Llangollen (Eleanor Butler [1739–1829] and Sarah Ponsonby [1755–1831]).[19] The latter, celebrities in their own lifetimes, had long since been models for female sexual and relational independence, including for medic, prison inspector and author Mary Gordon (1861–1941) who saw herself as their spiritual descendant and figured them centrally in her biographical novel *Chase the Wilde Goose* (1936). Historical figures clearly mattered to queer self-composure across the twentieth century.

Whilst social and sexual independence was taken for granted in the work on men, in these histories of women it was front and centre, connecting their cause tacitly or explicitly to a wider feminist politics. In other respects, the accounts of men and women were linked. Both largely depicted white, elite, talented individuals, whose prowess seemed intrinsic to their 'condition'. More broadly, the assumption was that 'the other love' was a transhistorical phenomenon running alongside an equally entrenched heterosexual norm. This seemed 'common sense' (that weasel concept underpinning much British and American political and historical discourse)[20] and helped further embed the binary understanding of sexuality which was gaining cultural purchase in the British and American postwar years (and despite Kinsey's findings to the contrary). Though this essentialism was being challenged by the late 1960s, until then it seemed to be the obvious way to understand the lineages outlined by Hyde, Foster or Braun, and also the obvious way to demand rights and equalities.

Gay history

A shift in approach to the 'homosexual' past is tangible in two books published in 1977. A. L. Rowse, best known for his work on Elizabethan England, published his *Homosexuals in History* after he had retired from Oxford University, and just as *Coming Out*, by newcomer Jeffrey Weeks, radically redirected modes of historical enquiry into the sexual past.[21] Rowse followed earlier precedents in detailing a lineage of culturally elite homosexuals – from Michelangelo to Noël Coward – and linking their intrinsic talents to their intrinsic sexuality. Weeks meanwhile charted the development and growth of homosexual and lesbian and gay politics across the late nineteenth and twentieth centuries in relation to wider social change, other social movements, and related class dynamics. Rowse seemed nostalgic for class-bound certainties which Weeks and his peers were trying to shake via their own rather different recourse to the past. In the contexts of youth, student and liberationist counter cultures there was, historian Lucy Robinson notes, a 'distrust of rigid structures [and] a focus on the experience of oppression and the politics of the inner mind'.[22] There was a profound challenge in this to established ways of doing politics and, also, history. So though work by Rowse, Hyde, Foster and the rest was groundbreaking in bringing homosexual histories into the public realm and represented considerable reputational risk-taking on their part as authors, it was also markedly different from that of a younger generation of scholars influenced by the women's and gay liberation movements and the 1960s and 1970s contexts which spawned and sustained them.[23] Whilst previously the onus was on individuals and the homosexual cross they bore, the emphasis now was on identity and community formation and the scope for radical social change.

British sociologist and soon to be Gay Liberation Front activist Mary McIntosh laid the groundwork for some of this new lesbian and gay historical work in her landmark piece, 'The Homosexual Role' (1968). She argued that the homosexual was best understood as a modern, socially constituted role rather than a psychiatric category or pathological type.[24] Deploying history and also anthropology she pinpointed three different modes of same-sex interaction over time – relating to gender crossing, intergenerational relationships and egalitarian partnerships. These modes had, she argued, been taken up unevenly depending on – and in relation to – social and cultural rituals, expectations and norms. Outside the modern West, same sex behaviour was rarely seen to be related to the kind of inborn impairment suggested by Bloch and other sexologists. Using historical examples from Africa and the ancient world, McIntosh observed that there was much homosexual activity but no homosexuals there and then. Instead same-sex sexual activity was related in these contexts to stage of life and differences in age. She thus concluded that most societies did not have a clear homosexual role and even where there was some approximation – as with male sex workers in temples of the ancient Middle East or the gender crossing / non-conforming Mollies of eighteenth-century London – same-sex sexual activity was not understood in the same way as it was in McIntosh's contemporary context (in which, she wrote, 'the polarisation of the heterosexual man and the homosexual man' was in any case 'far from complete').[25] On this basis, the interesting historical questions now related to why and how people understood and experienced homosexual roles in their particular social, cultural and historical contexts. Two US sociologists, John Gagnon and William Simon, added a further twist to this argument in 1974 by suggesting that the very idea of a fundamental drive, an intrinsic human sexuality, might itself have a history and have been conjured socially and culturally – foreshadowing the argument Foucault would present two years later in his *History of Sexuality*, vol. 1.[26]

These interventions invited different approaches to the history of homosexuality. Rather than tracking homosexuals through the past, the fresh imperative was to show how historical conditions had shaped understandings and experiences of same-sex intimacy. If the idea of an intrinsic, inborn sexuality was useful to the argument that rights were needed to protect a minority that had and would always exist, the social constructionist approach looked to the formation of different roles and understandings of sex and desire in the past in ways which suggested the scope for liberatory change in the present and future – an aim voiced in the UK Gay Liberation Front manifesto of 1971 in which McIntosh had a hand. 'We, together with other oppressed groups', it read, 'can start to form a new order and a liberated lifestyle' – and fundamentally by 'rid[ding] society of the gender-role system which is at the root of our oppression'.[27] In tune with wider liberationist debate – from the 1967 Dialectics of Liberation Congress in London to the 'Collective Statement' (1977) of the Combahee River Collective in Boston (1974–80) – these Gay Liberationists aspired to a cross-cutting, intersectional politics, challenging gender and sexual norms and ideologies. This politics inspired a rising generation of activist-scholars who worked, often collaboratively, with radical publishers and frequently beyond or in precarious relation to the academy.[28] Together they pushed at established ways of knowing; Weeks recollects being engaged in 'a practice of history against the grain, a collective activity that was both scholarly and political'.[29]

There was a new drive to campaign and also to construct knowledge 'from below' amongst those engaged in lesbian and gay history and in ways resonant with wider shifts in the academy. In the United Kingdom, the Birmingham Centre for Cultural Studies from 1964, especially under the directorship of Stuart Hall from 1969, opened a new field of interdisciplinary study and fostered collaborative, collective and less hierarchical approaches to research and writing, including, crucially, on dimensions of community and identity. The History Workshop movement from the late 1960s mirrored this approach, and when its journal launched in 1976 it was with the stated aim of bringing 'the boundaries of history closer to people's lives' by binding together social, public and popular history.[30] Given contemporary upheavals in sexual practice, identity and politics, it is no surprise that these were key themes taken up in historical perspective in *History Workshop Journal*, as well as in *Radical History Review* (from 1974) and adjacent liberationist British publications like *Spare Rib* (1972–93) and *Gay Left* (1975–80). History in these contexts was not sequestered but rather a tool for understanding the operations of patriarchy and the associated social organization of gender roles and sexuality.

This work was generally in social history mode and reflected some broader shifts in historical practice and themes in the 1960s and 1970s, evident in the new *Journal of Social History* (from 1967). 'Sociology m[et] history' here, and novel sources were deployed – from the folk ballads used by E. P. Thompson in his classic *The Making of the English Working Class* (1963) to the oral histories which began to gain equivocal traction in the discipline with the formation of the Oral History Association in the United States in 1967 and the Oral History Society in the United Kingdom two years later.[31] The authority of established experts was troubled by voices 'from below' and work of recuperation and gap filling. Historians working in the mode of 'thick description' (a technique developed in anthropology) informed a turn to microhistory which sought out the close texture of everyday life and of individual experience in particular places and times for their own sake and as a means of understanding the processes and effects of social and cultural change.[32]

Pathbreaking work appeared on gay history which took seriously these new disciplinary moves and epistemological shifts. Katz, for example, wrote in his *Gay American History* (1976) that 'beyond the most obvious fact that homosexual relations involve persons of the same gender, and include feelings as well as acts, there is no such thing as homosexuality in general, only particular forms of homosexuality.'[33] Through his commentary and the layering up of documents reproduced for the volume, Katz built a 'gay' history of the United States from the first settlers to his present. This was a history involving colonizers and colonized, and white, Indigenous and African American people. Katz suggested the particularity of homosexual experience, expression and politics in the United States in a shadow national history which took in the temporal and spatial span of colonized north America but examined it through a different lens. Later, he did something similar with heterosexuality, showing how it, too, was an invented category.[34] In 1983 D'Emilio illustrated the intimate connection between the political, social and economic by locating urbanization and capitalism as driving forces in the emergence of a homosexual identity and minority in nineteenth-century America.[35] He further demonstrated the consolidation and politicization of that identity postwar in the face of police oppression, witch hunts by the state department, and rhetoric about the so-called 'lavender menace'. The immediacy of the Civil Rights movement in the United States and the Combahee debate about the 'interlocking' systems of racist and sexist oppression,[36] together with a growing body of work on Black America (to which Katz and D'Emilio had themselves contributed), meant these histories were especially alert to intersections of race and sexuality and an associated politics.[37]

In the United Kingdom, class was more often the analytical pivot. Weeks was especially attuned to the effects of social stratification on same-sex behaviour, identities and communities in his *Coming Out* (1977) and *Sex, Politics and Society* (1981). With feminist historian Sheila Rowbotham in the co-authored *Socialism and the New Life* (1977), he explored the relationship between emergent British socialism and ideas about sex, sexuality and female emancipation. Weeks and Rowbotham did this via the lives and work of sexologist Havelock Ellis (1859–1939) and poet and romantic socialist Edward Carpenter (1844–1929), demonstrating that biography could be used to elucidate enmeshed social and sexual histories and was not only a way of showcasing heroic individuals.[38] Collaboration was key in this work and fostered a marked interdisciplinary openness. The collective working on the journal *Gay Left* in the United Kingdom from 1975 to 1980, for example, saw Weeks, film scholar Richard Dyer and art historians Simon Watney and Emmanuel Cooper collaborating in their reach for the sexual past in the interests of a radical present. Weeks and these other scholars marked out a history of the margins from the margins but also demonstrated how such perspectives shed fresh light on broader political and sexual cultures and called into question the 'obviousness' of normative sexual identity. Their historicization of sexuality demonstrated a mutable relationship between sex and society.

Lesbian history

There was a concurrent sense of possibility associated with women coming together under the banner of Women's Liberation and second wave feminism – in workshops, conferences, and to protest, write and edit. Pioneering work on lesbian history was appearing in interdisciplinary journals like *Spare Rib*, the *Journal of Feminist Studies* (both from 1972), *Signs* (from 1975) and *Feminist Review* (from 1979) and via a new tranche of radical publishers, including, in Britain, Virago (from 1973), The Women's Press (from 1977), and Brilliance Books (from 1982 and with funding from the Greater London Council). The first issue of *Signs* carried historian Carroll Smith-Rosenberg's piece 'The Female World of Love and Ritual'. This broke new ground by exploring relationships between women as part of the ordinary run of everyday life. Through letters and diaries written in the 120 years from 1760, she demonstrated that female friendships and intimacies arose in regular settings and were understood and experienced through a familiar language of affection. Like McIntosh, she argued that these women were not part of a deviant minority, and instead enlarged who might 'count' in lesbian history.[39] This potential was elaborated by American poet and activist Adrienne Rich in her 'Compulsory Heterosexuality and Lesbian Existence' (1980). Also published in *Signs*, and written amidst the intense debate about political lesbianism and lesbian separatism, Rich marshalled historical examples – including of the Beguine lay communities of Christian women in the Low Countries (loosely the modern day Netherlands, Belgium and Luxembourg) between the twelfth and fourteenth centuries – to make her case for a 'lesbian continuum' of which all women were part.[40] With this gesture, she broadened the field of lesbian historical vision to include all intimacy and relationships between women, regardless of any supposed inner truth of sexuality or indeed genital contact. Rich's intervention proffered historical tools to resist the compulsory heterosexuality confected through patriarchy.

A year later, Lillian Faderman provided grist to these arguments. In *Surpassing the Love of Men*, she traced multivalent expressions of female love and friendship over a longer period and in the kind of detail a book-length study allows.[41] Faderman showed that domestic space and rituals, conventions of letter writing, and a cultural affirmation of middle-class female friendship underpinned close relationships between women. Intimacy of all kinds – including in friendship – mattered to this history, laying the foundations for later work in lesbian, gay and queer history, which, in Weeks' phrase, 'dethroned erotic practices as an organising principle while offering affective intimacy in its place'.[42] The women Faderman identified might have been placed on Rich's lesbian continuum and were part of a community across time. 'Regardless of whether these women had genital sex together', Faderman wrote, 'by virtue of their passion and commitment, they can be claimed as foremothers by women in intimate relations with other women today.'[43]

Surpassing the Love of Men was both a detailed history and counterblast to the late nineteenth-century sexologists who 'morbidified' love between women and whose ideas gained ground in the West across the century that followed.[44] The book troubled whiggish idea of progress by showing how 'lesbian-like' women (to use Judith Bennett's later analytic) had made livable lives in a period prior to the scrutiny of science and sexology and the advent of social movements and a liberationist politics.[45] Faderman's contemporary Martha Vicinus elaborated and clinched these arguments in work in which she differentiated between romantic, platonic friendships and what she described as 'sexual Sapphism'.[46]

Smith-Rosenberg, Rich, Faderman and Vicinus's encompassing conceptualization of the potential for female-female sex, love and intimacy reflected the way in which lesbian history was part of a wider and burgeoning women's history.[47] The 'Big Berks' Women's History Conference from 1973 (a successor to the Berkshire Conference of Women Historians which had run from 1930) and the UK Women's History network (from 1992) regularly showcased lesbian history. There was no similarly encompassing umbrella for gay male history, and partly as a result gay histories were generally focused on a minority of men who had been decisively cast as marginal. Women's history in its conversation with lesbian history was showing how patriarchy, the distinct social roles occupied by men and women, and the power imbalance between the sexes had a profound effect on the ways in which same-sex intimacies were experienced and understood.[48] This underscored the need for a separate lesbian history distinct from that about gay men. Writing in the inaugural issue of *Women's History Review* (1992), Rosemary Auchmuty, Sheila Jeffries and Elaine Miller, three British lesbian historians, argued that lesbian history was too readily obscured by male-coded gay history and that gay male historians' frequent focus on the rights movement meant there was little consciousness of or challenge to patriarchy in their work.[49] Lesbian history, as part of women's and feminist history, necessarily involved a critique of the ways in which society and its institutions perpetuated the submission of all women, including women involved in same-sex relationships. Auchmuty, Jeffries and Miller insisted that this different impetus and focus needed recognizing in gay studies and promoting through separate lesbian publishing and courses.[50] There was a particular urgency to this call for visibility and recognition in the United Kingdom given the attempt to silence lesbian and gay voices with Section 28 of the Local Government Act (1988), which banned local authorities from 'promoting' homosexuality in their schools, libraries, and museums. British lesbian history of this period – including in the Lesbian History Group's anthology, *Not a Passing Phase: Reclaiming Lesbians in History, 1840–1985* and the Hall-Carpenter Lesbian Oral History Group's *Inventing Ourselves* (both 1989) – was part of the activist challenge to the measure and an attempt to counter the broader invisibility of lesbianism, certainly when compared to gay men. New journals, including *Gender and History* (from 1989) and *Women's History Review*, provided additional platforms.

There was nevertheless enduring concern that the queer umbrella of the 1990s threatened the visibility of lesbian-specific experiences of love, sex, desire and hate. Historian Donna Penn further cautioned that inclusiveness in lesbian history – potentially of all women – could mask the fact that oppression and hate were not felt equally.[51] The school girls involved in passionate friendships in English public schools examined by Vicinus (1984) and Annabel Faraday (1989) were, for example, differently and probably less directly targeted than the butches in lesbian bars in Buffalo, New York, described by Elizabeth Lapovsky Kennedy and Madeline Davis in *Boots of Leather, Slippers of Gold* (1993).[52] Penn's political point and her reminder to distinguish experience is important, but especially when taken as a body of work, lesbian history by this point was far from homogenizing. It instead signalled distinct experiences relating to outward presentation, to particular contexts and to race and class. Looking narrowly at the past to those who most ostensibly 'count' filters out too many others. Kennedy reflected on this issue in relation to *Boots of Leather*, noting very different investments in the Buffalo lesbian scene.[53] There were those for whom it was primary and enduring (Kennedy and Davis' obvious interviewees); those who had other strong community ties elsewhere (some of the Black women, for example); and those who came in and out of the scene or were part of it for only a short period. Did women who also or subsequently had male partners count? What about the women there who did not describe themselves or identify as lesbian or those who did but did not go to these bars at all? Butches were perhaps the most obvious lesbians here but were they necessarily more central to the story of these bars than their femme partners?[54] Later, trans historians would ask if it was right to presume the gender identities of these bar butches.[55] Kennedy and Davis' 'history from below' demonstrated how lesbian lives, even within a relatively tight network and community, could be markedly distinct from one another. As a result, same-sex desire, intimacy, friendship and love needed to be particularized and contextualized. *Boots of Leather* further showed the significance of oral history work, especially in the way it brought working-class voices into lesbian history-making.[56] It was a technique which revealed lives, communities and experiences in context and otherwise 'hidden from history' – an epithet used first by Rowbotham in the title of her 1973 work surveying 300 years of women's oppression, and then in an edited collection sixteen years later which sought to 'reclaim . . . the gay and lesbian past'. This shared usage neatly flags related impulses and approaches in women's, gay and lesbian history.[57]

Subsequent historians and theorists sometimes underplayed 'the major intellectual achievement' of this 'diversely productive crew',[58] historian Lisa Duggan observed in the mid 1990s. She saw them 'strip mining' the careful research of lesbian and gay activist-scholars and the prior generation of homosexual historians.[59] The debt was not only to this research material, but to the way those working in women's, lesbian and gay history had reformulated perspectives on the past and challenged essentialism and transhistoricism. Here were some of the crucial underpinning ideas for what would come to be known as queer history.

Social constructionism or essentialism?

In this work in the 1970s and 1980s there was a tension between the desire to populate the past with forbears on the one hand and, on the other, to signal the ways in which social and cultural contexts in the past produced very different understandings and expressions of same sex desire. There was a felt need, as Katz put it, 'to discover and disseminate our forgotten history'; 'to restore a people to its past; to itself'.[60] Joan Nestle, a New York friend and comrade of Katz and founder of the Lesbian Herstory Archive, worked to wrestle and protect 'our' history, a lesbian history, from 'patriarchal historians' and the injury inflicted by the supposed neutrality of academic history. Both Katz and Nestle rejected a transhistorical vision of sexual identity, saw the contingency and historicity of identity and community, and identified the challenges in deciding who and what counted in renditions of these things.[61] The 'our' they used in this sense referred to the broad community in their present which they were seeking to understand in historical perspective and in relation to inevitably different social configurations and understandings of same-sex desire and sexual activity in the past. The forebears imagined by Nestle and Katz did not have to subscribe to a specific identity to be part of 'our' broad history of same-sex passion. The same went for the descriptor 'lesbian and gay history' – conceived not as a search for lesbian and gays in history so much as furnishing a history for lesbians and gays in the present of the 1970s and 1980s.

If twentieth-century identities set off new histories, this did not mean historians necessarily expected to find those identities in the past. Those working on much earlier periods especially were demonstrating how sex and desire was understood very differently across time. Classicist Kenneth Dover showed in his *Greek Homosexuality* (1978) how sex and sexual roles between men in ancient Greece pivoted on differences of age and status (though more recent work has suggested this enduring characterization is too 'simplistic', 'polarised' and 'dominated by the phallus').[62] In Renaissance London, History Workshop collective member, Alan Bray, found that sex between men was part and parcel of the theatre, brothel and street cultures of London's Southwark. It was possibly also for many an extension of the ordinary practice of same-sex bed-sharing. Homosex was hidden in plain sight in these contexts because it did not have clear culturally understood credentials beyond the broader sense of pleasure-seeking in the capital or incidental physical contact at night.[63] Sodomy was certainly a vilified sin and crime, but was vaguely conceived and likely felt removed from what men were doing with each other casually and situationally. In this and the ancient Greek contexts, as in those highlighted by Mary McIntosh, male same-sex intimacy was not at the social margins.[64] Medievalist John Boswell similarly showed how gay history might be located in past practices and places that were socially and culturally central. He demonstrated the significance of religious and specifically monastic spaces to medieval cultures of homosexuality. In these contexts, male-male love and intimacy was conceptualized and experienced in terms of brotherhood (echoing the yearnings of gay liberationists) rather than the hierarchies of age and social status identified in other historical contexts.[65] Boswell looked at the Beghards, communities of men living together in lay Christian communities – similar to the female Beguines Adrienne Rich had discussed – and showed the 'slippage' between church doctrine and human behaviour. He demonstrated that the medieval church provided space for male-male love and intimacy, including for its celebration in forms of community and marriage. In the 1970s and 1980s, an era of secular liberation politics and deep suspicion of religions and their manifest intolerances, it seemed counterintuitive to look to the Catholic church for the reverse. This was Boswell's key intervention: histories of faith, religion and religious sites and institutions were, he showed, not only important to understanding the historical dynamics of hate and marginalization, but also to grasping the contexts and ways in which queer desires and structures of feeling were marshalled.[66]

Boswell envisaged the monastic cultures he described in essentialist terms. He acknowledged the effects of intense communal environments on love and desire, but he also saw them as places which drew a certain type of man. He was sceptical of social constructionism and its coherence as a mode of thinking about sexuality and desire in the past, working instead on the basis that there was indeed a minority of homosexually inclined men – then as before and after.[67] He refuted the simplistic caricature of essentialism in debate in the 1980s and early 1990s, not least by showing how the particularities of the time and place he was examining greatly mattered.[68] 'No reasonable person', he wrote, would disagree with the proposition that 'the social matrix' determines sexual experience 'in a largely irresistible way – including creating (or not creating) opportunities for sexual expression and possibly even awareness of sexual feelings and desires'. The more fraught question, he said, was 'whether society was itself responding to sexual phenomenon that are generic to humans and *not created* by social structures'. Boswell remained 'agnostic' about the basis on which human sexuality rested, suggesting it was likely a messy conjunction of biological, social and psychological factors.[69] On the one hand, this might be a moot point: whatever the origins of sexuality, there was broad agreement (including from Boswell) that social and cultural contexts mattered in the way it was understood and experienced. On the other hand, taking one view or the other directed the historian's gaze either to the search for this minority and type, or towards how and what same-sex acts, love and relationships came to mean at different times and in different places. In modern Europe, Michel Foucault argued, those acts and relationships had come to relate to the idea that there was a particular sort of homosexual person – one he saw his friend, Boswell, mistakenly trying to seek out in the medieval church.

2. Cultural theory and history

Boswell's thinking ran counter to that of deconstructionists and post-structuralists from the late 1970s who were looking closely at the ways language and discourse (including the language and discourse of history) produced meaning and 'truth effects' such that sexuality, the gender binary, or racialized categories seemed to be self-evident and transhistorical. Understanding the constitution and entanglement of these things meant examining discourse and culture instead of – or in addition to – social and economic structures which could not alone fully explain how norms and systems of power were sustained. This re-emphasis is evident in what became known as history's linguistic or cultural turn in the 1980s. It brought a fresh emphasis on the role of language and rhetoric, of art and architecture, and of community rituals and rites of passage in constituting (rather than merely reflecting) realities, norms and ways of being.[70] Lesbian, gay and especially gender and queer history emerging in the later 1980s and 1990s leant into these often highly theorized approaches, shifting the dial in history making in these areas further towards the academy. Katz, Weeks, Rich, Faderman and Smith Rosenberg had already challenged received wisdom in their historical work, which in different ways focused on the social and cultural modulation and production of sexual identities and meanings. This resonated through books and articles by Foucault, cultural anthropologist Gayle Rubin and literary scholar Eve Kosovsky Sedgwick who, from their different disciplinary and theoretical perspectives, elaborated ways in which sexual(ity) histories might be conceptualized and imagined. They staked further claims for the significance of sex and desire in understanding society, culture, and the operations of power, and in ways that made them foundational to queer theory and highly influential in the turn towards a queerer history.

Michel Foucault and the incitement to discourse

Whereas Anglo-American liberation movements and social history and history from below underpinned much of the work discussed thus far, Foucault's perspective emerged from a different context. Identity politics had a looser purchase in France and there was a strong literary and philosophical postwar tradition of deconstructing received ideas about subjectivity.[71] This was especially evident at Paris VIII, the radical new university founded in 1969 after the student ferment of the previous year, and where Foucault headed up the Philosophy Department.[72] In his bravura work on sexuality, he did not look in a focused way at particular contexts of same-sex intimacy, identity and community, but sought rather to identify a wider system of knowledge production and its powerful affects. Foucault took aim at the very concept of sexuality as Gagnon and Simon had done – and no less importantly at the popular conception that prudish Victorians had repressed it.[73] Sexuality in Europe, ran the argument, had come to seem an obvious and intrinsic component of identity, manifesting in tell-tale signs on the body, in gesture and in character (an understanding Hyde and Rowse had absorbed, for example). Foucault argued that these ideas took hold not because they were the truth, but because of a nineteenth-century 'incitement to [sexual] discourse' in authoritative sexological, psychoanalytic and legal texts and practices which confected a series of sexual archetypes – including the invert or homosexual.[74] Seen from this perspective, sexologists of the late nineteenth century were not describing a pre-existing homosexual type but rather inventing and pathologizing him as a distinct sort of person. Foucault insisted that this notion of sexuality was central to the exercise of power at a time when there was a felt need to manage, understand and categorize ballooning urban populations. Casual sexual acts and criminal sexual behaviour came increasingly to be seen as signs of inner truth – a truth some internalized and which others sought to treat and correct medically and psychoanalytically. Sexologists worked in dialogue with these 'homosexual' men and women (though largely the former) to formulate their categories, which in turn came to define others.[75]

Foucault was not in this claiming that identities associated with sex and desire were entirely new, but he was showing that a distinct nineteenth-century European choreography of meanings around sex took especially tenacious hold because it was associated with post-Enlightenment thinking about autonomous selfhood and what it meant to be human (or less than human). He argued that these meanings gained cultural purchase in part because of associated moves to advance rational knowledge via the professionalization and institutionalization of science, law, medicine, architecture and even history.[76] These powerful discourses encouraged individuals to assess and police themselves in what was effectively a diffuse mobilization of power. Sexuality in the Foucauldian conception was, explains classicist David Halperin, an 'amalgamat[ion of] desire and identity into a unitary and stable feature of the individual person', imparting 'a true self – a self that . . . functions as an object both of social regulation and of personal administration'.[77] In the wake of Foucualt's intervention, the historical task for some was to determine 'the discursive conditions that contribute to the construction of what comes to be regarded as true'.[78] In this formulation, 'coming out', that supposed moment of self-assertion and liberation, ironically became an accession to domineering ideas about what constituted the self rather than to the truth as such. This was an example of what Foucault described as 'reverse discourse', the process by which a newly imagined minority begins speaking and fighting on its own behalf, further shaping and firming up the invented minoritized category.

The history Foucault wrestled with was of the present. He was locating intersecting and overlapping ideas from the past about inner sexual truth and sexual types which unevenly inflected and shaped ways of being and acting in the now of the 1970s and 1980s. This was his take on 'genealogy', though in quite a different sense to its use either in conventional family history or by A. L. Rowse in his lineage of famous homosexuals.[79] Foucault pressed historians to think about how present understandings and categories, including the imperatives of their own discipline, directed and distorted their analysis of the past. He was pushing at established ways of knowing and at privileged knowledge production, shifting the methodological gears towards language, discourse and representation. This, he believed, allowed a broader-based history of sexuality to come into focus with the potential to explain far reaching operations of power and not only the specific repression of homosexuals. Retrospectively, the resonances with earlier and contemporaneous work by MacIntosh, Weeks, Gagnon and Simon are clear, but what Foucault added – and what was problematic in its way – was the broad-brush sweep across time, the West, and whole populations in an analysis of power which in its ambition rivalled that of Karl Marx.

The scale of this ambition resulted in deep engagement and ongoing critique. Reading Foucault, historians and theorists of sexuality came to challenge his failure to deal more fully with gender, race and empire. They worried over his focus on expert discourses like science at the expense of other less exclusive and elite 'genres' such as music hall or 'penny dreadful' scandal sheets which could produce popular ways of knowing beyond science.[80] Foucault's close attention to discourse had another ironic effect: to create a distance from the experience of sex itself, even as that experience was shaped by the ways in which it was described and understood culturally.[81] This worked against his call to turn from the constraints of an invented sexuality towards an appreciation and enjoyment of 'bodies and pleasures', a call couched as a hope for the future but which would also come to inform approaches to the queer past.[82] Foucault's intervention remains key because he opened out a fundamental historical question that queer historians have pursued in more local and contextual detail than he could do: that is, how have those random 'bodies and pleasures' been given meaning, been understood in particular ways, and become embroiled in structures and hierarchies of power? If Foucault's *de facto* case study was the nineteenth-century European invention of sexuality and the sexual types that came with it, his remarkable thesis invited analysis of other organizations of sex and desire and the rituals, traditions, and discourses which shaped them.

The 'charmed circle' and minoritization

Foucault had certainly not been the first to observe how power wove through the organization of sex. The feminist movement – in its first and second waves – had demonstrated decisively how patriarchal power was enacted and enforced through sex, and the positioning of women as sexual objects and sexual possessions. Women's history had been and continued to be a key tool in demonstrating this and also in showing how history was itself complicit in reinforcing these dynamics of power.[83] The analysis led some to campaign in the 1970s against pornography, penetrative sex and SM, and to explore different forms of intimacy which might swerve the re-enactment and entrenchment of patriarchal dynamics. At a 1982 conference on sexuality at the Women's Center of Barnard College in New York, these positions were challenged by so-called sex positive feminists in an eruption of the feminist 'sex wars'.[84] The arguments made at the conference matter to queer history because they circled and challenged what sex signified, and suggested the historical, social and cultural forces behind the accumulation of meaning. Sex in and of itself might be intrinsically meaningless. This was the position taken by Gayle Rubin, who was amongst the sex positive group at the conference. She argued in her paper for a re-thinking of sex and the meanings and judgements attached, sketching out a hierarchy with a 'charmed' inner circle of 'good, normal, natural, blessed sexuality' set against 'the outer limits of bad, abnormal, unnatural, damned sexuality'. In this way, she drew attention to oppositions between monogamy and promiscuity, same generational vs. cross-generational sex, using bodies vs. using toys, sex in private vs. sex in the park, and more besides. These hierarchies were, she showed, distinct from – though related to – those associated with gender.[85] Sexual and gender hierarchies were, for example, both in play in judgements passed on a sexually dominant butch dyke or a passive effeminate queen, but they were not coterminous. Sex and gender thus needed separate though relational analysis, Rubin contended, anticipating some later gender theory and history.[86]

Like and alongside Foucault, Rubin argued that sex was freighted with meaning accrued over time and in ways which were apparently necessary for social order. These culturally constituted meanings were powerful: people internalized them and they served as a means to include, exclude and hierarchize. Sex, or more especially 'bad sex', was a dumping ground for other social anxieties, with the general message that eradicating and marginalizing such activity would straighten out (in both senses) mainstream society. Rubin pushed against – and highlighted the dangers of – a sex negativity which reinforced this hierarchy of 'good' and 'bad' sex and of the 'good' and 'bad' people involved. Such judgements were pervasive and so mattered profoundly to lesbian, gay and soon queer history. They could make certain subjects of research – such as intergenerational sex and abuse – too toxic to engage with, given a context in which positive renditions of 'good' sex and sexualities were significant to arguments for rights and representation.[87] Rubin gestured instead towards an open field of investigation, beyond contemporary judgements, to consider the meanings and power dynamics that were culturally and historically associated with sexual acts, and which necessarily positioned the individuals involved in highly particular ways.[88]

With these arguments, Rubin troubled the utility of the gay/straight binary in understanding sexual and related social hierarchies in the past. Though heterosexual sex lay in the inner and homosexual sex in the outer circle, Rubin opened out many further complexities. The monogamy of a middle-class, white same-sex couple, for example, might give the pair an equivocal place in the charmed circle, whilst the promiscuity of a heterosexual and especially a heterosexual person of colour might be beyond the pale. These observations have been a spur to historical analysis – including my own. It was helpful to me in making sense of the queer artist couple Charles Shannon (1863–1937) and Charles Rickets (1866–1931). By acceding to some if not all elements of the charmed circle and adding the charm of creativity, they lived together their entire adult lives as a tolerated couple in Chelsea in central west London.[89] By contrast, the contemporaneous 'diffuse sexual and artistic bohemia' of ex-pat English folk in Florence, described by historian Rachel Hope Cleves, existed outside 'narrowly drawn' 'charmed circles' in Italy. This was not, she argues, because they were particular sexual types but rather because they were part of a deliberately transgressive heterosocial network.[90] For cases like these, Rubin's lens was more useful than sorting the heterosexual from the homosexual, indeed it allows heterosociality and cross-sexuality allyship to swim into view. Queer in this formulation is not in simplistic opposition to 'heterosexual'; it might indeed be possible to align with either and still oppose heteronormativity.[91] As the literary scholar Sharon Marcus argues, different forms of homosexuality can 'have less in common with one another than with their heterosexual equivalents'.[92] Age often structured relationships between older and younger men or boys *and* between older men and younger women or girls in nineteenth-century London, for example. Gender and class privilege gave a sense of entitlement and immunity to elite men in their relationships with and/or abuse of younger people.[93] Taking into account the sexuality binary which was beginning to come into limited cultural play in this period provides some insight into the thinking and behaviour of certain men, but exploitative sex also cut across emergent sexual typologies.[94]

From the mid-1980s, literary scholar Eve Sedgwick was making resonant arguments about male desire.[95] She saw universal and transhistorical potential for all people to engage in all sorts of sexual activities, but also that they were inhibited from doing so by the meanings that clung to them. These meanings mattered, and needed to be a focus of historicist enquiry, because they were central to the organization of culture and power. Following Foucault more explicitly than had Rubin, Sedgwick argued that sexual attraction between men became increasingly culturally pivotal in the West from the nineteenth century onwards. A distinct minority was conjured which served to define a 'normal' majority. Because the potential was for all men to desire and have sex with other men, the division was policed in paranoid fashion both personally and culturally. Sedgwick made her argument through careful literary analysis, showing how novels could expose and fuel such cultural 'tendencies' (to use the title of her 1994 book). In nineteenth- and twentieth century literary works by Herman Melville, Oscar Wilde, Henry James and Marcel Proust, she identified the play of homoerotics, sometimes via triangles in which a female character served as a cipher for the unspeakable draw between her two male suitors. Sedgwick demonstrated the acute anxiety of a culture governed through homosocial institutions in which the 'invisible, carefully blurred, always-already-crossed line' between being 'a man's man' and 'being interested in men' might be (and was often) traversed.[96] Rather as Iwan Bloch had suggested seventy years earlier, holding this line required a defensive homophobia. Normative masculinity was thus arraigned in opposition to the homosexual and his dirty secret. As a consequence, and given that normative masculinity was critical to the maintenance of nation and empire, this newly minoritized figure and the closet he occupied needed, ironically, to be visible; he and it became culturally central.

Here was a significant intervention which provided much needed oxygen to the argument that gay and lesbian studies and history were not minority pursuits but rather illuminated broad social and cultural norms and the ways in which they were sustained. Together with Foucault and Rubin, Sedgwick highlighted the significance of the production, and circulation of meanings to sex and desire, which in themselves had neither intrinsic truth nor a necessary connection to a particular identity or body. Their insights, which underpinned queer theory, reorientated historical questions. If lesbian and gay history had been focused on locating and enlarging our understanding of those engaged in same-sex sex and relationships in the past, it also now concerned the associated but more diffuse task of tracing the shifting meanings of sex and desire, and the ways in which 'regimes of the normal' operated in different times and places – regimes which sometimes included and sometimes specifically marginalized same-sex sex and relationships.[97]

Sedgwick's work followed and fed 'new historicism' in literary scholarship from the 1980s. This heralded a fresh focus in literary analysis on historical context and 'the historical webs in which . . . objects of study [authors and their texts] were caught'.[98] Read in this way, culturally specific preoccupations, hopes, fears and desires could be discerned in novels, poems and plays. In *Sexual Anarchy* (1990), for example, literary scholar Elaine Showalter teased out the homoerotics of Robert Louis Stevenson's *The Strange Case of Dr Jekyll and Mr Hyde* (1886) and Bram Stoker's *Dracula* (1897) in ways that elucidated interconnected late-nineteenth-century anxieties about degeneration, double lives and queer desires.[99] Literature could give some affective sense of a historical time and place and of coordinates of identification, power and passion. Fellow literary scholar, Alan Sinfield, built on these ideas to highlight the culturally active and instrumental role of literature and theatre. Working in the anthropological vein of cultural materialism, which has a sharp analytical focus on the technological, economic and political factors structuring and impacting culture, he argued that literature has often functioned to entrench power structures attendant to class, sexuality, race and gender. It was the genre of writing through which these structures became especially culturally visible at particular historical moments and also to subsequent historians and critics. But though literature promulgated and embedded power structures, Sinfield also argued that it could expose 'faultlines': moments in a text which suggested other ways of thinking and being. It was in this way that he distilled the radical potential of William Shakespeare's plays and Oscar Wilde's writing, and explained their queer appeal and import.[100] The arts – including literature, film, theatre, photography, sculpture and fine art – could provide a space where other worlds and possibilities might be imagined and where an alternative record of deviance might be amassed beyond (or unevenly overlapping with) science, the law and everyday interaction and gossip. Literary scholar Terry Castle thus conjured 'the apparitional lesbian' haunting literature of the past three centuries in her 1993 work. She suggested that this made lesbianism loosely imaginable for women readers then and gave it literary historical texture for those reading the works since.[101] She and others also alluded to the space for the queer imaginary in what went unsaid in literary work. Gaps, silences and the proverbial closet might be envisaged as queerly creative and productive.[102]

Historians met this literary turn with some caution. 'Readings', wrote historian and literary scholar Valerie Traub, 'are not the same thing as history; and deconstructive and psychoanalytic interpretations of literary texts, whilst they contribute importantly to historical understanding, do not necessarily conduce to a historical explanation' of why change occurred between one historical moment and another.[103] In her analysis of what she described as 'the discipline problem' in lesbian and gay history, Duggan similarly warned against the over-analysis of 'particular, privileged texts' and the 'overbroad' claims attached to them. Historians, she noted, 'are trained to collect a large number and variety of texts before making generalizations'. That approach 'would provide sounder grounding for the close textual readings by literary and cultural critics'.[104] Rubin participated here, remarking in an interview with Judith Butler in 1997 that: 'there is a common assumption that certain kinds of conceptual analysis or literary and film criticism provide descriptions or explanations about living individuals or populations, without establishing the relevance or applicability of such analysis to those individuals or groups'. 'I have this quaint, social science attitude', she opined, 'that statements about populations should be based on some knowledge of such populations, not on speculative analysis, literary texts, representations, or preconceived assumptions.'[105]

It was easier to get at the conditions for existence suggested in writing of a period than at existence itself, but the latter quest remained important if queer history was not to be populated only by the famous and notorious, or conceived solely in the interplay of discourse. The muddle of everyday life, including the physical, visceral act of sex itself, mattered too. There was no neat separation of the discursive and cultural on the one hand from the experiential and social on the other. But though historians of sexuality largely agreed that they were 'mutually constitutive', they struggled to find any neat way of assessing the relationship between the two.[106]

3. The history of sexuality

The radicalism of this body of historical and theoretical work resided in just how profoundly and variously it threw over biological and essentialist thinking and the idea of a binary sexuality. Scholars modelled a range of approaches to the past, including from social and cultural history and literary new historicism. From the later 1980s, this work came to be understood under the umbrella term of 'the history of sexuality'. Novel academic journals, especially the *Journal of the History of Sexuality* (*JHS*, from 1990) and *Gay and Lesbian Quarterly* (GLQ, from 1993), consolidated the emergent field's academic credentials, even though sexuality in the mid 1990s still tended to be 'locked out of history departments' and was seen to be peripheral to the 'central historical process'.[107] Much of the work, as we have seen, was undertaken either beyond the academy or in adjacent disciplines – in sociology, anthropology and literary and film studies, for example – cementing an interdisciplinarity that has been an abiding feature of the history of sexuality and especially queer history.[108] New work was deeply engaged in the wider 'cultural turn' of the humanities, invested in the history of ideas and the play of discourse and representation, tutored in part by scholarship from literature and film. Approaches from social history remained prominent too, though, and especially as oral history projects underway in the 1980s bore published fruit in the 1990s, and as historians grappled with that opaque relationship between self, society and culture in their analysis of, amongst other topics, sexual violence and safety, sexual and reproductive health, sexual advice, the dynamics of love and desire, social movements, and the modulation of sexual norms.[109] They did this initially largely in relation to the modern period and the United States and western Europe. Surveying the early years of *JHS* shows how unevenly research spanned the globe and centuries, though there has been developing reach in both respects over the last twenty years especially.

Queer history was strikingly dominant in this consolidating field. In each issue of *JHS* for its first decade (and indeed since) around a third of the review pieces and at least one (and usually more) of the five or six main articles relate to queer history. This included work on identity and community formations, biography, social movements, the transnational movements of people and ideas, localized and particular cultures and expressions, and the ways in which the state was implicated in the mobilization of hate and in strategically reinforcing a modern minority/majority model, not least through the law and policing. Throughout, the editors of *JHS* have granted extensive attention to queer, gender and postcolonial theory as historians wrestled with how best to historicise phenomena more often and popularly viewed transhistorically or in isolation. Such methodological and theoretical acuity provided some scholarly heft, a legitimacy perhaps, to a field which was still often seen as marginal or only of special interest. It allowed practitioners to build a sense of a collective project within history (albeit still precariously) and not only in other disciplines and outside the academy. By the 2000s some scholars (me included) were getting academic jobs because of, rather than in spite of, their work in the field, and in 2006 Matt Houlbrook and H. G. Cocks were able to assert with authority, in a state of the field collection no less, that the history of sexuality had become 'a protean discipline that allows us to enter a world of meaning, to understand the most fundamental assumptions of everyday life that shape social, cultural and political life'.[110]

A strong strand in such history of sexuality research concerns the situational play of desire (in shared bunks, between upstairs and downstairs, or between adjacent parts of a city, for example) and about the lived experience and configuration of intimacies and relationships which were sometimes in line with (and a product of) prevailing norms and identities and sometimes eccentric to them. Though historians of sexuality have been suspicious of finding types and identities in the past, this was not, in the words of literary and film scholar Annamaria Jagose, to 'discredit' identities like lesbian and gay and associated histories. It was instead to explore the conditions of their emergence and 'interrogate . . . [their] effects'.[111] People's behaviours at times fitted and at others exceeded circulating understandings of sexuality, desire and sexual identity. Houlbrook and fellow British historian Helen Smith, found working-class men having sex with each other as well as with wives and girlfriends in London and northern England in the first half of the twentieth century, for example. Most did not seem to attach the sex they were having to any interior sense of self or to a homosexual identity.[112] They instead saw themselves being within the normal or usual run of things, with bisexuality a common practice if not an identity. This was the case even as more elite contemporaries were beginning to mark a distinction in sexual types which then tended to compel the expert's – including the historian's – gaze. Such research decentring sexual categories led historian Victoria Harris to suggest that we take more historical notice of 'the acts of sex – those divisions of reproductive functions, the acts of intercourse . . ., the ways in which people experience the erotic and express themselves as human beings'.[113] This is especially salient if we accept Foucault's contention that sexuality has had a short historical pedigree as a nineteenth-century 'invention' and has not in any case had universal take up as a 'truth of self' globally or locally (as Houlbrook and Smith show clearly in the English context). In this sense, work in the history of sexuality has often exceeded the concept of sexuality itself, rather as lesbian and gay history went well beyond examining those who identified in these ways. It has done so most avowedly as queer history, taking in not only the peripheral, marginal, and radical, but also regular and reactionary everyday lives, cultures, and interactions, including the abuse of children and young people, slaves, and the imprisoned.[114] And yet if queer history has an intellectual home within the history of sexuality, it also has some alternate roots and sustained links beyond in both its origins and its journey since.

Conclusion

The final three decades of the twentieth century saw extraordinary intellectual ferment, reflecting – and reflecting on – rapidly shifting cultures of sex and sexuality. This chapter has sought to give some account, beginning with the legal and literary homosexual histories which enlarged awareness and understanding of historical figures, some of whom were key in later work. They formed a lineage of icons which had – and unevenly continue to have – significance for many LGBTQ+ people. Lesbian and gay historians in the 1970s and 1980s and queer scholars since have cautioned against the tendency to see these figures as intrinsically gay or lesbian. They have suggested instead how self-conceptions and broader understandings were of their time and not of all time, and also that unduly dwelling on our icons can obscure other ways of thinking about past queer behaviours and identifications. Social history, history from below, and oral history were foundational to such work and have continued to be hugely important in mapping out networks, communities and identities in relation to the social and economic forces and contexts of particular times and places. These approaches signalled the importance of class and social positioning – and so of the processes and impacts of capitalism and industrialization – to understandings of same-sex intimacy and desires. Socio-economics, social capital (or the lack of it) and consumerism have continued to be highly significant in analysis.[115] Historians working on the lesbian past, often in social history mode, and as much in the context of women's and feminist history as of lesbian and gay history,[116] meanwhile showed how 'any woman could'. This was a take on sex, desire and intimacy that can be traced through subsequent writers now considered foundational, notably Foucault, Rubin and Sedgwick. With these later interventions especially, approaches expanded as cultural history encouraged analysis of discourses, rituals and traditions which shaped meaning and so everyday behaviours and understandings. Those working within the new subdiscipline of the history of sexuality often melded these influences and perspectives in their work. The field has been persuasive in demonstrating the historicity of sexuality, bolstering earlier work in lesbian and gay history and consolidating the epistemological foundations of queer history.

This was not a total picture. Bi and trans dynamics and identifications received scant attention in this body of work – either directly or even in the ways gender transitivity and bisexuality were part of gay and lesbian histories in narratives of the self and networks of politics and sociability. Bisexuality, where it did figure in historical analysis, tended to emerge as a practice rather than identity and partly, historian Martha Robinson Rhodes suggests, because of the ways it was shut out of lesbian and gay liberation politics and cultures in the 1970s and 1980s.[117] There has in the last twenty years been more specific attention to the historical dimensions and formations of bi and trans identities and cultures, including in avowedly queer work looking beyond binaries of gender and sexuality and at periods and places where ideas of exclusive sexual identity have held less sway than they have in the Global North.[118] Further structures and regimes of power associated with race and gender have come into sharper focus, as have the possibilities and impossibilities of assessing subjectivity and emotions that inform everyday acts. These strands, perspectives and methodologies were by no means altogether absent before, but the 1990s and especially the 2000s would see them move front and centre, in the process challenging the Anglo- and US-centrism of much gay, lesbian and queer historical work.

Coda

My own route to queer history from the late 1980s, via literature departments, was both narrowly biographical and symptomatic of wider developments. In the late 1980s and 1990s, such departments were still more open to theorizing and thinking in historicist terms about queer themes than were most departments of history.[119] The MA in 'Literature Culture and Modernity' I took at Queen Mary, University of London, in 1993/4 included a course about AIDS literature and film as contemporary history. The timing mattered: the course was designed by a faculty member who died before he could deliver it, and two experienced colleagues stepped in to honour his legacy. It was sobering to witness academia, like other sectors, suffer grievous losses in the crisis, including by this time Michel Foucault and John Boswell. Such experiences wakened my sense of how meanings were produced around the virus, marshalling histories of abuse and pathologization explored in a second course I took about nineteenth- and twentieth-century gay and lesbian literature and its contexts. (It is worth noting that it was listed as a broader sexuality module to provide cover, the tutor said, for students worried that taking it might be seen as *de facto* coming out.) I found through this learning that history mattered to me in quite immediate ways. It provided anchor points for my new gay life in London and a deeper understanding of the confounding misogynist and racist dimensions of community I encountered on the scene and in my AIDS volunteer work. As a consequence, I leant into history for my PhD on homosexuality in late Victorian and Edwardian London, the project which became my first book, *London and the Culture of Homosexuality* (2003). Influenced by Foucault, Sedgwick and that literary historicist turn, there were chapters on the law and journalism, science and sexology, aesthetic and decadent literature, and Hellenism. The argument I made was that these powerful 'discursive fields' intersected with circulating expert and popular ideas about the city. I thus attempted critically to interrogate 'common sense' presumptions about the urban nature of the homosexual. The diary of the early campaigner for sexual law reform, George Ives (1867 – 1950), was a lodestone as I showed how these various texts and modes of expertise played out in one particular man's understanding of himself and others.

The discursive structure more or less survived for the book, though I added an epilogue focusing exclusively on Ives. It was a short chapter which one friend and colleague told me was in fact 'a breathless problematisation of my core thesis'. I had to concur. It is certainly the case that Ives' diary could be read as a textbook rendering of the interplay of the various discourses I had examined: we can see his preoccupation with sexology, the law and Hellenism, and also the way these ideas shaped his thinking and sense of self on a consciously articulated level. But what is also abundantly apparent is that Ives was not the sum of these parts. Some of his upper-middle class homophile and inverted friends and fellow Londoners lived related but very different lives, and saw him as an eccentric. One of the shortfalls was my stress on sexuality as the primary category for the analysis of his subjective experience, a predictably late twentieth-century tendency. Other of Ives' day-to-day lived experiences, understandings and articulations were, I conjectured in later work, as if not more significant in shaping his relationships and conceptions of desire.[120] Cultures and languages of class, for example, explained in part how Ives felt able to separate seemingly unproblematically the sexuality of his elite Cambridge University peers from that of some of his working-class lovers and house mates. It probably explains his desires for the latter. There were also the established generic and again class-bound conventions of diary writing which meant that Ives represented himself and his desires in particular ways.[121] My analysis of Ives in this first book did not ignore the significance of class, but I realized later that it could have been – needed to be – pushed further, and I sought to do that when I returned to him in *Queer Domesticities* (2014). This later book owed much to the social and cultural history I have discussed in this chapter, but it owed as much to the growing body of work in postcolonial and gender history and the history of the emotions which helped me to think differently again.

2

Identifications and Intersections

In her 1995 essay 'The Trouble with Harry Thaw', legal scholar Martha Umphrey considered the ways a young white playboy from early twentieth-century New York might best be understood: as protector of his wife's honour (by murdering the man who 'deflowered' her); as 'gay man' (on account of his male lovers); as 'bisexual', 'libertine', 'pervert', 'madman' or 'sadist'. She settled on 'queer' as a still inadequate way of acknowledging 'that the processes of history are unstable, and the search for exemplary historical subjects always incomplete'.[1] A queer history, she showed, was related not only to those who were avowedly or identifiably homosexual in whatever way but also those who refused 'to respect the laws of compulsory heterosexuality'.[2] Such a lack of respect, such sexual dissidence, did not necessarily give individuals a proud or radical place in history; they could just as easily be embroiled in the exercise of abusive power over others. Harry Thaw's way of being in the world owed much to his personal and family history and to the wider history of racialised, gendered and socio-economic privilege which allowed him to behave in the way he did with seeming impunity.

Many involved in the Black, feminist and lesbian and gay movements from the late 1960s had already flagged the need to think in interconnected ways in the analysis of identity, power, and oppression. As Umphrey was writing in the mid-1990s, however, queer, gender, subaltern and postcolonial theorists and historians were bringing the indices she highlighted into sharp focus in febrile contexts in the United States and United Kingdom alike. In the former, there had been a rollback of civil rights era political gains, especially in the workings of the justice system, and riots erupted in outrage – including in Miami (1980 and 1991), Los Angeles and Washington DC (both 1992).[3] In the United Kingdom, there was resonant unrest in cities in northern England in 1981, in Brixton, South London in 1985, and in Dewsbury, Yorkshire, in 1989. Demands to address institutional racism, especially following the police response to Stephen Lawrence's murder in south London in 1993, remained unmet.[4] Alongside, gay men and lesbians were cast afresh in the press and by government as dangerous to the social fabric. In the late 1970s and early 1980s, new gay rights ordinances were vociferously challenged in the United States and in some instances overturned following campaigns by the evangelical right concerned to 'save our children'. The UK government legislated in 1988 to limit the reach of 'gay propaganda'.[5]

AIDS was by this time exacting a heavy toll on gay and lesbian communities.[6] It was, wrote Paula Treichler (a scholar of women's studies and medicine), 'an epidemic of signification' in which earlier threads of meaning associated with homosexuals and people of colour – as diseased, corrupting, pathological and dangerous – were mobilized afresh in relation to HIV.[7] This prior storehouse of associations in part facilitated the swift escalation in contempt and with it the shame and fear which blighted lives as surely as the virus itself. Experiences of AIDS in the 1980s and 1990s were radically different depending on national and local regimes, politics, health systems and related embedded histories of colonialism, racialization, and organizations of gender. Situated at the intersection of multiple matrixes of oppression, queers of colour, for example, were both particularly vulnerable to the disease and neglected as potential care recipients.[8] Such differentials in power and in social and actual capital – including the histories that lay behind them – were a key concern of work emerging from postcolonial, subaltern, critical race and gender studies in these contexts. This in turn often tapped fresh scholarship on histories and theories of identification, agency and emotion, and on the challenge, indeed impossibility, of fully grasping these things and the subjectivities they imply in the past.

This chapter considers the impress of these adjacent and intersecting areas of work on queer history. They have together sharpened queer historical analysis of bodies, desires and identities, and of the way power operated on and through them, and have (paradoxically) clarified the limits of what we can know. As queer historians we have had to grapple with the conundrum of 'how to scrutinise taxonomy as a system and not allow its structuring habits to overdetermine our accounts of the past' (as queer literary scholar and historian Laura Doan deftly puts it).[9] The first section thus lays out concepts and approaches useful in troubling these 'structuring habits', and looks specifically at ideas of multiplying identifications, of unpredictable and individuated hauntings from the past, and of unruly emotion. These complicate notions of stable, coherent identity and subjectivity in the past, and underpin a messy, uncontainable (rather than formulaic) mode of intersectionality – the umbrella concept for this chapter also discussed in the first section and then in specific relation to race and gender in sections two and three (respectively). They show more specifically how historians have grappled with the complex entanglement of (homo)sexuality with other modes of categorization and identification, and how this relates to the exercise of power. The historical moves discussed in this chapter relate closely to the lesbian, gay, social, cultural and sexuality histories discussed in the previous one. Together and cumulatively they have helped towards an understanding of the complexities of lived and subjective experience, and disrupted totalizing ideas of cultural formation and unitary or simplistic accounts of identity and community in the past. In this way they have served to expand the queer historical imaginary.

1. Exceeding identity: intersections, hauntings and emotions

Intersections

Black feminist scholars in the 1970s and 1980s such as Angela Davis, Barbara Smith, and bell hooks noted with concern the frequent absence of race from the emerging scholarly conjunction of gender and sexuality. They argued that both gender and sexuality were racially coded and could therefore not be fully theorized and historicized without attending to race.[10] 'Actively committed to struggling against racial, sexual, heterosexual, and class oppression', these Black feminists set themselves the task of developing, in the words of the trailblazing Combahee River Collective to which Smith belonged, an 'integrated analysis and practice based upon the fact that the major systems of oppression are interlocking'.[11] In the late 1980s and early 1990s, legal scholar Kimberlé Crenshaw built upon this earlier activist-scholarship to show how racial and gender-based oppression could coalesce into particular forms of legal subjugation and discrimination for women of colour.[12] She argued that because racism and sexism were often viewed as separate forms of potential discrimination, the specific experience of these women at their confluence was obscured and diminished. As the Combahee

River Collective had contended, 'the synthesis of these oppressions creates the conditions of our lives'.[13] Vectors and hierarchies of power associated with race, gender and also class and sexuality needed to be analysed in their interaction with – and as co-productions of – each other, a necessity Crenshaw referred to as 'intersectionality'. This approach rapidly became key in thinking about how institutions (like the justice system) operated, how social and cultural norms were established and sustained, how oppression worked, and how people experienced the world, themselves and others.

These different threads in intersectional work were (and are) also entangled with each other and with complex histories. American literary and cultural critic Robert Reid Pharr thus wrote at the turn of the new century that 'even as we express the most positive articulations of Black and gay identity, we are nonetheless referencing the ugly historical and ideological realities out of which those identities have been formed'.[14] Exemplifying his point, he went on, 'I still had to resist the impulse to flinch when someone referred to me as queer and to positively run for cover when someone referred to me as a Black queer, as I have had to rid myself of the suspicion, left over from childhood, that I am being politely hailed as a n[word] and a faggot.'[15] Pharr shows how the cadence of queer, Black, 'faggot' and the 'n[word]' relate and morph in relation to his own positionality, identifications and emotionally laden experience, and result from a wider social, cultural and historical entanglement of racism and homophobia. Cathy Cohen and Scott Bravmann, writing in the United States of the 1990s, illustrated such imperatives to thinking intersectionally, including in historical research and writing, and not least in relation to, and in explicit and tacit critique of, LGBTQ+ history and politics which risked reinforcing rather than denuding structures and hierarchies of knowledge and power.[16] Cohen noted that 'for those of us who find ourselves on the margins, operating through multiple identities and not served or recognised through traditional identity politics, theoretical conceptualisations of queerness hold great promise'. But that promise, she went on, was not met when there was a failure to see heteronormativity as a system which 'intersects with institutional racism, patriarchy and class exploitation to define us as marginalised and oppressed subjects'.[17] There was, Bravmann noted in the same year, a pressing need:

> to examine gay and lesbian communities, subcultures and sites of resistance in complex, localised, and specific contexts, and to do so in relation to other kinds of social phenomena which mediate all sexualities: gender gaps and privileges, age and generational differences, racism and racial formations,

politics and national ideologies, the division of labour and class relations, to name just a few.[18]

This call, and resonant calls and critiques since, signal how enmeshed histories matter to the making of queer history and to an associated queer politics.[19]

These approaches gained uneasy traction on both sides of the Atlantic in the 1990s, and especially in contexts where interdisciplinary and cultural studies were finding space. At the University of Sussex on England's south coast, for example, the path-breaking Subaltern Studies Group were working alongside sexuality scholars including Alan Sinfield and Jonathan Dollimore. The Sexual Dissidence MA programme, which launched there amidst much controversy in 1992, was (and continues to be) notably intersectional and interdisciplinary.[20] If sex and desire in the past were being approached largely via the lens of sexuality, it was becoming clearer that other perspectives were needed too, and that in postcolonial and gender history, in histories of the body, the emotions and everyday life there was scope to broaden and diversify what was beginning to be known as queer history. Taking these perspectives can catch something of the complexity and play of power in identifications in the past, and provides tools for thinking askance, beyond identity, and also beyond sexuality – an imperative felt especially among those working on pre-modern periods before it had been 'invented'.[21]

Hauntings and identifications

The complexity of subjectivity arises partly from the entanglement of the past with the present – or, in our historical analysis, the past with the further past. When I have struggled with how to conceptualize this in my own work, which at its core is about quotidian queer lives and how they became un/liveable, I have often returned to historian and philosopher Michel de Certeau's 'Walking the City', which appears in his classic 1984 collection *The Practice of Everyday Life*. In this piece, de Certeau imagined Manhattan as a cipher for understanding subjectivity and agency within the social and cultural matrix, and in relation to hauntings from the past. He described surveying the island from the top of one of the World Trade Center towers – clearly, from that vantage point, delimited by the Hudson and New York rivers and organized with the grid system of streets and avenues. This ordering of the city served de Certeau as a metaphor for social and cultural control. The rivers certainly contained the population of the island, and the grid would logically also determine how people moved about there. And yet he noted that if people could not informally breach the watery boundary, they could and did negotiate the orderly system of roads and blocks in unpredictable ways. This, de Certeau argued, was because these spaces were haunted with the 'spirits' of individual and collective memory and history.[22] These allowed for or compelled eccentric navigations of the city, and cultivated some sense of agency and/or dissidence in the face of insistent modes of control, including orthodoxies relating to sexuality, race, gender and their intersections. To follow the Manhattan metaphor, this was akin to a refusal to follow the most direct or logical route across the grid in order to avoid or to pass by a spot inflected with personal or communal memory and meaning – a place of attack, flirtation, or protest perhaps. In addition, fractures in the grid of streets and avenues, as in the more uneven pattern around Greenwich Village, represent some flawed logic or dropped stitches in the wider social fabric. This creates an aperture to other ways of organizing society and culture, and other ways of being and behaving within the domineering structure.[23] And indeed, the actual street layout in that part of Manhattan allowed, even encouraged, those involved in the Stonewall riots of 1969 to take on the police, dodge them, regroup, and fight back from other positions.[24] Greenwich Village had long been associated with bohemianism and counter culture, haunting the collective consciousness of those rioting. This is partly why mechanisms of social, cultural and spatial control faltered here.

In the early 1990s, creative New Yorkers, including American gay science fiction author Samuel R. Delaney and the queer painter, photographer and writer David Wojnarowicz, captured a vivid sense of these possibilities in their work: identities proliferate, become radically unfixed or morph across a life course in relation to personal and collective histories associated with the city streets (and indeed, Greenwich Village). Fragments of the queer and Black past provided a means for everyday and more profound (joyful, erotic, tragic) departures from the grid of control viewed from the World Trade Center as was.[25] Art and fiction were shown again to be mediums which could capture something of the haunting presence of the past in the present de Certeau describes, and in ways 'conventional' modes of history making might struggle to do.

Such philosophical and creative work helps in thinking through the possibilities for eccentricity and difference within dominant social structures and in the face of powerful cultural expectations. These possibilities partially gather from the individualized play of the past in the present. This is a way of conceptualizing agency and deliberate deviation from norms and expectations but also of considering less purposeful difference. Sigmund Freud found in 'dreams, slips, jokes' clues to past wounds and formative events which directed behaviour unconsciously.[26] Historians can not fully explain such details (we can not psychoanalyse the dead) but we can hold, rather than override, the inexplicable in an individual's make-up and conduct in our historical analysis and perhaps see it as part of their queerness.[27] Umphrey thus reached for 'queer' to describe Harry Thaw because of her uncertainty in how to consider him. He can indisputably be explained in part through historically embedded and intersecting classed, gendered and raced relations and hierarchies of power, but his madness, sadism, violence, and multivalent desires are not fully elucidated in this way. Historians, most especially those working with queer themes and/or lenses, have increasingly allowed for an ineffability which they can glimpse but cannot clinch. [28] They have relatedly been reluctant to determine or label a sexuality in their subjects, and instead seek to take them on their own terms, in their own times, and as haunted by individual and collective memories and histories. In this way historians touch (even if they can not fathom) the complexity of subjectivity and everyday life – signified by those wayward navigations of Manhattan de Certeau observed.

Eve Sedgwick, in a deeply personal 1993 essay, used another metaphor, that of a pair of white glasses, to reflect on related ideas of identification. When wearing the glasses, borrowed from her friend Michael Lynch, Sedgwick saw differently and looked different. She reflected on this to reckon with her own cancer and Michael's AIDS-related illnesses, and with the ways in which culturally anticipated identifications and empathies shift in relation to these conditions and their historical and cultural meanings.[29] 'The white-rimmed spectacles', social anthropologist Silvia Posocco writes, 'were part of [a] critical project of envisioning social relations, affective attachments and knowledge practices that criss-cross gender and sexualities.'[30] Sedgwick showed how within her own life, as within most people's, such affiliations shift and change, challenging the continuity and stasis casually assumed to attach to identity, including sexual and gender identity, across a life course. It follows that we can not assume consistency or indeed coherence in the identifications of our historical subjects.

In psychoanalysis identification is described as a process through which 'the subject assimilates an aspect, property or attribute of the other and is transformed, wholly or partially, after the model the other provides.'[31] Sociologist and cultural theorist Stuart Hall, also writing in the mid-1990s, associated this process and experience with histories and cultures, with hauntings, which mobilize and sustain feelings of connection to a person, community, movement, or place. Those feelings might be fleeting or more sustained and part of an ongoing 'process of becoming rather than being'.[32] Thinking in these ways allows us to imagine people in the past having multiple and changing identifications, disidentifications or counter identifications.[33] These might have intersected, clashed and come in and out of focus at different times and in different places. This conception, Hall argues, is more helpful than the more singular and static idea of identity. In a similar vein, in work on Black queer men in the United States, literary scholar and queer theorist Kathryn Bond Stockton found the mobile concept of 'social holding' more helpful than 'community' in capturing feelings of belonging – from the sustained (in a church visited weekly, for example) to the more ephemeral (a cruising spot used occasionally).[34] Through the lens of community the former might get counted in, the latter most likely overlooked. But both might be as significant in 'orienting' a sense of self and identity (to deploy cultural theorist Sara Ahmed), and so in adjusting the way in which an individual positions themselves (or finds themselves positioned) in relation to prevailing norms.[35]

Apparent primary identities and communities – being gay or part of a gay community, for example – matter historically because they are part of the way people have understood themselves and those around them. But these articulations can divert us from historical complexity and the intersections that can make for very particular experiences of empowerment or oppression. Those experiences shifted for individuals in different places and times and in relation to other personal and collective memories and to wider histories.[36] Historians thus came to look at ways of describing people in the past which did not fix or singularize them nor homogenize the communities to which they belonged. This, for some, is why queer is so useful: it can be a descriptor of behaviour, of what a person did, rather than of who they were.[37] And it can signal an approach resistant to labelling individuals or assuming default cisness and heterosexuality. It suggests instead an openness to unexpected and cross-cutting identifications, organizations and experiences of sex, desire and gender.[38]

Being sensitive in historical analysis to the mobility of identification and its relationship to the play of power not only gives us a more nuanced sense of historic sexual subjectivities and the mesh of factors which shape them, but also exposes the fiction of a unitary or stable sexual identity then or since. Individuals might not have used identity descriptors even if they were circulating in their lifetime, and identities are in any case way more complicated than the labels we apply to them. There is, write H. G. Cocks and Matt Houlbrook, a 'part of identity and behaviour which cannot be categorised'. This, they go on, 'should tell us something about the inadequacy of dominant forms of representation for fully capturing and describing the nature of individual desires'.[39] Such desires vary through circumstance and in relation to changing wider cultures of eroticism and taboo. When people have acted on them this might have felt like an affirming or devastating confirmation of personhood, or alternatively like one of the random, fleeting 'twilight moments' fellow historian Anna Clark describes punctuating lives rather than being at their core.[40]

Emotions

Emotions orientate, sustain and disrupt identifications, and leaven the hauntings de Certeau evoked; they carry with them sometimes muted, sometimes sonorous, echoes of earlier lived experience. This 'archive of feelings' (as Ann Cvetkovich has it) is uniquely hard to grasp and navigate, and is a reminder of the ineffability of past subjectivities.[41] And yet, as historian Joanna Bourke notes, emotions have been a motor of social and cultural change and are 'at the heart of historical experience'.[42] They matter in queer historical analysis in particular because they modulated experiences of sex, desire and intimacy, and direct us to couching norms and expectations which prompted certain emotional reactions – like shame and anger – in those who didn't measure up.[43] Emotions were never 'only' personal but were mobilized in attempts to voice, prompt and persuade in contexts from the domestic to the governmental.[44] Bourke and others began to grapple with this significance from the late 1990s in the emerging subdiscipline of the history of the emotions, showing how feelings have changed in their dimensions and meaning over time.

Using emotions, including desire, expands queer history by leading us either away from types and identities or else into the complexity that lie beneath them. Historian Seth Koven, excavated 'deep structures of thought and feeling' in London's East End in the late nineteenth century in ways that threw up queer desires and dynamics illegible to historians looking through an identitarian lens.[45] Koven found a way into the texture of subjectivity by looking at how desires were mobilized in this specific context. He indicated that emotions might be felt, understood and corralled in particular ways by different groups of people, forming 'emotional communities' (as historian Barbara Rosenwein has it).[46] In her analysis of 'Oriental inscrutability', 'unsympathetic Blackness' and 'queer female frigidity', literary scholar Xine Yao captures a sense of how such communities formed and functioned at the interstices of gender, race and sexuality, and as a means of connection, survival and resistance in the nineteenth century United States.[47] Distinctive 'emotional communities' and 'styles' were instrumental in endorsing particular behaviours and identifications over others. In my work on AIDS in the United Kingdom in the 1980s, for example, I observed that the gay/straight divide was entrenched partly, even largely, because of the particular interplay of disgust, fear, and anger for groups of people bound by some shared sense of emotionality. Fear and shame had a different cadence for those identifying as gay than for those who were straight in this decade. This led these groupings to behave and respond in subtly and not so subtly different ways.[48]

Emotions clearly need a historical reckoning if we are to get closer to the dynamic relationship between queer and normal in and over time. This includes grappling with shame and other feelings related to 'unsettling or undignified aspects of homosexuality' which can tend to get bypassed in quests for prouder pasts.[49] As literary scholar Heather Love notes, queer lives in the past were routinely shaped and directed by a gamut of feelings, including 'nostalgia, regret, shame, despair, resentment, passivity, escapism, self-hatred, withdrawal, bitterness, defeatism, and loneliness'.[50] Such negative affects are compelling and important in analysis of the way individuals identifying or behaving queerly experienced themselves and lived their lives, but holding too fast to them as queerly defining risks reifying ideas of queer selfhood and blinkering us to the potency of other feelings. Joy and euphoria have also had a particular cadence in queer lives and histories, for example.[51] In the 'affectively dense mix' of emotions attending sex – that 'paradoxical domain of desire and dread, excitement and fear' (as US sociologist Janine Irving has it)[52] – we see emotional lives as multidimensional, pulling our historical subjects (and us as hisotrians) in contradictory directions.

Thinking intersectionally and with unruly emotion, multiple/multiplying identifications, and hauntings of the past, shows that discerning and analysing structures, hierarchies and taxonomies only gets us so far in thinking about past behaviours and subjectivities. Individuals were controlled and deeply impacted by these things but they also negotiated them in eccentric and unpredictable ways – ways which we, as historians, usually can't discern and can at best only signal. 'Find[ing] a body' in the archive, historian, Anjali Arondekar reminds us, does not mean 'one can recover a person' or 'formulat[e] . . . a subjectivity'.[53] There is perhaps some hope in envisaging people in the past finding their particular routes to liveable lives, and tacitly, fleetingly, sometimes deliberately and forcefully, resisting domineering forces and ways of knowing in their everyday. That they usually did this out of reach of the archive and the historian adds a frisson of evasion and of possibility in the past – and so perhaps also in the present.

2. Race, empire, and postcoloniality

LGBTQ+ histories have largely been written in and about Europe and settler North America, those places where the identities represented by the acronym formed and have had most purchase. They have in the process frequently embedded a eurocentrism, overextending the geographical reach and relevance of these categories and neglecting their raced and colonial dimensions. The casually assumed whiteness of these identities has usually passed unexamined, as have the ways in which racism, sexism, and homophobia have been entwined. The UK-based archivists and curators Ajamu X, Topher Campbell and Mary Stevens suggest this has been because of 'the splintering of activist historiography into discrete categories of a heteronormative Black history and an exclusive monochromatic queer history'.[54] In general, historians in the United States were quicker to analyse the implications for queer history of race and processes of racialization than those in the United Kingdom. As a consequence there has been a tendency in UK university curricula and popular history to look across the Atlantic for Black queer history.[55] This is even though historians of the British Empire and the postcolonial period have shown how gender and sexuality were centrally at stake in colonial rule and the processes of dehumanization and racialization in which the British had such a major role and which underpinned British state and imperial formations.[56] However, as opposed to the United States, the suffering of colonized and enslaved people took place largely away from British shores and has been scandalously peripheral to the British cultural field of vision. This is perhaps why the impact of empire, the slave trade, and associated processes of racialization and migration have all too often been absent in British LGBTQ+ (and broader) historical work.[57]

Recent queer work on Britain has taken more seriously the co-construction of class, race, gender and sexuality, demonstrating how these intersections must be understood as intrinsic to queer life, experience, representation, exclusion and silencing.[58] Work on postcolonial, subaltern, Black and Indigenous history and theory in the 1980s and 1990s laid some of the ground for this, challenging embedded eurocentric historical narratives, and signalling the importance of re-centring history so it is not told only via those worldviews, epistemologies, terms and frames of reference.[59] Key postcolonial analytics, including 'othering' (Edward Said), 'mimicry' and 'hybridity'(Homi Bhabha), 'identification' (Stuart Hall) and 'conviviality' (Paul Gilroy), have had some uneven purchase in queer history.[60] The 'othering' of queerly identified people sharpened a sense of a norm in opposition; the notion of mimicry resonated through considerations of 'passing' as straight or cis, and in ways that allowed a degree of access to normative power and privilege and equivocal avoidance of derision, violence and arrest. Hybridity and conviviality – connoting 'blending', interaction and also 'a radical openness' – invited a consideration of the cross-overs and co-productions of queer and normal, 'making a nonsense of closed, fixed and reified identity', as Gilroy put it.[61] What is certain too, though, is that these lenses applied in queer analysis also need to show how race and processes of racialization have mattered in that context. If queers in general have been othered, white queers have sometimes been shamefully instrumental in othering queers of colour, who, in turn have gained much less social capital through mimicry.[62] How to embrace nuance about intersections in modes of historical analysis, as with intersections in historic identifications? The two subsections that follow explore some of the ways in which historians have addressed these questions in relation to the colonial conjunction of race and (homo) sexuality.

Othering, silencing and nation-building

In *Orientalism* (1978), a foundational work of postcolonial studies, the literary and cultural critic Edward Said showed how the British and French exoticized populations of Asia and North Africa as a means of inscribing racial difference and exercizing colonial control. Said's examination of this cultural othering of 'the Orient' pulled desire, sex and gender into the examination of imperial power and dominion. He and subsequent scholars showed how this imagined Oriental 'other' (and the racialized 'other' more broadly) worked to confirm the restraint and moral righteousness of the European colonizer and fortified his 'right' to rule and 'civilize'. And yet the terms of this othering also made the colonial subject an object of erotic fantasy.[63] Historian Rudi Bleys showed in his 1995 work how nineteenth-century anthropological and other literature produced hierarchies of raced bodies with associated ideas of 'primitive' sexual appetites and propensities which were erotically captivating to some Western observers.[64]

Later in the decade historian, John Tosh, described a related and tacitly queer male 'flight from domesticity' in the mid- to late-nineteenth century in which colonial 'service' overseas became an extension of the homosocial and uneasily homoerotic worlds of public schools, universities and clubs which directly and indirectly sustained – and were sustained by – the proceeds of empire and its underpinning ideologies.[65] Alongside, and as I discussed in *Queer Domesticities* (2014), there was the fashion and passion for collecting, born in part of imperial adventuring, and bound into one version of British elite male queer culture.[66] Empires could in these ways set up particular homoerotic dynamics and institutionalize queer possibilities. Histories of (homo)sexuality, race and empire were conjoined – and in different ways in relation to different colonies and empires.[67] Decolonizing LGBTQ+ history thus proved to be much more than the inclusion of more queer people of colour and colonized peoples in analysis. It was also about showing how race and colonization matter in the emergence and understanding of categories of sexual identity, modes of identification and the broader play of desire and hate.[68] In an early edition of the *Journal of History of Sexuality*, for example, literary scholar Robyn Wiegman unravelled the 'sexual economy' and homophobia in play in the American South between white lynchers and their Black victims, who they often castrated before murdering.[69] More recently, cultural theorist C. Riley Snorton has demonstrated the particular dehumanization of Black trans people because they fell foul of white categorizations of both gender *and* sexuality.[70] Racism, homophobia and transphobia were enmeshed; these vectors of hate cannot be fully understood in isolation. 'Trans issues are never simply about gender,' historian Emily Skidmore notes, 'but always already about race, class, sexuality, citizenship, and national belonging.'[71]

Centring colonization brings alternate histories into particularly clear view. Historian Jamie Jesperson notes the ways in which a range of different (and differently named) trans feminine roles amongst the indigenous populations of southern California were collapsed under the single label 'Joya' by the invading Spaniards in their creation of New Spain in the 1520s. The *'aqi* (Chumash), *wergern* (Yurok), *iwop-naiip* (Yuki), *kwit* (coastal Acjachemen), *uluki* (mountain Acjachemen), *alyha* (Mojave), and *hwami* (Mojave/Yuma)', amongst others, had gendered roles wholly unintelligible to the Spanish colonizers.[72] Instead, the invaders saw their 'effeminacy' in relation to sexual passivity and indulgence in sodomy (often understood vaguely in this period and before to refer to 'a general miasma of sexual sin').[73] The elision of sexual practice with gender by the Spanish was used to justify the vicious hounding of the Joya in what scholar of Indigenous cultures, Deborah Miranda, describes as a 'gendercide' via 'murder, renaming, re-gendering and replacement'.[74] Distinct pre-conquest understandings of gender were in this way rendered barely legible to ensuing generations of Californians. They were reimagined in the terms and frames brought by the Spanish. The supposed 'primitivism' of these people was at the same time used as a foil to underpin the civility of the Spanish, obscuring and justifying the brutality of their conquest.[75] There was an intricate relationship here between race, indigeneity, sexuality and the dynamics of colonized and colonizer.

Anti-queerness was key to nation-building and colonization, including in newly independent former colonies. In early-twentieth-century Cuba, for example, effeminate men and masculine women (and associated sexualities) were linked with the colonizing other (first Spain and then the United States). Pepillitos, effeminate men, signalled passive 'submission to a foreign power', argues historian Abvel Sierra Madero.[76] The muscularity and reproductive virility of the postcolonial island was affirmed by way of contrast. In resonant ways fellow historian Mrinalini Sinha shows how for Bengali men in the late nineteenth century effeminacy was a symptom of colonization, a trait that could be shed once the British had been expulsed.[77] Anthropologist Basile Ndjio identifies a related othering of Western sexualities in Cameroon as part of an assertion of national character and a purification of its sexual past. It was a way, indeed, of forgetting an earlier sexual diversity.[78] This work reveals an emphasis on different modes of masculinity in the gendered and sexualized processes of modern state formation. It also illustrates the irregular global circulation and movement of gendered ideologies and systems and an uneven patterning of resonance and dissonance between Global North and South.

Though sociologist and gender theorist R. W. Connell assessed the inception of Spanish imperial adventuring in 1493 as a global watershed in how sex and gender were organized and governed, there may be a eurocentric tendency in overplaying the invasions as a thoroughly new beginning.[79] Colonialism was uneven in the way it played out, in its reach and its 'success', and historians have shown that there are contexts where it pays to think about histories of sex and gender beyond or adjacent to colonialism. In the later 1990s, historians Pete Sigal and Marc Epprecht described not an obliteration of native cultures of sex and gender, but rather cross-overs and something of the 'third space' of mimicry and hybridity Homi Bhabha had theorized a little earlier.[80] Sigal identified a seventeenth- and eighteenth-century hybrid queer culture that existed in the Mexican Yucatan between the Mayan people and late colonizers.[81] Epprecht suggested that colonialism, Christian and Muslim traditions, and shifting local popular culture created particular conceptions and expressions of (homo)sexual selfhood in parts of Africa.[82] More recent work by anthropologist Rudolf Pell Gaudio and historian Nwanda Achebe on Nigeria and by political scientist Joseph Massad on the Arab world, has signalled the endurance of cultures of gender and sex from periods prior to colonization and the arrival of Christianity or Islam.[83] In the Indian context, meanwhile, literary scholar Ruth Vanita has been able to show the use of Hindu rites in same sex unions and couple suicides from the fourteenth century – before, during and after British Imperial rule.[84]

These scholars have often had to work with archives in which the subaltern is refracted through the colonizer's gaze. The very idea that there might have been adjacent ways of knowing and feeling in the past is obscured in these hostile contexts. In a pivotal 1985 piece on 'reading the archives', literary theorist Gayatri Spivak argued for the need to hold a space of not knowing and to assess silences for what they tell us about the exercise of colonial power and about who and what gets hidden.[85] What existed behind those silences could barely be rendered or understood within eurocentric logics and the fiction of neutrality and authority in Western history.[86] We see this in the case of Joana Aguilar. Historian María Elena Martinez describes how Aguilar was tried in the colonial royal courts in El Salvador in the early 1800s for 'abominable sins' with women and was suspected of being a 'hermaphrodite'.[87] After fleeing to Guatemala, they came to the 'enlightened' attention of the surgeon Narciso Esparragosa y Gallardo. Gallardo was called on to examine Joana in 1803 and his findings were rehearsed in Aguilar's legal case, which is how the episode landed in the Spanish colonial archive and, later, came to the attention of historians. Gallardo had rubbed Aguilar's clitoris to study its enlargement and probed the other sexual organs before pronouncing that Aguilar had neither the full union of sex characteristics to make a 'hermaphrodite' nor an appropriate configuration to be classed as either man or woman. The surgeon concluded that without a sex designation, Aguilar could not be guilty of the crime of which they were accused. They were subsequently cleared. Martinez shows how the case was read in the 1930s as evidence of medical erudition and enlightenment in the face of brute laws. She re-read it in 2014 as an example of the imposition of European knowledge and reasoning. Martinez argues that Aguilar was rendered powerless and passive in the legal and medical context, and that the idea of a rational medical discourse obscured other drivers behind the surgeon's behaviuor and Joana's own subjective composure.

Acutely aware of silences in the archive, Martinez is able to suggest that the case opens out possibilities of different ways of being and knowing the self before and in the interstices of colonial dominion.[88] She signals a shadow mapping of gender and desire haunting official Spanish accounts, even if we still can not answer the question of how Juana thought of themselves in relation to their gender, desire and the sex they were having. In these respects Martinez' study relates to and is in tension with Anjali Arondekar's work on the limits and possibilities of the archive. Arondekar meditates on the impossibility of recouping subaltern subjectivities from objects in the archive. But she also engages the entrenched presumption that archives are marred by the absence of sex and sexuality and that recuperative work is necessary and urgent. She argues instead that the recuperative urge says more about the desire of the researcher and the particular cultural presumption that sexuality and sexual knowledge are hidden. She shows that the records in the Indian archives she explores are saturated, with these things: sexuality is central rather than marginal within them.[89] In this way, like Martinez, she denudes assumptions – or, perhaps better, fantasies – of obscured, veiled sexuality in the colonial archive.

Terms and frames of reference

Imperatives to categorize and hierarchize, characteristic of colonial governance and key to histories of racialization, lie behind nineteenth-century sexological terminology like 'homosexual' or 'transvestite'.[90] These associations echo through later understandings, such that gay, homosexual, lesbian and queer folk are often assumed white in Europe and North America to the exclusion of queers of colour who have been subject to other (and othered) typologies enfolding assumptions about indiscriminate 'primitive' desires and sexuality.[91] There is a significant strain in imposing Western terms and categories. In the early 2000s anthropologist Martin Manalansan found that the use of 'gay' by the Filipino-American gay New Yorkers he interviewed obscured diasporic and racial difference. It was an imprecise translation of Filipino terms which had other or additional meanings.[92] There is a need, Manalansan suggests, to think via adjacent ways of naming and knowing. Literary scholar Iman Al-Ghafari nevertheless makes an argument for the utility of the Western category 'lesbian' in the Iranian context. Aside from being internationally recognizable, Al-Ghafari sees lesbian as less perjorative and sexualizing than Iranian terms like 'grinder' and 'rubber', and even though these terms potentially capture better the physical rather than identitarian ways in which female-female desire and sex were being conceived, including as in some way tolerable.[93]

Running more and less explicitly through this work is the question of whether the discipline of history can ever account for other and othered ways of thinking and feeling – especially given its complicity in Orientalism and racialization.[94] Africanist James Sweet suggested in the mid-1990s that it is only by looking askance and sidelining Western Judeo-Christian tradition that the social and political significance of 'third sex' spiritual leaders in the sixteenth and seventeenth centuries can come into focus.[95] More recently, literary scholar Keguro Macharia advocates creative renderings of pasts for which few direct traces remain but which have a heavy impress on the present. In his work on the queer dimensions of the middle passage, he describes a historical duty to imagine the visceral impact of forced proximity on board the slave ships and of the abuse meted out by slave owners and others.[96] Suggestive in this process of informed, creative presumption can be the fragments circulating in oral traditions and folklore, in poetic and literary material, in gossip and anecdote, or in sculpture and material culture.[97] Amassing such counter archives and readings against the dominant archival grain has been a keynote of postcolonial and queer histories and their intersections.[98] Amidst all this, though, there is a need to avoid what Rahul Rao describes as 'homoromanticism' in which the time of the 'indigenous precolonial' is idealized as 'a spacetime of unmitigated tolerance', and as necessarily more 'authentic', free or unfettered.[99] We do not erase the history of violent imposition of colonial power and typologies when we also note that prior systems and conventions of sex and gender may have been differently or relatedly coercive and constraining.

Postcolonial work has been crucial in pushing those working on queer themes to be alert to and to challenge hierarchies of knowledge, language and perspective; to provincialize (rather than generalize from) European and North American contexts; and to pay attention to migration (forced and chosen) and to the processes, dynamics and lived experience of diaspora.[100] It shows that histories of racialization and colonization are entangled substantively, perspectively and methodologically with queer history, and this includes the way whiteness has been imagined and produced in relation to particular ideas about gender and sexuality. Work on contexts in the Global

South are therefore not 'just' an extension of work on the Global North (in what would be a replication of the metropole/periphery colonial dynamic). This was the key premise and concern in the 'Histories of the Sexualities in the South' project. Convened by Sephis, the South-South Exchange Programme for Research on the History of Development (established in 1994 amidst this upsurge in debate touched on in this section), the project created, from 2007, a network of historians working on sexuality within their respective regional and national contexts, and provided training and peer mentoring. The money came from the US Ford Foundation, tapping a neoliberal pulse in LGBTQ+ history-making. In execution, though, the emphasis was determinedly south-south. Project meetings were held in South Africa, Brazil, Bangladesh, Cairo and Indonesia and the essays in the resulting edited collection dislodge the Global North – and the United States and United Kingdom especially – as lodestones.[101] This work and more recent queer of colour historical critique insists that we are cognisant of who and what we privilege, eroticize, dismiss or ignore in our queer historical work. It insists too that we look at the structural ways in which race, gender, desire and sexuality intersected, and at how deviant or more specifically homosexual bodies were imagined within hierarchies of race, gender, place, class and related notions of respectability, acceptability, in/tolerance and homonationalism.[102]

3. Gender

Gender clearly mattered profoundly to processes of racialization, to the dynamics of national and colonial power, and so also to queer experience and identity and community formations. In conversation with precedent and ongoing work in women's history and feminist theory, gender history and theory burgeoned from the late 1980s alongside postcolonial work, driven by a similar deconstructive drive to question apparently obvious categories and transhistorical assumptions. Gender theorists and historians, notably Joan Wallach Scott, suggested that gender was contingent and multifaceted, with no singular model of what it meant to be a man or a woman; no one mode of femininity or masculinity enduring across time and space; and no *a priori* truth in the gender binary. Gender was a component in regimes, dynamics and structures of power, and in ways which incorporated but could not be reduced to patriarchy. The emphasis was increasingly on particular interdependent forms of masculinity and femininity, and the power that accrued to them. Connell, for example, investigated the idea of 'hegemonic masculinity' – that is, the concept that there were forms of masculinity that had most cultural purchase and power in a given place and time, and that stood in a relation of superiority to counter, complicit or subordinate masculinities. It is important, she suggested, not only to look at the power men had over women, but also at hierarchies of manhood and womanhood relating to age, class, race, sexuality, ability and also gender positioning and crossings.[103] Scholar of the African diaspora Hortense Spillers, in a similarly prominent intervention, argued that gender roles were firmly differentiated (socially, culturally, economically) between slave owners and their wives and daughters in the American South. These people and their bodies were seen to be sufficiently human to warrant this designation and division. Those gender differences narrowed, or were erased, amongst those they enslaved, Spiller controversially suggested.[104] This was because of their collective dehumanization and the same hard labour they were all forced to undertake on the plantations. In this context, power rested first and foremost in the hands of white men, not all men; white women, many of whom were also slaveowners, often also wielded significant power over the enslaved, including the power over their lives and deaths.[105] Related to these gendered positions were particular ideas about sexual propensities and orientations, sexual propriety and respectability, and sexual power and vulnerability.

Gender, Sexuality and the body

It is clear already that gender, viewed in non-essentialist terms, has been centrally at stake in the historical analysis of the (homo)erotics of race and colonialism, and associated hierarchies and dynamics of power. The body was the visceral site of this conjunction and can not be understood historically without a consideration of circulating ideas about gender. 'Bodies are not easily read', writes historian Annette Timm. 'Whether male or female or somewhere in between, they harbour no self-evident truths and no obvious clues as to how we should translate their differences into the fabric of our social and political lives.'[106] In this spirit, historians exploring gender, queer and trans formations in the past have sought to trace meanings attached to bodies and to explain how those meanings arose and with what affects – including in relation to how they were experienced erotically.[107] The determination of the body's gendered characteristics has been closely related to shifting understandings of sex and sexual preferences and has been shown to be markedly different in different places and times. Men in classical Greece and Rome had ways of thinking, feeling, and desiring which combined a distinct sense of corporeality and gender, for example. An athletic physique signified a honed balance of body and mind aligned with values of self-restraint, power and control.[108] His masculine elite status might be variously preserved and enacted bodily through the penetration of an enslaved person, an adolescent boy, a female sex worker, or a wife. The much-debated figure of the cinaedus was meanwhile effeminized by supposed sexual excess and a lack of self-control which made for a visible bodily contrast to other men. The cinaedus was, classicist Craig Williams argues, best understood as a gender deviant rather than as a sexual type akin to the passive homosexual.[109] In these contexts, the body, sexual activity, gender identity and social status were entwined, and in ways that followed no singular formula.[110] Looking at the subsequent period, artist and historian Leah DeVun traces waves of representation of non-binary bodies from the early Christian era to the fifteenth century, illustrating 'an embrace of the idea of nonbinary sex among the authorities in early Christianity, its rejection at the turn of the thirteenth century, and a new enthusiasm for its novel and expanded properties at the dawn of the Renaissance.'[111] In the process, DeVun casts fresh light on the way such difference was venerated and derided, and also related to intersecting depictions of sexual and religious alterity, such as in the putative animalism and sexual deviance associated with Jewish bodies and behaviour. In a related vein, Japanese Studies scholar Rajyashree Pandey shows how medieval Japanese texts had a fascination with the possibilities of the body in ways which evaded any strict binary between man and woman or, indeed, human and non-human (a further division troubled in recent queer historical work).[112] In this period and place, there was at least conceptual fluidity and porosity in the way gender was seen, and so also a queerness in the ways bodies were imagined interacting.

Drawing on medical and scientific texts, cultural historian Thomas Laqueur outlined a European shift in understandings of the sexed body between the early modern and modern periods.[113] In the former regime, he argued, women's bodies were seen as an imperfect version of men's, with inverted male genitals. In this 'one-sex model' women's desires were active like men's, with orgasm seen as necessary to conceive in a mirror of male ejaculation. An enlarged clitoris might signal heightened libido which could be satisfied by a man (for the virago) or another woman (for the tribade).[114] Crucially, the physical signs here were to do with sex drive rather than the direction of desire towards one gender or another. Meanwhile, humoral theory suggested that gender might be somewhat fluid, since the four bodily humors could be in and out of balance according to age, season, diet and a host of other factors.[115] These conceptualizations shifted with new directions in scientific thinking and the emergence of the idea of the autonomous enlightenment individual, Laquer argued. Male and female bodies were no longer conceived as inverted versions of each other but instead as disconnected opposites with desire directed from male to female across the divide.[116] Historians Laura Gowing and Karen Harvey offered serious caveats to this interpretation, on the basis that conceptual shifts did not translate straightforwardly into experience. Gowing showed that in the seventeenth century people understood their bodies through their own experience rather than via medical discourse, whilst Harvey, using eighteenth-century erotica, demonstrated the endurance of the idea that male and female bodies were in close relation rather than in opposition.[117] Together they underscored the unevenness of shifts in popular understandings and the frequent disconnect between expert writing and people's everyday experiences of their bodies.

The idea that women might have an independent and lusty sexuality does, however, seem to have receded across the eighteenth and nineteenth centuries in Europe as the concomitant notion that they needed 'completing' by men took firmer hold. It was only men and masculine women who were properly lustful. So whilst Valerie Traub argues convincingly that there was an 'amplified presence' of both erotic and romantic representations of relationships between women in sixteenth- and seventeenth-century England (often related to classical precedents), from the eighteenth century onwards this seemed more outlandish and 'against nature'.[118] Relationships between women were increasingly framed in terms of intimate romantic friendships, mobilized by love rather than desire, as Lillian Faderman had famously argued.[119] Sex without a penis and without penetration became almost unthinkable. Whatever women did together seems not to have been understood as sex in any 'true' sense. This is perhaps what made women 'slapping flat cunt' together acceptable to a late-nineteenth-century Norwegian judge who casually remarked that the practice was commonplace.[120]

Being a 'real' man increasingly meant desiring a woman or someone woman-like. London's eighteenth-century Mollies fell into the latter category, argues historian Randolph Trumbach, suggesting that they occupied a third gender position – in a muted echo of conceptualizations in classical Indian medicine of the second century and foreshadowing some strands of European sexology of the late nineteenth.[121] By this time, Trumbach averred, it became harder to maintain elite masculinity 'with a whore on one arm and a boy on the other',[122] even though the possibility of maintaining a sense of normality whilst having sex with other men unevenly endured in Britain and its capital until at least the 1950s.[123]

We do not know how Mollies actually understood themselves. It is tempting to assume that the queerer dimensions of their lives represented their 'real', 'authentic' sexual and gendered selves. Harking back to Hall's argument about identification, however, we might as much consider the ways they may have inhabited – perhaps relatively comfortably – different social roles as husbands, fathers, tradespeople and also as Mollies. Historians have suggested how Molly houses might for some have been places which allowed them to express felt gendered orientation or identification, bringing in ideas about sexual desire and practice alongside.[124] For others, the reverse might have been the case: these were houses where sexual desires could be indulged, underpinning gendered performance that seemed to go obviously with them, an angle taken by the historian Rictor Norton.[125] For others, Molly houses could have been one site amongst several for urban distraction and light relief, evoking desires and behaviours untethered to any profound sense of gendered or sexual selfhood. There may have been some mix of these things and also for some a mercenary element: there was scope to make some money in such places. What is certain is the extent to which gender was front and centre in a subculture in which marital relationships, childbirth, and domestic rituals were play-acted and parodied. Prevailing norms and gendered divisions were in these ways being pressed into the service of Georgian gender-queer revelry, involving the lower classes taking parodic aim at elite fashions and mores. When some of their number were prosecuted, those who received the roughest treatment in the pillory were apparently those who had crossed from being an 'athletic Bargeman', 'Herculean *coal-heaver*', and 'deaf tyre Smith' by day to being Mollies on some nights.[126] People were perhaps especially incensed by the way such burly convicts betrayed new norms of manliness. Their bodies, restrained in the stocks, became the focus of the crowd's anger.

Historians of the nineteenth and twentieth centuries have shown how bodies in Europe and North America in particular were read for signs of apparent gender and sexual difference, often identifying the latter through the former. Bodies were seen to betray deviance and also offered the means to straighten it out. Conversion therapies were an assertion of medical and scientific expertise on – and authority over – deviant bodies in procedures that historians Tommy Dickinson and Kate Davison have shown to be dehumanizing, pathologizing and shame-inducing.[127] They had profound effects on the way those being treated experienced their bodies subsequently.[128]

Surgeons 'corrected' sex indeterminacy in intersex people, and from the 1920s worked with some few patients to confirm a gender which differed to that assigned at birth.[129] Others remodelled their bodies without medical intervention to emphasize or de-emphasise gendered characteristics, through chest binding, for example. Starvation, multiple childbirth, luxurious foods, and cultures of drinking and exercise shaped and reshaped the body in gendered ways which related to experiences of and presumptions about desire and sex. Joanna Bourke shows that bodies prompted and compelled the quest for meaning because of what they did physiologically and the pain and pleasure experienced through them.[130] Such meanings in turn affected the way bodies felt and were understood. That they were associated with such a physical entity made them seem more obviously true and fixed – even though they demonstrably changed over time.

In addition to the substance of the body were the gestures, stance, walk, and voice which were part of a learned and repeated grammar of gender. Historian Robert Nye, for example, showed how upper-class French masculinity in the long nineteenth century was embodied through an adopted poise suggesting natural nobility.[131] More recently, Shakespeare scholar Will Tosh describes the ways in which gendered comportment was learnt in sixteenth-century England where boys of middling and elite families were differentiated from girls by being breeched and separated from them in dress and care at around the age of seven. Thereafter they learned how to be men – and in ways which also plunged them into a homosociality tinged with homoeroticism.[132]

Such ritualized and naturalized performances of gender are at the heart of Judith Butler's influential argument in *Gender Trouble* (1990), a work which has underpinned much queer as well as gender scholarship.[133] Our gendered comportment and identity, they argued, is not 'natural' or rooted in biology. Instead, we 'cite' other bodies in the way we conduct ourselves, layering up previous ways of being physical and in the process reinforcing a binary of gender necessary to the maintenance of heterosexuality and heteronormativity. Such bodily 'citation' or 'performance' is so sufficiently unselfconscious as to seem like the obvious way to be a man or a woman, making gender roles and behaviours (as well as the heterosexuality they summon) as hard to sidestep as if they were hard-wired. History is in this way written onto our bodies, representing an accretion across time in an imprecise embodiment of past intersections of gender and sexuality.

The imprecision in bodily citation or in following gender orientating 'speech acts' is significant, though. Therein lies the scope to see the historicity of the body, gender and associated understandings of desire, and to conceive of change over time. Traces of century-old bodily forms, gestures or voices find their way into later times in ways that not only reinforce but can also disrupt present-day norms and ideas of the naturalness of gendered behaviour. Camp draws particular attention to such shifts by deliberately seizing on and ironically replaying classic postures (from a 1930s Hollywood movie perhaps) or exaggerating gendered gestures (like the flicked wrist or pout). The division of the natural and unnatural crumbles when the performativity of gender is revealed. Gender is shown to be malleable and open to deliberate mis-citation in what Sedgwick came to describe as camp's 'prodigal production of alternative historiographies'.[134] Hauntings from the past (to loop back to de Certeau) allow for alterative navigations of gender and sexual norms in the present (or the present of the past).[135]

Trans historians have been especially attuned to such gender variance, including in its relationship to sexual 'deviance'. Robert Hill thus lists 'MTF and FTM transsexuals, drag queens, street queens, hair fairies, female impersonators, effeminate gays, butch lesbians, and transvestite clothing fetishists' in his account of trans 'before transgender' from the 1960s to the 1980s.[136] This intersection has been common in the characterization of sexual and gender minorities, though it has often been hard for historians to judge where the emphasis in analysis should or could be. This emerges in historical examinations of Victorian Londoners Fanny/Ernest Boulton and Stella/Frederick Park.[137] Their trial for attempted sodomy in 1871 rested in part on an examination of their bodies and the way they comported themselves with a theatrical effeminacy which sometimes seems to have been an attempt to 'pass' and sometimes to allude to but not quite follow feminized gendered expectations. In court, they abandoned their drag and demi drag in favour of a performance of ordinary masculinity, including masculinizing moustaches in a context when facial hair was all the rage for men.[138] That they were acquitted, historians have argued, was a sign that the jury did not decisively connect the evidence of effeminacy and cross-dressing to the crime of sodomy with which they were charged.[139] Their defence of overenthusiastic playacting might also have been accepted by jurors reluctant to land heavy punishment on them.[140]

Historical analysis of the case, perhaps because of the sodomy charges, has tended to focus first on the pair's sexuality, rather in the way 'female husbands' have often been read as lesbians.[141] Literary scholar Simon Joyce suggests reversing the direction of analysis or, rather, envisaging both queer and trans embodiment and subjectivity in such cases.[142] Historian Mo

Moulton concurs, noting how reading sexuality off gender presentation 'privileges identity founded on sexuality and assumes a stable sexed body to anchor it'.[143] This neglects the way in which historical actors like Fanny and Stella and Moulton's own case study of historian Muriel St Clare Byrne (1895–1983) form a sense of themselves which does not align neatly with prevailing categorizations then or now. This might mean withholding the urge to put either gender or sexuality first.[144] It might also mean allowing for the contingency of these things and for past lives to 'operate . . . according to other logics'.[145] As Jen Manion notes in her *Female Husbands* (2020), 'our contemporary belief that gender and sexuality are identities individuals articulate has dramatically skewed our view of the long-ago past'.[146]

Whilst, as Rubin and Sedgwick insist, there are different hierarchies and regimes relating to sexuality and gender, we do not get far if we analyse one without the other or without other intersections (of race, class or dis/ability, for example).[147] We do not get far either if we think about bodies only conceptually and not as visceral entities central to experience, as Butler acknowledged in *Bodies that Matter* (1993) in part response to criticism of *Gender Trouble*.[148] Given that we don't have bodies from the past physically in front of us, historians have struggled to capture a sense of them, how they looked, felt and were experienced, and also how their abilities and disabilities were judged and made to signify differently at different historical moments – including as erotically freakish or as de-eroticized.[149] We can look to texts, images, statues and film to get some sense, but of course these representations will often present idealized and/or conventionalized bodily forms.[150] These are themselves telling and historically significant but they do not get us to the physicality of sex. Indeed if sex in the present of the past was more body than text (if the two can at all be separated), queer and gender history has often been more text than body.[151]

Binaries and beyond

The entrenched Western binary perspective has tended to mean that much queer historical work looks at either men or women. There are good reasons for this separation. Social and economic structures have divided men and women in ways that then also structured the scope and nature of same-sex sex and relationships. This includes in pre-industrial Europe where the pervasive (and unevenly enduring) idea was that women were not the mistresses of their own bodies but the property of fathers and then husbands – a patriarchal regime that affected the way women and men behaved and understood themselves and each other.[152] Historians have shown that industrialization, urbanization and the expansion of trade shifted some of these entrenched gender regimes and ushered in others, relating, for example, to the division of home from work which altered queer dynamics once more but, again, often in specific ways for men and for women.[153] Men in modern Europe have generally been better resourced and able to buy, socialize, gentrify and travel in ways that has shaped gay male cultures and networks differently from those of lesbians.

Such tangible economic and social divisions, together with associated cultural presumptions about – and productions of – gender, have affected trans analysis too. Kit Heyam shows how masculine dress and identification amongst people assigned female at birth has often been explored by historians in relation to economics and the scope for better pay in traditionally male work.[154] That such behaviour might also or instead be about gender crossing, confirmation, or trans identification gets less consideration than for those assigned male at birth identifying and/or presenting as female. There has tended to be more of a presumption of a distinct taste, passion or inherent character for these historical figures. The stakes were different for each of these loose groupings, and chiefly because of the different social and economic positions accorded to the gendered positions they were embracing.[155]

With legal, social and economic change in the direction of gender equality in twentieth-century Europe, there was more conceptual scope to assess shared ground and alliances across the gender divide, even as very significant fractures remained. Experiences of same-sex desire and relationships nevertheless continued to be in need of singular historical attention.[156] Historian Rebecca Jennings shows this in her recent work on lesbian intimacy and family-making since 1945 in Australia and the United Kingdom. The intimacies she describes have been fundamentally shaped by gendered roles, positioning, and reproductive capacity.[157] In her study of suburban US 'lesbian desire within marriage' in the 1950s, fellow historian Lauren Jae Gutterman suggests that balancing suburban heterosexual marriage with homosexual lovers was a different experience for home-based wives than for husbands who commuted to work and might have had their queer flings in the city.[158] Whilst both Jennings and Gutterman demonstrate that heterosociality was often significant to lesbian friendship and kinship networks, the ways in which lesbians have been un/able to make family and forge intimacies has been fundamentally structured by the social roles and cultural positioning accorded to men and women. Whatever enforces the gender binary and however much we might see it as a fabrication, it has had very real social, economic and personal effects. It is this that makes women's and lesbian history enduringly significant.

Bucking the single-sex approach to research poses particular challenges and yields different perspectives. In her 1991 study of the close friendship of Noël Coward and Radclyffe Hall, Terry Castle suggested the particular intimacies that could emerge between queer people across gender lines, and especially in relation to a shared sense of artistic and sexual bohemianism.[159] Anthropologist Esther Newton also looked at gay men and lesbians together in *Cherry Grove, Fire Island* (1993). She nevertheless tellingly identified the need to rebalance the dominance of men in the book with a chapter dedicated solely to women's experience.[160] Taking this two-gender approach allowed her to show how rupture between men and women could be overstated, but also how lesbians 'remained a distinct and separate group whom gay men recognized as alien kin, sisters yet strangers'.[161] Such authorial decisions often reflected a sense of personal political solidarity and allowed for a grounded analysis of difference, divergence, and conviviality.[162] They bring into focus heterosocial friendships, alliances, and households, and their importance in many queer lives past. There is a larger aperture in such an approach for acknowledging the ways in which queer lives often involved cross as well as same-sex sex and relationships – whether experienced as desired, despised, companionate, sexual, necessary or a mix of these things.[163] Queer but cross-gender couples and households were bound together variously by political commitment and joint or collective care-giving for children, each other, or frail adults long before gay adoption, surrogacy and acknowledged queer co-parenting and care-giving arrangements gained more visibility.[164] Bisexuality has often been a lived experience across a life course or in a particular period of a life.[165] That it was often not claimed as a label means it can be missed in identity-based histories or in histories blinkered by contemporary typologies emphasizing gay and straight and men and women.[166]

Sidelining the social and cultural power of the gender binary (however much we might want to unsettle it) can underplay the ways in which it structured desire and relationships – from the Molly houses of the eighteenth century to the butch-femme bars of 1950s Buffalo and London.[167] Historians have shown that this was true in relationships across generational, racialized and class divides in which the positions on either side were envisaged as more or less masculine or feminine by those involved or those commentating from the sidelines. In the late nineteenth and twentieth centuries, southern European, north African and working-class teenagers and young men were often described as embodying an earthier or more robust masculinity which made them desirable to the older 'cultured' northern European men who desired them.[168] Gendered difference mattered in such same-sex sex and relationships, including in assumptions about who had an associated intrinsic homosexual identity and who did not. This, Alan Sinfield argues, put the modern figure of the homosexual in a fix because it could seem that desire flowed only in one direction – across a gender divide from the flawed (effeminate) to the idealized (masculine) man.[169] The homosexual wanted a 'real' man but a 'real' man would surely not want or desire a man imperfect in body and masculinity.

There is, though, a difference between theorized positions like Sinfield's and historically lived realities. Houlbrook shows that 'regular' 'masculine' guardsmen rent boys had sex with middle class and tacitly or explicitly feminized queer 'brown hatters' in Hyde Park as a way of earning some extra cash, having fun, and perhaps asserting some power. But he also observes that these casual contacts sometimes resulted in sustaining and lasting friendships and relationships and on terms which may not have felt unequal in gendered terms (even if they were unequal in other ways).[170] Gender differences between female lovers have tended to be overstated historically, argues historian Leila Rupp, and possibly because butch-femme couples have been especially visible and culturally legible.[171] Timm argues that the idea of gender difference structuring same-sex relationships in any case began to recede in Europe after the Great War. She suggests that the experience of conflict validated the idea of brothers-in-arms (and on the home front sisters-in-arms) and that there were then subsequent equivocal moves towards gender equality and fairness brokered by some social democratic European states taking on a more 'caring' role. This unevenly shifted the ground on which relationships were built and desires were felt.[172] Companionate marriage became increasingly common and desired in the second half of the twentieth century in Europe, and this seems to have been matched in same-sex relationships oriented around a shared rather than differentiated sense of masculinity and femininity.[173] Post-gay liberation there was a greater articulation of this ideal (if not the reality) of mutuality in sex, pleasure and relationality.[174]

Whilst the power of the gender binary historically is evident, holding it too firmly in our historical analysis obscures the very different ways in which gender was understood and experienced across the globe from ancient to more recent times. In a 2013 piece, anthropologist Mary Weismantel describes her dismay at a colleague who cut off a whole swathe of understanding of the

Çatalhöyük people in southern Anatolia around 7000 BC by splitting them into male and female and assuming social roles which accorded to our contemporary understanding. Weismantel argued instead that they were a society in which this division would probably have made limited sense given that there was 'very little evidence of socially assigned gender'.[175] This is partly because people we would now divide biologically as either men or women do not seem to have had particularly different social roles, and, secondly, because 'ancient people did not think of themselves and their own bodies in the modern western sense, as individual bodies with individual identities'.[176] Weismantel demonstrated the historical insight that can flow from withholding or holding very provisionally a default binary position in relation to gender. Kit Heyam, for example, has looked at contexts and circumstances of gender dissonance in the past where a two-gender system did not make the most sense. As they write, 'it's history that shows us that – notwithstanding the outraged claims of anti-trans commentators today – what constitutes a man, a woman or gender itself has continually been defined, contested and redefined'.[177] Universalizing categorizations need to be subverted to the ways gender non/conformity was experienced and understood at a local level, gender scholar Shraddha Chatterjee argues in relation to histories of the Hijra in India.[178] This echoes the queer historical move to withhold assumptions about sexual identities (and binaries) and to historicize and particularize gender alongside and in relation to sexuality, sex and desire.

In their work Chatterjee, Heyam and also Snorton suggest the utility of deploying a trans lens, of transing the past, and of using 'trans' as a placeholder or indicator rather than an identity.[179] This brings an openness to past understandings, experiences and regimes beyond the organizations and types we might anticipate. It also allows us more easily to think about queerness and transness together as well as on their own terms. This includes where gender crossing and confirmation, gender indeterminacy, and third gender and intersex might not have been seen or experienced as culturally troublesome or subversive but instead acknowledged as part of a run of possibilities or in relation to particular social roles.[180] This approach brings a recognition that trans identities can not be fixed or idealized in a timeless tradition and further that the 'oddly gendered subject' existed 'in the world and in relation to others'.[181] Transgender history, gender studies scholar Jay Prosser argues, is usually constituted of everyday stories forged in particular everyday contexts.[182] These can nevertheless feel extraordinary to us now, as with the upbeat accounts of trans men Skidmore found in north American newspapers at the turn of the twentieth century and which 'focused on individuals who excelled at embodying not simply masculinity but a particular type of masculine identity: that of the white, economically independent citizen'.[183] In this we circle back to the contextual intersections of race, class and gender where this chapter began and which gave Harry Thaw his social position and power in New York at around the same time.

Conclusion

The history of the emotions and postcolonial and gender history, together with theoretical work on identification and subjectivity, spurred new queer histories in the 2000s. These increasingly took account of intersectional dynamics in the workings of power and the ways individuals conceptualized and conducted themselves. Thinking in these ways showed that people were not only passive constrained consumers or 'subject positions defined entirely within a discursive web'.[184] Intersections of sexuality, race and gender have been, along with class,[185] the elements most frequently marshalled to such queer analysis. But there is a growing awareness of how widening our historical lens further, broadening our sense of intersectionality, can only enrich understandings of identity and identification, as well as of community and social holding, past and present. There is more to say about how understandings of disability, patterns of faith and religion, the more than human world, and cultures of education and work (amongst much else) modulated experiences and conceptions of sex and desire in different ways in different times and places. Crip studies scholars, for example, point to the physical and/or mental infirmity that attended 'diagnoses' of inversion or homosexuality. They also signal the way in which homosexuality became a form of disablement in capitalist economies focused on heterosexual reproduction. In the late twentieth century, in the context of the AIDS crisis, there was a notable tendency for gay men to associate themselves with fitness and able-bodiedness, and attribute asexuality or latent heterosexuality to the visibly disabled.[186] What was considered dis/ability also changed over time and individual levels of dis/ability have routinely shifted across the life course – like other facets of everyday life, experience and identity.

Taking intersectional analysis seriously, and so also the ways in which racism, misogyny and transmisogyny were wrapped into queer dynamics, opens out difficult histories, as powerful recent doctoral work has shown.[187] Jo Brydon, for example, demonstrates how folk musicologist Percy Granger's sense of sexual and gender selfhood was shaped and shot through with racism, white supremacism, and fantasies about violence, incest and child abuse.[188] Will Jones' work demonstrates just how endemic male-male rape and sexual abuse was in the Nazi extermination camps. This, they show, was facilitated by the organization of space and by hierarchies of power in the camps which gave some prisoners authority over others. Combined with the intensified racism, anti-Semitism, homophobia and misogyny of this period, this rendered some men and boys at once subhuman and 'rapable'.[189] This work, as with that on the middle passage, lynching, and abusive individuals and groups in other contexts, matters historically because it demonstrates how queer histories and dynamics are necessarily enmeshed with other vectors and hierarchies of power and identification.[190] These histories cannot be separated and sanitized, and they indeed speak of the need to look beyond LGBT history narrowly conceived. Regina Kunzel thus describes being 'drawn to subjects who are not always legible as "LGBT" and who sometimes stretch the limits of what we might think of as "queer"'.[191] In her work on prisons and hospitals she thus deals with those who are 'marginal to the enterprise of LGBT history: reluctant subjects afraid that they're homosexual; unpalatable subjects, attracted to young children; unheroic subjects, debilitated by shame and self-loathing'.[192] This is a not a proud history but it is a queerer one which challenges the utility of simplistic notions of identity in approaches to the past and crucially develops our understandings of the multiple dimensions and complex affects of power.

Coda

My daughter was born in 1999; my eldest son in 2002. Becoming a father meant adjusting my sense of self in relation to home and family in profound and more prosaic ways. Daily life changed as additional places came into focus. It was playgrounds I now headed for in the park and kids clubs at the cinema and theatre. New networks formed, others loosened or tightened. A domestic circuit of play dates and familial socializing edged out the round of bars and clubs – though not entirely: the way we divvied up the week between the mothers, myself and my then partner meant I still had some time for that (though less inclination than before). Having thought in my teens and early twenties that being gay and being a father were incompatible identities, I now found them coming together in ways that changed the dimensions of each for me. That being both felt possible in the late 1990s owed much to unevenly shifting social, political and cultural contexts in Britain. There was a partial recession in the homophobia that had braced my earlier adulthood, the result perhaps of new visibilities and the 'legitimation' that sociologist Dennis Altman argues came through the 'disaster' of AIDS.[193] A new Labour government was gesturing to the repeal of Section 28 (with its talk of 'pretended families') and to same-sex adoption (both of which transpired in 2003). More broadly the shape and make-up of families was changing, providing an aperture for queerer configurations.[194] These contexts suggested I might step more fully into my own family story and tradition: my parents were both from large families, I was one of six, and by this point (in the late 1990s) my siblings had already had eleven children between them. Deciding to have my own might have seemed like a radical, unconventional step to some, but it was also in keeping with family life as I knew it. There was then the passing luck of being asked to co-parent by a friend I made on my MA, inspired, with her partner, by pioneer lesbian parents of the 1980s and by others they knew personally. In addition I had secure housing and the promise (if not yet the reality) of a stable income.

As a way of thinking all this through for myself, I turned to history. I wanted to understand the historical circumstances of queer home and family making for earlier generations. Influenced by the historical and analytical moves I have explored in this chapter, I began research on what would ultimately become *Queer Domesticities* (2014). In the book I held categories lightly and alongside other ways in which my case studies thought about themselves and people around them. I avoided looking at a collectivity of queers but at historically couched individual stories of identification and allegiance which often fractured and complicated notions of shared identity and community. What emerged was a partial decentring of the sexual and of sexuality as other modes and patterns of identification, belonging, rejection and affiliation relating to class, race, gender, locality, bohemianism and the arts, health, familial cultures and history swam into view. My case studies did not propel me 'towards a general understanding . . . towards a model that is prevalent, mainstream' (as Carlo Ginzberg has it).[195] Instead, they allowed me to chart distinctive negotiations of norms and cultures of home and family which made for some difference, some agency, some eccentricity, but not a thoroughgoing outsiderness. And despite their differences from each other, I did find something that linked my bohemian collectors and designers of the late nineteenth century to my bedsitter tenants of the fifties, squatters of the seventies, and 'modern' family makers of the 2000s. This related to a shared self-consciousness. The 'orientation' of all of these men to varying degrees away from projected norms in London and England made them especially alert to the way their domestic practices allowed them to fit in or stand out.[196] This helped me towards an understanding of felt difference and marginality across a century of profound change and amongst those who had little otherwise to connect them. It also allowed me to discern the dimensions and potency of circulating norms and the imperative individuals felt to align with them 'by desire, by habit, by survival' – something I was feeling in new ways as a parent.[197]

3

Space and Time

Those touched by the AIDS crisis in its first decade sometimes experienced time in changed ways. They entered rhythms of care giving and receiving, timed drug regimens and hospital visiting hours, and saw lives – perhaps including their own – speeding to a premature end. If gay lives were often narrated around the supposed temporal pivot point of 'coming out', an HIV diagnosis brought another moment of potential disclosure, another temporal marker for those receiving and giving the news. Relationships with space shifted in tandem as new sites (clinics, hospitals, crematoria) entered people's daily and weekly circuits, and familiar places (home, bars, the workplace) changed their tenor or began to recede in significance. Some hospitals wards became notably 'gay' in terms of patients and the staff opting to work with them.[1] Whole areas or cities were laced with a sense of risk; a correspondent to the UK's Mass Observation Project in 1987 was not alone in sharing her fears of infection in London's public places: 'I have to admit that in rush hour we felt very much aware that we might be in a hazardous zone.'[2] The impacts of AIDS were felt at a local level in different ways, modulated, intensified and ameliorated by policy made nationally and by transnational flows of information, modes of activism, and the virus itself. The rank inequality in the global economy meant some had treatment and most did not; death came sooner for them. Temporal ideas of development, progress, stasis and backsliding were linked with these spatial dimensions, and in ways which marked out particular groups – Haitians, drug users, gay men – from the rest and from each other.

Later, the crisis reconfigured historical time, with the 1980s as a decade accruing heightened queer relevance and resonance, with a new 'before' and (supposed) 'after',[3] punctuating accounts of queer life and collective memory. This did not happen for everyone but rather for those most immediately affected. When Covid struck, Western journalists tended to hark back to the devastating Spanish flu of 1918–20 rather than the ongoing AIDS pandemic.[4] This touched queer thinking itself. The art historian Christopher Reed and literary scholar Christopher Castiglia identified a form of traumatized forgetting in queer theory's 'anti-social' nihilistic turn inwards, to the psyche and to the present, in the 1990s and 2000s.[5] With this, they wrote, came the risk of turning from history and of 'wip[ing] out memories … of the remarkably vibrant and imaginative ways that gay communities responded to the catastrophe of illness and deaths and sought to memorialise our losses'.[6]

These warped spatial and temporal experiences highlighted how perceptions and experiences of time and space were significant in people's everyday and emotional lives, in exclusions and inclusions, and in a wider associated politics. The imbrication of space and time, therefore, came to matter immensely to the writing of queer history, in ways that both exceeded and rested upon more mainstream developments. Contemporaneous spatial and temporal turns in history, and in the humanities and social sciences more broadly, provided tools and perspectives. Historian Stephen Kern's landmark *The Culture of Time and Space* (1983) was a resource in conceiving how space and time were historical and ideological co-constructs, often marshalled – quite literally in the manipulation of the built environment and time zones – to divide and rule.[7] What we think of as modernity, and especially the coming of the railways and telegrams, dramatically shifted the ways in which time and space were experienced, Kern argued. The circularity of time in pre-industrial contexts gave way to a different sense of temporality in nineteenth-century Europe and especially its urban centres, with 'progress' and the accumulation of capital significant for some, whilst others had lives parcelled up between factory and home and their different temporal rhythms. Rather than being steady, predictable backdrops to historical action, space and time were increasingly seen to be formative. Historians began to show how they shaped and modulated human behaviour, relations and subjectivities.

What did this mean for queer analysis? Concepts from cultural geography and queer theory, the topic of the first section of this chapter, were foundational to queer historical explorations of sequestered sites (like bars, monasteries, prisons, ships or homes) and the division of space into urban, suburban and rural. These are visited in the second section which also examines geo-political units (such as nation, continent, and Global South and North) and the queer import of voluntary and enforced movement between places, which has had both crushing and enabling effects on sexual and relationship lives. In accounting for the effects of space and time in such a rich variety of ways, queer historians have questioned entrenched ideas in the history profession about origins, turning points, periods and historical time – the focus of the final part of this chapter. The choices we make about working in relation to particular places or much larger units of space (or both together), to longer or shorter periods of time (or the ways the former surface in the latter), have thus fundamentally determined the way the queer past is configured as history.

1. Grounding ideas: cultural history and queer theory

In a 1991 article for *Marxism Today*, the cultural geographer Doreen Massey showed how her local high street in north-west London was one node in a global social and economic network. With its specific transnational traffic in people, goods and ideas, she demonstrated that places could be both intensely local and particular *and* be linked into national and international networks which contributed to making them so. 'Place' seen in this way was always in process, shaped by events, behaviours and shifts in those wider networks. This created what Massey's fellow cultural geographer Ed Soja conceptualized (leaning on sociologist Pierre Bourdieu) as a dynamic 'habitus of social practices'.[8] He suggested that discerning the layered meanings and historicity of places gives us some sense of how ways of being were shaped, supported and troubled (in ways resonant with de Certeau).[9] In turn, people's everyday lives and behaviour modulated the meanings and associations of place. Sometimes these were in line and sometimes at odds with the intentions of planners and architects.[10] London's Trafalgar Square, laid out between 1829 and 1844, was intended as a celebration of British military prowess, for example. The architect, John Nash, probably did not anticipate that its northern walkway would become a cruising spot in the 1930s, subculturally known as 'the meat rack'. The men who met there queered this site of national pride after sundown, and, as word spread, this new association became entrenched such that even when this part of the square ceased to be used for pick-ups, it continued to be a subcultural reference point.[11] The materiality of the square – the balustrade, street furniture, and surrounding architecture – was also part of its particularity, funneling, inhibiting, and freeing people in different ways. The balustrade on that northern edge at the time prevented direct descent into the square itself – perhaps encouraging the queer traffic back and forth and providing somewhere to lean and linger. The physical environment mattered as surely as what the square had come to symbolize.[12]

Across the 1990s and 2000s, scholars from different disciplines increasingly centred queer formations and experiences within such dynamics of space, and considered how queer behaviour inadvertently or intentionally changed the way places were used and what they meant.[13] Geographers and sociologists considered the queer significance of liminal spaces which fell betwixt and between those that were more clearly designated as public or private (though this classic and apparently clear division of space was in lived experience porous and uncertain).[14] Back alleys, hotel rooms, clubs, the Trafalgar Square meat rack at dusk – each had an air of liminality which might affirm or modify a person's existing sense of themselves or prompt behaviours and ideas outside the ordinary run of their life.[15] Adjacent to Trafalgar Square, meanwhile, the National Gallery, the Coliseum Theatre, the church of St-Martin's-in-the-Fields and the Charing Cross Hospital were sites in which other places were evoked and time could feel very different again. Foucault described such places as 'heterotopias' and saw them embodying contradictory potential. On the one hand, they mirrored and reaffirmed cultural norms (in the presentation of a national art collection and the rehearsal of age-old church dogmas, for example) and so had symbolic, controlling and definitional cultural power. On the other hand they could be disorientating. The millennia they evoked might concertina in both church and gallery in a dizzying experience of time.[16] Like liminal spaces, heterotopias are often associated with problematic bodies or bodies perceived to be in transition in some way: the dead in crematoria, the diseased in hospitals, the mad in asylums, or those moving through the life stage rituals of church, temple or mosque. There was in this way often a concentration but also a problematization of cultural meaning in heterotopias. They could signal something going wrong, the scope for dissent, or some vision of alternative worlds and ways of being. For these reasons heterotopic space, like liminal space, had a particular queer significance.[17]

Such spaces did not exist in isolation. They were what they were because of their situation in a wider material and cultural landscape. Liminal spaces relied on the idea and lived realities of the public and the private, for example. Thinking in terms of spatial connections, networks and overlaps between such spaces reveals complex facets of queer identification and experience. Cruising grounds like the Trafalgar Square meat rack or places for indoor socializing like the nearby Salisbury pub on St Martin's Lane (whose queer reputation was cemented in *Victim*, the 1961 film of homosexual angst) were each significant to the men who went there. So too was the short walk between them, the journey home, home itself in whatever form it took, workspace the following day and, perhaps, St Martin's church or some other place of worship on a Sunday. Other queerly iconic places – by the sixties including Brighton, Amsterdam and San Francisco – may have had an orienting significance whether or not our loosely imagined subject had actually visited them.

Different conceptions and experiences of time came in and out of focus alongside; pub, church, work, and home, were each associated with different temporal rhythms, times of day and days of the week. Church evoked centuries of sinners and held out hope of eternal salvation. Home came with the circularity of domestic labour and child rearing in ways which have been gendered and consolidated as 'women's time'.[18] On a much larger spatial scale, whole continents were marked out temporally. Africa (large parts of which were governed from Whitehall, spitting distance from Trafalgar Square) became pre-modern, primitive and 'traditional' in the eyes of British and other colonizers in the nineteenth and twentieth centuries. In European novels, anthropology and the press, this vast continent and the people who lived there were frequently associated with traditional pasts and stasis, at odds with the elite colonizer's putative lockstep with the march of history and progress, a developmental notion of time connected firmly to European modernity.[19] Indeed typologies of race and sex in the later nineteenth century emerged not only in tandem with each other but in relation to colonial divisions and characterizations of space and time.[20] There was in this what Leah DeVun and Zeb Tortorici helpfully describe as a 'denial of coevalness', whereby groups of people were (and are) disempowered by being imagined linked to the past rather than the present of the powerful.[21]

Cultural geographers' ideas about time, space and their relationship to gender, race, sexuality and 'civilization' were taken up by queer theorists in the late 1990s and 2000s.[22] Leading figures such as José Estaban Muñoz, Jack Halberstam and Lee Edelman highlighted the temporal and spatial positions of those othered and minoritized in terms of gender and sexual dissidence, flagging other modes of life (or aspects of life) lived on alternate temporal tracks and in relation to other, often liminal, places. Through such lenses we see how clubs, countercultural squats and communes, or secluded bathing or cruising spots might be experienced and might represent a step out of the run of progressive, capitalist 'chrononormativity'.[23] Through his reading of George Eliot's *Silas Marner* (1861), Alfred Hitchcock's film *The Birds* (1963) and other cultural texts, Lee Edelman contrasted heterosexual 'reproductive futurity' to a queer stuckness and failure to progress. He argued that embracing this might allow for a queer refusal of – and ironic stance towards – chrononormativity and the heteronormative social and political order it supports.[24] In some related ways literary scholar Katherine Bond Stockton envisaged queer children not growing up and reaching forward but instead 'growing sideways'.[25]

The queer present, others argued, could be liveable, bearable, because of a particular queer investment in the past. 'We might imagine ourselves haunted by [past] ecstasy and not just by loss', wrote Freeman; 'residues of positive affect (erotic scenes, utopias, memories of touch) might be available for queer counter (or para) historiographies'.[26] Such an eroto-history does not gather into a neat sequence or fit a progress narrative but rather 'fattens' the present with the past, allowing for 'touch[es] across time' which affirm a 'shared marginality' (to quote medieval scholar Carolyn Dinshaw).[27] Gestures, words and icons from the past, whether mobilized in the present or imagined in a queer future, can come to constitute a counter heritage allowing for difference, defiance, community, and connection now and going forward.[28] Halberstam suggested that playing consciously with time and 'place making' was a means through which queer folk gained a measure of agency in a quest for liveable lives, communal connection, and the resistance of normative logics and expectations.[29] We can glimpse something of this in the Paris voguing scene and the Black drag houses in Manchester of the late 2010s and the 2020s. Dancers deliberately referenced in moves and in content the voguing balls of 1980s New York and the loss, grief, solidarity and politics which braced them.[30] They 'quoted' those moves and tapped into a past vein of defiance, fostering a sense of being 'out of time' and of escape to earlier moments of experienced or fabled solidarity.[31]

These debates are associated with the present – including theorizing how the past resonates, or fails to resonate, through it. They matter to history and to history-making because they prompt us to think about how time and space were experienced by people in the past and about the difference this made to their lives. The prompt helps us to discern some queer alterity – in the drive of decadent and aesthetic *fin de siècle* literary figures (such as Walter Pater, J.-K. Huysmans and Oscar Wilde) to offset the developmental pitch into the future by cultivating beautiful aesthetic, decadent moments in their present, or in the nostalgic reach by the Uranian poets of the same period for the ancient Greeks.[32] The queer theoretical invitation also helps clarify investments in and accessions to normative ideas of time and space – on the part of that artistic elite but also more broadly: there were not many queer aesthetes and decadents revelling in beautiful moments; there were not, either, many queer Victorian men harking back melancholically to classical times or to pastoral spaces.[33] Most men who had sex with other men did not consciously revel and reach back in these ways, nor did they identify or idealize what they were doing with such temporal disjunction. Moreover, conventional understandings and experiences of space and time, including ways of understanding and rendering the past, substantially structured queer experiences and lives. If the segmentation of time for many nineteenth-century British upper-middle-class men (into periods of public school, university and travel) prepared them for colonial governance and power, that same temporal and spatial patterning could open out and structure their homoerotic desires and experiences.

2. Scales of spaces and time

Places and times apart

This theoretical work does not provide an historical roadmap but it has fostered an alertness to the affects of space and time in queer history. In the British context historians have honed in on medieval monasteries, the theatres and 'stews' of Renaissance London, eighteenth-century bog and Molly Houses, and nineteenth- and twentieth-century hospitals, asylums and boarding schools – all of which can be revealed, in different ways, as liminal and/or heterotopic spaces. Bars and clubs recur in work on the second half of the twentieth century, and from rich oral histories we get a sense of their look and feel and of how they couched and directed ephemeral pleasures and queer embodiment.[34] These places reflected and created certain ways of experiencing identity and community – as secretive and discreet (the basement bars with spy holes for entry), as highly gendered (the butch-femme bars), as liberatory and euphoric (1970s disco), as fetishistic and sexually prolific (the backroom bars and leather joints), as overtly feminist and separatist (some women-only bars).[35] Indeed, as historian Mori Reithmayr has argued, the 1960s gay bar scene functioned as a crucial origin point for the very idea of a 'gay community' in its different dimensions.[36] Such places suggested the scope to sidestep the orderly progression of time through an inversion of day and night and a turn into the moment and fleeting pleasures (in a muted echo of those *fin de siècle* decadents).[37] In interviews, patrons recalled a sense of escape, as well as feelings of safety, joy, rivalry, jealousy, discomfort, and also exclusion (relating, for example, to age, race, gender, and dis/ability) – observations important to queer affective histories, and to histories of identity and community formation.[38]

If bars and clubs have been a rich seam for investigating the fabric of lesbian, gay, butch, femme or queer identification in the twentieth and twenty-first centuries especially, historians have also shown that they were certainly not the only or even the prime places for queer self-making. They have pointed at the significance of gay and lesbian bookshops, the headquarters of charities and political groups (writ large in social movement and institutional histories), archival and library spaces, as well as video stores, saunas, bathhouses and sex joints largely geared, though not exclusively, towards men.[39] These are in different ways identifiably queer spaces and invite analysis on that basis. But there has been mileage too in looking at all or any spaces queerly. In his work on Liverpool, and in particular Liverpool 8 (the Toxteth area of the city), from the 1960s to the 1990s, historian Khalil West finds multiple social spaces – including shebeens, 'regular' bars, gay bars, people's homes – 'charged by a capricious, promiscuous erotic force' which eludes neat summary via sexual taxonomy.[40] He shows through his innovative use of oral history that these 'fugitive', 'superpositional'[41] erotic dynamics were forged and modulated through the dimensions and make-up of specific venues and what they invited; through their location within Liverpool, with its multivalent histories of slavery, uprising, and inward and outward migration; and through the local lived dimensions of class, deprivation, blackness, queerness, conviviality, insiderness, outsiderness and more besides. West's focus on the space – and social spaces – of Liverpool 8, and the ways they have been organized, lived, felt, and become meaningful, elucidates (homo)erotic dynamics presumed to be absent or elsewhere (in the city's gay quarter most obviously), whilst showing too that there has been no settled sense of queerness here.[42]

Sequestered carceral and curative institutions which likewise eschewed queer labelling also had queer affects. From the early modern period in Europe the imposing presence and architecture of hospitals, prisons, workhouses and asylums promulgated and policed norms and so also what was considered deviant.[43] Historians have shown how institutions facilitated the observation, assessment, cure and punishment of the sexually transgressive, producing a typology of sex and positioning those interned as socially and culturally marginal – even as they were also crucial to broader definitions of what was normal and moral. In his *Curing Queers* (2015), historian Tommy Dickinson shows how in hospitals in Britain in the 1950s doctors and nurses deployed presumptions and speculation about queer bodies and responses to erotic stimuli and pain. The hierarchies of power in these places (of doctors over nurses, and of both over patients) evoked a complex knot of emotion experienced with particular intensity by – and with lifelong legacies for – the queers confined.[44] In her exploration of dynamics of regulation and permissiveness in prisons, historian Regina Kunzel observes the way some prisoners behaved at odds with the attitudes they held on the outside, as when racist white women embarked on interracial same-sex relationships during their time inside.[45] Such situational homosexuality – observable in barracks, workhouses and extermination camps – has been interpreted by historians via institutional layout, management and homosociality.[46] Sexual acts were often non-consensual and abusive, undertaken with a sense of impunity on the part of perpetrators empowered by their position of authority or by hierarchies amongst the inmates.[47] In other instances, sexual and intimate relationships were experienced as pleasurable and sustaining in bleak circumstances.[48]

Public historian Jo Stanley and linguistics scholar Paul Baker found through their oral history work an extension and intensification of queer sexual and social lives on board twentieth-century civilian ships. Crew members were at a distance from land-based policing and social control, giving them an enhanced sense of possibility.[49] Earlier, crews stranded in the arctic ice in the late nineteenth and early twentieth centuries entertained each other by cross-dressing and using black face.[50] There was in this an intensification of wider racist cultures and also a loosening of some strictures around sex and gender. Historians have identified similar dynamics in theatres and other carnivalesque sites on land and in terms both of what such spaces permitted and what appeared on stage.[51]

These various sequestered sites might function as 'home' to those who had signed up, been imprisoned or certified mentally ill. Oral histories show how theatres, cinemas, pubs and other such spaces could conjure a sense of being 'at home' – and perhaps more so than in actual homes.[52] They have often not felt safe and have been seen as factories of normativity rather than places significant in queer lives and the formation of a queer sense of self. There has nevertheless been a recent turn to the domestic as an arena where people formed understandings of themselves, their bodies and their desires.[53]

At home opinions were voiced loudly, secrets were kept, guilt and shame were acutely felt, and in/tolerance was articulated explicitly or more tacitly. Families might model various relationships; unmarried aunts and uncles perhaps offering a glimmer of queer possibility to children who in the modern period have been considered heterosexuals in waiting.[54] The architecture of homes might press ideas of privacy and individualism – and with queer consequences. Bedrooms in elite homes from the mid-nineteenth century in Britain were increasingly accessed separately (rather than from one room to the next). The nursery was set apart, often in the liminal space of the attic alongside servants and nanny.[55] Back and front stairs in such homes separated adult family members from servants (home was also a workplace for many) – a materialization of hierarchies of power which might prompt desire as well as offer a setting for its indulgence, as literary scholars Peter Stallybrass and Allon White illustrated in their *Politics and Poetics of Transgression* (1986), which showed how such spaces might be central to historical erotic analysis.[56] Historians since have demonstrated that homes were sites of abuse and transgression, and of concern about both. There were acute fears in the mid- to late-nineteenth century about servants corrupting children in their care into masturbatory pleasures which might lead to queer and other horrors, for example.[57] Homes without such elite spatial division – as in the cramped shared rooms of the poor – were suspect in the same period and subject to surveillance because of what they might provoke or portend.[58]

Homes were viewed in Britain as the engines of empire in the way they could ferment ideologies of gender, race and sexuality.[59] They were also places where these ideologies might be disrupted and questioned. There was scope for those with the resources to organize homes in ways that allowed them to stand out rather than fit in; they could be used quite deliberately to build, frame and sustain identity. Having an apparently regular home was, on the other hand, a way of finding some acceptance or of passing as 'normal'.[60] Historians of the United States and United Kingdom have shown that creating village, small town and suburban homes could even enable queer lives.[61] Scholar of the Black diaspora Nadia Ellis thus found in a domestic partnership in the rural English Cotswolds 'an accommodation between black queerness and domesticity that the race relations scholars were unable to imagine'.[62]

As a relatively new site of queer historical enquiry, the 'home' has opened out dynamics beyond those witnessed and imagined in other sequestered spaces. Historians Rebecca Jennings and Amy Tooth Murphy suggest that bars, for example, only get us so far in understanding historic butch identification; queer domestic and workplace histories take us further.[63] This serves as a reminder that none of these places 'apart' operate in isolation. People invariably related to a range of places either actually or in their imaginations, and in different ways depending on their circumstances and intersecting identifications. Their feelings and experiences in one place (of pleasure and relaxation, for example) depended on contrasted or related feelings and experiences in others (perhaps of fear and discomfort). These feelings were couched and shaped by the wider spatial contexts in which they were situated and which came with a further cache of social and economic imperatives and cultural and subcultural meanings.

City, suburb and countryside[64]

In his pioneering *Gay New York* (1994), George Chauncey showed how the city's docks, patterns of immigration and settlement, workplaces, bar cultures, overstretched accommodation, and associated mythologies (not least about opportunity and escape), made for distinct queer identities and subcultures there. The way the city developed – with its public, civic, liminal and curtailed private spaces – prompted desires and particular sexual dynamics.[65] European and North American modernity and capitalism created the conditions for homosexual communities and identities to form in distinct ways, and, suggested Chauncey, John D'Emilio and sociologist Henning Bech, in specific relation to cities like New York.[66] Their contention was borne out in a raft of subsequent studies of the queerness of other major urban centres, including Sydney, San Francisco, Los Angeles, Chicago, Philadelphia, Berlin, London and Paris. These histories tacitly or explicitly highlighted some shared queer urban dynamics but also uncovered much that was city specific, arising from their particular geographical, demographic, economic, administrative and national contexts.[67] I found in my work on late-nineteenth-century London that 'modern' facilities and spaces like train stations, department stores, public toilets, community halls, museums and galleries, fostered novel social, cultural and (homo)erotic connections. The inception of the underground and invention of the bicycle transformed queer sexual and social opportunities, with the latter becoming a symbol of – and practical tool in – women's independence socially and sexually.[68] These innovations were part of the fabled new pace of modern life in the city. Neurasthenia and degeneration (evolution in reverse) emerged in the late nineteenth century as racialized urban maladies relating to such temporal acceleration. They were closely associated with a sexual dissidence which seemed to be proliferating in the city,[69] and which was also associated with London's position as centre of empire and of global trade. The resulting traffic in people, ideas, attitudes and things shaped and inflected queer life during and after the colonial era, not least in the way foreign-ness and race were (homo)eroticised.[70]

The first wave of queer urban history responded to the iconic queer status and significance of particular cities. The next included work on cities and towns which had little queer infamy but much queer import. *Queer Cities, Queer Cultures* (2014) carried essays on Copenhagen, Ljubljana, Budapest and Helsinki, for example. The authors deployed a range of approaches to the queerness of urban life – including through the lens of literature, individual testimony, memorialization, and birds-eye mapping to suggest and illustrate disparate queer urban dynamics.[71] It became clear in this work that men's queer histories were often easier to track through the public spaces of a city than women's. This was the case even though, in different and related ways, public city life created conditions for women's social, political and sexual independence too – including in the permissive urban 'pink twilight' described by art historian Kate Flint in a piece which counters the presumption that to find female same-sex love and desire we need to look indoors.[72]

Looking at work on the queer dimensions of European urban centres together showed how deceptively homogenizing the epithet 'European' could be: queer identities and communities formed and functioned in vastly different ways from city to city depending on regional, national, political, demographic and cultural contexts.[73] French scholar David Caron showed how the queer dynamics of the Marais area of central Paris were modulated by intersecting Jewish, bohemian and wider Parisian and French histories.[74] The place-based focus allowed him to specify resonant dimensions of queer and Jewish identities more often understood separately. In the process he also demonstrated that cities can sometimes best be understood queerly not as a whole but as a series of differently scaled localities experienced in some overlapping but also very different ways. Parallel work on queer London, for example, showed the distinct queer cadences of Notting Hill, Brixton and Soho.[75] It is only in the wider imagination that the UK capital had and has a more homogenous queer sheen.

Cities in their various forms have been the go-to places for queer adventure and also (not coincidentally) for queer historical research.[76] But what of other types of space side-lined for their putative heteronormativity and conservatism?[77] Studies on suburbs and countryside have called out the metrocentrism and 'metro-normativity' of queer history and showed that queer lives were lived in these other places too, and in distinctive ways precisely because of the spatial context.[78] Suburbs have represented entrenched norms and the status quo. For these reasons, they have often been judged as crushing places for those who felt different. Though these ideas are powerful, they belie a sense of suburban liminality which suggests some queer potential. Alison Oram, for example, stressed the significance of suburban spaces to gender crossing and to a discrete lesbianism in the inter- and postwar years in Britain. 'In the sexually fluid 1950s', she wrote, 'same-sex desire flourished in the same suburban spaces as heteronormativity, in the frayed edges of marriage.'[79] Suburban homes could be facilitating and discreet places to meet friends and lovers whilst husbands were at work and the kids at school.

There is work to be done to 'deconstruct suburbia as implicitly heterosexualized' and respectably middle-class, but even as such it had queer import.[80] The queer significance of suburbs in twentieth-century England is evident when we note that around 80 percent of the population grew up in a suburb or suburban town.[81] For good or ill, these were the places which shaped ways of feeling and being queer. We see the particular shame (that 'stickiest' of emotions)[82] which comedian Tom Allen circles in his memoir of suburban Bromley in south-east London in the 1990s.[83] Caution and concern about the neighbours and also a quiet sense of accommodation were a common refrain community historian Alan Butler heard in his oral history work on suburban Plymouth.[84] And then there were the erotics and risks of local parks and 'cottages'[85] (which we can discern in the frequent reports of arrests in the local press) and the excitement of going 'into town' on public transport for queer fun away from family. These and other feelings feature in testimonies and in fictional/ized accounts of growing up in the suburbs and they can be traced into adult attitudes and behaviours.[86] Suburbs may not have had a good queer press but historians have begun to show through such material how they have been embedded in queer lives nevertheless – and in ways also distinct between national contexts, given that, for example, English suburbs have a different meaning and substance to those of other parts of Europe or North America.[87]

Fantasies about moving to the suburbs in queer literature and testimony have been rare; the countryside has been a different matter. Whilst the classic queer trajectory has been into the city,[88] queer moves in the other direction have also been celebrated and idealized. Historians have shown that amongst elite homophile men in the late nineteenth and first half of the twentieth century, the countryside and the coast suggested freedom, escape, and some legitimization.[89] There could be a queer sense of being part of 'natural', 'circular' seasonal rhythms, beyond urban temporalities associated with degeneracy, speed and a future-focused productivity.[90] Focused queer historical analysis of the countryside was nevertheless slower in coming. The American historian John Howard's *Men Like That* (1999) was the first book substantially to break the mould by looking at the specificities of rural life in the southern United States. Performer and historian E. Patrick Johnson subsequently demonstrated in his oral history work how queer possibility and expression were bound into racialized rural southern cultures, identities and dangers over a similar period.[91] More recently historical geographer Caroline Bressey and historian Gemma Romain have shown how Black queer women artists and bohemians were distinctly 'out of place' in interwar rural England and, given that they are still under-represented in the rural heritage circuit, can feel so now too. Class and race mattered and matter profoundly to feelings of belonging and alienation as much in rural as in urban space, though differently so.[92] There have been significant limits on freedom and significant degrees of social control in rural communities, even if the fantasy of liberty and escape has been strong.

These freedoms and fantasies have had a different complexion in different national contexts and depending on the extent of rural space, the nature of land ownership, and historic patterns of killing, displacement and migration. In England for the last two hundred years few people have lived far from a significantly-sized city in what is a heavily urbanized nation. This, together with the near ubiquitous cultivation of the English countryside, is part of what distinguishes rural experience here from, say, the United States and Canada, where there are vast expanses between cities,[93] engendering their own queer dynamics. There was an appeal, for example, in supposedly 'virgin'[94] North American terrain for lesbians seeking to establish lives and communities at a physical distance from compulsory heterosexuality and patriarchy, especially in the 1970s and 1980s. They could get far further away from the city than could women escaping to rural England and Wales in the same period.[95]

Histories of queer rural life – surveying (amongst other places) the southern US states, the Florida panhandle, the Canadian prairies and New Zealand – have taken the focus off cities and shown that what lay beyond was no queer wasteland.[96] In the process, historical subjects who engaged more casually in homosex have come into view amidst others who held particularly tightly to a queer identity and sense of queer rural community.[97] Alongside much else, these studies have suggested that whilst rural to urban migrations have tended to compel queer historians, looking at movement in the other direction reveals the draw of the rural and the sense of community and belonging it could bring. In such migrations, origin as well as destination mattered to the way queer subjects conceived of themselves and inhabited and forged connections in their new surroundings.[98]

National, global and transnational histories

The queer lives lived in relation to particular sites, cities, suburbs and countryside were also lived within national borders and in ways that responded to a transnational and global traffic in goods, ideas and people. These wider spaces and spatial dynamics have consequently needed a historical reckoning. The damage done to queerly identified people by the nation-state has made other spatial starting points and dynamics especially appealing. Looking past the nation at specific localities or also at transnational movements and circuits shows how people have found additional coordinates to identity and community at odds with national strictures.[99] And yet, building from George Mosse's classic *Nationalism and Sexuality: Respectability and Abnormal Sexuality in Modern Europe* (1984), historians have shown how national boundaries matter profoundly to queer experience, and in some overlapping but also distinct ways to those highlighted in relation to particular places and the urban, rural and suburban. National histories, cultures and legal structures shaped sexual and gender norms and ideas of deviance. National entry points, and docks in particular, have often been liminal, male dominated spaces, fostering fleeting queer contact and more sustained (homo)erotic subcultures.[100] Borders have regularly been points where individuals have been judged for their perceived homosexuality or gender non-conformity (or both) in attempts to maintain and bolster the fiction of a heterosexual state. Queer exclusion at these borders and from certain institutions of the state (as well as forced inclusion in others) have been important components in sustaining that fantasy.[101] Historians have thus signalled that race, gender and sexuality were centrally at stake in the ideological formation of nations. André Fernandez, in exploring the creation of modern Spain, for example, showed how sexual deviance prosecuted by the Aragonese inquisition in the fifteenth century in neighbouring jurisdictions became a means of defining the new kingdom as cleansed of – and standing in moral opposition to – such behaviour.[102] In Sweden, Jens Rydström found that the particular trajectories of the nation's welfare state 'created, transformed and dissolved identities'. They helped forge a conception of Swedish nationhood around an equivocal notion of tolerance which existed in tension with related and constraining ideas of acceptable citizenship – at issue in the criminalization of HIV transmission there, for example.[103] Other historians have shown how in France cross-cutting civic ideals of liberty, egality and fraternity took precedence over distinct sexual identities. The latter have consequently had relatively less significance than in the United Kingdom or the United States where identitarian individualism held more sway, socially, culturally and legislatively.[104]

Work which has used the nation as a unit of historical analysis has shown how queer dynamics are modulated by national systems of law, policing, governance, education and health provision, as well as by national histories and mythologies linked to war, conquest and colonization. National character and identity configure around these things, and, spread through daily interaction, folklore and powerful print cultures, inflect ideas about sex and desire in particular ways – as Charlotte Ross, a scholar of Italy, found in her study of lesbianism there from the 1860s to the 1930s.[105] Different dynamics of possibility and restraint emerge in Rebecca Jennings' *A Lesbian History of Britain* (2007) and Tamara Chaplin, *Becoming Lesbian: A Queer History of Modern France* (2024). Reading these texts side-by-side suggests the significance of alternate national cultures of class, religion and individual liberty.[106] Climate – and what it meant practically and symbolically – likely also had a part to play.

There are clearly national queer stories to tell, but they are never straightforward. For *A Gay History of Britain* (2007; the companion volume to Jennings'), Robert Mills, Randolph Trumbach, H. G. Cocks and I had to take into account the changing composition of the United Kingdom and varying relations of power between its now four nations.[107] Laws have not been rolled out evenly. Homosexual sex remained illegal in Scotland, Northern Ireland and the Channel Islands well after partial decriminalization of sex between men in England and Wales in 1967 (though historian Jeff Meek's study of Scotland shows that this should not be taken to suggest a more repressive climate there; prosecutions before and after 1967 were relatively few).[108] Northern Ireland's queer past was structured around dynamics of colonialism, civil war and a deep religious divide in ways that differentiate its queer history from other parts of the United Kingdom.[109] The four nations have in addition been typed and caricatured in distinctive ways, shaping judgements, suspicions and ways of relating – sexually, emotionally and otherwise. Britain's colonial history and role in globalization have meanwhile acted on the queer imaginary, on the dynamics of desire, and on actual encounter. These affects have been unevenly felt, understood and experienced across the UK's nations, however, and not least because of the respective experiences of colonizing and being colonized.

Using the nation as a unit of analysis can be productive but also blinkering. My British perspective made the end of the Second World War in 1945 seem the obvious starting point for *Queer Cities, Queer Cultures* (2014), which I edited with Jennifer Evans. But alternate moments emerged in the chapters as equally or more nationally and queerly significant: the formation of modern Turkey in 1923, the assent of Franco in 1939, or the reunification of Germany in 1990, for instance. It was certainly possible to track historical connections between queer cultures across European nations, as well as a collective and shifting sense of Europeanness. But the national differences were as – if not more – pressing. Other edited collections on larger political and continental groupings – including on the Soviet Union, Asia, Eastern Europe and Eurasia, Latin America and Africa – have similarly exposed queer differences between neighbouring nations and across regions.[110]

Thinking globally and transnationally, as queer historians began increasingly to do from the 2000s, sharpened understandings of difference within and between different nations, continents and empires, partially decentring the West and putting Europe and North America in their respective places.[111] This is one of the achievements of Leila Rupp's *Sapphistries: A Global History of Love Between Women* (2011) and of the multi-authored *Gay Life and Culture: A World History* (2010), which, if still weighted to the Global North (not least in the terminology of the title), shows some of the uneven traffic of ideas between places and across time.[112] More recently cultural historian Heike Bauer has traced the significance of sexologist Magnus Hirschfeld's global tour to the development and spread of his theories and observations.[113] Latin American studies scholar Jorge Salessi's work on Argentina in the late nineteenth and early twentieth centuries demonstrated how such foreign ideas were taken up in particular ways as Buenas Aires underwent rapid change and 'modernization'.[114] As notions about elite homosexual identity consolidated in the West, so did the impression of his transnational rather than national allegiance. Homosexuals, like Jews, were apparently natural traitors and by the mid-twentieth century, as historian Gregory Woods shows, there was a conception of active international homosexual conspiracy; a 'homintern' entangled with the 'comintern'.[115]

With cheaper international travel and more efficient modes of transnational communicaton in the final third of the twentieth century and especially with the inception of the internet, there was a greater general and specifically queer mobility in fashion, music, film and art suggesting a deceptive proximity in sexual subcultures, experiences and politics.[116] Media studies scholar Hongwei Bao notes the retitling of the TV series 'Queer as Folk' to 'Queer Comrades' for the 2009 Beijing-based iteration, signalling a Chinese socialist twist on the likewise culturally particular UK and US versions which launched in 1999 and 2000 respectively. 'Queer Comrades' is, he writes, both 'an acknowledgement of the programme's close link to transnational queer culture and a conscious departure from it'.[117] Shared reference points have not necessarily had shared meanings, and Stonewall is another case in point. It became, through its memorialization and mythologization, a symbol of inclusion and a seemingly common rallying point on both sides of the Atlantic.[118] A closer look, however, shows that it has been taken up in divergent ways or barely at all in different urban and national contexts. Places other than New York, San Francisco and the United States have mattered in rethinking sexual worlds.[119] This speaks to the need to think about the local in the global (and vice versa) and to follow Chauncey and fellow historian Elizabeth Povinelli's call to assess how – and the extent to which – the transnational 'mobility of people, media, commodities, discourses and capital' changed 'local, regional and national modes of sexual desire, embodiment and subjectivity'.[120] Ultimately, this pushes us to consider how global mobility played out unevenly and could be bypassed or resisted in particular contexts.

Chosen and enforced travel, and imagined and desired movements, have been a keynote in these various histories. Some eighteenth- and nineteenth-century British men were exiled and transported for their sodomitical crimes and effectively became refugees because of anti-queer persecution at home.[121] Later, Paris and Weimar Berlin seemed to offer enlightened contexts for elite queer men and women (though historian Laurie Marhoefer shows how the fantasy was not matched by the reality).[122] Others travelled to southern Italy and North Africa for sexual pleasure, predicated often on predation and the abuse of power over those who did not have the resources to be as mobile.[123] Migration matters not only to the site of departure (leaving a gap) and to the place of arrival (a new presence) but also in and of itself; desires might emerge from, rather than being the reason for, movement. Trains, boats and planes opened out various queer possibilities in and of themselves.[124] Travel took time (which can be transformative) and marked a caesura – with the before in that place and the after in this. Such ruptures are often engrained in the way LGBTQ+ individuals narrate their lives to oral history interviewers.[125] Looking at transit between countryside and city, between nations, and across continents brings a historically rich queer diaspora into view in which experiences, memories and behaviours were drawn from place to place.[126] This can be a way of seeing queerness in complex relation to other intersecting motivations and imperatives for movement (apart from the manifestly queer) and also other histories (of, for example, empire, war, trade and work).

Focusing on a single place can mean missing some of these dimensions, though historians and cultural geographers have also shown how focusing in that way can bring into sharp relief the local affects of transnational movements, forces and flows.[127] Anthropologist Martin Manalansan's work on the Filipino diaspora in Manhattan, for example, demonstrates how multiple histories are at stake for his subjects – of New York and the United States, of Manilla and the Philippines, of globalization and travel, of language, of racialization and Orientalism, and of the cojoined homophobia and racism in US governance.[128] In this way, other national and urban cultures concertina in the singular context of New York City, showing how working transnationally does not mean abandoning the local. Manalansan's transnational perspective instead reveals how and why local cultures are particular given the ways other places and times intersect there.[129] In a similar way, global queer history is not necessarily about covering the globe. It can also involve using a global lens on a particular place and considering how it was affected by global flows.[130]

There can be an exhilaration in ideas of transnational liberation and of 'queer nation'; of rising above reactionary local and national political debate. But they can also flatten the queer contours of different places and obscure the social, economic and cultural power dynamics in play in social movements.[131] They can tend towards a historical metanarative told through American and European lenses and via 'world' cities at the expense of other places. This can feed homonationalism and replay celebratory ideas of western liberal progress, benefiting queers who fit particular conceptions and expectations of coupledom, productivity and respectability.[132] And yet queer historians have shown that thinking globally and transnationally can also do the reverse, challenging such narratives and delivering nuanced, multivalent accounts of the past.[133]

3. Historical time: progress, periods and turning points

Postcolonial historical work challenged conventional periodization (with historical time divided into ancient, medieval, early modern and modern) and the knee-jerk use of the national state as the obvious, pre-eminent unit of analysis. These ways of organizing knowledge about the past placed the powerful and the colonizers front and centre. Subaltern studies scholar and historian of India, Dipesh Chakrabarty, argues that the idea of progress embedded in such accounts underpins and validates eurocentric narratives of success and civilization which were aligned with the accumulation of financial capital.[134] This renders secondary those understandings and experiences of time and space which do not account for progress but which might yet open out the dynamics and texture of the queer past and other ways of being. Chakrabarty shows that historical convention in these respects has embedded political divisions of space and time and accompanying hierarchies of power and modes of oppression. This is one of the reasons why queer and postcolonial theorists have tended to resist progressive historical conceptualizations of time and identified the radical potential of using other temporal lenses. They have sharpened awareness of the tendency to see historical change as necessarily trending towards the circumstances of our present, missing the loose ends which cannot be tied into a more sweeping narrative of advance or change.[135] Such stray or dissident elements matter to understanding experiences, desires and relationships and might also provide some clues to later eccentricity even if they do not fit clearly into that broader temporal sweep. One way to work with this is to take on board the temporal frameworks and understandings of our historical subjects. Another has been to focus on shorter periods which allow for more detailed analysis and thicker descriptions which can show and build argument.[136] There is scope in this to flesh out broader historical claims but also nuance and tug at them by delving more deeply into lives, thinking and ways of being from the perspective of people who did not know what the future would hold.[137] We can conceptualize in this way the contradictions of a particular time and place and, in Carlo Ginzburg's words, 'grasp what eludes a comprehensive viewing.'[138]

The payoff for the richness of focused period studies can be an evaporating sense of 'why then?' and also of how these located modes of thought, feeling and behaviour came about and mattered (or not) to what happened next. The answers have often been provided by historians of sexuality and gender working with longer periods but who, rather than succumbing to progress narratives, look to what Traub calls 'cycles of salience' and 'recurring patterns'.[139] In *The Shape of Sex*, for example, DeVun surveys 1,500 years, stopping substantively with the Renaissance but also encouraging us to bring the premodern she deals with 'into conversation' with the modern to '[allow] us to recognize a pattern of thinking about human bodily diversity that continues, or perhaps recurs, in science and medicine across a long chronological framework'. There is no doubt, she writes, that 'premodern ideas about nonbinary sex are temporally remote from us and yet also strikingly proximate'.[140] Foucault's development of 'genealogy' suggests just such an irregular accumulation of ideas and ways of being.[141] Gathering these up helps us understand something of the processes of subjective composure and cultural change, and shows too that now as then there was usually less consensus and shared understanding, more fractures and contradictions than sweeping historical accounts can suggest (ironically, like some of Foucault's own). Different generations of people with different experiences, memories and histories existed in the same place and time.[142] This accounts for some of the 'uneven developments' literary scholar Mary Poovey identified in her work on gender in the nineteenth century. She demonstrated how older and newer understandings circulating within and between literary texts, parliamentary debate, medical texts, and periodicals prevented a single ideology from taking decisive hold. Possibilities for dissent and difference became visible as a result – with implications for women's social, cultural, economic and, indeed, sexual lives.[143] This work was important in terms of women's and lesbian history and came as a reminder that in no era or place are meanings, ideologies and ways of being homogenous or sealed off.

Poovey's 1988 argument was given a queer twist a decade later by Elizabeth Freeman, who conceptualized the 'temporal drag' which allowed 'stubborn identification with a set of social co-ordinates that exceed one's own historical moment'.[144] In this vein, and to specify a fractured genealogy of homosexuality, David Halperin identified four conceptual threads weaving in irregular fashion through late-nineteenth and twentieth-century understandings of male homosexuality. These related to effeminacy; active (and the act of) sodomy; male friendship and love; and innate passivity and congenital 'inversion'.[145] Though these threads were interwoven, they related to different histories and traditions, and they played out unevenly in the way individuals understood themselves and others – even in the same place and time.[146] Laura Doan notes, for example, that whilst there are 'good queer critiques of the sexological apparatus' as it emerged in the late nineteenth century amongst an elite, 'far less attention has been paid to events or individuals resistant to this way of knowing' and so to 'the system of classification itself'.[147] Works of sexology and psychoanalysis were peripheral to most and unread by all but a very few at that time.[148] Doan thus suggests the need to be guarded in accepting broad accounts of change over time even as we try to answer questions about how and why changes in cultures of sex and gender occurred and what they meant for people living through – and contributing to – them.

Marking out periods for queer historical work – as for much historical work – is complex. For *London and the Culture of Homosexuality*, I focused on the twenty-five years from 1885, but my subjects from this period took me to other times and places. My analysis was dependent on understanding a longer durée (the course of urbanization in Britain) and a distant period altogether (the classical era which was a lodestone for some of the men I was discussing). Historical figures I dealt with from my period also had an afterlife in later decades, most famously Oscar Wilde.[149] The endpoint for the book was 1914, not a queer date as such, but a point when the dynamics of male-male friendship and comradeships shifted dramatically in the context of horrific trench warfare.[150] In this sense, the start of the war and the years that followed were more significant to an encompassing queer social history than the passing of the Labouchere Amendment of the Criminal Law Amendment Act in 1885 under which Wilde was prosecuted and where I began the study. This date is much touted in British queer history because it was when all acts of 'gross indecency' between men were criminalized. But Charles Upchurch suggests that in following Foucault's lead and Wilde's celebrity to the late nineteenth century, historians have missed an earlier set of debates among parliamentarians and elite others in the 1820s and 1830s which lightly sketched a modern homosexual figure.[151] He does not dispute the significance of later moves in sexology, amongst lawmakers and in journalism to the consolidation of this type, but he warns against seizing supposed starting or turning points too definitively. Upchurch's caution is well placed, and British queer historians have needed to exercise it in relation to another much-deployed key moment: 1967 and the partial decriminalization of male-male sex in that year. If this has become a date to commemorate because it apparently signals 'progress' towards a more liberal state, historian Frank Mort and others have also pointed to vibrant queer cultures before and to the upsurge of arrests and prosecutions afterwards.[152] By the time it passed many queer folk had been acting 'as if' their behaviour was legal and acceptable. The earlier roll out of the welfare state, or the end of national service in 1963 probably mattered more directly in the everyday realities of postwar queer lives.

Overly insistent dates and periods can in these ways obscure earlier and adjacent queer histories. Bravmann argues that taking Ancient Greece as the cradle, beginning or 'epitome' of European culture and accommodation of homosexuality neglects the impacts of earlier Phoenician and Egyptian colonizations. This particular 'fiction' arising from the way we have divvied up time has the affect of inscribing whiteness into eurocentric stories of queerness.[153] He, like Upchurch and Mort, encourages us to consider the queer shades of thought, feeling and desire which lie either side and across such purported pivotal moments and periods. Classical Athens, Renaissance Florence (and Italy more broadly), and Shakespearean and Late Victorian London have each been queerly mythologized through a historical repetition loop which reinforces and perhaps over-determines their significance. Asking why and for whom these periods have and have had emotional resonance and particular significance are worthwhile historical questions.[154] But we can clearly hold onto the importance of these times whilst drawing others into our queer historical consciousness.

On a more individual level, honing in solely on those who 'live[d] up to temporalities of self-actualisation, progress, and identity' does related injustice to queer history. We need, Jennifer Evans argues, to be cognizant of those in the past who did not align in these ways and did not make remarkable social and cultural interventions. By working with what Halberstam describes as 'the queer art of failure' we might bring alternate queer histories and temporalities into focus.[155] Queer theorists and historians (following and in conversation with their postcolonial peers) have seen dominant conceptions of time, chronology and period being directly connected with the marginalization and subordination of particular groups of people and areas of the globe. This goes to the heart of discussion of what queer history might be and even if such a thing is possible or desirable. There is certainly a queer need to critically engage with the ways conventionally periodized histories have coalesced to entrench ideologies of race, gender, sex and sexuality, highlighting the dates and stretches of time that pertain to some but not all people. Though there may be some coincidence, different periods and moments will matter to minoritized groups and matter differently to men and women.[156] Literary scholar Madhavi Menon thus describes the very notion of periodization as a heteronormative straitjacket, squeezing queer alterity out of the past.[157] And yet to periodize, Traub observes, is not 'inevitably problematic – as long as it is understood to be contingent, manufactured, invested, and not produced by othering what came before'.[158] Not all individuals, groups, regional, urban or national stories fit given frames and we need to reflect on who gets excluded and for whom given dates would be especially arbitrary or irrelevant. This includes the way periodizations and turning points deployed by queer historians inevitably obscure others. The queer call might thus be to hold our temporal choices especially contingently and to remember – and account for the fact that – time as ordered for a historical narrative is different from time as it is experienced and understood in the everyday.

Whether through focused study of a particular moment or analysis of stasis or change over time, work on the history of sexuality and queer history tends to show that the idea of progress is fundamentally flawed. What counted as progress and success has in any case been difficult to measure; there is plentiful evidence of people enjoying queer pleasures in apparently oppressive times and suffering trauma in eras of supposed permissiveness and liberation.[159] An important strand of social movement history has shown that generations prior to Stonewall were not as quiescent as some have assumed. There was earlier resistance and examples of individuals and groups asserting their felt difference long before 'liberation'.[160] These queer histories complicate pat popular narratives of journeys from darkness into light, and of the 'after' ('after Stonewall', 'after 1967') being better than the 'before' ('better' on what and whose terms?, we should ask). They show, too, that whatever the trajectory, it differs markedly between national, regional and urban contexts.[161]

We need to hold norms and expectations of period and place within history to account and to engage with them reflexively. But they can also feel inescapable because they are so culturally legible and have such a grip on the way the past has been made into history. Our historical queer subjects, including those schooled in history, often understood their worlds in these domineering ways of organizing knowledge. Drawing in alternate postcolonial and queer ways of thinking about time and about space to our historical work is richly productive, but will also require a dialogue with – and some critically engaged replication of – those conventions, which are, to Chakrabarty, 'at once both indispensable and inadequate'.[162]

Conclusion

Viewing space and time through a queer lens and as active components in queer historical analysis allows us to understand and imagine further ways in which (homo)sexuality has been modulated and controlled in the past. In terms of space, this is true of particular places and institutions in a material and architectural sense, but it is true too of much larger geopolitical spatial units – of nation, continent, first and third world, Global South and North – through which individuals and groups orientate their sense of sexual selfhood and through which wider structures of power are marshalled to define and police. In terms of time, and at a local level, particular sites can be associated with an intensification or escape from time or a step into the past. In addition, distinct temporalities attach to those larger units, with backwardness, degeneration, progress or enlightenment characterizing the sexual too, though in ways that do not necessarily relate to experience. Homonationalism trades on these perceptions of time in locating who is in and who out in the narrative of LGBTQ+ 'advance'. This is something historians need to be alert to in the narratives they construct. As we 'fatten' the present with the past, to what extent are we affirming or complicating the vision of liberal progressive nationhood or metropolitanism set against supposed 'backward' 'others' in the Global South or in rural areas? One way in which queer historians have addressed this has been to expand their analysis from 'obviously' queer times and places (Stonewall, the Victorian *fin de Siècle*; the queer bar, the iconic gay city) and to work on the basis that queer is everywhere but is everywhere different. This is an elaboration of the work of early lesbian historians discussed in chapter 1 who found queerness in regular places and in tune with familiar temporal rhythms of putatively heteronormative spaces like the home. We should of course take heed of marginal, exceptional and liminal spaces, but also remember that such spaces existed alongside and in connection to those which were ordinary and orderly. People's everyday lives were in different ways parcelled up between them.

Coda

All my projects have rested on a fascination with space and its affects. This formed through some stellar high school geography teaching which led me fleetingly to consider studying architecture – especially when, captivated by a David Hockney painting, I designed a swimming pool in a technical drawing class which ended up on the workshop pinboard (the queer impulse behind this creation oblique even to me). I soon learnt that watery settings in art and literature, as well as in real life, frequently had a queer cadence. In Alan Hollinghurst's *Swimming Pool Library* (1988) that watery-ness was linked into London, and the city became even more alluring to me when I read this novel slack-jawed as an undergraduate in Sheffield. It seemed the obvious place to move when I graduated, and not only because of its queerly tinged pools and ponds.[163] Gay life, from what I had read, clustered there, and gay life, as a newly out twenty-year-old, was what I was after. Six months later, I moved into the housing association flat of my first boyfriend in the south-central suburb of Battersea. London was on the cusp. It was still possible to find cheap places to live; social housing like ours was more available than it was soon to be. This gave us some freedom as a couple: my boyfriend opened a café which just broke even; I took poorly paid work at a centre for actors, drank too much after work in the nascent gay village in Soho and did an MA which opened up new vistas intellectually, and not least in the introduction it gave me to then new work in cultural geography – work which adjusted my sense of the spaces I moved through and engaged with in the city.

Would I have found London so captivating if I had been bought up there and not made that quintessential move from village upbringing to urban queer adulthood? I relished the newly felt frisson of travelling on the tube with exchanged and 'backward glances' (like those literary scholar Mark Turner charts in London and Paris of the nineteenth century)[164] and I found myself looking up from my book especially at those stops fabled for their indoor or outdoor scenes – Clapham Common, Hampstead Heath, Earls Court, Leicester Square. The penultimate carriage on Piccadilly Line trains between those last two stops was supposedly the gay one. Many journeys later I realized this was either queer urban myth or a tradition that had faded with the Earls Court scene itself; AIDS was taking a particularly heavy toll there and Soho was emerging as London's pre-eminent gay hub in the early 1990s. A younger clientele drank there in new 'continental style' bars replete with plate glass windows that spoke to a defiant visibility. This was in contrast to the basement and clandestine venues which still existed here and there. To some, this new scene marked a loss of a seedier erotic underground and enacted further exclusions. For me at that time, it provided some ballast alongside other more mixed, indie bars and clubs around Kings Cross and Angel just to the north.

My new bike meant I evaded the routes and timetables of the tubes, buses, and especially night buses. A single bike ride might take me from home through the civic Victoriana of Battersea Park (complete with cruising ground), past iconic building of government and empire in Whitehall and Trafalgar Square (focus also of Pride and protest) and on to lose myself in books at the circular reading room of the old British Library (apparently perfect for a 'promenade', an established queer historian told me euphemistically). 'Alternative' queer films and plays were often on at the National Film Theatre on the South Bank and Drill Hall in Bloomsbury in the 1990s, and I would go on from shows and screenings there to Soho, Kings Cross or Angel. Each of these places conjured particular associations for me and adjusted my sense of self a little as I passed by or lingered – and to the extent that in the introduction to my first book I projected parts of this journey backwards to 1890s London as a way of imagining how it might have felt to traverse these and other spaces in the city then.

It is telling that when I sat down to write this coda I returned directly to the 'gayest' period of my life, and not to the shifting spatial co-ordinates and temporal rhythms that came with my weekly commute to my first academic job at Keele University in the English midlands, with parenthood and new partnerships, and with the advent of the internet and smartphones. And yet I was queer through all that too, with a cumulative and also changing sense of what that meant for me and the way I interacted with the city which had become my home. The act of coming out (invariably a multiple and selective process rather than singular event) shades out such reorientations across the life course, and yet the gay man I came out as to my parents at twenty feels markedly different from the gay man I see myself as at fifty-six. The shifts in my sense of self in-between have been modulated by – and lived through – different spaces and temporal rhythms which also directed me towards new projects. From work on Londons public queer cultures, I turned (with parenthood) to domestic spaces and then to the localized and emotive dimensions of the AIDS crisis in work which was a reckoning with my early years in the capital.

In the later 2010s I became disenchanted with London. With a third child newly arrived and in middle age I found myself engaging less with what the city offered and more with places beyond. A spell living in Brighton with my new partner sparked an interest in the way different provincial cities fostered alternate understandings and experiences of queer identity, community and politics, and in ways which dislodged London's putative queer pre-eminence. 'Queer Beyond London', a project I embarked on with Alison Oram and Justin Bengry, followed. We imagined the capital might dominate the wider queer imaginary, though we found it did so only very unevenly in our examination of the different queer dynamics and temporalities of Manchester, Leeds, Brighton and Plymouth, and the social, economic, demographic, occupational, geographical and historic contexts and forces which lay behind them. We found in naval Plymouth that partly because of the ban on homosexuality in the military (which lasted until 2000), the city's vibrant underground scene functioned largely below the proverbial radar long after partial decriminalization of homosexual sex in 1967. In Brighton, however, there was already by the time of that supposed national watershed a much-touted visibility and individualism which in the 1970s became the hallmark of wider gay liberationist politics. If the call to 'come out' was articulated loudly nationally and internationally in the 1970s, it was clearly taken up very unequally. One Plymouthian visitor to Brighton in the 1990s saw that you 'could be gay there'. This was not, though, an identity he owned when he was in his home city, even though what he was doing there was markedly queer.[165] These different watery cities, and the temporalities aligned with them, fostered very different queer dynamics.

4

Queer History/Public History

In 2014, film-maker Siobhan Fahey began recording oral histories of the Rebel Dykes, a loose grouping of young, lesbian, feminist punk women in 1980s London. This eventually grew into the Rebel Dykes History Project, with a three-month Art and Archive Show (2021), events across the UK – including talks, meet ups, and a Dykes-inspired club night[1] – and a collaboration with London's Bishopsgate Institute, which now holds the project archive as part of its growing LGBTQ+ collection.[2] The feature-length documentary, *Rebel Dykes* (2021), freely available on the net, was a further project output which built a picture of the Rebel Dyke 'family' in the 1980s and 1990s, forged through shared activism and sex and SM positivity, and in reaction against the cultural and political mainstream and other strands of lesbian feminism. The film includes footage of the notorious women-only BDSM sex club Chain Reaction which some of the Dykes ran in Vauxhall, south London, and follows their activism at Greenham Common, for ACT UP and against Section 28. The group pre-empted 1990s 'queer' defiance, claims one of the film's talking heads; 'we didn't want to be 'straight gays', remarks another. The film was financially supported by the Heritage Lottery Fund (HLF), the Arts Council and by individuals keen to tell a story that 'has so far been unheard', as contributor Karen Fisch put it. The project overall, the film, plus Fisch's additional comedy and performance work, has helped bring the history of the Rebel Dykes into contemporary lesbian and wider queer historical consciousness in Britain.[3]

The Rebel Dykes Project is a quintessential piece of UK LGBTQ+ public history. It represents a journey of historical discovery and reclamation outside of the academy, involving and representing a community, and with creative, artistic, archival, documentary and virtual components. It is fundamentally collaborative – amongst the Dykes themselves and with partners like the Bishopsgate. And it is one of a wide range of projects in the

UK benefitting from a switch in the HLF's protocols in 2003 to allow for funding of small-scale community-based ventures. This was a step which significantly increased the profile of LGBTQ+ public history across the entire country; by 2019 the HLF had funded 130 LGBTQ+ projects to the tune of £5.4 million in total.[4] The Rebel Dykes Project aligns with much of this wider work because of what it does in and for the present. It serves individual Rebel Dykes from the 1980s, affirming personal memories and heightening a sense of how experiences then informed life choices since. It also revitalizes a sense of community between the Dykes, and animates connections with subsequent generations of lesbians and queer women. Fahey notes that the film and intergenerational project events since its release have inspired a sense of possibility and hope, not least by centring lesbian and feminist experience and complicating assumptions that the feminism of that moment was necessarily trans-exclusionary.[5] Like other such projects, it establishes wider contexts by demonstrating the shaping power of culture, economics and politics: of the Thatcher government and its legislative actions, of the rank homophobia of the 1980s, and of the effects of financial precarity.

This chapter takes its cue from the Rebel Dykes History Project and others like it to explore the significance of LGBTQ+ history-making outside the academy, and the problems and possibilities arising from the especially intimate relationship between queer and public histories, the subject of the first section. In conjunction, that is as queer public history, this has been work almost invariably from below, from the margins and in ambivalent relation to wider audiences, though there has been a recent tardy uptake by some major mainstream museums and heritage bodies. Partly as a result local contexts have mattered profoundly and have almost invariably been the focus of work. Sometimes queer public history rehearses and further embeds an established iconography, familiar turning points and well-honed narratives This is a tendency discussed as part of sections two, three and four – on places (and in particular streets and museums); on people (who visit and collect for queer archives, and who arise from them as LGBTQ+ icons); and on the creative arts. But these sections show too that much of this work has artfully complicated such pat narratives and the status of the infamous, and suggested other ways of thinking about and sitting in relation to the past.

The range and extent of queer public history over the last fifty years is vast – and way more extensive than the canon of books and journals which previous chapters have touched. Extra academic work dwarfs the academic, and for this reason the chapter is not remotely comprehensive. My case study choices are eclectic and arise from my own encounters with, and involvement in, queer public history over the last thirty years. This is why the chapter moves between streets, exhibitions, museums, and archives in North and (fleetingly) South America, South Africa, Scandinavia and the United Kingdom, and how Yorkshire landowner Ann Lister (1791–1840) – a long-time companion in my teaching – compels my discussion of icons. It is also why the closing examination of how national contexts modulate the relationship between public history and the creative arts, centres on Britain, the place I know best. This is certainly partial and random, but the restricted field of vision already speaks to the power of public history to steer attention: I spent time in Berlin and San Francisco (which take up the bulk of the discussion of section 2 on 'Places') *because* of the historically accrued queer notoriety of these cities. I moved to London and Brighton (which also feature heavily in this chapter) partly for the same reasons. What went on in these places in terms of queer public history queered them further and so formed part of a historical environment which directed my work as a queer academic historian. That work in turn led me to advisory roles on creative and heritage projects in various places with less queer notoriety but as much queer import. The extent of queer public history means there are myriad other people and places I could have drawn into the chapter. They would have helped me to speak about some of the same issues and dynamics but they would also have led me in other directions, to other shaping contexts, and into other creative queer historical realms. This is the invitation of such queer historical abundance.

1. Queer history/public history

The US National Council of Public History has a usefully embracing definition: 'Public history', they write, 'describes the many and diverse ways in which history is put to use in the world.'[6] These include in museums, historic houses, memorials, tours and TV documentaries, and in public policy, education, activism and the arts. Public history is seen, traditionally, to be the work of professionals – historians, curators, archivists – in and for various publics. However, Raphael Samuel, a driving force behind the History Workshop movement and a pioneer social and public historian, saw it also as the work 'of a thousand different hands'.[7] He argued that history-making is or should be democratic, and by way of example touted the growing engagement with – and participation in – history and history-making in Britain from the Second World War and especially from the 1970s. In his landmark *Theatres of Memory* (1994), he charted the rising popularity of family history and of historical film, literature and drama. He also traced a shift in museum, archival, and heritage practices designed to engage visitors more actively and in relation to the digital realm which was just emerging at the point of his untimely death. Samuel skirted the reactionary work and potential of public history as 'a tool of establishments' in what was instead a hopeful vision of a radical, collective practice. This is resonant at least with the aspirations of much queer public history, even if its radicalism is not guaranteed just by dint of dealing with marginality and sexual subjectivity and community.[8] As will become clear, queer public history can also toe a homonormative line and be blind to its exclusions.

If the practice of public history has a long – indeed ancient – pedigree, it became a more specifically acknowledged and professionalized mode of history-making from the 1970s. The first postgraduate course launched at the University of California, Santa Barbara in 1976 and the first dedicated journal, *The Public Historian*, appeared from 1978. It promised to democratize history in terms of the subjects it dealt with and the audiences it addressed. Public history resonated with social history, history from below, and activist and community driven histories which were gaining traction at around the same time. Though the practice is defined in relation to where and how history is mobilized rather than in relation to particular themes or periods, the focus has tended to be on areas that are perceived to have immediate current appeal with a wider or particular group of people. The emphasis has consequently tended to be on histories of people, families, places and communities of the recent past, with evidence frequently gleaned from oral history, letters, diaries and photos.

The resonances between public and queer history are easy to recognize. Early lesbian and gay history *was* public history in its emergence outside the academy (there was precious little space within it) and also in the way it was put to use in consciousness raising and politics, and to make space for identity and community. The onus on collaboration and reaching out were public history hallmarks too. Since the 1990s, queer historical work 'in public' has continued in multiple directions with an especially porous boundary between queer history-making in and beyond the academy. This academic/public interface is characteristic of history more broadly in comparison to many other disciplines. But for those working on queer historical themes and with queer approaches it has been especially close. Jack Halberstam describes the necessary mutual commitment 'between the minority academic and the minority subcultural producer [which] can play a big role in the construction of queer archives and queer memory'.[9] Queer public history has been used to tout kindred spirits, to forge a sense of legitimacy, and to make queer lives imaginable. It has been deployed by lobbyists, activists and health and educational professionals. And it has been mobilized in literature, film, theatre and art; in museums, galleries and archives; in works of sexology, sociology and policy; in walking tours, public talks and memorials; and in multiple creative ways on the web. This work has often felt particularly immediate, and it has been a tool for fostering belonging and community for the present and into the future.[10] Indeed, showing how prospective projects might forge or support communities is an explicit part of the United Kingdom's Heritage Lottery Fund bidding process.[11]

This conscious process of gathering the past into the present as 'history' (in museum exhibitions and books, for example) shades into a broader sense of being surrounded by images, music, fashion, and fantasy which are historically resonant and provide more diffuse but nevertheless historically rich points of identification and belonging.[12] Historian Mark Pendleton describes something of this in his visits in the 1990s to a club in Kyoto called Diamonds are Forever. He wrote that 'newly gay, and newish to Japan I knew little of the culture and community I was stepping into, but I sensed that coming out would require an embrace of histories that were not yet mine'.[13] Diamonds as a material space, the music played there, the dancefloor moves, and the lip-syncing and embodiment of dead icons provided some tools for Pendleton's acculturation. He suggests in his poignant rehearsal of this process that bars and clubs are not only of the present and for present socializing, but are themselves venues for – and a means of sustaining – queer public history. In London this came into sharper focus as queer venues began closing in the 2010s and became more directly reconceptualized as being of 'historical significance'.[14]

There is queer potential in looking beyond history in intentional and disciplinary terms and instead leaning into a heightened consciousness of these more accidental, ephemeral brushes with the past. This speaks to queer conceptions of finding 'touch[es] across time' and everyday sustenance through the past in the present.[15] It is also one way of thinking about the tension between public history 'proper' and those engaged less formally in the queer past 'in public'. The tension (and associated challenge) arises primarily because the idea of the 'public' – as a mass of people, as a set of places, as a sphere of discourse – is deeply contested. Queer lives have frequently been excluded from or marginalized and traduced in each of these versions of the public.[16] Meanwhile, 'history' has tended to serve queer lives and publics poorly. Should those working with the queer past engage in its conventions? And if so, which public can and should queer history invoke and address? Is it 'for us' or for everyone? And, if the former, who is included in the 'us'? There is a related tension in formal spaces of public history like museums and archives. Here the established categorizing logic is at odds with a queer drive to trouble and disaggregate prevailing organizations of knowledge and space.[17] Because of this, queer theorists and others have asked whether a queer museum or queer representation within a museum is even possible, whilst others, especially those working from Latinx and queer of colour perspectives, have looked for their pasts in other places, embedded in gesture, voice, bodies, and sexual practice, and circulating in gossip and anecdote, for example.[18]

Such counter histories refute dominant and exclusionary ways of accounting for and narrating the past and touch a longstanding tendency amongst the queerly identified to infer historic resonance. In the absence of direct representation, many got used to habitually reading for queers and queer dynamics between the lines and seeking out signs and symbols in art and artefact that might hint at a queer past and provide a queer frisson and sense of connection in the present. This could happen in regular, established museums. The Uranian poets in late-nineteenth and early-twentieth-century London, for example, drew out the homoerotics of classical statuary in the British Museum in their verse and – we can suppose from the erotic intensity of the writing – in their fantasies.[19] Their knowledge of the ancient world, accrued in the homosocial environments of English public schools and universities, allowed the museum's collections to signify queerly and to cement a bond between some of these men. The context of the British Museum and wider value accorded to Classical culture by Victorians and Edwardians elevated the fascination of these visitors from the 'merely' lustful.[20] It was possible for a queer elite to find both their privilege and their desires reflected, consolidated and produced in this and other forums of national culture, even though the institutions of state derided them. For others, this made these places doubly excluding, as E. M. Forster suggests in his novel *Maurice* (written 1914; published 1971). Gamekeeper Alec Scudder is alienated in the British Museum when he meets his upper middle-class lover (the eponymous Maurice) there. The statues wobble and he reaches towards blackmail in a refraction of the class dynamics the museum endorses. It is, in this rendition, a space of negative, equivocal queer affect and does not deliver the positive endorsement the Uranian poets found there. That, for Alec and Maurice, comes in the natural and mythic affirmation of the English greenwood – another historicized fantasy realm – to which they retreat at the end of the novel.[21]

Forster and these contemporaries each observed – albeit in different ways – that museum and heritage sites could speak obliquely, for good or ill, to queer audiences. The heritage houses of Plas Newydd in North Wales (home of the Ladies of Llangollen), Shibden Hall in Yorkshire (Anne Lister), and, in Kent, Charleston (the Bloomsbury set) and Sissinghurst (Vita Sackville West), were valued by women for their lesbian histories before they were widely avowed in labelling, tours and guidebooks.[22] That acknowledgement has more recently come with special exhibitions, integrated displays and self- and person-guided tours of these and other historic sites. In London, the British Museum and Victoria and Albert Museum both now have queer routes through their collections and the Tate Britain held a large-scale exhibition on 'Queer British Art' in 2017.[23] The reconfigured Museum of London, launched in 2026, integrates queer stories into its account of the city, showing how queer and urban life have long been enmeshed. The People's History Museum in Manchester, the Brighton Museum and Oxford's Pitt Rivers anthropological museum have attempted something similar, in the latter case with a particular reflexivity about museological tradition and practice. Their 'Beyond the Binary' project reworked catalogues and displays to trouble the gender binary imposed on othered cultural contexts by Western anthropologists.[24] Historic England's 'Pride of Place' work meanwhile shifted authority and expertise from the heritage professional and curator to queer and trans individuals and community groups who were invited to pin places of particular personal and communal historical significance on a digital map. The initiative allowed queer histories and past ephemeral queer experience to connect via this mode of shared authority.[25]

This work – usually initiated by queer employees rather than the higher ups – has widened the constituency and appeal of these museums and heritage organizations, and made more generally visible those queer threads that have long run through their work and collections. There has been a real value for queer audiences in being part of and having space within institutions that have traditionally been unrepresentative and exclusionary but which have now often become significant in sustaining and showcasing a tight relationship between queer and public history. They have contributed to queer historical consciousness and a consciousness of queerness in the broader historical imaginary. The critique is that these venues have come late and sometimes grudgingly and too cautiously to the queer history party. Distinction and difference can be compromised and sanitized in these contexts, squeezed into a conventional mode of knowledge production and presentation, and so un-queered and folded into a mainstream account in ways that can reflect and entrench homonormativity. Though equipped with less resources, history made and deployed at the cultural margins sometimes has more latitude. The sections to come lean more into the latter whilst also signalling the developing dialogue with mainstream museological and heritage spaces and practices.

2. Places

Berlin

The ALMS (LGBTQ+ Archives, Libraries, Museums and Special Collections) conference of 2019 took place in Berlin's House of World Culture (Haus der Kulturen der Welt) – a hopeful sixties edifice predicated on global bridge-building and connection. It sits on the banks of the River Spree on the edge of the Tiergarten, near the former site of Magnus Hirschfeld's Institut für Sexualwissenschaft (Institute for Sexual Science; 1919–33), the 'first known effort to fill the queer void in the world of museums'.[26] The institute saw the intersection of subculture, art and science – a place where queer collecting was seen to serve scientific 'advance' as well as queer legibility and affirmation.[27] If collecting was, by the 1920s, a relatively common part of elite scientific and medical practice in Europe,[28] the Institute differed in its sharper focus and in its accessibility in a period when Berlin was seen to be at the sexual vanguard (a story that has endured in popular memory, though one which historians have sought to nuance).[29] The Nazis' destruction of the Institute in 1933, including the burning of its papers and books, signalled just how threatening such spaces were seen (and are still seen) to be by some and how vulnerable public markers (and makers) of queerness were (and are) in the face of regime change and shifts in political climate.

It was only much later that Hirschfeld's work was embedded again in the fabric of the city. The riverbank opposite the House of World Culture was renamed in his honour in 2008, with information points installed about the man and his work. A ten-minute walk away, Karl-Heinrich-Ulrichs-Strasse commemorates another nineteenth-century political and sexological pioneer, and speaks to Berlin's particular place in the history of sexology. 'Stumbling stones' were meanwhile added into the fabric of Berlin's pavements from 1992, marking those deported and lost to the Nazi's extermination camps, and including some 'homosexual' men and 'antisocial' women. A monument dedicated to those same men and women was unveiled in 2008 near to the memorials to the Jews (2005) and Roma (2012). Set into the Memorial to Homosexuals Persecuted under Nazism is a screen showing alternating films of men and of women, signalling endurance beyond the horrors of the period, and signalling too the subsequent onus on lesbian and gay identities (and so also binary gender). The decision to rotate films came after fraught debate over who should be memorialized and how, highlighting a felt need for representation in the terms of the 2000s rather than of the 1930s and 1940s.[30]

Together, these various urban markers come as a riposte to the Nazis and subsequent reanimations of their hate. They make the brush of queer history especially tangible in this city, and sustain its 'hallowed place in the global queer historical imaginary'.[31] Queer history 'looms large', writes Jennifer Evans: 'it is pressed into the landscape, it adorns the buildings and it is worn in the faces of each generation of city dwellers tasked with finding some way of coming to terms with its heinous past'.[32] This came into especially sharp focus in two walking tours I took during the ALMS conference week. They each sketched a trajectory from the putative liberalism of Weimar era (1918–33) to the horrors of the thirties and forties; from possibility and permissiveness to brutality and despair.[33] Beyond the persecutions of the Nazi era, the guides described the struggles of queer people in the years to decriminalization in East Germany in 1968 and in West Germany in 1969. And they showed how more or less consciously consumed histories had shaped queer identities and communities in the earlier periods they described as well as in the time since. One guide pointed out the Nazi modifications to 'decadent' buildings around the infamous Weimar El Dorado Club (1928–32) on the corner of Motzstrasse in Schöneberg, suggesting how the look and feel of the German capital changed for those traversing these queerly notorious streets as the regime rose to power. (The club itself is now a natural food supermarket.) A nearby gay sex and clothing store we passed had military regalia on display in its window; history embedded there in troubling fetishism. These tours suggested a particular way of knowing the history of queer Berlin and something of how that knowledge might inflect the queer present.

Retracing my steps alone later in the evening, I found the area haunted by these earlier cultures, people and politics, the past echoing round the present in ways both moving and deceptively immediate. If some of the same buildings lined the street, the gay men I clocked in this area were not ciphers of queer men of Weimar or Nazi Germany. The moves to make evident the queer pasts and tragedies of these streets mobilizes history, but they are also where some histories overtake others.[34] Rent controls in the city, artist and squatting communities, and music and club scenes – each part of or emerging from the shattered, split and then reunified city – also provided contexts for distinctive queer feeling, expression and kinship here. But though more recent, these facets of Berlin's history are feinter in the queer historical imaginary and memory than the searingly tragic earlier period.

Berlin's queer Schwules Museum has pushed at some of these issues since it was established in 1985. It has rehearsed 'the pink triangle narrative' (which recalls the way 'homosexual' extermination camp inmates were badged) but has also sought to extend the city's queer history beyond it.[35] Housed initially in a courtyard adjacent to a gay café and community space in Mehringdamm in Kreuzberg, it was very clearly of and for 'the community'. It emerged from a temporary exhibition in 1984 at the Märkisches Museum (of the History of Berlin) entitled 'El Dorado: homosexual men and women, 1850-1950'. Curated by a group of lesbian and gay activist-scholars, this was the first attempt to present queer history in a major German museum. Four of the men involved quickly formed a group called the Friends of Schwules Museum to organize for the permanent iteration. Working at an impressive pace, it opened in the following year. The museum's trajectory comes as a reminder of the importance of temporary exhibitions which can be more deft and responsive than permanent staging of collections and can be a means of testing the water, raising consciousness and prompting further action.[36]

If the El Dorado exhibition had been a significant moment in recalling and recording Berlin's queer past, the queer museum and archive embedded this past more firmly in the history and culture of this city and its people. This was underscored when the city authorities allocated enhanced funding to facilitate and sustain a move in 2013 to a former printing factory in Lützowstrasse in the Tiergarten area, at a distance from gay Kreuzberg (and Schonberg) but close to Nollendorfplatz, the historic heart of queer Berlin, and to the Potsdammer Platz entertainment and former red-light district. (The latter was incorporated, via guided walks, into the museum's exhibition on sex work which showed how queer life was enmeshed in the city's street culture and sexual commerce.)[37] The city funding authorized and legitimized the museum and the queer histories it showcased and produced. It also gave it the means to innovate and to take queerer approaches in its elaboration of the past. This included the 2020 exhibition '100 Objects: An Archive of Feelings' which focused on the emotional texture of some of the 1.5 million items held in the museum's archive and referenced Ann Cvetkovich's eponymous work.[38] Rather than a chronological progression, the exhibition was sectionalized according to 'desire', 'joy', 'anger', 'care' and 'fear', reflecting a turn to affect, the ephemeral, and eroto-history in queer historical work. The exhibition was a wry nod to the British Museum's 'A History of the World in 100 Objects' initiative (2010). In this incarnation, though, the objects were not being used to map decisive moments in history but rather to give a more diffuse sense of the queer emotional terrain of the past – wrestling in the process with the impossibility of representing queer affect and subjectivity.

In this last respect, the 'Archive of Feelings' show riffed on an earlier decolonizing exhibition of 2017: 'Odarodle: An Imaginary Their-Story of Naturepeoples, 1535–2017'. Odarodle is an inversion of 'El Dorado' – the Weimar-era queer venue, the name of the exhibition that had galvanized the formation of Schwules Museum, and also the mythical 'city of gold'. The latter was, curator Ashkan Sepahvand noted, 'one of the fantasies that fueled early modern Europe's race for wealth, power and territory', signposting the often-submerged historical relationship between colonialism, the development of racist typologies, and the emergence of the homosexual 'other'. Sepahvand pointed out the way in which the original El Dorado exhibition recreated queer 'habitats' in separated male and female sections. It included 'the gay boudoir, the lesbian café, and the cruising area of the Tiergarten', deliberately or otherwise echoing classic ethnographic and natural history exhibits that showcased colonial and historical subjects. He thus suggested that the El Dorado exhibition merely inserted another theme into familiar modes of exhibiting and knowing. The curators, he argued, had not taken the opportunity to 'shatter . . . perspectives altogether' and to 'dismantl[e] . . . a unified view'. This latter is what Sepahvand sought to do for Odarodle by inviting sixteen artists to respond to Schwules Museum and Archive and so 'sensualise and complicate seeing, showing, reading, thinking'.[39] Again, the temporary exhibition became a tool for deft critique – not least of the museum itself. This commission was part of an imperative felt by the museum's Board of Directors actively to engage with debate in queer history and to explore the dimensions and possibilities of a queer museology. This was evident, too, in the 'Archive of Feelings' exhibition and the 2018 'Year of Women' which invited reflection on the museum and its focus (raising heckles amongst those who saw this as a gay male space).[40] This experimentalism is sustained by the museum management structure, with an elected Board of eight, 300 members, and dozens of volunteers. There is in this a muted echo of the community history-making of the 1970s and 1980s from which the museum emerged.

San Francisco

Curators at the GLBT Historical Society Museum just off Castro Street in San Francisco have been similarly reflexive and critically engaged. Its inaugural 'Our Vast Queer Past' exhibition (2011–14) positioned 'our' history in relation to 'theirs' but refuted pat assumptions about its coherence or homogeneity. Queer history 'does not form a single narrative', read the introductory panel; 'our history is too varied and unruly to be limited in that way. Instead, we bring together multiple stories, sometimes interlinking, sometimes isolated, sometimes in conflict.'[41] Underlying this was an attempt to make apparent 'the filtering, interpretative and disciplinary frames of perception through which we come to – or lose – embodiment, subjectivity, rights and affect'.[42] The small museum space provides focused attention on queer lives, separating them out from a mainstream, whilst also demonstrating a dance with wider social and cultural contexts. It illustrates, for example, the significance of the Californian goldrush to emergent and enduring queer dynamics in the city and wider region. In the inclusion of sex toys from the 1930s to the 1980s, the curators refused to skirt queer sex and so be complicit in the shame associated with it. Instead they 'boldly retained the centrality and materiality of sexual performance to queer heritage'.[43] The debate about this inclusion centred on what queer history should be about, what it should do, who it might be for, and whether it mattered that visitors might be offended by a small display of dildos.[44] Occluding such sex positivity would for some have been a frustrating re-packaging of San Francisco's queer history and culture – and not least of the museum space's own former erotic life as a cruisy laundromat in the queerly exuberant Castro District.[45]

The notably enmeshed lesbian, gay, bisexual and trans movements in the city have roots in the gay bars, queer performance cultures and homophile groups of the 1950s, which raised an associated historical consciousness well before the Castro emerged as a gay area in the later 1960s and became a local, national and international LGBTQ+ focal point.[46] The San Francisco Lesbian and Gay History Project was formed in 1978 as a loose-knit study group but soon turned outwards with public-facing talks, slide shows and discussions held across the city. From 1985, the GLBT Historical Society was established as an archival project, based initially at co-founder Willie Walker's apartment in the Castro District (on 17th Street), before expanding to storage lockers, a building in the Mission District (on 16th Street, in the building where the LGBTQ+ Theatre Rhinoceros was then also located), and on to a more permanent home, with a first paid archivist, in Market Street, downtown San Francisco from 1995. The reading room doubled as a gallery, and the society staged temporary exhibitions there and in borrowed venues, including on 'Queer and Kinky Danger: Art of San Francisco's Leather/SM/Kink Worlds' (1998); 'Making a Case for Community History' (1999; featuring case studies of Asian Americans, Pacific Islanders, African Americans, Latino/as, bears, and the leather and transgender communities) and 'Saint Harvey: The Life and Afterlife of a Modern Gay Martyr' (Susan Stryker's landmark exhibition of 2003 on the assassinated gay activist and city supervisor Harvey Milk [1930–78]).[47] A temporary 'pop up museum' on the corner of 18th Street and Castro in 2008 showcased some of the Society's by then vast and wide-ranging collection.[48] It drew around 25,000 people in its eleven-month run, suggesting the appetite and providing the impetus for the permanent museum which followed in 2010. It was sited – as with the first Schwules Museum – in the midst of the fabled gay neighbourhood and has since hosted a further tranche of temporary exhibitions alongside its more longstanding displays.[49]

The GLBT Historical Society Museum became part of the intense memorialization in the Castro. The area is palpably drenched in history – its own, and, given its status as a national and international queer hub, that of other places and people. There is a triangular garden commemorating LGBTQ+ people lost in the Nazi extermination camps, with an invitation to take a piece of rose quartz from the memorial to further the idea/l of international connection, communion and solidarity in the face of a murderous past. (My stone is in front of me on my desk as I write; a piece of material culture freighted with collective and personal memory). There are also memorials in this neighbourhood to local tragedy – to the generation lost to AIDS in the city and to trans people killed. There are commemorative murals on side-streets and plaques marking Harvey Milk's camera shop and apartment; the plaza at the head of the Castro is also named after him. A 'rainbow honor walk' of plaques embedded in neighbourhood sidewalks on Market, Castro, 18th and 19th Streets celebrate iconic lesbian, gay, bisexual and trans forebears from around the world.[50] The non-profit 'honor walk' project has helped fashion the Castro as a site of international memorialization.

Many of the stores on the Castro are marked as LGBTQ+ 'legacy businesses': local, for-profit enterprises of more than thirty years standing.

The LGBTQ+ history guided tour I went on here was one such; a hardware shop and sex store were two others. Heritage in these instance signals the status and value of the pink pound but is also a means of preserving the 'character' of the area. The designation affords protections which help to prevent takeovers and the arrival of chain stores. Herein lies a tension between serving a community and a neoliberal servicing of 'tourist economies' by creating 'spectacles for consumption' – a complex circle to square when the aspiration is for more to visit, to comprehend, and to connect (something a brand new, much larger, GLBT Historical Society Museum, Archives, and Public History Center, due to open in 2027, aims also to facilitate).[51] Queer heritage has been strategically useful and also profitable: the area trades actively on its own history and place in collective memory in ways that are moving and empowering as well as inevitably selective. Evidence of the presence of two-spirit people in this part of California went unmentioned on the guided walk, for example.[52]

Capturing the 'polyvocality of [this] place' is a challenge. This is true, too, of the Tenderloin district across town, part of which was designated as the Compton's Transgender Cultural District in 2017 (later renamed The Transgender District).[53] This was a welcome recognition of the August 1966 riots at the local Compton's Cafeteria branch which predated Stonewall, and of the venue's significance as a sustaining part of a trans social scene in that decade. The naming makes a bold claim on public space, ensuring that people passing through brush consciously against queer and trans history. More pragmatically, like legacy business status, it gives some local protections and allows the city authorities to tout their inclusive credentials. However, other queer historical dimensions of the area have been shaded out in the process, including the route of the Christopher Street Liberation Day March in 1970, which skirted the western side of the Tenderloin, and the youth, AIDS and gay parenting support offered at the Glide Memorial Church under the leadership of Pastor Cecil Williams, and Reverends Ted McIlvenna, Don Kuhn and Lewis Durham from 1963.[54]

Designations, tours, and memorializations are lodestones for many and can establish and render permanent shared reference points and meaning in relation to a minoritized sense of community.[55] There is a clear value in this, especially in the face of historic and contemporary attempts at erasure. But there can also be a loss of those queer identifications, dynamics, cultures and histories which extend beyond such permanent markers and the communities they represent, making this memorialization unevenly meaningful and even exclusionary. Curators and public historians, including at the GLBT

Historical Society, have long observed and tasked themselves with tracking the multivalent queer histories of this city. But the queer iconic status and significance to collective memory of places like Berlin and San Francisco also entrench more simplified narratives or mythologies which can narrow a sense of the history of these places – to sexology, Weimar sexual liberalism and fascism with the former, and, with the latter, to sixties and seventies counterculture, the devastation of the AIDS crisis, and the Castro.

Bergen, Tromsø, Bogota, and Helsinki

What of places with less queer international repute and fewer infamous stories writ large? In Norway there is not a dominant queer narrative to offset or complicate, or rather there has been a baseline presumption of liberal acceptance over recent years, with a related sense that addressing queer histories and making them visible is not a politically urgent task. Building on the growing body of work from other national contexts assessing the everyday dance of queer and normal, the Queerdom (Queer Domesticities) project (2021 - 2025) drew out the particular Norwegian dimensions of everyday queerness. In this way it historicized those presumptions of ordinariness and embeddedness – and in ways that might be surprising to those who anticipate the extraordinary or that the extraordinary would cause more ructions. Bringing the queerness of the Norwegian everyday into public consciousness does not simply affirm the status quo, however. Instead, making it apparent troubles embedded assumptions about default heterosexuality and robust masculinity in this nation oriented in the cultural imaginary more towards mountains and sea than cities where queer life and difference are seen to flourish. The Polar Museum in Tromsø in the Arctic Circle and the Maritime Museum in the port city of Bergen, each with curators actively involved in the Queerdom network, mounted special exhibitions in 2023 and 2024 which tug at such assumptions. At the Polar Museum, the team rethought museum artefacts and props through a queer lens to suggest ways of thinking beyond the machismo of Arctic exploration.[56] Selected items were displayed in boxes with 'standard' and 'queer' commentaries and different 'peep holes' to bring alternate perspectives on arctic drag on ships (a tradition on crossing the meridian), on arctic domesticity, and on the bakers and designers who provided food and clothing. Explorers' letters revealed links between the sexological, anthropological and botanical drives to categorize and differentiate in the late nineteenth and early twentieth centuries (and in ways which resonate with the connections made by Odarodle). The exhibition design communicated the double vision of many queerly identified people and the double meanings of familiar, often banal objects.

The Maritime Museum exhibit was underpinned by an oral history project with twenty men and women working in passenger ships and oil and other cargo vessels.[57] These accounts were divided between sections on, first, queer possibilities on ship and in port, and second, on the danger and fear of exposure many felt in the cargo ships especially. This was all couched in the story of Norway's particular relationship with the sea and the economic boom of the 1960s and 1970s which drew more men to work in the sector. Ship models from the museum's wider holdings gave a vivid sense of the physical environment in which sailors were living and working, fostering an understanding of the everyday and material experience of queer life on board vessels which were pivotal to the Norwegian economy and muscular self-image.

Queerdom in its various dimensions has sought to awaken a sense of queerness reverberating through multiple aspects of Norway's quotidian past. The broader project has worked in the longstanding spirit of uncovering queer and trans lives, but it has also sought to queer a set of embedded mainstays of Norwegian history and to invite a queer second look. The interest in approach as well as substance has underpinned other recent queer public history interventions. In Bogota, Colombia, the non-profit, volunteer-driven Museum Q initiative operates as a 'museum without walls', intervening in established collections and online to 'recover ..., communicat[e] and mak[e] visible the stories and memories of LGBTQ+ people as part of the national narrative'.[58] Since its inception in 2014, it has staged exhibitions on coming out, same sex marriage, and historic and contemporary violence against queer people. It has intervened in high profile collections, with a contribution to the new 'Social Fabric, Voices and Confrontations' room in Colombia's National Museum, and a residency at the MAMBO (the Museum of Modern Art) exploring the sex trade and 'furtive encounters' in the surrounding streets. It has set up online projects (including on Instagram) to queer conventions in heritage practice and to give curated space to artists engaged in queer history.[59] Museum Q's model is swift-footed and multivalent – working with and also up against established museums and cultural sites and practices. The virtual environment is key: Museum Q is just one of many online initiatives taking advantage of the scope to reach new and international audiences at relatively little cost (crucial given the limited resource available). Such projects can be deft in the face of authoritarianism, if also risky precisely because of their reach. Those doing their queer public history work virtually seem, anecdotally, to receive more abuse and sustained attack than the rest of us.

Seeking something of this democratic accessibility and engagement on the ground, the 2017 Queercache project in Helsinki, Finland, embedded a sense of the queer everyday by focusing on minoritized and excluded queer people rather than turning up the volume further on the already queerly iconic – the twin figures of Touko Valio Laaksonen and Tove Jansson, creators, respectively, of Tom of Finland and the Moomins.[60] Queercache wrestled with the challenge of keeping meaning loose rather than fixing it in permanent public memorials or repeated, well-rehearsed narratives.[61] The team placed twelve boxes strategically across the city containing case studies, characters, quotations and objects from a span of 150 years plus. These touched multiple dimensions of Helsinki's queer past, including as it pertained to refugees, Romani and trans people. Material was presented in Finnish, Swedish and Arabic – the country's third most spoken 'foreign' language after Russian and Estonian because of immigration primarily from Iraq, Syria and Morocco. The inclusion is a notable gesture of solidarity with especially minoritized migrants; the omission of Russian might be differently significant given historic tensions with Finland's neighbour to the east. The boxes also included a pencil and notebook so that those tracking and finding the boxes could add their own thoughts or memories. This created dialogue and built meaning and association in ways that resonate with broader aspects of Finish nation-building and modes of popular public history practice here.[62] If the 'cache' technique is not new, it resonates particularly with queer experience, as archaeologist Visa Immonen argues, including in the dynamics of visibility and invisibility, im/permanence, and cruising and searching. The boxes might be encountered randomly, out of order, and do not together form a coherent narrative; some might easily be missed. The project in this way validated a sense of the randomness of the queer past and touched intimacies, friendships and solidarities, as well as ephemeral experience and fleeting desires.

The nation-state and its administrative subdivisions are prominent in the themes and framing of much queer public history. Even as this work can shake up national, including queer national histories, these geopolitical units remain powerful arbiters of queer life.[63] Public and community historians inevitably engage in the contexts which have the most immediate impacts on them and those around them, and which they might be most actively engaged in challenging. More pragmatically, money allocated to such work by national or regional bodies may come with the explicit or tacit expectation of a focus on that national or regional frame – as with community history awards from city authorities in London (to the Hall-Carpenter archive) and in Berlin (to the Schwule) in the 1980s and 1990s, or from the Norwegian government for the Skeivt (Queer) Archive in Bergen and the Queerdom project (via the Norwegian Research Council) in the 2010s and 2020s. And yet projects are increasingly reaching beyond these bounds, especially in explorations of transnational migration. Queercache was highly attuned to movement within but also from outside Finland. The Bergen Maritime Museum specifically highlighted the significance to ship workers of travel experience elsewhere, most especially in the United States, in consolidating a sense of what a gay identity might mean and implicate in the 1960s. The 'Transtrans: Transnational Transgender Histories' exhibition at Schwules Museum in 2020 had itself travelled across the Atlantic from its first showing at the Nickle Gallery of the University of Calgary. A huge opening panel mapped the international movement of people and ideas.[64] ALMS has sought to bring projects with a national focus alongside each other and so into conversation. The 2016 iteration in London was named Without Borders, looking to transnational connections in the practices of and themes in queer public history. The second day of the conference was overshadowed by the results of the United Kingdom's vote to leave the European Union, underscoring the ways in which the re/affirmation of national borders collide with aspirations to queer transnationalism.

There is a huge gulf between places where queer history making has been possible, even prolific, and those where such work remains impossible. At a 2019 New York conference focused on public history and heritage, and marking the fiftieth anniversary of the Stonewall riots, Michael Ighodaro, an HIV and homelessness activist who moved to the United States as a refugee from Nigeria in 2012, spoke of the luxury of being able to debate and critique queer public history in and of our particular contexts. For him, histories and memories of queer Nigeria – relating, for example, to a space under a bridge where men met to socialize – could only be shared through word of mouth. There is no paper or digital trail to follow. It was challenging and dangerous there and in many other parts of the world to speak out for sexual rights, justice and experience in the present, or to deploy history as a tool of activist struggle and individual and communal sustenance. The thirst for that history is part of what made the subsequent US documentary *Legend of the Underground* (2021) so significant. The film follows and historicizes the lives of a number of queer Nigerians, including Ighodaro, in their decisions creatively to seek out liveable lives and to confront rank discrimination and homo and transphobia. Here was a celluloid trace, accessible virtually worldwide, including, for those with internet access, in Nigeria.[65]

3. People

Exhibitions, queer and queered museums, and walking tours are rich in individual stories, providing the personal hook that is a consistent feature of queer public history and public history more broadly. This makes queer history relatable, tangible, even as it also risks taking experience, action and personhood as unproblematically retrievable and at face value, rather than in relation to or as a product of historic social and cultural contexts and dynamics. In the United Kingdom there is a roster of white, elite icons – Radclyffe Hall, Oscar Wilde, Alan Turing, Edward Carpenter and Anne Lister – who have been routinely celebrated in LGBT History Month since its inception in 2005. Turing and Wilde have their own memorial statues; Lister and her lover Ann Walker, a plaque outside the church in York where they 'married' in 1834; Hall and Carpenter have a now dispersed LGBTQ+ archive named after them, containing, in its oral history component, dozens of testimonies of individuals much more thoroughly 'hidden from history' than they. LGBTQ+ community and public history projects have almost invariably pivoted on such testimony. The cluster of queer and trans projects and exhibitions in Brighton on England's south coast, for example, have all been centrally focused on the stories and treasured objects of Brighton locals.[66] Items for the Museum of Transology (from 2014) and Queer Looks (from 2018) at the Brighton Museum were crowd-sourced or gathered by queer and trans peers. Workshops and feedback boards accompanying these exhibitions drew further voices into the space of the museum.[67] Popular queer history books (for sale in the museum's bookshop) tend to unfold their themes via the stories of individuals. This focus in public and popular history echoes a biographical pulse in queer historical work more broadly as people in the past are reanimated to 'meet' those in the present – sometimes with a sense of familiarity, at others of baffling disconnect from present ways of thinking, feeling and behaving. Lister provides a case study here for thinking through some of these dynamics, but first to those whose passion for people in the past – iconic and otherwise – is expressed by forming, collecting for, and visiting queer archives, a further space of queer public history.

Archives and collecting

Collecting has in itself been construed as a particularly queer pursuit: a way for individuals to construct a sense of legitimacy and of difference, to suggest a superior queer taste, or to mark marginalized lives through material traces.[68] Those with sufficient wealth bought stuff for their homes, imbuing the domestic with queer historical markers in ways which couched the resident and communicated something about them to visitors.[69] If sometimes this was about keying into and contributing to wider collecting trends, Neil Bartlett, the writer, director and collector, also associates it with a 'tradition of drag', 'of radical second-hand taste', with 're-discoveries of stuff from the past which nobody else wanted, which gay men in particular have discovered and loved, and cherished'.[70] There can be a sense of queer inheritance to this, with things passed down not through the conventional kinship routes, but from friend to friend or lover to lover. A photograph once owned by Wilde, for example, passed to his friend and executor Robbie Ross, to Bloomsbury artist Duncan Grant, to art historian Simon Watney and on to Bartlett. The tiny late-nineteenth-century erotic image now carries with it associations of its journey through these various hands. Such items, and a broader gathering up of queer 'bricolage', materializes and gives some value to desires and relationships which have been derided or ignored, 'considered trash'.[71] This is not the elite sensibility of the queer stately home-owning collector, but it hits a similar note in terms of finding a sense of distinction and difference through accumulated things – from camp ornaments and pieces of art to photographs, scene newspapers, safe sex leaflets, badges and much more besides.

Such collections have been amassed under beds, in attics or on shelves and mantlepieces; others formed in relation to early gay publishers and were based around the material people were reading. These archival endeavours were rooted in a consciousness that what gay men and lesbians were living through was itself historic and mattered to history – a consciousness then that is also seductive now. We are repeatedly drawn to the gay liberation moment as a historical turning point partly because it was understood as such then and in ways that focused collectors' attention in particular ways. Amongst the first were the Western Gay Archive, established in 1971 by *ONE Magazine* contributor Jim Kepner in his Los Angeles apartment; the Canadian Gay Liberation Archives which began in a cupboard in the Toronto offices of Pink Triangle Press in 1973; and the Australian Lesbian and Gay Archives (now the Australian Queer Archives) founded in Melbourne in

1978 following the fourth annual Australian Homosexual Conference. The Western Gay Archive grew rapidly and merged with the archive of the ONE Press to become the ONE National Gay & Lesbian Archives, presently probably the largest LGBTQ+ archive in the world. It is held at the University of Southern California in LA with an associated museum in the queer West Hollywood neighbourhood. The Canadian Gay Liberation Archives became ArQuives: Canada's LGBTQ2+ Archive in 2018, housed, complete with exhibition space, in a nineteenth-century sessions (court) house – a neat repurposing given the criminal dimensions of queer history and the archive's own brush with the law through a 1977 police raid.[72] These archives have developed from community organizations to established institutions with more stable funding and professional support. More recently, further grassroots archives, often developed online, have begun to address the deficit in collections in the Global South, including the volunteer-run online Queer Indonesia Archive (from 2020) and Acervo Bajubá (from 2010 in Brasilia and 2017 in San Paula).[73]

With an onus on creating a clear public interface, such LGBTQ+ archives have become anchor points because of what they symbolize as much as for what they hold in their vaults. Their individual and community origin stories matter. Lesbian history pioneer Joan Nestle talks about how her experiences in the 1950s as a working-class dyke in the Bronx, New York, mobilized her intersecting activist and historical work. It drove her determination to collect and preserve in her New York apartment in the early 1970s in what became the Lesbian Herstory Archives.[74] Nestle shelved books by first rather than patriarchal surname in line with a contemporary feminist politics and she describes being guided by her consideration of what lesbian visitors to the archive in the present might be looking for. Partly as a result the archive, now in a Brooklyn brownstone house, has longstanding significance as a place of assurance and possibility.[75] Jen Jack Gieseking 'marvel[led] how you can climb on a chair, take down [Audre Lorde's] boxes, and leaf through drafts of her poems, books and letters on your own'.[76] There is an immediacy, intimacy, and sense of connection here often missing in more formal archival settings. The past has been touchable in a way that mattered especially to women whose pasts had been denied, derided and sidelined. Lesbian archives have for this reason sometimes been reserved exclusively for women's use.[77] Ben Power Alwin, archivist at the Minorities Archive (formerly the New Alexandria Lesbian Library, established in 1974) in Chicago described how in the 1970s and 1980s it 'felt like the only safe place to do an LGBT collection was in my home', and how since then the 'domestic, anti-institutional environment' has provided sustenance for him and for queer researchers and visitors. 'People [come to listen to music or watch a video and] want to be surrounded by their own materials … It nurtures them the way it nurtures me to live here.'[78] The shift in the archive in this case especially reflects personal and subcultural change. As Alwin confirmed his male gender so the archive changed from a lesbian to a minorities collection: the Herstory shelf re-labeled Ourstory. There is a powerful sense in Alwin's testimony about 'passing on and handing down' history to a 'family' who will value rather than demean it. This sense is especially vivid in collections formerly or still held at home, as with this collection, the Lesbian Herstory Archive, and the rukus! Black Queer History Archive assembled and held first in the south London flat of photographer Ajamu X. Ajamu's home became a multipurpose space for archiving, art-making, and social and sex parties (for the Black perverts' network), reflecting his sense that these things were necessarily interconnected in the formulation and sustenance of Black queer history. His sex parties, for example, were part of a process for him of redirecting 'archives' of Black bodily pain towards pleasure.[79] The archive, now held at the London Archives, takes seriously the idea of 'creating a rukus', causing a disturbance, to more mainstream currents in both LGBTQ+ and Black history.[80] Like the Two Spirit Archives in Winnipeg, it forges space through history for those marginalized within LGBTQ2S communities and representation. GALA in Johannesburg has worked to do something similar by reorientating and rebalancing the initial overrepresentation of cis white men in the foundational collection of 1988.[81]

Accession and collection policies vary considerably from archive to archive but in community contexts they are often broad and inventive – valuing what in the rubric of more traditional collections might count as 'mere' personal ephemera. Nestle joked that anything touched by a lesbian has its place in the Lesbian Herstory Archive; Alwin still goes 'street collecting' for the Sexual Minorities collection.[82] These archives recognize the significance of people's everyday, the domestic, the mundane and the pornographic, and hold these things alongside books, journals and materials relating to movements, campaigns, iconic lives, and in/famous events. Collections donated by individuals are often kept intact rather than being disaggregated or weeded for material duplicated elsewhere in the archive. At the Skeivt Arkiv (Queer Archive) in Bergen (constituted by the Norwegian Parliament in 2015), the collection of Rolf Løvaas, the founding member and first chair of the Norwegian Homophile Group of 1948, includes material from the organization as well as his porn and physique magazines.

A few shelves along is what archivist Runar Jordåen describes as an 'archive of feelings' of the disabled art critic, Bjørn Hatterud, including a sweater from his first date, a ski trophy from a humiliating school trip, patient records, emails, drawings, children's toys, and CDs. The Schwules Museum Archive kept together the contents of a drag queen's closet and furniture bequeathed from a queer man's Berlin flat. These accession and archiving decisions make the Skeivt and Schwule archival vaults into extraordinary treasure troves which speak to the complexity of queer individuals and the multivalence of the queer past.[83]

These various archives are further people-focused in their active outreach and engagement. Several, as we have seen, have an associated museum or exhibition space. Most have been innovative in the use of the web to build audiences and collaborative networks.[84] The Transgender Archives at the University of Victoria in Canada (from 2013) has become a hub for international community organizing and research by and for trans people, including at the biannual Moving Transhistory Forward conference.[85] It has sought in this work, as in its collecting, to offset the medicalization of trans bodies and also to facilitate conversation and comparison with other strands in the LGBTQ+ acronym (and beyond). GALA's collection has been mobilized in township AIDS outreach, prompting internal debate about the balance between collecting and preserving on the one hand, and being a resource for activism and health education on the other. The line has been hard to determine or to hold, especially in the period of AIDS denial under the presidency of Thabo Mbeki (1999–2008), and given the archives' wider mission to become inclusive and reflective of African (homo)sexualities.[86] It has sought to do this via publications and mobile exhibitions about, for example, gender-crossing hairdresser Kewpie (1942–2012), whose personal story unfolds a queerer history of Cape Town's District Six during the apartheid era.[87]

GALA elaborates and sustains a diverse community in relation to the collection and the space of the archive itself, which is housed in University of Witwatersrand premises but faces the street rather than the campus.[88] Maintaining focus and space amidst archival moves into local government, museum or university settings (a typical transition for many collections) has often been fraught, especially as community archives move from being self-governing to being controlled by larger institutional protocols, blunting a community-feel or queer or radical edge. London's Hall-Carpenter Lesbian and Gay Archive, which started life in 1980, was split in three with much hand-wringing when it became clear in 1988 that its home, the London

Lesbian and Gay Centre, might not survive the dissolution (by Margaret Thatcher's government) of the left-wing Greater London Council GLC which had provided partial funding. Such precarity has been the key driver in the transition of community archives to better-resourced institutions (though a lesson from the United States currently is that such institutions might themselves be in a precarious position). In Hall-Carpenter's case, the oral histories went to the British Library, the politics boxes to the London School of Economics, and the news media collection first to the University of Middlesex and then to Bishopsgate Institute. As the collection was split, there was a sense for archive volunteers, donors and visitors of a loss of home and distinctiveness, though Bishopsgate especially has sought to reforge this. The reading room is now replete with protest banners and the neon signage from a defunct gay sauna. LGBTQ+ volunteers meet weekly and a talks and workshop programme draws specific attention to the expanding collection. Partly as a result, the Bishopsgate LGBTQ+ collection has grown exponentially with acquisitions from individuals, groups, charities and others. This collection sits within and resonates with Bishopsgate's wider radical holdings, including the papers of Raphael Samuel.

Anne Lister and the queer icon

The naming of Hall-Carpenter after a cutting edge (though elitist and conservative) lesbian author and a pioneering Romantic Socialist 'intermediate type' affirmed the place of these particular individuals in the British queer historical imaginary in the 1980s when the archive formed. They have served as a kind of shorthand for issues, causes and identities precisely because they are already known and their stories are easily accessed. Icons and martyrs (often one and the same) serve an important communal function across time. Mobilised in biographical, historical and fictional writing, art and performance, they become part of queer collective memory.[89] Oscar Wilde has been re-imagined in literature, film, theatre, and sculptures, casting him variously as a shameless decadent, flawed husband and father, homosexual victim and gay martyr.[90] Each incarnation further cements his iconic status and tells us more about the context of those cultural productions than about Wilde and his late-nineteenth-century milieu. His celebrity can thus be misleading. Literary scholar Simon Joyce observes that Wilde so dominates understandings of late Victorian queerness, that we miss the gender transitivity that seems to have been important for Charles Taylor, Wilde's largely forgotten co-defendant.[91] That Wilde and other icons are connected to our contemporary identity categories – as gay, lesbian or trans forbears – also means we lose a sense of what the sex and relationships they were having meant to them and how this related to other parts of their life.[92] Why, in Wilde's case, do we take his same-sex relationships as indicative of his 'truth', over and above his relationships with women, including his wife Constance?

Celebrating once vilified figures can be a way of signalling liberal credentials and progress, papering over the cracks of enduring inequality. Alan Turing, the World-War Two code breaker, is now lauded as a national hero, including through a posthumous pardon issued in 2013 in respect of his prosecution for the sex he had with another man.[93] The memorialized past is part of a dynamic via which what was once unconscionable becomes ordinary and banal (though the process can easily also reverse). Turing, Wilde and others in the British queer pantheon have been linked by their queerness, virtuosity and martyrdom, less so by their whiteness and class status. They are figures who do not threaten or make uncomfortable anymore, though they can 'obscure the continued oppression of those queer individuals who remain, simply put, too deviant to be recognized and protected by the nation'.[94]

The journey of Anne Lister into posterity is instructive in these various respects and more. Lister was a Yorkshire landowner and industrialist, a Tory and devout member of the Church of England. She also had a series of intimate, sexual relationships with other women – from Eliza Raine, the daughter of an East India Company surgeon and his Indian wife, and with whom Anne devised a secret diary code, to Ann Walker who moved into Lister's home at Shibden Hall and outlived her. Lister was a prolific diarist, writing around four million words detailing her everyday life, reading, research, social visits, business dealings, and romantic and sexual relationships. Through this record of her life, we can see Lister composing herself for herself and also for a distantly envisaged reader. She was doing this in a period when understandings of the self and the relationship of the self to the social were shifting post-Enlightenment and in the contexts of the romantic movement and rapid social change accompanying industrialization. The idea of an inner life and truth was gaining cultural purchase,[95] signalled by the very act of writing so extensively not only about her social world and interactions but about her feelings, desires, and ways of couching and understanding them. In the absence of other scripts or defined roles, Lister marshalled classical and other historical fragments to make herself legible and legitimate to herself and, tentatively, to her lovers.[96] She also protected and projected herself via the established church, Tory, and landed traditions and histories, and followed the male fashion for European travel and self-conscious consumption of culture and history.[97] Home at Shibden Hall signalled public status and family lineage and gave her some space – not least a room – in which to build her library and to write privately. Lister used all this to carve out her difference by fitting into something that was at the same time culturally and historically recognizable. If her landed position, 'masculine' dress and demeanour, and relationships with other women were notably eccentric, she rendered them possible, liveable and understandable to herself and others through established conventions and historic referents. She used history instrumentally in these respects, foreshadowing more recent queer uses of the past.

That the diaries survived for public interpretation is down to John Lister (1847–1933), the last Lister resident of Shibden Hall. He found and then re-hid Anne's diaries when he realized what they revealed. His friend Arthur Burrell recalled that 'Mr Lister was distressed but he refused to take my advice, which was that he should burn all 26 volumes'. This was perhaps because of the later Lister's sense of fealty to Anne as family – that same dynastic impulse – or perhaps as well because he identified her as a queer kindred spirit.[98] Alternatively, he may have kept the diaries because of his Fabian socialist politics and their social commitments, a marked departure from Anne's. His contemporary, the Fabian Society co-founder Edward Carpenter (1844–1929), then living relatively openly with his lover just outside Sheffield, saw in sexual 'honesty' and comradeship a path to social change. Destroying the diaries would be the reverse. Scandals around Wilde and others at the same time suggested the need for discretion, even though John may have judged that Anne's testimony would have its time. He was, finally, a keen local antiquarian: the idea of burning the diaries probably 'seemed sacrilege'.[99] If John Lister had a sense of the significance of this past to his present and to future generations, the cultural and legal climate in which he made his discovery made continued secrecy the best policy – a secrecy that was itself telling. After his death, the sympathetic Burrell passed the diaries and the cipher on to the Halifax Corporation, enabling subsequent researchers to unlock their content. They are now held by the West Yorkshire Archive and are a cornerstone of its expanding LGBTQ+ collection. Early researchers bypassed 'the purely personal' as not relevant to history, whilst latterly, and following local historian and teacher Helena Whitbread's painstaking transcription of the coded sections in the 1980s, it has been these parts of the diaries that have been most picked over.[100]

One context for this was the familiar and urgently felt need in the 1970s to make lesbians historically visible. The journey of these diaries into the archive provided proof positive not just of love but of sex between women, heralding a shift in analysis.[101] As such, Lister was described as an exemplar of the first modern lesbian and placed in a lesbian genealogy stretching from Sappho to Radclyffe Hall.[102] She provided historical ballast for contemporary lesbian identity and politics, anchored in a historic home open to the public and hosting, from the 1980s, special events linked to its most famous resident. 2010 saw BBC radio and TV programmes on Lister,[103] UNESCO recognized the diaries' significance in 2011,[104] and then from 2019 the sexy fast-paced TV series *Gentleman Jack* garnered a wide audience. Lister's story as told in this series was exceptional but also made comprehensible through the contexts of industrialization, a rising middle class, family and gender conventions, and norms of courtship and marriage.[105] Since then, there have been proliferating workshops, talks, and commemorative walks in Halifax. The Anne Lister Society formed in 2020, with the aim of 'build[ing] conversations between scholars and Lister's wider readership and an expanding network of invested enthusiasts'.[106] The society's first two meetings were held in the United States, signalling Lister reach; the third, in 2024, in Lister's hometown.[107] Shibden Hall earns additional income as a lesbian civil partnership and wedding venue. Lister, in short, has become an industry involving the kinds of public and academic history cross-over that is so often a hallmark of queer historical work.[108]

Uncertainty – or rival certainties – in what to make of Anne Lister emerged in the 2018 controversy over the decision to publicly mark with a plaque her commitment to her lover Ann Walker at Holy Trinity Church in York in 1834.[109] The first plaque unveiled described Lister as a 'gender non-conforming entrepreneur'; the 2019 replacement as 'lesbian and diarist'. This was a shift in emphasis from her outward presentation and what she did towards identity and private writing. The change was a response to protest which made national news and included an online petition acknowledging that Lister was gender non-conforming but that 'she was also … a lesbian'. 'Don't let them erase this iconic woman from our history', the petition concluded.[110] This campaign came in the midst of the wider upsurge in tension from 2016 around trans rights and visibility in Britain and the United States. History mattered in relation to issues of silencing and public representation, and in terms, too, of who 'owns' certain pasts; 'they' should not be allowed to take Lister from 'us', the petition read. If Lister was clearly a woman and lesbian to many,[111] Kit Heyam describes Lister with they/them pronouns and Joyce suggests the need to hold both possibilities, given that Lister's masculine presentation might relate to a desire for other women, to a sense of gendered selfhood, and also to a quest to preserve and present a particular class position.[112] What would Lister herself have made of her celebrity as a lesbian or as gender non-conforming as opposed to, say, her erudition or status as a land and mining entrepreneur? Those former elements are front and centre now, the latter more incidental, but in her lifetime the sex she had was a secret; her masculine attire initially kept private and described in code.

Anne Lister's path into posterity and into lesbian, queer and public history owed much to chance and investments which changed over time and may have been charged with shame, hope, pride and loyalty, and then a thirst for knowledge, a desire to educate, a quest for precedent and visibility, and an opportunity to profit. Her story has been bound into lesbian politics and history, into the seminar, lecture and conference room, into the space of the archive, into a heritage property, and into fictional re-imaginings – on the small screen and most recently in Emma Donoghue's rendition of Lister's school girl relationship with Eliza Raine.[113] The path of the diaries – the code, the hiding place, the work of deciphering, the decisions taken on whether or not to reveal them to a wider public – became part of the story and its appeal (and is part of what has made Lister iconic). This trajectory speaks to the silences, secrecies and guesswork which are a particular part of queer history making – in and beyond the academy – and the creativity often required to address them.

4. Creative histories

Queer historic consciousness has long been fostered in the creative arts – and perhaps more overtly (and explicitly) than elsewhere. There can be a particular latitude in art, film, theatre and fiction, even in contexts of censorship, because queer audiences have unevenly learned to read inference and suggestion, to join dots and make connections. Authors, artists, playwrights and film-makers have found the scope to communicate historically in these forms, and with a creativity that can address gaps and silences and texture and elaborate what little we know of the past. Imagination and creativity have been little valued (if much deployed) in history as a discipline, though those working on under-represented histories have tended both to appreciate history made in and through the arts and to value creative tools in their own work. Story-telling and other artistic interventions 'on the limit of the unspeakable and the unknown' provide a means of working through, rather than merely signalling, the silences and hostilities of the archive.[114] African-American Studies scholar Saidiya Hartman thus deploys modes of 'critical fabulation' and 'informed speculation' to address historic erasure of the lives and experiences of those sold into trans-Atlantic slave trade. Audre Lorde's much earlier use in *Zami: A New Spelling of My Name* (1982) of what she called 'biomythography', a weaving together of autobiography, history and myth, was a means for her to render Black lesbian life amidst the silencing racism, misogyny and homophobia of inter- and postwar America.

Lorde and Hartman validate and redeem the imaginary and the creative in historically orientated work and encourage us to think about what they can add to history (rather than how they fall short of it). Historian David Dean thus talks about theatre and performance as a 'neglected site' of public history that can open up central questions to the discipline relating to 'memory, narrative, identity, agency, archive/source, time and space, re-enactment, representation, and performance'.[115] He suggests that theatre and film provide a means of visually imagining and embodying past gestures and physical and erotic dynamics, drawing the past vividly into the same time and space as that of audiences and participants in ways the written word struggles to do.[116] This mode of capturing past experience underlines historian Peter Bailey's argument about the importance of physicality in the past and more specifically the 'knowingness of gesture' which might – in the instance of his research – make an apparently innocent music hall song lyric wantonly crude.[117]

Finding a way into such past gesture and movement, into past bodies, gives us layers of meaning and a sense, too, of a community of tacit knowledge and feeling beyond words. This is true in general, but is especially significant in representations of the queer and trans past where bodies, sex and desires are so centrally at stake.[118] In Ajamu X's last exhibition, 'Archival Sensoria', the archive of its title was constituted by his photographic work. But the archive was here also comprised of the bodies the work depicts. It is, Ajamu X writes, 'through our bodies that we bring our archives with us', in an oblique riff on Judith Butler's conception of bodily citation.[119] Relatedly, pornography can be seen as a form of public history in the way it trades in and deploys the past and past motifs to erotic effect and to forge erotic community.[120] Historical novelists meanwhile often use the same tools as historians, but with the creative scope to texture and fill out historical knowledge. It is, writes Heike Bauer, 'an area that allows writers to explore the full affective complexities of the relationship between past and present. This includes the traumatic undercurrents of LGBTQ+ life but also its pleasures, joys, and mundane aspects.'[121]

Such work is invariably a response to contemporary social, cultural and political contexts. In postwar Britain, for example, history was deployed in the arts to make a tacit argument for legal reform. Oscar Wilde was reanimated in two films of 1960 and Mary Renault reached for ancient history in her novels of the period.[122] Work set in the contemporary deployed the past to frame and underscore the respectability of tortured homosexual characters.[123] In the years following the liberalizing Sexual Offences Act of 1967, writers and artists continued to reach for history as the dial shifted towards celebrations of lesbian and gay difference in the face of enduring homophobia and inequality under the law. Gay and lesbian film and theatre co-ops, reading and writing groups and photography and art workshops became forums for historical exploration. The repertoire of Gay Sweatshop Theatre (1974–97) frequently hinged on the recuperation of the lesbian and gay past, sometimes supported with small grants from metropolitan councils and national bodies like the Arts Council. These were nevertheless still transactions at the cultural margins, involving experimental films and fringe theatre, geared to give 'our' history back to 'us' in performance mode. There was a powerful sense of possibility and empowerment in this, which 1980s funding cuts, the abolition of metropolitan councils, and Section 28 of the Local Government Act compromised though did not crush. Indeed, there was an especially angry queer creative and historical surge in the late 1980s and early 1990s in the context of those moves, wider homophobic disdain, and serial losses to AIDS. British film-makers like Isaac Julien and Derek Jarman re-inflected established historical narratives to cleave queer space and insist on visibility in the present. Julien's *Looking for Langston* (1989) was a peon to poet Langston Hughes and the Harlem Renaissance, and spoke to entangled histories of homophobia and racism, history's relationship to the present and the impossibility of telling a straightforward story of ephemeral queer pasts. Derek Jarman landed on a series of historical figures for his films – Michelangelo in *Caravagio* (1986), Christ and Judas in *The Garden* (1990) and the eponymous protagonist of his *Edward II* (1991) – and played fast and loose with history through politically expedient anachronism to insist on queer differences then and push at constraining norms and attempts to silence in his present.[124] Jarman had a sense of urgency in engaging with the past, shared by Bartlett, who 'seized history by the throat and made bitter love to it' in his landmark work on Oscar Wilde and late Victorian London in *Who Was That Man* (1988).[125] Via a creative mix of autobiography, biography and history he insisted on the past queer pleasures of the city, and suggested how they were distinct but resonant with those he enjoyed there. Since then other authors – Sarah Waters in *Tipping the Velvet* (1998), Patrick Gale in *A Place Called Winter* (2015) and Tom Crewe in *The New Life* (2022) – have also honed in on this period which historians have described as pivotal in the formation of modern Western sexual identities.[126] In their writing, they provide emotional surround to historical detail and suggest how different historical registers – costume parties or classical texts, for example – might have mattered to their imagined subjects.

These last authors were writing in a less febrile British context. Whilst in the late 1980s and most of the 1990s queer public history had come angrily from the margins and via counterculture, by the late 1990s fewer people were dying of AIDS-related illnesses because of triple combination therapy (from 1996), there was an equivocal recession in homophia, and a government had come to power with a stated commitment to enshrining equality in the law. The repeal of Section 28 (in 2003 and as part of that commitment) opened the way for local authority-funded schools, libraries, archives and museums to engage more directly with LGBTQ+ historical work and with community groups, something they did unevenly and often primarily in relation to LGBT History Month which was launched in 2005 (and which travelled internationally).[127] The Heritage Lottery Fund's change in protocols provided a further funding source for LGBTQ+ community projects hinging on history and heritage, and frequently including a creative component. Directives on social inclusion and the Equalities Act of 2010 subsequently pushed arts and heritage organizations to be more broadly representative and engage wider audiences.[128] Meanwhile, under the university funding regimen from 1986, academics had to demonstrate their impact beyond the academy. For historians this often meant engaging more actively with the museum, heritage and archive sectors. This all had an effect on the range and geographical spread of the UK queer community and public history projects, and it had an impact, too, on historically oriented queer creative projects and interventions.

In 2016, the club and performance collective, Duckie, re-enacted one of Lady Malcolm's Servants' Balls, an annual benevolent extravaganza for the servant class in the 1920s and 1930s detailed in Matt Houlbrook's *Queer London*.[129] The project won HLF funding and drew together creatives, historians and club producers, culminating in two balls at Bishopsgate Institute. Bartlett conducted a séance, conjuring a butler who recounted his queer adventures in the interwar years (a period Bartlett had carefully researched for his historical novel *Mr Clive and Mr Page* [1996]). The costumes of the punters (as in the 1920s and 1930s) were a reminder of how these events offered fleeting scope to be someone else and to play a role – often a historical role – that could speak to a sense of self and to an escape from the present. This immersive historical extravaganza – one of a number masterminded by Duckie – outed a different, more exuberant queer interwar, evoking a history of difference, sensual possibility, fun and escape rather than the litany of misery that can emerge through court records.

The recreation of Lady Malcolm's Servants' Ball was decidedly queer in organization and execution but more broadly by this time queer history had become uneasily mainstreamed, encountered by broad audiences in their museum, gallery, theatre and cinema visits as well as at home on TV. Art commissions accompanied the National Trust's work to mark the fiftieth anniversary of the 1967 Sexual Offences Act, for example, including a prominent installation at Kingston Lacey Hall in Dorset, former home of William Bankes, Member of Parliament and avid collector, who fled England after his tangles with the law over the sex he had with other men. Fifty-one nooses were installed representing each of the largely lower-class men executed for sodomy in Bankes' lifetime; they lacked his means to self-exile.[130] The film *Pride* (2014) about the 1984/5 campaigning group Lesbians and Gays Support the Miners, the TV series *Gentleman Jack,* and the AIDS drama *It's a Sin* (2021) all reached huge audiences. This was queer public history in a different mode from that of the 1970s and 1980s when it was almost invariably community-produced and community facing. High production costs meant that for these particular queer outings there was little room for the experimentation and risk-taking of those earlier decades. If they were risqué in content they were also sanitized. Community-facing work continues – in the hands of the Rebel Dykes, for example – but it is now part of a broader offering that is enlarging a particular queer historical consciousness in the United Kingdom.

Conclusion

Queer public history in Britain was a means, in the 1960s, of pressing for reform, in the 1970s of becoming visible, and in the febrile 1980s and 1990s of fighting back. In the 2000s, the more active engagement of heritage bodies and museums gave a deceptive sense of queer cultural accommodation, integration and acceptance. Though welcome, public representation can contribute to a repetition loop marking only certain people, places, turning points and progressive timelines at the expense of others. Such celebratory renditions gesture to battles won and a movement beyond difficult pasts, obscuring the ongoing challenging facing LGBTQ+ people.[131] Queer public history in its various forms, and especially as consumed without much controversy by a 'general public', can feed a certain smugness about progress made. It can, though, also challenge, and perhaps especially when it invites consideration of other (and othered) contexts and different ways of thinking about the past. The part documentary / part fiction film Deseos/رغبات, released in 2015 and thereafter on the film festival circuit (including in the United Kingdom), is a case in point. Film-makers Maya Mikdashi and Carlos Motta imagined a correspondence between two figures, Martina and Nour, living nearly a century apart but both in imperial contexts – of the Spanish in Bogota for Martina and the Ottomans in Beirut for Nour.[132] The fictional letters draw out the webs of empire, science, law, tradition and culture in which Marina and Nour were caught and which shaped their sense of themselves and others' sense of them. The film, Mikdashi and Motta said in interview, comes as a 'rejection of any imperative to be entirely faithful to the historical record' in order, ironically, better to conjure the transnational historical forces playing out unevenly on these figures and to imagine some historical community.[133] Cultural theorist Macarena Gómez-Barris suggests that it is in such work in the arts, especially as deployed in queer, trans, Indigenous and anti-capitlist movements, that different vectors of history and a transformative transnational politics might emerge.[134]

Coda

I watched the Merchant-Ivory film adaptation of E. M. Forster's novel *Maurice* and Stephen Frears' *Prick Up My Ears*, the biopic about playwright Joe Orton and his lover Kenneth Halliwell, a couple of months apart in 1987. For the first, I was with my mum and dad in our local cinema in Burton-on-Trent in the English midlands, covered with embarrassment. I went on my own to the second. Emerging from the Holloway Road Odeon in central-north London afterwards, I was thrilled to realize how close I was to some of the scenes of Orton's sexual adventures, though as a nervy and nerdy eighteen-year-old I swerved back to the surety of my brother's flat. Orton's sixties offered a glut of urban sex; Maurice and Scudder's more rural affair and escape was just about watchable with my parents. There was less sex and a hint of the socialism with which they aligned. I was drawn by the irreverence of the one and the sugar-coated comfort and wider politics of the other. Whatever I came to think of these films later, these first viewings sparked a sense of possibility. Certainly their rendition of the past suggested some cultural and historical anchorage to the identifications I was beginning to own.

A year later, studying English and Drama at university in Sheffield, I was too nervous and uncertain to join the Student Union's Gaysoc, but I did (daringly!) write an essay on two gay plays I had just seen: Martin Sherman's *Bent*, which unfolded the horrors of the holocaust for 'the men with the pink triangle', and Gay Sweatshop Theatre's production of Noël Grieg's *The Dear Love of Comrades,* exploring the intersecting desires and politics of Edward Carpenter, a friend of E. M. Forster. Part of the excitement of the latter was sitting in Sheffield's part-council funded Leadmill Arts Centre with a packed audience of gay men – more than I thought there could possibly be in Yorkshire, let alone in the city where I was studying.[135] The 1989 West End run of *Bent*, with soap star Michael Cashman in the lead opposite theatre legend Ian McKellen, was a landmark theatrical moment. It reminded the much more mixed audience of the tragedy and dangers of erasure in the context of the AIDS pandemic and Section 28, a measure aimed at 'loony left' local authorities like the GLC (which part funded the Hall-Carpenter archive) and Sheffield Council (which supported the Leadmill).

It was such filmic and theatrical engagements with the past, rather than history 'proper', that forged my queer historical consciousness and drew me into historical work. However, during my PhD in the late 1990s and first years as a history lecturer at Keele University in the early 2000s, I experienced a disconnect between the theory-laden work emerging from academic queer studies and history and the historically-inflected queer fiction, film and theatre I was consuming in my spare time. This began to change in 2005 when I moved to a role leading a programme of short, open access history courses at Birkbeck, the University of London college established in 1823 as part of the workers' education movement and still, when I joined, focused on teaching working Londoners. Five years later I became co-director of the Raphael Samuel History Centre, whose central mission was to democratize history and to bridge the popular / academic history divide. These twin contexts orientated me back towards public history, and, as I wove queer history through the programming of courses and events, I began to think in more concerted ways about who we are speaking to as queer historians – and how. Alongside, and in the changing UK contexts discussed in this chapter, I was taking up invitations to contribute to some of the growing number of LGBTQ+ community, museum, archive, heritage sector and media projects. Other university-based queer historians in the United Kingdom were doing the same. The gap between queer academic and queer public history was narrowing. This was palpable at LGBTQ+ history conferences, most obviously the ALMS gatherings which were focused on histories made in and for non-academic publics, but also at those which were university-based but now often involved collaboration with museums and archives, and frequently featured films, performance, walks and reflections on public history in the programme.[136]

Witnessing and doing this work led me to some of the case studies discussed in this chapter. They happily reminded me that there was no queer academic monopoly on theoretical and methodological sophistication, but they also sometimes put me in two minds. There was a thrill in seeing histories made clearly visible in contexts where, previously, we were squinting to discern queer traces. And yet there was a sense of loss when elusive histories became readily consumable and easily digestible (a neo-liberal product, perhaps). Given wider historical convention, curators, producers and editors sometimes voiced understandable unease with supposition and cadence. It was, for example, the need for a verifiable queer figure or link that led the editor of the National Trust's queer guide book, *Prejudice and Pride* (2017), to drop spreads I had written about the expanse of beach and dunes in Studland Bay, Dorset, and about the back-to-back houses in central Birmingham, both in the care of the Trust.[137] These were spaces which had a queer tinge in the past and invited queer conjecture in the present. But without a specific case or name they didn't make the final cut. Similarly, when a piece I wrote about the queer dimensions of a house in Hammersmith was taken up for a BBC radio show, the ineffable and ephemeral gave way to the strictly verifiable.[138] Again, I understood the logic, the desire to present 'robust' history to the 'general public'. And yet after my, our, own formative experiences of reading signs and between lines I found myself hankering after suggestive histories made up of feint traces and haunted spaces. For me, these ironically often spoke more directly of queerness past.

5

Archives and Sources

Queer historians have often had to rely on speculation and guesswork amidst the archival patchwork of absence and presence. They have picked over traditional and community collections and pushed at established conceptions of what might count in the making of a historical narrative. This magpie quality and the particular way materials have been assembled and used is part of the distinctiveness and creativity of queer historical work. But this concluding chapter also extends an argument running through the book about how queer history is enmeshed within broader and surrounding historical practice. If queer historians question and push at the edges of history as a discipline, their methods are also indebted to it. This becomes clear in the main part of this chapter which surveys the queer potential and pitfalls of different sources – specifically, official sources and data, books and printed materials, visual culture, ephemera, and, finally, 'the evidence of experience'.[1] Each 'genre' of source sheds a different sort of light on the past, positioning historical actors in particular ways and suggesting alternate modes of thinking about sex, desire, gender and power at different historical moments and over time. Surveying them here summons themes, issues and arguments from the preceding chapters and so allows this one to act as a conclusion of sorts. It is also an elaboration: whilst chapters 2 and 4 glanced the archive conceptually and as a space (respectively), here it is re-centred as a resource for researchers, beginning with an account of the so-called archival turn and of my own archival journeys.

1. Archival encounters

The archival turn from the mid 1990s was barely a turn in the sense that historians, and especially social and postcolonial historians and those working 'from below', had already interrogated the status of official repositories and of printed and state materials that have traditionally been given more credence than, say, images, music, or oral testimony. But in *Archive Fever* (1996), deconstructionist philosopher Jacques Derrida made an especially strident intervention, arguing that archives were bound to the exercise of power and were a way of controlling knowledge and cultural memory – a mode of control disrupted, he suggested, by the virtual world that was just then emerging.[2] At around the same time those working in subaltern and postcolonial studies showed how the archive represented and embedded colonial authority. In modes of acquisition, sorting and categorizing, archivists had 'the power to exalt certain stories, experiences and events and to bury others.'[3] Zeb Tortorici describes, for example, how the 'ritualistic record-keeping' of the Spanish colonial government in its Central and South American dominions maintained some fiction of 'colonial hegemony'.[4] He also shows, though, that such official documentation can provide glimpses of deviant and disobedient lives lived at odds with elite Spanish sexual and gender norms. The colonial archive might thus speak of an equivocal rather than assured grasp on power – a place where we can see the reach of empire and nation but also its limits.

Tortorici's analysis of archival structures and contents exemplifies the queer turn towards the play of power, the haunting silences, and the 'abundance' of archives, and so what they might reveal in spite of themselves.[5] Queer scholars have looked at ways of resisting the limiting and obscuring 'routine grammars and logics' of categorization and research processes.[6] They have sought to tune more fully into the contexts and immediate experience of archival encounters – into the accidental, the evasive, the emotive, the sense of overwhelm, and to the absences which shadow every archival fragment. There is often a tension between, on the one hand, the desire to know, to be certain, to be a 'good' historian, and, on the other, the uncertainties that proliferate as a grasp for 'truth' turns to a handful of archival 'dust'.[7] These desires, dynamics and tensions have braced my own archival experiences, and in ways which can speak to queer historical work more broadly; they exemplify something of the quotidian variety of the research process.

In the coda to Chapter 1 I talked briefly about George Ives, the early British law reformer, who became a lodestone in my work. Jeffrey Weeks' mention of Ives' diaries in his *Coming Out* (1977) nudged me to apply for a travel grant to look at them at the Harry Ransom Humanities Research Center (HRHRC) in Austin, Texas. His reference to Ives' scrapbooks sent me on their trail in London and, finally, to an antiquarian bookseller in London's Mayfair just before they were sold to the Beinecke Library at Yale University in New Haven, Connecticut. To this piece of luck was added the generosity of the bookseller who allowed me to set up camp at the back of the shop with unrestricted use of his xerox machine (this was 1998), tipping me into an unsystematic copying frenzy. By now I had my flight booked to Austin, so as I copied pages from the scrapbooks, I also noted the dates of striking scrapbook items to allow me to cross-reference them with diary entries when I got there. These dates directed me in my first pass at the diaries in the much more formal context of the HRHRC reading room, where the paraphernalia of archival research – including the obligatory (and, Barry Reay notes, almost fetishistic) white gloves – ratcheted up my imposter syndrome.[8] I had three weeks in Austin, staying in the Dodi Al Fayad memorial room in a lesbian-run guest house. I was fortunate to have even this stretch of time and this (decidedly camp) space to process my notes outside HRHRC hours. But it was nowhere near enough to read and digest the diaries from start to finish, and so aside from the list of dates I wanted to cross-check from the scrapbook and the index Ives constructed for the benefit of the 'future reader' he confidently envisaged, I decided to read the same two months of each year (April and December) so I could at least reach across his life in the time I had. The rewards of working through an entire diary – as Helena Whitbread did with Anne Lister – are immense. More often such time, patience, or resources to do that are short, and this was the case for me with Ives.

For my queer domesticities project, I made a second visit to the HRHRC and also to the scrapbooks, by this time at the Beinecke some 1,830 miles from Austin. On my first visit, eureka moments came by accident: the page that fell open, the stray letter or photo that fell out. For my second pass, I tried to embrace such randomness, swerving off-piste to take in whatever else caught my eye in the mode of archival cruising.[9] This helped me to think more expansively about intersecting interests and identifications which contributed to Ives' sense of himself and which made his queer life liveable. Behind different approaches to searching are different ideas about what constitutes queerness and what might or might not be relevant. In the case of Ives, for example, I shifted from searching out the specifically sexual in my first visit, to having an eye to the multiple anchor points of his life and daily rhythm in my second. Throughout, whether working systematically or more randomly, I wondered what other stories I might be drawn to telling if I had decided to look to other months and other pages in these volumes. I wondered what connections I might have been able to make if I had had the diaries and scrapbooks side by side rather than looking at them weeks and miles apart.

In other research contexts, it was the conjunction rather than the separation of materials that shaped my work. When, for example, I first looked at the Brighton Ourstory Lesbian and Gay collection in their cramped premises above a shop in Hove (the English south-coast town adjoining Brighton to the west), I found diverse voices across different kinds of material brought into oblique dialogue by virtue of being stored in the same box or folder. Other materials joined the conversation when this community collection transferred to the Keep, the state-of-the-art archival centre at Falmer on the edge of Brighton which opened in 2013 and brought together East Sussex county records and the special collections of the universities of Sussex and Brighton. There, I got drawn into the testimonies of the National Lesbian and Gay survey of the 1980s and others from the Mass Observation archive which, in its second iteration, garnered the voices of 'ordinary' Britons from 1981 to the present (the first had run from 1937 to the early 1950s).[10] These materials had been amassed as I was growing into a sense of who I might be and beginning a tortuous process of coming out in the febrile context of the late 1980s and early 1990s. This is probably one of the reasons why I felt a series of emotional punches as I sampled and skimmed this material. I did not go to the Keep to begin a project on emotions in queer history but I was led down this path by the affective interplay between these sources, by the emotional realms of my early adulthood which they touched, and by the wider context in which I was doing this research: the first election of Donald Trump to the presidency of the United States of America, the Brexit referendum in the United Kingdom, and what Judith Butler called 'the emancipation of unbridled hatred' at this time against those who apparently threatened 'our' values, 'our' economy, 'our' bodies and 'ourselves'.[11] The experience was a reminder that archives are a pandora's box which evidence a gamut of emotions in the past and mobilise others in the present.[12]

If at the Keep I got lost in a profusion of voices, in my earlier pursuit of playwright Joe Orton (1933–67) it was the silences and evasions that struck me most. In the papers deposited by Orton's first biographer, John Lahr, at the University of Boston, in the Orton Collection at the university in his home city of Leicester, and in the papers of Orton's agent, Peggy Ramsay, at the British Library, I did not find the intimacy I was after. Instead I got a replay of the distance the playwright so adeptly maintained between himself and his various audiences in his lifetime and which obliquely spoke to cultures of queerness in the sixties. There is precious little in Orton's own hand or typescript in these various archives, most of the original diary is missing, and folder after folder contains letters (often duplicated, with copies held in each of the three sites) documenting disputes over his legacy. Orton slips from view amidst these controversies – a reprise of his own shifting account of himself and his life. The questions I took to these archives remained pretty much unanswered, but new ones emerged about the agendas in play for those who felt they had a stake in Orton after his death and who in various ways controlled the material. These are questions which have haunted the legacies of various literary and public figures, and especially those who have apparently had something queer to hide.[13] These archival encounters were frustrating in part because I was romantically looking for some illusive queer truth about the playwright. It took me a while to see the archival blockages as revealing in themselves.[14]

This sense of accident, luck and lack of control has been seized queerly by other historians and scholars in accounts of 'cruising' sources, of 'feral pedagogies' and of 'scavenger methodologies'. They are particularly relevant in work on dissident desires and fleeting pleasure which sometimes demand the piecing together of fragments and anecdotes and what Anjali Arondekar describes as 'reading practices that are meandering, ragged, and unfamiliar'.[15] These descriptors touch the muddle of the research process, something queer theorists encourage us to surrender to but which also challenge entrenched expectations about the historian's role in finding patterns, making sense and tugging disparate evidence into narrative shape. In their work in the Lesbian Herstory archive in Brooklyn, Jen Jack Gieseking found and categorised nearly 400 lesbian and queer organizations in New York from 1983. But they noted that doing so imposed a logic and coherence which evaded those involved at the time. Gieseking captures the paradox of systematically researching and ordering a past that was, in the flesh, more inchoate. Relatedly, and at around the same time, Lesley Wood, coordinator for the 'Queer in Brighton' community history project (2012–14), described trying to embrace the sense emerging from project interviews and other materials of a 'delirious museum' of 'memories, experiences, opinions, the historical anecdotes and arcane facts' which she nevertheless drew together into an account 'of our community, of our kind'.[16]

Some materials invite more 'cruising' than others. I started my surveys of newspapers specifically looking for court cases involving homo-sex, but my eye was repeatedly drawn to apparently disconnected articles and images which yet framed and contextualized those cases. Looking at adjacent books on shelves, other folders in archive boxes, other links on websites can helpfully refocus and draw us down different paths (as well as rabbit holes). The digitization of newspapers and courts cases has been a revelation in allowing swifter, more systematic searching of particular crimes and characters (for example), throwing up instances that would otherwise have remained obscure, as historian Marthe Glad Munch Møller found in relation to a series of interwar trans cases in Norway.[17] The downside is that scanning through the search results pulls us away from what is adjacent and contextually fattening.[18]

The digital revolution was an important context for the archival turn and seemed to answer some of the problems with the material archive. The internet provided more democratic access to a world of material. It promised 'big history' with a vast sea of data which also held the tiny details and individual stories otherwise lost to time;[19] 'We must prepare to be more regularly astonished by the people whom we will be able to find in the past', wrote historian Julia Laite.[20] The internet means individuals and organizations can curate their own public archives – from collections of images on flickr or Instagram to personal or institutional blogs and websites. For those with internet access, there is scope to search these resources; no travel grant needed. The expansiveness and randomness of research on the net is enticingly suggestive of ephemeral queer lives, desires and dynamics. But the internet is also overwhelming and anxiety-provoking in terms of verification, dating, digital editing and authenticity (that slippiest of concepts). Charles Upchurch notes the challenge of cross-checking and spotting errors in digital inputting, labelling and text recognition software.[21] It can be hard with digital searches to find the logic (or illogic) of a collection and its organization. The institutional power we are encountering is often less obvious than in the physical environment of a reading room. Library search engines (and those rolodex indexes pre-internet) reveal their categorizations and operations relatively clearly. In web-based research we need to keep querying our own search terms and navigation methods, recognizing that 'to choose one descriptor is to diminish the possibilities of another'; we need to consider 'what gets lost when data becomes so accessible'.[22] Processes of selection, curation and labelling in digital archiving projects remain as pertinent as in material collections, and with an accompanying series of ethical choices and conundrums.[23] Individuals and institutions have had to ask what should be digitized as a priority, what should be left out as problematic or offensive, and what needs particularly careful contextual couching.[24]

Amidst all this are the manifest gaps. Joan Nestle observes that 'the roots of the [Lesbian Herstory] archives lie in the silent voices, the love letters destroyed, the pronouns changed, the diaries carefully edited, the pictures never taken, the euphemized distortions that patriarchy would let pass'.[25] 'Like so many other vices', John Howard wrote relatedly of the queer southern USA, 'homosexuality and gender insubordination were acknowledged and accommodated with a pervasive, deflective pretence of ignorance.'[26] Nestle and Howard each stress in different ways the need to read askance for these signs, to extrapolate them from obscurity by looking to what is not explicit, and to follow the oblique coordinates of queerness through the archive – not least for what they might communicate about the contexts in which such euphemism felt so important. There is nevertheless a common nagging sense of missing something – true of historical research in general, but especially in the pursuit of the elusive queer past. In the whirl of paper, the visceral 'residues of sleaze' are easily lost – and perhaps intentionally so.[27] And even if we can find evidence of sexual acts in the archive, the desires, emotions, and relationships in play at that sexual moment remain largely obscure to us now.[28] This can be deeply frustrating, but it is perhaps also how queerness is best represented – as out of reach and uncertain, suggestive rather than fully graspable. As Arondekar notes, 'a homosexual is most himself when he is most secret, most absent from writing'.[29]

If this is the case, do we do our duty better to the queer past by signalling the potential for queerness in particular contexts rather than by exposing those who may have spent their lives in an obscurity they deliberately sought?[30] As with Orton, the desire to evade might tell us more than pinpointing what lay behind the evasion. Silences might not only be defensive but actively deployed so as to live differently (the closet, historians Dominic Janes and H. G. Cocks suggest, might in this sense be a productive and creative space rather than necessarily a repressive one).[31] Sedgwick calls for us to hold the space of not knowing rather than submitting to a 'consensus of knowingness' in which what is tangible about the past can end up standing in for all that we do not or can not know.[32] This runs counter to the recuperative tradition in lesbian and gay history and to the felt imperative to fill silences that for some signal oppression and so, apparently, failure. Jack Halberstam nevertheless suggests that such failure might itself be 'a queer art' and strategy of refusal in a culture where success and visibility are king. There is a queer counterblast in not according to the grammar of success and the imperative to be out, proud and tangible.[33] In terms of an approach to the past, this suggests a recalibration of who and what we are looking at and so also of how we might assemble and analyse fragments and silences across an array of sources.[34]

2. Sources

Officialdom: counting, courts, and governance

With European imperial expansion and the consolidation of nationhood came a new drive to measure and quantify – goods and trade, birth, death, marriage and literacy rates, population densities, socio-economic status, and more. The archival residues of this piecemeal shift give historians of the early modern and modern periods different, additional, materials to consider in their work on the queer past than medievalists or classicists. Decisions about what and how to measure communicate something about prevailing ways of thinking and can give clues to pressing political concerns or sensitivities. Queer behaviours and identities barely register directly in this material. If marriage and fertility rates have helped historians to discern dimensions of reproduction and opposite sex activity and to identify the differences between regions and nations, there is little on the face of it to help with queerer activity. The data is stark and impersonal and can seem distant from diffuse questions of desire and sexuality. Historians have nevertheless also suggested how data on birth rates might signal changing sexual habits, cultures and moralities, which in turn give us some context for thinking about queer sex and relationships and how (im)possible they may have felt.[35] Literacy and occupancy rates help in other ways. To be literate meant being able to read the newspapers and other texts which cultural historians have shown to be so significant in shaping sexual codes and behaviours.[36] Occupancy figures give us clues about access to private space and the extent to which people were cheek-by-jowel with others. We can at least suppose what each context might have meant for the fleeting or more sustained expression of queer desires and the emergence of associated identities, especially when triangulated with other sources. Demographic data on urban growth and migration provides further grist and context. A gender imbalance in a particular place, for example, might allow conjecture about homosocial living, working and socializing, and form an important backdrop to what court papers and newspapers reveal about specific sexual and social infractions.[37]

On the basis of such data, we can not know what the people who were counted felt or imagined or did, but we can build some sense of the world in which they lived and guess at some of the dynamics of familiarity and strangeness. The data can in these ways spark our sense of what might have been possible and substantiate or problematize ideas emerging through other archival material. For *Queer Beyond London*, for example, information derived from a mapping of British demographic data from 1801 to 2011 by geographers at the University of Portsmouth pointed to the socio-economic and occupational make-up of the four case study cities, helping partially to explain the queer differences between them.[38] Business directories and census returns (the latter now easily searchable online) capture the composition of particular streets and so the households, shops, pubs and other outlets which would have been familiar to our historical subjects. We can build a picture of what people saw as they went on their way.

Ecclesiastical, military and civic courts and surrounding commentary instructed citizens in good behaviour and guided them to informal judgements of others. It was partly in these forums that church and state attempted to regulate sex and gender, steadying a moral compass as a means of exercising control.[39] Legal documentation and press coverage of court cases situate the sexual deviant as a subject forfeit to their dogmas and laws. Historians have used this material for what it shows explicitly about the exercise of power and also more obliquely and between lines to discern the voices and sometimes the agency of those in the dock or witness box. In records of what happened in the courtroom (and of the performances of witnesses and the accused), in the priorities given to certain pieces of information over others, and in the rhetoric and arguments used by prosecutors and judge, we can discern the formation and deployment of diverse sexual and moral codes. Court documents can also reveal how different state actors could promote competing understandings of gender and sexuality, disagree over the boundaries of permissible sexual practices, and fight over the limits of anti-gay policing.[40] Libel cases reveal the centrality of sex in the making or unmaking of an individual's reputation. Through them, historians have been able to track shifting concepts of decency and the role of such cases in sharpening public sensitivity to what was considered indecent.[41] They have used arrest and prosecution figures (including sometimes telling gaps between the two) and shifts in the type of crime on the charge sheet to signal an unevenness in the application of the law between places and across time.[42] Historian Michael Rocke triangulated the detailed records of the Office of the Night in Renaissance Florence with estimates of population to show that sex between men was a common and casual occurrence. Around half of men under thirty had been arraigned before a court for sex with another man. The statistics were the basis of Rocke's argument about the tacit acceptance of such activity (even as the

Office of the Night was trying to curtail it) and about homosex being a matter of taste and habit relating to life stage rather than necessarily being a lifelong tendency or orientation.[43] Such material, especially when read alongside other sources, has helped to elaborate changes in local and national sexual cultures, as well as to spell out the dangers these changes could bring for some.[44] Civic and ecclesiastical legal pronouncements, including those conveyed via the press, might set a tone or expectation but they did not comprehensively suppress sexual 'deviance'. As a result, courts of various sorts became forums for revelations which helped guide as well as deter those interested in queer pleasures and possibilities. They could give a broader public specific details, places, names and faces to abstract injunctions and vices.[45] Such 'hostile' sources, though 'fragmentary, one-sided … and dangerously inaccurate',[46] gave people then and historians since access to voices rarely heard in the public record.[47]

These sources are distinct in terms of time and place. The way Rocke examined Florence was facilitated and prompted by the presence, record keeping and particular telling vigilance of the Office of the Night there. The preponderance of male-male encounters in that type of evidence – and in legal evidence more broadly – substantially affects the sorts of histories we can make about men, women and those whose gender did not conform to the binary. Women's lives – and their lives with each other – were certainly circumscribed by the law in multiple ways, but lesbianism itself tended to enter the courts only more obliquely thorough divorce cases, libel actions or the occasional literary sensation.[48] Records of such cases frame queer women differently from the much more prolific and prosaic prosecutions of men for the sex they were having with each other. Defendants assigned male at birth presenting as women sometimes appeared in court charged under soliciting, cross-dressing, gross indecency and sex work legislation, giving us some glimpse of possible trans lives and a sense, too, of how presumptions about sexual practice and orientation intersected with those about gender presentation.[49]

Far from being monolithic and homogenizing, the profusion and muddle of surviving legal records, like those of local council licensing and public recreation committees, can provide a route to understanding the exigencies of sexual governance.[50] They do not lend themselves to a 'tidy history', writes historian Stephen Robertson, 'instead they dramatize confusions and different ways of understanding and acting sexually' – including locally and in relation to dynamics of class, race and gender.[51] Government records which chart the processes of making laws meanwhile sharpen our understanding of prevailing presumptions about sexuality and also suggest the accident and personalities behind legislative change.[52] Though lesbians were far from free of legal regulation in Britain,[53] repeated debates in parliament about criminalizing sex between women came to nothing partly because of a reluctance to believe in or to advertise such activity.[54]

Printed words

Newspapers, periodicals and magazines, and texts from the literary to the sexological have been further building blocks for queer history. These are often the easiest sources to reach for online or from library or bookshop shelves. They have apparent authority and have given voice and influence to those with power, specialist expertise or creative prowess. The cultural capital of most writers – in whatever genre – is an important part of the analysis of such texts; so too is the fact that most people did not or could not get their ideas into print, or read the work of those who did (this is why knowing about literacy rates can matter). The texts that did get published provide snapshots of their moment of production and publication. Introductions and prefaces to successive editions allow us to identify the enduring and shifting significance and influence of work (as we saw with Bloch's *The Sexual Life of England* [1908] in Chapter 1). The content matters too, of course, and so do the generic and disciplinary conventions which shaped ideas and the way they landed with the readership.

The newspaper press has been a key source for historians pursuing opinion, attitudes, cases, voices and the rhetoric around sexual deviance. If we can lean into census returns, passenger lists, business directories and workplace records to track individuals and their networks, newspapers can help us towards the social, cultural, political and actual climate in which they operated and the local or wider events and contexts that might have preoccupied them. The press is deeply partial and provides no straightforward access to the truth of what happened or to the public opinion papers frequently claimed to represent. We need, Alison Oram shows in her work on lesbianism and gender-crossing in Britain, to become attuned to the generic conventions which positioned queer and trans people in particular ways through the repetition of cultural scripts and tropes.[55] Changes in journalistic writing practices significantly changed the way news of queer conduct was presented and consumed. The so-called new journalism of late-nineteenth-century Britain, for example, ushered in more sensationalism and fearmongering.[56] These changes matter in our analysis, as do the proprietors, publishers and, again, the anticipated and actual readership. Historian Justin Bengry shows, for example, how publishers and particular publications cultivated new readerships and the pink pound in 1950s and 1960s Britain.[57]

Alongside national and local newspapers are the sub- and countercultural newsletters, zines, papers and magazines which historians have used to trace the queer significance of particular places, to identify the dimensions of politics and activism, to trace social and sex scenes (not least via lonely heart ads),[58] and to explore the significance to queer lives and subcultures of dancing, music, the arts, history and gossip.[59] Some publications courted a queer audience under cover of art, film or fitness (associating queerness with these things in the process). Others did this through high production values emulating more mainstream publications.[60] These different modes of queer expression and communication link us to countercultural hopes and aspirations, as with the privately circulated *Urania* magazine which ran from 1916 to 1940, and which radically questioned gender roles and norms.[61] Though its readership was tiny, it allows us to discern counter currents of thinking in relation to apparently deeply entrenched norms. Which publications we take seriously is meanwhile telling. Historian Marc Stein observes that Jonathan Ned Katz largely overlooked gay commercial and porn magazines in his work on the 1970s, even though they had a much larger circulation than the community newsletters and papers which he drew on more fully. It was the latter that were closer to Katz's heart and politics and he uses them to enlarge our understandings of activist battles and ideals.[62] The glossier, sexier titles tell us something different again and highlight the wider dynamics of homosex and desire which often functioned at odds with, or at a distance from, community and countercultural aspirations and output.

Expert works – of sexology, anthropology, sociology and history – attracted a more niche readership but give a sense of currents of thought which unevenly shaped ideas about queer types and passions, including for those actively seeking coordinates for a sense of self. Such people, testimonial evidence suggests, were often avid readers of this material and the literary work it influenced.[63] Connections between text and subjectivity are of course not direct. Although sexological texts made broad, universal claims – usually extrapolated from examinations and testimonies of European urban elites – their reach and relevance were much more localized. Most people would have been unaware of these new arguments, may have rejected them, or else used them strategically to justify and excuse whilst following other grooves in queer self-presentation and understanding. The privileged cultural position accorded to science and medicine means that their impact – individually and collectively – can be overstated. Trans historian Jules Gill-Peterson thus discerns the damage the 'overexposure to medicine' has done to transgender history and especially to the 'intelligibility' of trans people of colour.[64] Conversely, religious texts have often been under-examined in the insistent secularism of much LGBTQ+ politics and history of the last forty years. This is despite their powerful effect on the way individuals considered themselves to be immoral, sinful, righteous, or in/explicable in the eyes of their deity/ies. Some found a sense of belonging and peace rather than animosity and rejection within the pages of religious texts and the structures, rituals and communities related to them.[65] We see again how the immediate social, cultural and political contexts of research direct the researcher's gaze.

Historians working on the queer past have tended to read these various works not for the truths they purport to convey but for the particular ideas and ways of knowing and engaging with the world they reveal at that particular time. Literature has been an important source in these respects too. A good quarter of pieces in the *Journal of the History of Sexuality* are anchored in literary texts. A novel might brush against what was imaginable, preoccupying or anxiety-provoking at a particular time and so allow us some sense of the texture of thought and feeling then.[66] It might allude to culturally specific preoccupations, hopes, fears and desires; to queer and gender dynamics; and to the co-ordinates of identification, power and passion. Heike Bauer writes that literature is thus 'an important source for understanding the processes by which ideas about sex have been articulated, translated and transformed'.[67] This includes pornographic literature in which we can see shifts in what was desirable, imaginable and erotic at a cultural and also individual level.[68]

Literature and the arts more broadly provided some scope to pitch imaginatively beyond the sometimes traumatic and constraining present and for historians in turn to examine what was conceivable at the time the authors were writing. Russian poet Marina Tsvetaeva (1892–1941) used poetry to imagine escape and amazon companionship and reproductivity. Her British contemporary Virginia Woolf (1882–1941) swept through history in a flight of literary fancy to conceptualize shifts in gender for her eponymous protagonist in *Orlando* (1928) – a more public articulation of the gender 'disturbance' explored in the pages of *Urania* in the same decade.[69] Woolf's novel, published in the same year as Radclyffe Hall's *Well of Loneliness,* and just as women gained the vote on equal terms to men in the United Kingdom, encouraged a double take on social and cultural norms and their relationship to the past, history and tradition. Such work, especially when examined in relation to other texts and sources, gives us a sense of the sexual zeitgeist of a particular time or – in a comparison with earlier or later texts – over time.[70]

Things, images, and ephemera

Archaeologists and architectural and art historians have demonstrated how objects, spaces and visual cultures underpin queer historical work. The built environment and the way space was organized helps towards an understanding of the organization of society and culture, as well as of how people might have functioned in their everyday.[71] The architecture of the workhouse, prison, school, asylum and home – and the way it changed over time – communicates past expectations and understandings about sexual and gendered behaviour and ways of controlling it. Government and civic architecture embedded hierarchies and structures of power related to entangled ideas of masculinity, femininity and sexual normativity. Architects, urban planners and interior designers also challenged hegemonic styles and heteronormative spatial organizations, giving us insights into other ways of thinking and behaving and signalling circulating aspirations for change.[72] The Romantic Socialist designers and architects of the Arts and Crafts movement in Britain in the late nineteenth and first part of the twentieth century, for example, represented an avowed 'honesty' in design, which for some was linked to a frankness in sexual relations and a rejection of contemporary ideas of propriety and respectability.[73] Material spaces can thus prompt fertile historical questions; wandering through historic streets, alleys, rooms and corridors can suggest some answers.

Objects, statuary, painting, photos and films can similarly signal prevailing norms and/or attempts to counter them. These were the visual and material resources people had to orientate themselves and their desires in the past and as such are historically telling. Historians have, for example, used religious art and iconography to track sensual intensity, desire, homoerotics and shifting ideas about sex, gender, deviance and sin across the past two millennia.[74] This is not only about identifying the directly homoerotic or queerly iconic – or what might have been seen as such in a particular context – but also about broader visual economies and queerly coded visual motifs. Clare Barlow's curation of the Tate Britain's 'Queer British Art' exhibition in 2017 located the queer tinge of flowers, watery settings and dramatic natural landscapes, and through them illustrated shifting queer visual dynamics over a century and more.[75] The exhibition also demonstrated how photography, film and portraiture were a way of representing and affirming selfhood on terms eccentric to prevailing norms. For the historian, they suggest something of how people presented and comported themselves – or rather, how they were expected to do these things.[76] They can also capture otherwise illusive moments and events in queer lives, from fleeting street interactions to impromptu domestic performances.[77]

Like a written text, an image can be read in multiple ways: for what the content communicates directly and indirectly, for the generic expectations it follows or disrupts, for the way it relates to and reveals surrounding social and cultural context, and as an object in itself that might be held, displayed, gifted or hidden.[78] These modes of analysis are not unique to queer historical work but they are especially relevant to it because of the heightened significance of being made visible, of needing or wanting to hide, of the play of secrecy and revelation, and of the significance of embodiment. If we look at a photo of a happy family or carefree friendship group, for example, we can identify what was culturally expected of photographic images and the pressure to come into line (literally) for the moment the shutter clicked. What lay in the moments before and after the photo was taken might be very different, making the family photo album potentially an 'amnesia' archive: a collection of images which airbrushes the queerness out.[79] We might yet observe queer strategies for being and relating in such social formations which resist erasure. This is something film-maker Adrian Goycoolea explores in relation to his family album replete with images of his great uncle, the autobiographer, artist's model and film critic, Quentin Crisp.[80] Single, possibly queer, relatives in family photos might have given a flickering sense of other ways of being.[81] Photos taken with friends and lovers served as mementos and as creative tools in making and affirming family in various guises, as Mo Moulton argues in relation to the albums of twentieth-century Irish pianist and music teacher, Dorothy Stokes. They include photos of friends, lovers and many, many dogs. In this collation, Moulton sees Stokes etching out her emotional world in the interstices of Irish familial normativity.[82]

Illicit images have meanwhile been analysed for what they say about shifting sexual cultures and scripts – including changing fantasies, fetishes and desires, and what pornographers imagined might fuel them.[83] Such pictures were erotic prompts, a turn on, and they allow us to engage with the visceral nature of the queer past.[84] Evans argues that such visual cultures push us to consider dimensions to queer lives which are otherwise often sanitized or airbrushed from the public record and representation (including historical representation). She calls for historical analysis not only of the 'provenance and circulation' of such material but also of its content, of the 'aesthetic conversation' they instate and how 'this too has evolved and changed over time'.[85] In this vein, a new research project, 'The Europe that Gay Porn Built, 1945–2000', is looking at what the circulation and content of pornography reveals about the relationship between politics, transnational networks and the erotic, including in the formation and conceptualization of European-ness and particular European erotics.[86]

New technologies changed the ways such visuals were produced and consumed, ushering in different erotic formations again. Cameras went from being in the hands of the few to being, in a digital age, virtually ubiquitous, with attendant queer import in terms of self-representation and sexual exchange. The sex cinemas where films were projected to groups of strangers set up a different dynamic to those viewed at home on video, then DVD, now via streaming. Historians have traced the commercialization of sex and bodies in relation to the pink pound and such technological shifts, and have identified ways in which the porn industry has sometimes been a form of communal identification and support.[87] That it has often also been abusive and exploitative, and has peddled imagery that is sometimes overtly so, has made many wary of using it in research. These dynamics of sex and desire are nevertheless a significant component in queer history – as is the analysis of how the grotesquely overpowered and least powerful might grasp some agency through imagery of sexual embodiment and pleasure.[88] There is resonant analytical potential in the demeaning images taken by police, medics and prison officials. They provide a record of coercion and the exercise of power but can also reveal small gestures of self-assertion on the part of the subject, in a defiant gaze or posture, for example.[89] This is hardly redemptive but we glimpse something of the individual through it. Photographs, paintings, rolls of cine film, or video cassettes, as with books or newspapers, have been objects to collect, display or hide away, and in ways that also bears historical analysis. Changes in technology allowed for the mass reproduction of images and for people to accumulate them.[90] What was kept and how (in a frame, an album, under lock and key, in an envelope, slipped into a book) provides clues to its status and significance in a life. This was the stuff of self-fashioning and allows historians to read the social and cultural contexts of that assemblage of self.

Other objects have also guided historians. An item of clothing, ornament, piece of furniture, make-up bag, pill box, pipe or sex toy give us some clues to the queer everyday, a tactile sense of how things might have felt to handle, and how they might have mattered.[91] Several of the queer archives discussed in the last chapter demonstrate a particular commitment to material culture, recognizing that it can prompt us to think about how ordinary and extraordinary things were significant in queer or trans lives, how they marked difference accidentally or more deliberately, and so also how they became the stuff of individual and subcultural expression or of a wider visual and material encoding of difference. Art historian Lauren Fried pushed her analysis of gender and glam rock in the 1970s further than photos or film footage allowed by handling costumes held at the Victoria and Albert Museum: the sensuality of fabric, the intricacy of stitching, and conjunction of materials that hugged and emphasized crotch and arse gave her a sense not just of how these clothes looked but how they might have felt to wear for these artists and for the many who emulated them.[92] Political scientist Jane Bennet similarly celebrates the 'vitality of materiality' and the 'curious ability of inanimate things to animate, to act, to produce effects dramatic and subtle'.[93] The shock for Houlbrook of finding a tissue streaked with rouge in the British National Archive gave him a visceral sense of the policeman drawing it across the cheek of the man he had arrested.[94] When historian Chris Brickell and Judith Collard 'open[ed] up a mid-twentieth century make up box', by contrast, they were drawn to imagine the start rather than the end of a queer evening: 'we may wonder what the thick oily pastel would feel like on our own skin and then imagine our way into the world of theatrical glamour and exotic personae'.[95] Their edited collection, *Queer Objects*, includes reflections on more such stuff of everyday life. The items were either seen generally as intrinsically queer or became personally or collectively invested in that way. An action man, a pair of speedos, a waistcoat and a portable record player all fall into the latter category. My entry for the collection was about the rotary dial telephone and its place in queer lives (and hands) from the 1960s through to the 1980s. A subsequent chapter by Simon Clay picked up the story with smart-phones and the adjustments to behaviour and perception they prompted and represented.[96]

The random ephemera of life – fliers, a doodled cigarette packet, tickets, postcards, and tokens of fleeting or sustained affection – have frequently been taken up by queer historians for the traces they provide of lives otherwise undocumented (officially or otherwise). Sexuality studies scholar Juana María Rodríguez in her work on Proyecto Contra SIDA por Vida (Project Against AIDS for Life) in San Francisco describes the value she places on 'flyers, notes, objects, images, manifestos, party debris, art' to elucidate the lives of Latinx queers and queers of colour. 'Folks were dying every day', she wrote, 'so the urgency to preserve and remember was palpable.'[97] Hoarding and collecting such stuff has itself been taken as a sign of queerness and queer folk have oriented themselves via acts of intentional or accidental curation.[98] In a bedside table 'archive', a crowded mantlepiece or a box of keepsakes, we might trace contours of love, desire and queer culture.[99] The 'thingness' of these items, the fact they were kept (privately or collected by a museum) and their significance in signalling or forging community and connections makes them tools for historical interpretation.[100] The randomness and fragmentariness of ephemera also allow us to glimpse and signal queer lives lived through 'twilight moments' and 'below radars'.[101] This material and approach embraces uncertainty and incompleteness and so refuses to accord to disciplinary expectations of being sure.[102] Validating such stuff because it is suggestive rather than conclusive resists the drive to know and the heteronormativity of empiricism and traditional historical practice.[103]

Ephemera, like visual and material culture, can seem to close a gap between past and present in ways that is both exhilarating and deceptive. It might not, after all, have had the resonance then that it does now. The rotary dial telephone to me now is a slightly camp and barely used accessory in my home. It was a practical and differently significant item in my youth. If its physicality can still give a sense of how it felt to cradle the handset and move the dial, we need to layer that immediate sensation with other evidence. When I wrote about it for Brickell and Collard's collection, I drew also on newspapers, and on literature and film to reach for a sense of how these phones occupied a distinctive place in queer lives then. The 'evidence of experience' guided me to a sense of how it might have felt when such phones rang.

The evidence of experience (i): diaries, memoirs and autobiographies

Personal testimony in various forms offer tantalizing glimpses into everyday lives, desires, sex, and relationships. It allows us to texture our sense of particular times, places and events, and gives some voice to people absent or historically and culturally marginalized. It is where past lives can feel tangible and imaginable. As with material culture, though, the sense of immediacy is deceptive. In a key intervention in 1991, Joan Walloch Scott insisted that 'the evidence of experience' cannot give us unmediated access to personal and everyday 'truths' in the past in what fellow historian Nan Alamilla Boyd described as an 'implicit critique of self-knowing and self-telling'.[104] Experience was not outside of culture and discourse and neither were the ways in which that experience was narrated. 'How can we rely on historical narrators as coinvestigators or interpretative agents?', asked Boyd rhetorically; 'aren't [they]always already enmeshed in the social conditions that produce their own articulations of self through desire?'[105] Testimonial evidence, in Scott's argument, is a means of understanding those social conditions rather than the inner truth of the individual giving the testimony. The danger, Laura Doan later noted, is in 'reinscribing and naturalising the terms of difference' rather than 'exploring how difference is established'.[106]

Scott's intervention complicated the urge to 'grab a tape recorder and go out and record the memories of our elders before they were lost' (as Kennedy put it).[107] And yet Lisa Duggan argued soon after 'The Evidence of Experience' appeared that the piece set up something of a straw doll. She pointed out that the first generation of lesbian and gay historians who were leaning so substantially on oral history were also largely working within a social constructionist paradigm. They were, Duggan writes, 'plac[ing] the project of historicizing and denaturalizing the categories of sexual identity at the center of their agendas'. She added that downgrading 'the evidence of experience' and with it the category of experience in historical work 'reproduces the privilege of the elite academic voice over the writing of those who have laboured with far less support, reward, and recognition for their work'.[108] In this, Duggan was reaffirming the significance of those researching lesbian and gay history beyond the academy, often by gathering testimonies from those whose voices might imminently be lost.[109]

The critique of oral history and testimonial evidence is well made, but theory can disable our practice because there is of course an impossibility, an inadequacy, in any attempt to render past sexual subjectivities. Practitioners – Boyd prominent among them – impress by holding that imperfection, doing the work anyway and showing why it matters.[110] The fruits of their labour allow us to work through ways in which the social, cultural and the subjective meet and to what queer effect. Testimonies in various forms can shed light on the muddle of the everyday and trouble neat accounts of past societies and cultures and the people who populated them. They demonstrate that the 'bell-curve of "normally" and "usually"' does not explain all lives in all places.[111] And they give us some scope to think about lives on their own terms and as valuable on those terms – whether or not they can tell us something more broadly about past societies and cultures.[112] Testimonial evidence can loosely be divided in two. First, there are the testimonies that were written at the time. These include diaries, letters or accounts written for surveys like Britain's Mass Observation project. Second, there is the recounting in retrospect that comes in memoir and autobiography, in courtroom or sexological testimony, and in oral history. The division is loose and imprecise, not least because these retrospective accounts are also evidence about the moment the testimonies are given.

Whatever the genre of testimony, the person was writing or speaking in relation to a real or imagined interlocutor and this necessarily affected the resulting narrative. First-person accounts in court were moulded for the judge and jury in order to justify, exonerate or implicate. Charities and local and national government (especially as they became more bureaucratic from the 1800s) demanded testimonies from supplicants for housing, financial support, a drinks or entertainment licence, to adopt, and far more besides. It behoved those supplicants to tailor their accounts in ways that gave them the best chance of getting what they wanted. Those offering their histories to sexologists would pick out the details they thought would be most significant, perhaps influenced by the expert's earlier work or the questions they were asking. Memoirists and autobiographers did the same for their life course: composing their lives in a way that made them explicable and perhaps more palatable to themselves and others. They also included or excluded detail according to what seemed most relevant to the context in which they were writing. The new field of psychoanalysis guided British writer and broadcaster J. R. Ackerley's (1896–1967) account of his homosexuality, for example, with a striking rehearsal of his relationship with his father. More rarely non elites have used memoir to make their voice and version of themselves heard. In the case of the Hijra in India this work has come as a counter and corrective to 'expert' sociological and anthropological writing about them.[113] Cultures of class, gender and race play out explicitly and implicitly in these testimonies, and a close reading can locate not only a sense of the individuals 'speaking' but also the pressures operating on them to constitute and understand themselves and their stories in particular ways. We can start to grasp the rhetorical and other resources available or unavailable to individuals as they compose, frame, edit or account for themselves in relation to their social worlds.

Diaries are a way of making the self comprehensible to the self (the first imagined reader) and were also often written in fear or anticipation of others taking a look. We sometimes get sexual details in these sources which are hard to find elsewhere. The Irish nationalist Roger Casement had a balance sheet of his expenditure on sex in his diary alongside details of the cock size, nationality and hair colour of his pick-ups. The manner of this record not only signals the relative ease of casual homosex in Edwardian London but also the extent to which it was possible for Casement to compartmentalize and rationalize this aspect of his everyday life and to commodify the working-class, Irish and southern European men he was especially drawn to.[114] Using the explicit detail in the 1980s diaries of David Louis Bowie (a transport worker, not the pop star), Reay illustrates how fetishes and desires were often plural and changed across a life course. There is not, he argues, a singular truth of Bowie's sexual self. The diary form also comes as a reminder to avoid reading lives only through their endings. Bowie was writing without any direct knowledge of what that ending would be and his death from an AIDS-related illness in 1993 thus becomes 'an unwelcome postscript to diaries long begun'.[115] For filmmaker Derek Jarman, the diary was a way of clocking a continuing present and presence in the context of the AIDS crisis in Britain and his own illness. 'Still here', he writes in one of his final diary entries.[116] In Bowie's and Jarman's testimonies, we see queer coordinates of selfhood beyond sex, including the significance of friendship, solitude, caring and much else besides. These other currents in their lives helped define their sense of difference and were sometimes part of an accompanying investment in what was ordinary – as, indeed, was the very act of keeping a diary. Straight testimonies, often undervalued in LGBTQ+ work, help towards an understanding of that ordinariness as well as of how queerly tinged ordinary lives could be.[117] Thus, if the British press and government rhetoric in the eighties entrenched divisions between gay and straight, the Mass Observation testimonies suggested less rigidity in thought and feeling. Individuals surprise in their accounts of themselves and those around them, showing that there were other ways of thinking and behaving than more public materials suggest.[118]

The evidence of experience (ii): oral history

Testimony delivered retrospectively in carefully edited and published memoir or autobiography can lack the emotional intensity of recorded or videoed interviews. Though these are also edited and sometimes oft-rehearsed accounts, changes in voice, gesture and posture gave historian Will Jones additional insight into the emotional worlds of interviewees who had experienced same-sex sexual abuse in the Nazi extermination camps.[119] It is partly for such reasons, partly because of the frequent deficit in other evidence, that oral history has been writ large in LGBTQ+ historical work and been used to fill out our understandings of particular events, organizations, people and places; to track social, cultural, political and attitudinal contexts and change over time; and to think about the place of the remembered past in the present. It has been a tool in LGBTQ+ history from below and social history since the 1970s, and the practice has been shaped by cultural history, history of the emotions and memory studies. Creating such testimonies remains a political act. New knowledge is produced which is unavailable via other sources and is often at odds with official records. Queer oral history collections can thus be 'archives of disruption' (as Clare Summerskill, Amy Tooth Murphy and Emma Vickers have it in the subtitle of their recent collection). Oral history interviews are co-productions between interviewee and interviewer, and sometimes across an epistemological divide.[120] Many have lived with the assumption that sexuality is intrinsic and fixed, and experience it as such in their everyday and world view. For this reason, rather than for its truth, essentialism matters profoundly in the histories that emerge.

There can be a particular feeling of responsibility to interviewees and their stories because we have heard their voices and made connections with them in ways that affect the histories we go on to write. It is the one historical source which allows us to check back in for 'clarification, expansion or confirmation'.[121] Interviewees also give us clues to wider, collective ways of thinking, remembering, or telling which can be tested out through other sources or further interviews. Kennedy and Davis suggest that you need confirmation from between five and ten oral histories to confidently conclude something about a particular place, movement or historical moment, whilst also getting a sense of the significant differences in the way individuals felt and behaved there and then.[122] More often projects have involved many more interviews than this.[123]

The context of the interview and the distance of time creates a scrim through which the past is viewed. Historian Afsaneh Najmabadi found that the diasporic Iranians she interviewed in the 1980s and 1990s filtered their recall 'through the lens of later identities' such that 'earlier sexual and gender subjectivities and practices came to be seen as problematic and backward'.[124] In the process, she argues, the particularity of Tehran in the 1960s and 1970s was diluted. Relatedly, John Howard's attempt to pursue desire rather than identity in his work on the rural southern states of America was compromised by the identitarian lens through which his interviewees had come to understand their lives. The sex and desires they remembered became retrospective evidence of the process of becoming they wanted to describe, creating a problem for Howard in his interpretive work. Boyd captures this deftly. 'How', she asks, 'can the researcher of sexuality move beyond the limits of identity politics if historical narrators cannot verbalise their same-sex experiences outside the paradigm of gay and lesbian identities?'[125]

The very structure of lesbian, gay or bi oral history narratives often invites a familiar story of queer becoming, with 'coming out' as a key punctuating moment (though the lived reality is usually of a rolling process rather than singular announcement). This can set up a tension. When I interviewed Plymouth-based naval submariner, Dennis, he talked of his appreciation of the political and cultural distance travelled in the United Kingdom since the 1980s and his coming out in the early 2000s. But that appreciation strains against the pleasures of queer Plymouth and naval comradery he felt as a new recruit in the ostensibly less liberated seventies and early eighties. The story he felt he should tell about progress in the 2000s was saturated with a nostalgia for a period and way of being that felt more connected, communal and pleasurable to him.[126] We see in such interview moments how collective and individual memories are entangled but also often in tension.

'Memories', Christopher Reed and Christopher Castiglia remind us, 'are not retrievals of an archived past but something more imaginative and driven by present needs.'[127] If we can collect, read and analyse oral history as much for these complexities of memory, nostalgia and story-telling as for the moment described, then we get a vivid sense of how the past is gathered into the interviewee's present. In this way, the vicissitudes and tangle of memory become something to work with rather than against or around. This encourages oral historians and those working in the field of memory studies to consider 'the social and cultural contexts shaping memories of the past'.[128] I got some sense of this in my work with a group of gay squatters in Brixton in south London whom I interviewed in 2011 but who had interviewed each other twice before – in 1983 and 1997.[129] Many of the same details came up in each interview round, though with telling additions and omissions. By the time of the third round with me, there was a sense of a narrative well-rehearsed, perhaps remembered from the previous tellings as much as from the original moment. But as interesting were the different dynamics in each set of recordings. The 1983 round was conducted collectively as the squats dissolved. The intimacies of communal life had only just been relinquished, and they played out in these conversational testimonies in which both interviewer and interviewee shared their experiences.[130] There was palpable frustration and anger about the fragmentation of the squatting community;

several related this to the wider context of economic depression and Margaret Thatcher's governance. When former squatter Ian Townsen undertook the second round of interviews fifteen years later, some of the men from the first round had died, and there was more reflection, some regret and much nostalgia for a putatively freer time before the AIDS crisis. The 1970s seemed tougher in the first round than they did in this second. The interviews I recorded in 2011 had a different dynamic again. I was younger than the men I was interviewing and was engaged in politics in a different way than the squatters had been. I was also a tenured academic and had had some rudimentary oral history training which meant I attempted (often unsuccessfully) to hold back from the conversational and from my own reminiscences and anecdotes. Though I told my interviewees I was gay, I was still an outsider to this community of thirty years standing, linked not only by their queerness and lives together in that decade but by grief and memories shared over the decades since. Some may have been suspicious of me. They were certainly protective of each other and their formative experiences as a collective. Deep disagreements aired in earlier interviews were now smoothed, signalling a collective loyalty as well as the healing of time. In talking about their lives, these men were often deeply insightful. This was perhaps because people who have been marignalized and minoritized have had to engage in serious critical reflection 'to find and redefine [their] identities' and to think about their relationship to the world around them.[131] The interviews were in this sense both raw materials for what I went on to write and already historicized and analytical accounts.[132]

The sense of being within or beyond a community, of sharing a sexual, gender or ethnic identity (or not), of being a professional, an expert or an amateur, or of being older or younger than the interviewee will each effect the resulting narrative.[133] The gender of the interviewer seems (anecdotally) to affect the level of sexual detail, with queer men more reticent in such revelation to female interviewers and vice versa. Such dynamics might suggest prevailing ideas about appropriacy and shame and perhaps also a protectiveness of a sexual life and culture. And then there is the emotional dynamic of the interview itself – usually factored out of analysis but, suggests Esther Newton, important precisely because these interviews revolve around sexual difference and desire. She wrote: 'information has always flowed to me [in interview] in a medium of emotion, ranging from passionate – although never consummated – erotic attachment through profound affection to lively interest'. This, she went on, 'empowers me in my projects and, when it is reciprocated, helps motivate informants to put up with my questions and intrusions'.[134] There is in this a dramatization of the emotions prompted in our encounters with other kinds of evidence and which likewise matter to the way we go on to analyse them.[135]

Oral histories have, by convention, been one-on-one, reflecting our cultural onus on the individual. They have also focused on voice and the voice transcribed, sometimes tidied up for publication though as often now with the telling pauses, hesitations and repetitions left in. Video interviews, like those gathered by the British National HIV Story Trust, have brought physical presence and gesture into the picture.[136] Others have taken that physicality further. Artist and historian Harrison Apple describes how their project on Pittsburgh's after-hours queer social clubs was informed by interviewees 'remembering' and recounting via physical re-enactment – moments in which we can glimpse the body as archive and, in the emotion expressed through it, as an 'archive of feelings'.[137] The process extended a sense of the physicality of the remembered scene and also constituted a new moment of community between those involved when Apple went on to restage one of the events.[138]

Group interviews and witness seminars can help elucidate networks, communities and shared experiences, especially when recorded alongside solo interviews. Participants riff off each other in ways that affirm, correct and contradict information, or sometimes replay past conflict. In a witness seminar I conducted in Leeds, divisions of forty years prior resurfaced when one of the men referred to the city's 'gay girls' and bemoaned lesbian separatism.[139] What emerged for me from this and other experiences is the tension between group connection (and the desire for connection) on the one hand, and, on the other, the way in which individuals in groups 'are mobilised through different paths, perform different duties, develop different social ties, and are given different degrees of power and prestige'.[140] These tensions might echo those in the past (as in the Leeds case), they might surface through differing memories and understanding, and they might reflect and underscore immediate and wider contexts of the group interview (as in some of the anti-immigrant sentiment which was contentious in a witness seminar I facilitated in Plymouth).[141]

Whatever choices we make in gathering and sharing new testimony, queer historians have been acutely conscious of the ethical dimensions of this work – not least in relation to the politics of naming or anonymizing and the capacity for interviews in whatever form to reanimate and trigger grief, upset and hurt as well as desire and pleasure, years after the events described. Care and solidarity, like that fostered in Apple's work, are important components of queer oral history work and are one of its manifold pleasures. It is a strand of history-making in which feelings in the present, for the past and for each other tangibly matter.[142]

Conclusion

This chapter has stressed the significance of archival encounters to queer historical work, tugging through a thread which runs across the book. We saw in Chapter 2 that the the archive came under sustained examination for its colonial patterning, seeming to obscure (homo)erotics and queerness (even though they might be there in abundance, as Arondekar suggests).[143] Chapter 4 looked at the archive, and more particularly the community archive, as a site of public history which might be a place of positive recourse for people in the present. This chapter has looked in a more focused way at how we might read the past through archives and the particular sources they contain. Such sources, however compelling, should not overwhelm an acknowledgement of what is missing and yet deeply meaningful. Sometimes this invites a departure from historical convention in replacing 'what was' with 'what might have been', as Saidiya Hartman has it.[144] This and other queer historical tendencies highlighted in my Introduction are apparent in the way queer historians approach source material and in the particular sources they tend to lean into. Oral history has, for example, been especially appealing because it facilitates a vivid communion with the past in and for the present, amplifying an impulse amongst queer historians more broadly.[145]

For all queer history's particular tendencies, though, practitioners remain indebted to wider modes of history-making. Across the preceding chapters I have highlighted especially the relationship with social, cultural, political, legal and urban history; with history from below, postcolonial and gender history; with the history of sexuality, of ideas, and of the emotions; and with historicist approaches in other disciplines – in literature, geography, anthropology, sociolology and law. The cultural, spatial and archival turns in history and the humanities have impacted queer history too. We can not, therefore, decisively separate out queer historical methodology as a distinctly coded practice. It is relatedly, Reay writes, 'all too easy to dismiss the "traditional archive" as reactionary and unhelpful in explorations of queer life and lives'; 'I want to advocate', he goes on, 'for the richness of the sexual histories, the pockets of recorded desire, located in the most respectable repositories'.[146] He, like others, has worked through collections held in multiple official and counter archival settings and not only in those specifically denominated as LGBTQ+. It is, indeed, by reading across such archives that historians have shown queer history to be enmeshed with other histories and other ways of doing history. A queer openness and open-endeness in these respects has been productive in reaching a more complex understanding of sex and desire, and their relationship to culture and society.

Queer has served history well as a term and lens which can loosen the edges of identity and encourage cross-cutting, intersectional work. But we also need to hold it provisionally and be prepared to let it go if its meanings and use (generally and in the academy) drift from those which have pushed us towards new questions and modes of enquiry. This might be especially the case if, as queer history becomes more embedded in the academy and is shuffled into a conventionalized disciplinary deck, it loses its deftness, reflexivity, and capacity to be transgressive. We have seen how it can cement rather than call into question a Western sexuality binary and how gender and race have sometimes seemed add-ons rather than intrinsic to queer historical analysis. These troubles with queer history do not necessarily negate its utility (especially as historians are increasingly working to address them), but we need to be mindful that the lived experience of the current and coming generation may spark other ways of thinking about the past, rather as earlier uneven shifts in identification, community and politics prompted homosexual, lesbian and gay and then LGBT and queer history. What is certain is that whatever it is that emerges in historical and critical enquiry, it will be in conversation with – and will owe a debt to – the work this book has surveyed.

Epilogue

Queer history very frequently circles individuals. There are a plethora of biographies and person-centred case studies which, in the manner of micro-history, layer up intricate details to build a picture of a person and groups of people in a particular time and place. This makes for good story-telling and can grip the reader. It is also a way of taking up historical space and producing a fuller sense of people who have often been marginalized, derided or dismissed. The detail is in this sense worth it in and of itself and as a way of 'doing justice'. But it also does wider historical work by complicating ideas of identity and subjectivity (people when viewed so fully rarely fit a mould) and by showing (rather than merely telling) how that complexity relates of historic social and cultural contexts and dynamics. Joe Moran notes how fellow historians have generally been cautious of such approaches. Description is meant to feed argument not be the argument, and the superfluity of detail can make it feel more like reading fiction than authoritative history. He nevertheless observes the power and utility of the 'burgeoning' genre of detailed 'speculative biography', work which 'seek[s] to redress the historical record by writing more imaginatively about those with poorly documented, barely remembered lives'.[1] This is why obsessive collecting, the careful patchworking of detail and sources, and conjecture have been so important to many queer historians and to the writers and artists who have been prominent in forging a queer historical consciousness. Queer lives become more than occasional blots on the historical landscape. They are instead painted into – shown to be part of and to emerge from – such scenes. Person-centred queer work might risk becoming a shadow version of the 'great [white] man' approach to the past in which exceptionalism feeds a fiction of individual autonomy. But this is not how queer history has tended to operate, perhaps because queer historians and creatives have felt all too acutely the troubling impress of those 'great men' and of the worlds they created and sustained. Even in queer dealings with icons like Anne Lister we usually get a deep sense of place and time. If there is a tantalizing resonance with now, Lister could also only be of Yorkshire in the 1800s.

In the course of this book and especially in the codas to each chapter, I have tried to think about my own work and, relatedly, my sense of queer selfhood, in such wider contexts. To tie up this autobiographical thread, and as an extension of the last chapter on sources, I have reorientated the perspective for a reflection on the ways in which the detritus of my life, including my memories, might be read as an archive.[2]

And memory is a good starting point.

Reaching back to the mid-seventies, I recall one of my many aunts telling me that I would not want to end up being a hairdresser. This did not come from nowhere. I remember that I was sitting wrapped in a flowery bedspread pretending to blow dry my hair (I did not have much – even then). Perhaps the clarity of this mental image has endured because my aunt's comment pinched a little, as if I had been exposed – though I did not know for what. On another, slightly later occasion, my dad said that he didn't like that gay no longer just meant happy. He said homosexual was the proper term – one perhaps less cluttered for him with those new, discomforting gay voices 'from below'. This might have been the first time I had heard either word, or heard either word with a sense of some judgement attached, albeit gently articulated by a gentle man. Thinking of these two instances conjures two more: another aunt telling how she got the giggles when she encountered an effeminate man dressed 'in something like a baby grow', and yet another aunt (there were lots) who told my mum about befriending 'the most beautiful woman she had ever met'. These were hardly startling moments; fragments of memory from a busy household where visitors and chat were constant. That they stand out amidst the rest suggests that I was already alert to some sense of difference and was honing in on clues and coordinates. I picked up on a tone in my first aunt's voice which suggested she had detected something shameful or embarrassing in me. My dad and aunt number two highlighted a sense of otherness under a contested name and a hilarious look. Both flagged possibilities that seemed separate from and somehow troublesome to the lives they were living. My mum's remembrance about aunt number three, on the other hand, touched the possibility of finding and frankly acknowledging beauty in someone of the same sex.

Another way of thinking about these memories is to say I tugged them forward as a firmer sense of my own desires configured in my teens and I dredged my memory bank for clues to my difference. This was me plotting a story of my own queer emergence, a story I am rehearsing again now – grasping and reshaping distant memories for the present purpose, as i might for an oral history interview.

I did not know about the pioneering early activist-scholars of the 1970s until much later, but the circumstances of my upbringing meant I was absorbing some of the wider context and debate. The tiny local labour party met in our living room (excruciating for me in my teens because it was composed mostly of my teachers). Through my siblings I felt some sense of new styles of engagement with life, learning, politics and counterculture. I remember 'Nuclear Power No Thanks' and 'Rock Against Racism' stickers appearing in the centre of our rotary dial telephone at home.[3] Feminism was a regular riff round our dining table when everyone descended for Christmas – my siblings' stance sometimes tugging at my parents' more class-oriented socialism. In the late 1970s and first half of the 1980s, I would go with my parents to visit my older brothers and sisters – in a lesbian-feminist co-op in Leeds, in squats in London, in student houses in Manchester. Kicking my heels in these places as the adults talked, I remember feeling a vague stirring of possibility looking over bookcases or flicking the lesbian and gay listings sections in the *Spare Rib* and *Time Out* magazines that lay around. Here was a different world from the one I knew, suggesting an apparent ease with an identity I was beginning to feel some affiliation with.

These memories and these magazines could help piece together the contexts and reference points for that queer becoming. Other texts – including the plays, films and novels I described in the coda to Chapter 4 – might provide clues to the ways in which I was more deliberately thinking about my newfound sense of self in relationship to particular histories in my early adulthood. Meanwhile, my 'coming out' letters to my parents which I found again when my mum died, together with my stray attempts to keep a diary (each lasting only a few days or weeks) might touch some of the uncertainty I felt in these early years. On the one hand, I experienced my body and sex with a strange mixture of defiance, pride and enjoyment (I had imbibed the liberationist anticipation of pleasures guiltlessly sought and mutually experienced). On the other hand, there was fear and embarrassment. I felt self-conscious because of my cracked, red skin which I also feared (wrongly) might make me additionally vulnerable to the HIV virus. I worried about what a diagnosis might reveal about me. Shame, to use Sara Ahmed, was particularly 'sticky' in the new context gay men found themselves in and there were pressing histories which made that feeling insistent.[4] I found myself 'straighten up' with straight men to ameliorate what I felt to be my deficient masculinity. There were, in short, contradictory feelings in play behind the proud, out persona I also confected (and owned). This might be tangible in those letters and diary fragments from the first half of the nineties.

Triangulated with other materials, this testimony could provide ways into thinking about the social and cultural contexts associated with the 1980s and 1990s. Resources to draw on would be the boxes, albums and hard drives of photos which might give a sense of what it was like to be brought up as part of a large, loosely middle-class, left-wing family in a deeply conservative village in the English midlands. Interests, travels, passions and attachments to family and friends would emerge from this too. Accumulated small details from ephemera and possessions could bring another perspective: the books, DVDs, the pin board in my office with its layers of postcards, photos, drawings, and badges (all rich in association for me) provide clues to some of the coordinates of my sense of self. Somewhere they might find a tattered A–Z with which I first navigated London. 'Xs' marked different destinations. Various pages were missing, torn out so I could find my way without the whole book in my back pocket. The future historian might guess at what the 'xs' flagged and so trace the fragmented clues to the significance of this city in my shifting sense of myself in my twenties. This old A–Z, the randomness of the pinboard, the books and DVDs piled and unorganized, the folders of random papers would all also speak to my disorganization – a sign of the way I muddle through in my encounters with the present and past.

Official records relating to this life might tell another story again. Our application to adopt in 2015 tells an oddly coherent life narrative of myself and my husband and follows a formula well-crafted by social workers. We sought to provide what ours needed for that document and I emerge from it as a 'dual heritage English-Welsh gay man'. This was a surprise when I read it back because my Welsh heritage has never felt core to my sense of myself. This was an aspect of my 'life story' which instead spoke strategically to some children our social worker thought might be well matched with us. What this document does not record – but which could maybe be read between lines – is how conscious we were of being seen through straighter eyes. My will, entwined with my partner's, speaks of the multiple dimensions of my queer family and the responsibilities and love that bind it. This might all suggest an orderliness and coherence that belies my experience of everyday life, yet could say something, too, of the strong need I have felt to protect myself and my kin; the nagging interior voice that I should do things 'properly'. At more of a distance, the census will make my successive moves legible – from east Staffordshire to Sheffield, and then from south to north London. It would not capture my year in Brighton, which fell between censuses. Depending on the moment it was taken, entries would find me in coupledom, living solo, with my kids or some of my nieces and nephews who stayed for extended periods.[5] The 2031 census would likely find me still living just outside Oxford. An online search would reveal I probably moved there for a newly created professorship in the history of sexuality. It would not show the additional factors that persuaded us to move from London: some serious ill-health, a growing disenchantment with London, my younger son's looming high school years, and my partner's horticultural passions.

My historical preoccupations and influences would emerge from my publications. Just from the titles this imagined researcher would spot my enduring interest in different spaces – spaces that had a shifting significance and meaning in my own life too (as other documents would suggest). They might note a growing emotionality in my work by the 2010s, reflecting shifts in wider historical questions that were being asked and also a time in my life when I was taking stock and reflecting back to the exciting, febrile, and grief-stricken period of my early adulthood in the 1990s – still writ especially large in my memory bank with first loves, tight friendships formed, and losses in my birth family and, through AIDS, my London circles. They might guess that I perhaps also felt a little freer to write more from the heart than I did earlier in my career.[6] And they might just connect this to the nostalgia that is probably evident in this book for earlier, passionately collaborative gay and lesbian history-making in the 1970s and 1980s.

These latter sources might lead to module outlines and official versions of myself on institutional web sites. Colleagues, friends, lovers, siblings, partners and children could provide alternate and resonant takes on my life, riffing off and contradicting each other and those other materials. With more probing, they would find the difference age and generation might make. One of my older sisters saw her upbringing as more working class than I did mine, and we had different reference points when we came out partly as a result: my sister's were in Leeds, living with largely working-class women in squats and co-ops in the 1970s and early 1980s; mine were in the early 1990s, newly attached to a middle-class Londoner.

This imagined archive of material could be read for what it communicates directly, for what we might discern between lines and in the silences, and for how it relates to wider social, cultural and political contexts couching and shaping sexual identifications and communities in England at these points in the twentieth and twenty-first centuries. It could reveal subtle and dramatic changes over time by looking across this life course or comparing it with others. An alert sift through my chaotic filing cabinet might throw up the life insurance policy my fearful parents took out for me in the late 1980s, but also show that I cashed it in to pay for my civil partnership in 2013 – a paper trail signalling wider, shifting social, cultural and political ground around me.

What, though, would the queer historical point be of such a narrow and singular case? Social and oral historian Penny Summerfield writes that 'even the most ordinary life makes it possible for the reader to visit other worlds through the prism of another person's memories, feelings and perceptions'.[7] Looking at this particular conjunction of materials with a breadth of vision incorporating surrounding contexts and adjacent cases might take us into more interesting terrain, giving some perspective on forms of late-twentieth-century subjective composure, on particular ways of identifying and finding community, and on the imperatives which shaped and directed experiences and ways of being in that queer place and time. The project might expose the self-consciousness of queerness in the late twentieth and twenty-first century. And in the entanglement evident across these records – of the personal, the political and historical, of this life with diverse others – it might also complicate reactionary contemporary attempts to use history to simplify, separate and vilify. But whether or not the project did these things, it would at least demonstrate the significance of the past to queer self-composure – and of writing queer history to this particular historical subject.

Notes

Preface and Acknowledgements

1 Section 28 of the Local Government Act of 1988 stated that UK local authorities 'shall not intentionally promote homosexuality or publish material with the intention of promoting homosexuality' or 'promote the teaching in any maintained school of the acceptability of homosexuality as a pretended family relationship'. See Local Government Act, UK, at https://www.legislation.gov.uk/ukpga/1988/9/section/28/enacted?view=plain (accessed 20 June 2025).

2 'Feature: Stonewall in Global Perspective', *History Workshop Journal* 89 (Spring 2020); 'Stonewall 50 Years On: Gay Liberation and Lesbian Feminism in its European Context', conference at Manchester Metropolitan University, Manchester (6 December, 2019); 'Stonewall 50', Columbia University, New York (6 April 2019). On homonationalism see especially: Jasbir Puar, *Terrorist Assemblages: Homonationalism in Queer Times* (Duke University Press, 2007); and Puar, 'Rethinking Homonationalism', *International Journal of Middle East Studies* 45, no. 2 (2013): 336–9.

3 See Elizabeth A. Armstrong and Suzanna M. Crage, 'Movements and Memory: The Making of the Stonewall Myth', *American Sociological Review* 71, no. 5 (2006), 724–51.

4 'Love and Resistance: Stonewall 50', exhibition at New York Public Library (14 February 2019 – 15 July 2019).

5 Armstrong and Crage, 'Movements and Memory'. On the shifting meanings of Pride (in relation to Brighton, England, and Dublin, Éire), see Kath Browne, 'A Party with Politics? (Re)Making LGBTQ Pride Spaces in Dublin and Brighton', *Social & Cultural Geography* 8, no. 1 (2007), 63–87.

6 Joanna Walter, 'New York City: Dueling Pride Marches to Mark Stonewall's 50th anniversary', *Guardian* (28 June 28 2019).

7 Matt Cook, 'Entangled Tales: Making Queer History Since the 1960s', Inaugural Lecture for the Jonathan Cooper Chair in the History of Sexuality, Mansfield College, Oxford, 20 May 2025. https://www.youtube.com/watch?v=4hRnTcAz_fc (accessed 30 June 2025).

Introduction

1   A borrowing from Eve Kosofsy Sedgwick, *Tendencies* (Routledge, 1994).

2   Jennifer V. Evans, *The Queer Art of History: Queer Kinship After Fascism* (Duke University Press, 2023), 4.

3   On queer and trans historicism see especially Valerie Traub, 'The New Unhistoricism in Queer Studies', *PMLA* 128, no. 1 (2013), 21–37; Leah DeVun and Zeb Tortorici, 'Trans, Time, and History', *TSQ: Transgender Studies Quarterly* 5, no. 4 (2018), 518–39.

4   On the uses and abuses of history more broadly see especially Robert Gildea, *What is History For?* (Bristol University Press, 2024).

5   On this point see Estelle B. Freedman, '"The Burning of Letters Continues": Elusive identities and the historical construction of sexuality', *Journal of Women's History*, 9, no. 4 (1998), 181–200.

6   Anna Clark, 'Twilight Moments', *Journal of the History of Sexuality* 14, no. 1 (2005), 139–60, at 156 and 145.

7   On this see Regina Kunzel, 'The Power of Queer History', *The American Historical Review* 123, no. 5 (2018), 1560–82.

8   On these points in relation to British queer history see Laura Doan, *Disturbing Practices: History, Sexuality, and Women's Experience of Modern War* (University of Chicago Press, 2013); and Matt Houlbrook, 'Thinking Queer: The Social and the Sexual in Interwar Britain', in *British Queer History: New Approaches and Perspectives,* ed. Brian Lewis (Manchester University Press, 2013), 134–64.

9   On these points see especially Julia Shaw, *Bi: The Hidden Culture, History and Science of Bisexuality* (Canongate, 2022); Nan Alamilla Boyd, 'Bodies in Motion: Lesbian and Transsexual Histories', in *Transgender Studies Reader,* eds Susan Stryker and Stephen Whittle (Routledge, 2006), 420–33, at 422; Heather K. Love, 'Selections from "Spoiled Identity": Stephen Gordon's Loneliness and the Difficulties of Queer History', in *Transgender Studies Reader,* 521–36, at 523.

10   On the relation of contemporary identity categories to colonialism, see Laurie Marhoefer, 'Was the Homosexual Made White? Race, Empire, and Analogy in Gay and Trans Thought in Twentieth-Century Germany', *Gender & History* 31, no. 1 (2019), 91–114; Marhoefer, *Racism and the Making of Gay Rights: A Sexologist, his Student, and the Empire of Queer Love* (University of Toronto Press, 2022). On the relation of sexual identity categories to race science, see Siobhan B. Somerville, 'Scientific Racism and the Emergence of the Homosexual Body', *Journal of the History of Sexuality* 5, no. 2 (1994), 243–66; Somerville, *Queering the Color Line: Race and the Invention of Homosexuality in American Culture* (Duke University Press, 2000); Jennifer Terry, *An American Obsession: Science, Medicine, and*

Homosexuality in Modern Society (University of Chicago Press, 1999). On the relationship of sexual identity categories to gender, see Alan Sinfield, *The Wilde Century: Effeminacy, Oscar Wilde and the Queer Moment* (Cassell, 1994); Roger N. Lancaster and Micaela Di Leonardo, eds, *The Gender/Sexuality Reader: Culture, History, Political Economy* (Psychology Press, 1997); Karen Harvey, *Reading Sex in the Eighteenth Century: Bodies and Gender in English Erotic Culture* (Cambridge University Press, 2005); A. Najmabadi, 'Beyond the Americas: are gender and sexuality useful categories of analysis?', *Journal of Women's History*, 18, 1 (2006), 11–21; Elizabeth Kennedy and Madeline Davis, *Boots of Leather, Slippers of Gold: The History of a Lesbian Community* (Routledge, 1993); Helen Smith, *Masculinity, Class and Same-Sex Desire in Industrial England, 1895–1957* (Palgrave Macmillan, 2015). For discussion of these conjunctions see chapter 2.

11 See Martin Duberman, George Chauncey and Martha Vicinus, *Hidden from History: Reclaiming the Gay and Lesbian Past* (Meridian Books, 1990).

12 Carolyn Dinshaw, *Getting Medieval: Sexualities and Communities, Pre- and Postmodern* (Duke University Press, 1999), 36, 40.

13 On this point see Evans, *Queer Art of History*, 16; Doan. *Disturbing Practices*.

14 See Sophia Rosenfeld, *Common Sense: A Political History* (Harvard University Press, 2011).

15 On the relationship between queer history and collective memory see especially Laura Doan, 'Queer History / Queer Memory: The Case of Alan Turing', *GLQ: A Journal of Lesbian and Gay Studies* 23, no. 1 (2017), 113–36.

16 Clark, 'Twilight'; Deborah Cohen, *Family Secrets: Living with Shame from the Victorians to the Present Day* (Viking, 2013); Evans, *The Queer Art of History*.

17 Cathy Cohen's critique of queer politics was that it had come 'to reinforce a simple dichotomy between heterosexuality and everything "queer"'. Cathy Cohen, 'Punks, Bulldaggers and Welfare Queens: The Radical Potential of Queer Politics', *GLQ: A Journal of Lesbian and Gay Studies*, 3, no. 4 (1997), 437–65, at 348.

18 On the history of the term 'queer' see Marc Stein, *Rethinking the Gay and Lesbian Movement* (Routledge, 2012), 8–9, and Siobhan Somerville, 'Queer', in *Keywords for American Cultural Studies,* eds Bruce Burgett and Glenn Hendler (New York, 2007), 187–91. See also Matt Cook, *Queer Domesticities: Homosexuality and Home Life in Twentieth Century London* (Palgrave, 2014), 7–8.

19 A borrowing from Michael Warner, *The Trouble with Normal: Sex, Politics and the Ethics of Queer Life* (Free Press, 1999).

20   Sedgwick, *Tendencies*, 8.

21   On the cultural potency of this model, see Eve Kosofsky Sedgwick, *Epistemology of the Closet* (Harvester Wheatsheaf, 1991).

22   On these issues see Cohen, 'Punks, Bulldaggers, and Welfare Queens'; Cohen, 'The Radical Potential of Queer? Twenty years later', *GLQ: A Journal of Lesbian and Gay Studies* 25, no. 1 (2019): 140–4; Joseph M. Pierce, María Amelia Viteri, Diego Falconí Trávez, Salvador Vidal-Ortiz, and Lourdes Martínez-Echazábal, 'Introduction: *Cuir*/Queer Américas: Translation, Decoloniality, and the Incommensurable', *GLQ: A Journal of Gay and Lesbian Studies* 27, no. 3 (2021), 321–7.

23   Manuela L. Picq, 'Decolonizing Indigenous Sexualities: Between Erasure and Resurgence', in *The Oxford Handbook of Global LGBT and Sexual Diversity Politics,* eds Michael J. Bosia, Sandra McEvoy and Momin Rahman (Oxford University Press, 2020), 168–184, at 169. See also Manuela L. Picq and Josi Tikuna, 'Indigenous Sexualities: Resisting Conquest and Translation', in *Sexuality and Translation in World Politics,* eds Caroline Cottet and Manuela L. Picq (E-International Relations, 2019).

24   On these points see Holly Cashman and Marilyn Martin-Jones, *Queer, Latinx, and Bilingual: Narrative Resources in the Negotiation of Identities* (Routledge, 2017); Heike Bauer, *Sexology and Translation: Cultural and Scientific Encounters across the Modern World* (Temple University Press, 2015); Kadji Amin 'Taxonomically Queer? Sexology and New Queer, Trans, and Asexual Identities". *GLQ: A Journal of Lesbian and Gay Studies* 29, no. 1 (2023): 91–107.

25   Howard Chiang, 'Archiving Peripheral Taiwan: The Prodigy of the Human and Historical Narration', *Radical History Review* 120 (2014), 204–25, at 208. See also Chiang, *Transtopia in the Sinophone Pacific* (Columbia University Press, 2020).

26   On this point see also Martin F. Manalansan, *Global Divas: Filipino Gay Men in the Diaspora* (Duke University Press, 2003); Cashman and Martin-Jones, *Queer, Latinx, and Bilingual*; Bauer, *Sexology and Translation.*

27   Scott Bravmann, *Queer Fictions of the Past: History, Culture, and Difference* (Cambridge University Press, 1997), xii.

28   On this point see Marc Stein, 'Canonizing Homophile Sexual Respectability: Archives, History, and Memory', *Radical History Review* 2014, no. 120 (2014), 53–73.

29   Jane Gallop, *Anecdotal Theory* (Duke University Press, 2003), 18.

30   Nancy K. Miller, *Getting Personal: Feminist Occasions and Other Autobiographical Acts* (Routledge, 1991), xi, cited by Gallop, *Anecdotal Theory,* 156.

31   For reflections on this point, see the interview with Black queer archivist and photographer Ajamu X at https://www.frieze.com/article/ajamu-pleasures-darkroom, (accessed 10 December 2024).

32   The dance metaphor is deployed by Roy Porter and Lesley Hall in their explanation of Michel Foucault's argument. Porter and Hall, *The Facts of Life: The Creation of Sexual Knowledge in Britain, 1650–1950* (Yale University Press, 1995), 8.

33   See Rachel Gelfand, 'Between Archives: Yerushe, Intergenerational Collaboration, and Aging in Queer Family', *Radical History Review* 139 (2021), 200–10; Gerard Koskovich, 'The History of Queer History: One Hundred Years of the Search for Shared Heritage', in *Preservation and Place: Historic Preservation by and of LGBTQ Communities in the United States,* eds Katherine Crawford-Lackey and Megan E. Springate (Berghahn, 2019), 30–84, at 30; on (queer) erasures in the family photograph see Julia Hirsch, *Family Photographs: Content, Meaning and Effects* (Oxford University Press, 1981).

34   See Martin Meeker, '"You Could Argue That They Control Power": Politics and Interviewing across Sexualities', in *Bodies of Evidence: The Practice of Queer Oral History,* eds Nan Alamilla Boyd and Horacio N. Roque Ramírez (Oxford University Press, 2012), 220–36, at 227. Huw Lemmey and Ben Miller provide a playful corrective to this heroic drive in their 'Bad Gays' podcast and book: Huw Lemmey and Ben Miller, *Bad Gays: A Homosexual History* (Verso Books, 2022). For a general discussion of community history's 'celebratory impulse', see Linda Shopes, 'Oral History and the Study of Communities: Problems, Paradoxes, and Possibilities', *The Journal of American History* 89, no. 2 (2002), 588–98, at 591; and Robert Mills, 'Queer is Here? Lesbian, gay, bisexual and transgender histories and public culture', *History Workshop Journal,* 62 (2006), 253–263.

35   A term coined in Raymond Williams, *Preface to Film* (London, 1954) and then elaborated as a mode of cultural and historical analysis, on which see Devika Sharma and Frederik Tygstrup, eds, *Structures of Feeling: Affectivity and the Study of Culture* (Walter de Gruyter, 2015).

36   For an examination see Marhoefer, *Racism and the Making of Gay Rights*; William Jones, '"So Then . . . He Raped Me": Male Experiences of Sexual(ized) Violence in the Nazi Concentration Camps' (DPhil diss., University of Oxford, 2024), 245; Jan-Henrik Friedrichs, 'Transnational Networks of Child Sexual Abuse and Consumerism: Edward Brongersma and the Pedophilia Debate of the 1970s and 1980s', *Journal of the History of Sexuality* 31, no. 2 (2022), 169–91; Lemmey and Miller, *Bad Gays.*

37   On this point, see Ellen Lewin, 'Who's Queer? What's Queer? Queer Anthropology through the Lens of Ethnography', *Cultural Anthropology* 31, no. 4 (2016), 598–606.

38   Sara Ahmed, *The Feminist Killjoy Handbook* (Random House, 2023), 161.

39   Ahmed, *Feminist Killjoy Handbook*, 178.

40   On the mismatch of theory, history and culture see Kadji Amin, *Disturbing Attachments: Genet, Modern Pederasty and Queer History* (Duke University Press, 2017), 4; Amin, "Taxonomically Queer?".

41   Gallop, *Anecdotal Theory*, 164.

42   Sedgwick, *Tendencies*, 8.

43   See Richard Sandell, Rachael Lennon, Matt Smith, and Anna Lincoln, *Prejudice and Pride: LGBTQ Heritage and its Contemporary Implications* (University of Leicester, 2018); Nicole Ritchie, *Queering Museums: Questions of Space, Affect, and the (non) Normative* (University of Toronto, 2015); Robert Mills, 'Theorising the Queer Museum', *Museums and Social Issues* 3, no. 1 (2008), 41–52. Khalil R. West, 'Dark Matter: Sociality, Space, and the Haptics of Queer (Il)legibility in "Black Liverpool", 1967–1997' (PhD, European University Institute, Florence, 2025), introduction.

44   Susan Stryker and V. Varun Chaudhry, 'Ask a Feminist: Susan Stryker Discusses Trans Studies, Trans Feminism, and a More Trans Future with V. Varun Chaudhry', in *Signs* 47, no. 3 (2022), 789–800, at 797.

45   Kunzel, 'The Power of Queer History', 1579. See also Kunzel, 'The Flourishing of Transgender Studies', *TSQ: Transgender Studies Quarterly* 1, no. 1 (2014), 285–97.

46   Claire Sears proposed the use of trans as a verb, building on Susan Stryker, Paisley Currah and Lisa Jean Moore's 2008 call to consider trans in relation to mobility and movement between positions. Andrea Long Chu and Emmett Harsin Drager criticized the loss of a sense of trans personhood in these moves. Claire Sears, *Arresting Dress: Cross-Dressing, Law, and Fascination in Nineteenth-Century San Francisco* (Duke University Press, 2015); Susan Stryker, Paisley Currah and Lisa Jean Moore, 'Introduction: Trans-, Trans, or Transgender?', *Women's Studies Quarterly* 36, no. 3/4 (2008), 11–22; Long Chu and Harsin Drager, 'After Trans Studies'. With thanks to Jo Brydon.

47   See Jamey Jesperson, 'Trans Misogyny in the Colonial Archive: Remembering Trans Feminine Life and Death in New Spain, 1604-1821', *Gender & History* 36, no. 1 (2024), 91–111; C. Riley Snorton, *Black on Both Sides: A Racial History of Trans Identity* (University of Minnesota Press, 2017).

48   On this latter point see Jeffrey Escoffier, 'Inside The Ivory Closet: The Challenge Facing Lesbian and Gay Studies', in *American Homo: Community and Perversity* (University of California Press, 1998), 104–17.

49   Simon Joyce, *LGBT Victorians: Sexuality and Gender in the Nineteenth-Century Archives* (Oxford University Press, 2022).

50   Evans, *Queer Art of History*, 142.

51 Diarmaid Hester, *Nothing Ever Just Disappears: Seven Hidden Histories* (Penguin, 2024).

52 Mo Moulton, 'Our Mushroom Moment? On the Trans Possibilities of a New History of Communal Life', inaugural lecture, University of Birmingham, 23 October 23 2024.

Chapter 1: Foundations

1 Lillian Faderman, *Surpassing the Love of Men* (1981; Harper Collins, 1998), 17.

2 Martha Vicinus, 'The History of Lesbian History', *Feminist Studies* 38, no. 3 (2012), 566–96, at 589; Jonathan Katz, *Gay American History: Lesbians and Gay Men in the U.S.A.: A Documentary* (Crowell, 1976), 2.

3 These other pioneers included, in the US, Estelle Freedman, Joan Nestle and Alan Bérubé, and, in the UK, Annabel Faraday, Jeffrey Weeks and Alan Bray.

4 John D'Emilio, *Sexual Politics, Sexual Communities: The Making of a Homosexual Minority in the United States, 1940–1970* (1983; Chicago University Press, 1998), xiii–xiv. For discussion see Regina Kunzel, 'The Power of Queer History', *The American Historical Review* 123, no. 5 (2018), 1560–82, at 1561–2.

5 Iwan Bloch, *Sexual Life in England* (1908; Corgi Books, 1965).

6 Magnus Hirschfeld, *Urnish People: Causes and Nature of Uranism*, trans. M. Lombardi-Nash (1903; Urania Manuscripts, 2022); Hirschfeld, *The Homosexuality of Men and Women* (1914; Prometheus Books, 2000); Havelock Ellis, *Studies in the Psychology of Sex, Vol. 1: Sexual Inversion* (Wilson and Macmillan, 1897).

7 Bloch, *Sexual Life*, 124.

8 The Corgi editions appeared in 1958 and 1965.

9 On the 'homosexual problem', see Michael Schofield, *Society and the Homosexual* (Gollancz, 1952); Homosexual Law Reform Society, *Homosexuals and the Law: An Examination of this Human Problem* (HLRS, 1958); Charles Berg and Clifford Allen, The *Problem of Homosexuality* (Citadel, 1958). Historically-oriented reformist fiction and film of this period included Mary Renault, *The Charioteer* (Longmans, Green and Co 1953) and the two biopics about Oscar Wilde of 1960: *Oscar Wilde* (dir. Gregory Ratoff, 1960) and *The Trials of Oscar Wilde* (dir. Ken Hughes, 1960). Other work set in the present of the 1950s and 1960s used history and an investment in tradition as a way of legitimizing respectable middle class homosexual characters. See, for example, Rodney Garland, *The Heart in Exile* (1953; Milliveres, 1995) and the film *Victim* (dir. Basil Dearden,

1961). For discussion see Richard Hornsey, *The Spiv and the Architect: Unruly Life in Postwar London* (University of Minnesota Press, 2010).

10 See: Chris Waters, 'Havelock Ellis, Sigmund Freud and the State: Discourses of Homosexual Identity in Interwar Britain', in *Sexology in Culture: Labelling Bodies and Desires,* eds Lucy Bland and Laura L. Doan (Polity, 1998), 165–79.

11 Alfred Kinsey, *Sexual Behavior in the Human Male* (W. B. Saunders, 1948); Alfred Kinsey, *Sexual Behavior in the Human Female* (W. B. Saunders, 1953).

12 Herbert Marcuse, *Eros and Civilization: A Philosophical Inquiry Into Freud* (Beacon Press, 1955). See also Wilhelm Reich, *The Function of the Orgasm: Sex-Economic Problems of Biological Energy*, trans. Theodore Wolfe (Orgone Institute, 1942).

13 Jeffrey Weeks, *Sex, Politics and Society: The Regulations of Sexuality since 1800* (1981; Longman, 2012), 274. On the troublesome concept of sexual revolution see essays in Gert Hekma and Alain Giami, eds, *Sexual Revolutions* (Palgrave Macmillan, 2014).

14 Phyllis Grosskurth, *John Addington Symonds: A Biography* (Longmans, Green and Co, 1964); Brian Reade, ed., *Sexual Heretics: Male Homosexuality in English Literature from 1850 to 1900* (Routledge & Kegan Paul, 1970); T. A. Smith, *Love in Earnest: Some Notes on the Lives and Writings of English 'Uranian' poets from 1889 to 1930* (Routledge & Kegan Paul, 1970).

15 H. Montgomery Hyde, *The Other Love* (Heinemann, 1970); Hyde, *The Trials of Oscar Wilde* (Dover, 1973); Hyde, *The Cleveland Street Scandal* (W. H. Allen, 1976).

16 Hyde, *The Other Love*, 37–44. For a more direct argument in this respect see Ricard Davenport-Hines, *Sex, Death and Punishment: Attitudes to Sex and Sexuality in Britain since the Renaissance* (Collins, 1990).

17 Jeannette Foster, *Sex Variant Women in Literature: A Historical and Quantitative Study* (1952; Naiad Press, 1985); Henry Wharton, *Sappho: Memoir, Text, Selected Renderings and a Literal Translation* (David Scott, 1885). For discussion of the impact this translation had on elite women readers of the late nineteenth and twentieth centuries see Heike Bauer, 'Literature and Biography as Sources for LGBTQ Lived Experience', in *The Oxford Handbook of LGBTQ History,* eds Dominic Janes and Howard Chiang (Oxford University Press, 2026).

18 Walter Braun, *Lesbian Love Old and New: The History of the Other Love and its Ramifications Today* (Luxor Press, 1967). With thanks to Alison Oram.

19 Alison Oram, 'Lesbian History', in *Companion to Women's Historical Writing*, eds Mary Spongberg, Barbara Caine and Ann Curthoys (Palgrave

Macmillan, 2005), 304–15; Elizabeth Mavor, *The Ladies of Llangollen: A Study in Romantic Friendship* (Viking, 1971); Mavor, *Life with the Ladies of Llangollen* (Viking, 1984); Nigel Nicolson, *Portrait of Marriage: Vita Sackville-West and Harold Nicolson* (Weidenfeld and Nicolson, 1973).

20   On this see Sophia Rosenfeld, *Common Sense; A Political History* (Harvard University Press, 2011).

21   A. L. Rowse, *Homosexuals in History: A Study of Ambivalence in Society, Literature and the Arts* (Weidenfeld and Nicolson, 1977); Jeffrey Weeks, *Coming Out: Homosexual Politics in Britain from the Nineteenth Century to the Present* (Quartet Books, 1977).

22   Lucy Robinson, 'Three Revolutionary Years: The Impact of the Counter Culture on the Development of the Gay Liberation Movement in Britain', *Cultural and Social History* 3, no. 4 (2006), 445–71, at 445.

23   On these contexts see Weeks, Sex, Politics and Society, chapters 13 and 14; Hekma and Giami, *Sexual Revolutions*.

24   Mary McIntosh, 'The Homosexual Role', *Social Problems* 16, no. 2 (1968), 182–92.

25   McIntosh, 'The Homosexual Role', 182.

26   John H. Gagnon and William Simon, *Sexual Conduct: The Social Sources of Human Sexuality* (Routledge, 1973). For an account of these shifts and those that followed see Joseph Bristow, 'Remapping the Sites of Modern Gay History: Legal Reform, Medico-Legal Thought, Homosexual Scandal, Erotic Geography', *Journal of British Studies* 46, no. 1 (2007), 116–42; and Jeffrey Weeks, *Sexuality and its Discontents: Meanings, Myths, and Modern Sexualities* (Taylor & Francis, 2022).

27   *Gay Liberation Front Manifesto* (London: 1971), Bishopsgate Institute Archive https://www.bishopsgate.org.uk/gay-liberation-front-manifesto (accessed 13 October 2024).

28   See Marc Stein, *Queer Public History: Essays on Scholarly Activism* (University of California Press, 2022), introduction.

29   Jeffrey Weeks, 'Queer(y)Ing the "Modern Homosexual"', *Journal of British Studies* 51, no. 3 (2012), 523–39, at 528.

30   'Editorial', *History Workshop Journal* 1 (1976), 1–3, at 1. See also Matt Cook and Marybeth Hamilton, 'Virtual Special Issue: History of Sexualities', *History Workshop Journal* (2019), https://www.historyworkshop.org.uk/virtual-special-issue-history-of-sexualities/ (accessed 14 December 2024).

31   See Charles Tilly, *As Sociology Meets History* (Academic Press, 1981). On the origins of oral history and its relationship to social history see Paul Thompson, *The Voice of the Past: Oral History* (Oxford University Press, 2017).

32   On 'thick description' and its first use in this sense see Clifford Geertz, *The Interpretation of Cultures* (Basic Books, 1973). The classic work of microhistory remains Carlo Ginzburg, *The Cheese and the Worms: The Cosmos of a Sixteenth-Century Miller* (Johns Hopkins University Press, 1976). See also Carlo Ginzburg, 'Microhistory: Two or Three Things That I Know about It', *Critical Inquiry* 20, no. 1 (1993), 10–35, at 33; Jill Lepore, 'Historians Who Love Too Much: Reflections on Microhistory and Biography', *The Journal of American History* 88, no. 1 (2001), 129–44.

33   Katz, *Gay American History*, 6.

34   Jonathan Katz, *The Invention of Heterosexuality* (1995; University of Chicago Press, 2007). See also Lynne Segal, *Slow Motion: Changing Masculinities, Changing Men* (Virago, 1997); Hanne Blank, *Straight: The Surprisingly Short History of Heterosexuality* (Beacon Press, 2012).

35   See John D'Emilio, 'Capitalism and Gay Identity', in *Powers of Desire: The Politics of Sexuality*, eds Ann Snitow, Christine Stansell and Sharon Thompson (Monthly Review Press, 1983), 100–14; D'Emilio, *Sexual Politics, Sexual Communities*. D'Emilio provided a queer twist on Friedrich Engels, *The Origin of the Family, Private Property and the State* (1884; C. H. Kerr, 1902). For more recent interventions on this theme see Amy Gluckman and Betsy Reed, eds, *Homo Economics: Capitalism, Community, and Lesbian and Gay Life* (Routledge, 2012); Christopher Chitty, *Sexual Hegemony: Statecraft, Sodomy, and Capital in the Rise of the World System* (Duke University Press, 2020).

36   Cohen, 'Punks, Bulldaggers and Welfare Queens', esp. 441.

37   See Jonathan Katz Ned, *Resistance at Christiana: The Fugitive Slave Rebellion, Christiana Pennsylvania, 1851* (Crowell, 1974); John D'Emilio, *The Civil Rights Struggle: Leaders in Profile* (Facts on File, 1979).

38   Weeks, *Coming Out*; Weeks, *Sex, Politics and Society*; Sheila Rowbotham, *Socialism and the New Life: The Personal and Sexual Politics of Edward Carpenter and Havelock Ellis* (Pluto Press, 1977). Rowbotham later published a magisterial full-length biography of Carpenter, Sheila Rowbotham, *Edward Carpenter: A Life of Liberty and Love* (Verso, 2008). On the enduring significance of person-centred social history see Jim Downs, '"Like People in History": why social history matters for the LGBTQ+ community', in *Reckoning with History: Unfinished Stories of American Freedom*, eds Jim Downs, Erica Armstrong Dunbar, Thomas Kenneth Hunter and Timothy Patrick McCarthy (Columbia University Press, 2021), 18–45.

39   Carroll Smith-Rosenberg, 'The Female World of Love and Ritual: Relations between Women in Nineteenth Century America', *Signs* 1, no. 1 (1975), 1–29.

40   Adrienne Rich, 'Compulsory Heterosexuality and Lesbian Existence', *Signs* 5, no. 4 (1980), 631–60.

41   Faderman, *Surpassing the Love of Men*.

42   Jeffrey Weeks, *What is Sexual History* (Polity, 2016), 93. Weeks was referring specifically to Alan Bray, *The Friend* (University of Chicago Press, 2003), but see also Sharon Marcus, *Between Women: Friendship, Desire, and Marriage in Victorian England* (Princeton University Press, 2007).

43   Faderman, *Surpassing the Love of Men*, 19.

44   Lillian Faderman, 'The Morbidification of Love Between Women by 19th-Century Sexologists', *Journal of Homosexuality* 4, no. 1 (1978), 73–90. On the growing popular traction of sexology see Waters, 'Havelock Ellis, Sigmund Freud and the State'.

45   Judith Bennett, 'Lesbian-like and the Social History of Lesbianisms', *Journal of the History of Sexuality* 9, no. 1/2 (2000), 1–24.

46   See Martha Vicinus, 'Distance and Desire: English Boarding-School Friendships', *Signs* 9, no. 4 (1984), 600–22; Vicinus '"They Wonder to Which Sex I Belong": The Historical Roots of the Modern Lesbian Identity', *Feminist studies* 18, no. 3 (1992), 467–97; Vicinus, *Intimate Friends: Women who Loved Women 1798-1928* (Chicago University Press, 2006).

47   Vicinus, 'History of Lesbian History'; Annamarie Jagose, 'Way Out: The Category "Lesbian" and the Fantasy of the Utopic Space', *Journal of the History of Sexuality* 4, no. 2 (1993), 264–87.

48   See Chapter 2, section 3.

49   Rosemary Auchmuty, Sheila Jeffreys, and Elaine Miller, 'Lesbian History and Gay Studies: Keeping a Feminist Perspective', *Women's History Review* 1, no. 1 (1992), 89–108.

50   A pioneering lesbian history course was, for example, taught by Alison Oram and Annabel Faraday for University of London's extra-mural department from 1985.

51   Donna Penn, 'Queer: Theorizing Politics and History', *Radical History Review* 62 (1995), 24–42, at 24.

52   Vicinus, 'Distance and Desire'; Annabel Faraday, 'Lessoning Lesbians: Girls' Schools, Co-education and Anti-Lesbianism between the Wars', in *Learning our Lines: Sexuality and Social Control in Education*, eds Carol Jones and Pat Mahony (Women's Press, 1989), 23–45; Elizabeth Lapovsky Kennedy and Madeline Davis, *Boots of Leather, Slippers of Gold: The History of a Lesbian Community* (Routledge, 1993). See also Alison Oram, '"Embittered, Sexless or Homosexual": Attacks on Spinster Teachers', in *Not a Passing Phase,* ed. Lesbian History Group (Women's Press, 1989), 99–118.

53   Elizabeth Lapovsky Kennedy, 'Telling Tales: Oral History and the Construction of Pre-Stonewall Lesbian History', *Radical History Review* 62 (1995), 59–79.

54   Kennedy, 'Telling Tales'.

55   Jack Halberstam, 'Transgender Butch: Butch/FTM Border Wars and the Masculine Continuum', *GLQ: A Journal of Lesbian and Gay Studies* 4, no. 2 (1998), 287–310; Hannah Rossiter, 'She's Always a Woman: Butch Lesbian Trans Women in the Lesbian Community', *Journal of Lesbian Studies* 20, no. 1 (2016), 87–96.

56   Kennedy and Davis, *Boots of Leather, Slippers of Gold*. Other pioneering lesbian and gay oral history work includes: Esther Newton, *Cherry Grove, Fire Island: Sixty Years in America's First Gay and Lesbian Town* (Beacon Press, 1993); Allan Bérubé, *Coming Out Under Fire: The History of Gay Men and Women in World War II* (Free Press, 1990); Brighton Ourstory Project, *Daring Hearts: Lesbian and Gay Lives of 50s and 60s Brighton* (QueenSpark, 1992).

57   Sheila Rowbotham, *Hidden from History: 300 years of Women's Oppression and the Fight Against It* (Pluto Press, 1973); Martin Duberman, George Chauncey, and Martha Vicinus, *Hidden from History: Reclaiming the Gay and Lesbian Past* (Meridian Books, 1990).

58   Lisa Duggan, 'The Discipline Problem: Queer Theory Meets Lesbian and Gay History', *GLQ: A Journal of Lesbian and Gay Studies* 2, no. 3 (1 June 1995), 179–91, at 183. See also Jeffrey Escoffier, 'Inside the Ivory Closet: The Challenges Facing Lesbian and Gay Studies', *Out/Look: National Lesbian and Gay Quarterly* 10 (1990), 40–8, at 44.

59   Duggan, 'The Discipline Problem'.

60   Katz, *Gay American History*, 8.

61   Jonathan Ned Katz, *The Invention of Heterosexuality* (1995; University of Chicago Press, 2007), viii–ix; Katz, *Gay American History*, Introduction; Joan Nestle, *A Fragile Union* (Cleis Press, 1998).

62   K. J. Dover, *Greek Homosexuality* (1978; Bloomsbury, 2016); James Davidson, *The Greeks and Greek Love: A Radical Reappraisal of Homosexuality in Ancient Greece* (Phoenix, 2008), 150. For an analysis of Dover in relation to Foucault see James Davidson, 'Dover, Foucault, and Greek Homosexuality: Penetration and the Truth of Sex', *Past and Present* 170, no. 1 (2001), 3–51.

63   Alan Bray, 'Homosexuality and the Signs of Male Friendship in Elizabethan England', in *History Workshop Journal* 29 (1990), 1–19; Bray, *Homosexuality in Renaissance England* (Columbia University Press, 1995). For a more recent analysis see Will Tosh, *Straight Acting: The Many Queer Lives of William Shakespeare* (Sceptre, 2024).

64 On this point see Victoria Harris, 'Sex on the Margins: New Directions in the Historiography of Sexuality', *The Historical Journal* 53, no. 4 (2010), 1085–1104.

65 John Boswell, *Christianity, Social Tolerance, and Homosexuality: Gay People in Western Europe from the Beginning of the Christian Era to the Fourteenth Century* (University of Chicago Press, 1980). On some of those other contexts see Bret Hinsch, *Passions of the Cut Sleeve: The Male Homosexual Tradition in China* (University of California Press, 1990); Michael Rocke, *Forbidden Friendships: Homosexuality and Male Culture in Renaissance Florence* (Oxford University Press, 1996); David M. Halperin and John J. Winkler, *Before Sexuality: The Construction of Erotic Experience in the Ancient Greek World* (Princeton University Press, 1990).

66 Ralph Hexter, 'John Boswell, 1945–1994', *Radical History Review* 62 (1995), 259–61.

67 John Boswell, 'Categories, Experience and Sexuality', in *Forms of Desire: Sexual Orientation and the Social Constructionist Controversy*, ed. Edward Stein (Routledge, 1992), 133–73, at 136–7.

68 On the essentialist/social constructionist debate see especially Stein, ed., *Forms of Desire*.

69 Boswell, 'Categories', 135.

70 The pivotal piece in history's 'turn' was Gareth Stedman Jones, 'Rethinking Chartism' in his *Languages of Class: Studies in English Working Class History, 1832–1982* (Cambridge University Press, 1983), 90–178. See also Roger Chartier, 'Text, Symbols, and Frenchness', *The Journal of Modern History* 57, no. 4 (1985), 682–95; Alun Munslow, *Discourse and Culture: The Creation of America, 1870-1920* (Routledge, 1992). There was a heated debate about the linguistic turn in successive issues of the *Journal of Social History* (1991–6, vols 16–21).

71 For an account see Tilottama Rajan, *Deconstruction and the Remainders of Phenomenology: Sartre, Derrida, Foucault, Baudrillard* (Stanford University Press, 2002).

72 Rick Dolphijn, 'An Apprenticeship in Resistance May '68 and the Power of Vincennes (Universite de Paris VIII)', *New Horizons in Education* 55, no. 3 (2007), 22–33.

73 Foucault took particular aim at Ronald Pearsall, *The Worm in the Bud: The World of Victorian Sexuality* (Penguin, 1971).

74 Michel Foucault, *History of Sexuality Volume 1: An Introduction*, trans. Robert Hurley (Allen Lane, 1979), 17.

75 See David Halperin, *How to Do the History of Homosexuality* (University of Chicago Press, 2004), especially chapter 1.

76   For an account in broader perspective see Faramerz Dabhoiwala, *The Origins of Sex: A History of the First Sexual Revolution* (Oxford University Press, 2012).

77   David M. Halperin, *Saint Foucault: Towards a Gay Hagiography* (Oxford University Press, 1997), 95.

78   Laura Doan, *Disturbing Practices: History, Sexuality and Women's Experience of Modern* War (Chicago University Press, 2013), 140.

79   On this sense of genealogy see Halperin, 'Introduction: In Defense of Historicism', in *How to Do the History of Homosexuality,* 1–23.

80   See Mark Haugaard, 'Foucault and Power: A critique and retheorization', *Critical Review* 34, no. 3/4 (2022): 341–1; Stephen Legg, 'Beyond the European Province: Foucault and Postcolonialism', in *Space, Knowledge and Power: Foucault and Geography,* eds Jeremy Crampton and Stuart Elden (Routledge, 2016), 265–89; Carolyn J. Dean, 'The Productive Hypothesis: Foucault, Gender, and the History of Sexuality', *History and Theory* (1994): 271–96; Jeffrey Weeks, 'Remembering Foucault', *Journal of the History of Sexuality* 14, no. 1/2 (2005): 186–201.

81   On these points see Dean, 'The Productive Hypothesis'; Didier Eribon and Michael Lucey, 'Michel Foucault's Histories of Sexuality', *GLQ: A Journal of Lesbian and Gay Studies* 7, no. 1 (2001), 31–86; Harris, 'Sex on the Margins', 1103.

82   Foucault, 'Sex, Power, and the Politics of Identity', in *Ethics: Subjectivity and Truth: Essential Works of Foucault, 1954–1984,* ed. Paul Rabinow, trans. Robert Hurley (Penguin Classics, 2020), 163–74. For more on this tension theoretically and in the archive see Jason Glynos, 'Sex and the limits of discourse', in *Discourse Theory and Political Analysis: Identities, Hegemonies and Social Change,* eds David Howarth, Aletta J. Norval, and Yannis Stavrakakis (Manchester University Press, 2000): 205–18; Zeb Tortorici, 'Visceral Archives of the Body: Consuming the Dead, Digesting the Divine". *GLQ: A Journal of Lesbian and Gay Studies* 20, no. 4 (2014): 407–37. Tortorici's article appears in a special issue 'On the Visceral' and the place of the body in queer studies and history.

83   From this period, see, for example, Rowbotham, *Hidden from History*; Ann Ferguson, 'Patriarchy, Sexual Identity, and the Sexual Revolution,' *Signs: Journal of Women in Culture and Society* 7, no. 1 (1981): 158–72; Judith R. Walkowitz, *Prostitution and Victorian Society: Women, class, and the state* (Cambridge University Press, 1982); and Sheila Jeffreys, *The Sexuality Debates* (Routledge, 1987). Particularly influential feminist texts on sexual politics from the same period include: Andrea Dworkin, *Woman Hating: A Radical Look at Sexuality* (E.P. Dutton, 1974); Catharine MacKinnon, *Feminism Unmodified: Discourses on Life and Law* (Harvard University

Press, 1988). For an overview see Alice Echols, *Daring to Be Bad: Radical Feminism in America, 1967–1975* (University of Minnesota Press, 1989); Dorothy Sue Cobble, Linda Gordon and Astrid Henry, *Feminism Unfinished: A Short, Surprising History of American Women's Movements* (Liveright Publishing Corporation, 2014).

84 Elizabeth Wilson, 'The Context of "Between Pleasure and Danger": The Barnard Conference on Sexuality', *Feminist Review* 13, no. 1 (1983), 35–41; Rachel Corbman, 'The Scholars and the Feminists: The Barnard Sex Conference and the History of the Institutionalization of Feminism', *Feminist Formations* 27, no. 3 (2015), 49–80.

85 Gayle S. Rubin, 'Thinking Sex: Notes for a Radical Theory of the Politics of Sexuality', in *Culture, Society and Sexuality*, eds Peter Aggleton and Richard Parker (Taylor & Francis, 1999), 143–78; Rubin, 'Blood Under the Bridge: Reflections on "Thinking Sex"', *GLQ: A Journal of Lesbian and Gay Studies* 17, no. 1 (2011), 15–48. On Rubin and Sedgwick and these overlaps and distinctions, see Simon Joyce, *LGBTQ+ Victorians: Sexuality and Gender in the Nineteenth-Century Archives* (Oxford University Press, 2022).

86 On this see Gayle Rubin with Judith Butler, 'Sexual Traffic: Interview', in *Feminism Meets Queer Theory*, eds Elizabeth Weed and Naomi Schor (Indiana University Press, 1997), 68–108, at 100–1; for discussion of Butler and gender theory see chapter 2, section 3.

87 On these issues see also Scott De Orio, 'The Invention of Bad Gay Sex: Texas and the Creation of a Criminal Underclass of Gay People', *Journal of the History of Sexuality* 26, no. 1 (2017); 53–87.

88 For an especially incisive account of Rubin's argument see Kunzel, 'The Power of Queer History', at 1561.

89 Matt Cook, *Queer Domesticities: Homosexuality and Home Life in Twentieth Century London* (Palgrave Macmillan, 2014), 29–54.

90 Rachel Hope Cleves, 'A "Queer Collection": The Anglo Colony in Florence, 1840s–1950s', in *Locating Queer Histories: Places and Traces across the UK*, eds Justin Bengry, Matt Cook and Alison Oram (Bloomsbury, 2023), 159–77.

91 On this point and on what an identitarian lens might occlude, see Cathy Cohen, 'Punks, Bulldaggers and Welfare Queens: The Radical Potential of Queer Politics', *GLQ: A Journal of Lesbian Gay Studies*, 3, no. 4 (1997), 437–65, at 454; Cohen, 'The Radical Potential of Queer? Twenty Years Later', *GLQ: A Journal of Lesbian Gay Studies* 25, no. 1 (2019): 140–4.

92 Sharon Marcus, 'Queer Theory for Everyone: A Review Essay', *Signs* 31, no. 1 (2005), 191–218, at 205.

93 See Seth Koven, *Slumming: Sexual and Social Politics in Victorian London* (Princeton University Press, 2004).

94   On this point see Morris B. Kaplan, 'Who's Afraid of John Saul? Urban Culture and the Politics of Desire in Late Victorian London', *GLQ: A Journal of Lesbian and Gay Studies* 5, no. 3 (1999), 267–314; Koven, *Slumming*; Jo Brydon, 'Percy Grainger and Trans Identity in Edwardian London' (PhD diss., Birkbeck, University of London, March 2025).

95   Eve Kosofsky Sedgwick, *Between Men: English Literature and Male Homosocial Desire* (1984; Columbia University Press, 2015); Sedgwick, *Epistemology of the Closet* (Harvester Wheatsheaf, 1991); Sedgwick, *Tendencies* (Routledge, 1994).

96   Sedgwick, *Between Men*, 89.

97   See Michael Warner, *The Trouble with Normal: Sex, Politics and the Ethics of Queer Life* (Free Press, 1999).

98   Lynn Hunt, 'Introduction: History, Culture, and Text', in *The New Cultural History*, ed. Lynn Hunt (University of California Press, 1989), 1–22, at 22.

99   Elaine Showalter, *Sexual Anarchy: Gender and Culture at the Fin de Siècle* (Viking, 1990).

100 Alan Sinfield, *Faultlines: Cultural Materialism and the Politics of Dissident Reading* (University of California Press, 1992); Sinfield, *The Wilde Century: Effeminacy, Oscar Wilde and the Queer Moment* (Cassell, 1994); Sinfield, *Shakespeare, Authority, Sexuality: Unfinished Business in Cultural Materialism* (Routledge: 2006)

101 Terry Castle, *The Apparitional Lesbian: Female Homosexuality and Modern Culture* (Columbia University Press, 1993). See also Deborah T. Meem, 'Eliza Lynn Linton and the Rise of Lesbian Consciousness', *Journal of the History of Sexuality* 7, no. 4 (1997), 537–60. For similar uses of literature in the early 1990s, see Arthur Flannigan-Saint-Aubin, '"Black Gay Male" Discourse: Reading Race and Sexuality between the Lines', *Journal of the History of Sexuality* 3, no. 3 (1993), 468–90; Joseph Bristow, ed., *Sexual Sameness: Textual Difference in Lesbian and Gay Writing* (Routledge, 1992); Jonathan Dollimore, *Sexual Dissidence: Augustine to Wilde, Freud to Foucault* (Clarendon, 1991). On ideas of queer haunting see also Carla Freccero, 'Queer Spectrality: Haunting the Past' in *The Spectralities Reader: Ghosts and Haunting in Contemporary Cultural Theory*, eds Maria Blanco del Pilar María and Esther Peeren (Bloomsbury 2013), 335–59.

102 On this point, see Harry Cocks, *Nameless Offences: Homosexual Desire in the Nineteenth Century* (I.B. Tauris, 2003); Dominic Janes, *Picturing the Closet: Male Secrecy and Homosexual Visibility in Britain* (Oxford University Press, 2015).

103 Valerie Traub, 'The New Unhistoricism in Queer Studies', *PMLA* 128, no. 1 (2013), 21–39, at 30.

104 Duggan, 'The Discipline Problem', 189.

105 Rubin and Butler, 'Sexual Traffic', 100–1.

106 On this point in relation to gender see Laura Lee Downs, *Writing Gender History* (Bloomsbury Academic, 2010), 76.

107 Duggan, 'The Discipline Problem', 180.

108 Duggan, 'The Discipline Problem'.

109 For a sense of this breadth, and in addition to the *Journal of the History of Sexuality*, see H.G. Cocks and Matt Houlbrook, eds, *The Modern History of Sexuality* (Palgrave Macmillan, 2006); Weeks, *What Is Sexual History?*

110 Cocks and Houlbrook, 'Introduction', in *Modern History of Sexuality*, eds Cocks and Houlbrook, 1–18, at 3.

111 Annamarie Jagose, *Queer Theory* (Melbourne University Press, 1997), 131–2.

112 Helen Smith, *Masculinity, Class and Same-Sex Desire in Industrial England, 1895–1957* (Palgrave Macmillan, 2015); Matt Houlbrook, *Queer London: Perils and Pleasures in the Sexual Metropolis, 1918–1957* (University of Chicago Press, 2005); Houlbrook, 'Soldier Heroes and Rent Boys: Homosex, Masculinities, and Britishness in the Brigade of Guards, circa 1900–1960', *Journal of British Studies* 42, no. 3 (2003), 351–88.

113 Harris, 'Sex on the Margins', 1103.

114 Including, most recently, Jan-Henrik Friedrichs, 'Transnational Networks of Child Sexual Abuse and Consumerism: Edward Brongersma and the Pedophilia Debate of the 1970s and 1980s', *Journal of the History of Sexuality* 31, no. 2 (2022), 169–91; Will Jones, 'So Then . . . He Raped Me': Male Experiences of Sexual(ized) Violence in the Nazi Concentration Camps, (DPhil diss., Oxford University, 2024); Regina Kunzel, *Criminal Intimacy: Prison and the Uneven History of Modern American Sexuality* (University of Chicago Press, 2022). On the broader point see Harris, 'Sex on the Margins', 1103.

115 See, for example, Justin Bengry, 'Courting the Pink Pound: Men Only and the Queer Consumer 1935-9', *History Workshop Journal* 68, no. 1 (2009), 122–48; Amy Gluckman, and Betsy Reed, 'The Gay Marketing Moment', in *Homo Economics*, eds Gluckman and Reed, 3–10; Chitty, *Sexual Hegemony*.

116 Jagose, 'Way Out'.

117 Martha Robinson Rhodes, 'Bisexuality, Multiple-Gender-Attraction, and Gay Liberation Politics in the 1970s', *Twentieth Century British History* 32, no. 1 (2021), 119–42.

118 On bisexuality, see Steven Angelides, *A History of Bisexuality* (University of Chicago Press, 2001); Lachlan MacDowall, 'Historicising Contemporary Bisexuality', *Journal of Bisexuality* 9, no. 1 (2009), 3–15; J. Taylor, 'Out of the Darkness and into the Shadows: The Evolution of Contemporary Bisexuality', *The Canadian Journal of Human Sexuality* 27, no. 2 (2018) 103–9; Julia Shaw, *Bi: The Hidden Culture, History, and Science of*

Bisexuality (Canongate, 2022). On trans history, see Susan Stryker, *Transgender History: The Roots of Today's Revolution,* 2nd ed. (Seal Press, 2017); Kit Heyam, *Before We Were Trans: A New History of Gender* (Basic Books, 2022); C. Riley Snorton, *Black on Both Sides: A Racial History of Trans Identity* (University of Minnesota Press, 2017).

119 Duggan, 'The Discipline Problem', 179.

120 Cook, *Queer Domesticities.*

121 Matt Cook, 'Sex Lives and Diary Writing: The Journals of George Ives', in *Life Writing and Victorian Culture,* ed. David Amigoni (Ashgate, 2006), 195–214.

Chapter 2: Identifications and Intersections

1 Martha Umphrey, 'The Trouble with Harry Thaw', *Radical History Review* 62 (1995), 9–23, at 20. For further discussion see Matt Cook, 'Squatting in History: queer pasts and the cultural turn', in *Social Research After the Cultural Turn,* eds Sasha Roseneil and Stephen Frosh (Palgrave, 2012).

2 Umphrey, 'The Trouble with Harry Thaw', 22.

3 See Michelle Alexander, *The New Jim Crow: Mass Incarceration in the Age of Colorblindness* (The New Press, 2010); Susan Olzak, Suzanne Shanahan and Elizabeth H. McEneaney, 'Poverty, Segregation, and Race Riots: 1960 to 1993', *American Sociological Review* (1996): 590–613.

4 On these points, see especially John Solomos, *Race and Racism in Britain,* 4th edn (Palgrave MacMillan, 2022), chapters 1, 5, 6 and 7.

5 Neil J. Young, *Coming Out Republican: A History of the Gay Right* (University of Chicago Press, 2024), 98–126; Michael Bronski, *A Queer History of the United States* (Beacon Press, 2011), chapter 10. On Section 28 of the Local Government Act (1988) see Paul Baker, *Outragious: The Story of Section 28 and Britain's Battle for LGBT Education* (Reaktion, 2022).

6 See Elizabeth Fee and Daniel Fox, eds, *AIDS and the Burdens of History* (University of California Press, 1988), introduction; Sarah Schulman, *Let the Record Show: A Political History of ACT UP New York, 1987–1993* (Farrar, Straus and Giroux, 2021); George Severs, *Radical ACTS: HIV/ AIDS Activism in the Late Twentieth Century* (Bloomsbury, 2024).

7 Paula A. Treichler, 'AIDS, Homophobia and Biomedical Discourse: An Epidemic of Signification', *Cultural Studies* 1, no. 3 (1987), 263–305.

8 See Cathy Cohen, *The Boundaries of Blackness: AIDS and the Breakdown of Black Politics* (University of Chicago Press, 1999); Kevin Mumford, *Not Straight, Not White: Black Gay Men from the March on Washington to the*

AIDS Crisis (University of North Carolina Press, 2016); Horacio N. Roque Ramírez, 'Gay Latino Histories/Dying to be Remembered: AIDS Obituaries, Public Memory, and the Queer Latino Archive', in *Beyond El Barrio: Everyday Life in Latina/o America*, eds Gina M. Pérez, Frank Guridy and Adrian Burgos (New York University Press, 2010), 103–28; Schulman, *Let the Record Show*. With thanks to Mori Reithmayr.

9   Laura Doan, *Disturbing Practices: History, Sexuality, and Women's Experience of Modern War* (University of Chicago Press, 2013), 129.

10 See, for example, Barbara Smith, 'Toward a Black Feminist Criticism', *The Radical Teacher* 7 (1978), 20–7; Angela Davis, *Women, Race and Class* (Random House, 1981); bell hooks, *ain't i a woman? black women and feminism* (South End Press, 1981); Gloria T. Hull, Patricia Bell Scott, and Barbara Smith, eds, *All the Women Are White, All the Blacks Are Men, But Some of Us Are Brave* (Feminist Press, 1982); Cherríe Moraga and Gloria E. Anzaldúa, eds, *This Bridge Called My Back: Writings by Radical Women of Color*, 2nd edn (1981; Kitchen Table: Women of Color Press, 1983).

11 *The Combahee River Collective Statement*, April 1977, https://americanstudies.yale.edu/sites/default/files/files/Keyword%20Coalition_Readings.pdf (accessed 10 January 2025). For discussion and analysis see Keeanga-Yamahtta Taylor, ed., *How We Get Free: Black Feminism and the Combahee River Collective* (Haymarket Books, 2017).

12 See Kimberlé Crenshaw, 'Demarginalizing the Intersection of Race and Sex: A Black Feminist Critique of Antidiscrimination Doctrine, Feminist Theory and Antiracist Politics', *University of Chicago Legal Forum* 1 (1989), 139–67; and Crenshaw, 'Mapping the Margins: Intersectionality, Identity Politics, and Violence against Women of Color', *Stanford Law Review* 43, no. 6 (1991), 1241–99. For an astute deployment of Crenshaw's theorization see Rahul Rao, *Out of Time: The Queer Politics of Postcoloniality* (Oxford University Press, 2020), 24–5; for an influential reconsideration, see Jennifer C. Nash, *Black Feminism Reimagined: After Intersectionality* (Duke University Press, 2018). With thanks to Mori Reithmayr.

13 *Combahee River Collective Statement*.

14 Robert Reid-Pharr, *Black Gay Man: Essays* (New York University Press, 2001), 137.

15 Reid-Pharr, *Black Gay Man*, 102–3. See also Reid-Pharr, 'Extending Queer Theory to Race and Ethnicity', *The Chronicle of Higher Education* 48, no. 7 (2002), 7–9.

16 Cathy Cohen, 'Punks, Bulldaggers and Welfare Queens'; Scott Bravmann, *Queer Fictions of the Past: History, Culture, and Difference* (Cambridge University Press, 1997); see also Robyn Wiegman, 'The Anatomy of Lynching', *Journal of the History of Sexuality* 3, no. 3 (1993), 445–67.

17 Cohen, 'Punks, Bulldaggers and Welfare Queens', 440.

18   Bravmann, *Queer Fictions of the Past,* 127.

19   For more recent interventions, see especially: Rao, *Out of Time*; Cathy
      Cohen; 'The Radical Potential of Queer? Twenty years later', *GLQ: A
      Journal of Lesbian and Gay Studies* 25, no. 1 (2019): 140–4; and three
      recent deeply intersectional doctoral theses: Mori Reithmayr, 'Community
      before Liberation: Theorizing Gay Resistance in San Francisco, 1953-1969'
      (PhD diss., Oxford University, 2022), esp. 55–63; Ben Miller, 'In Search of
      Lost Time: Primitivist Homomythopoetics and the Self-Invention of the
      White Gay Man' (PhD diss., Freie Universität Berlin, 2024); Khalil R. West,
      'Dark Matter: Sociality, Space, and the Haptics of Queer (Il)legibility in
      'Black Liverpool', 1967–1997' (PhD diss., European University Institute,
      2025).

20   See Jonathan Dollimore, *Sexual Dissidence: Augustine to Wilde, Freud to
      Foucault* (Clarendon, 1991); Alan Sinfield, *The Wilde Century: Effeminacy,
      Oscar Wilde and the Queer Moment* (Cassell, 1994). On the controversy
      surrounding the MA, see Alan Sinfield, 'Playing the System: The Sussex
      MA, and an Anxiety.' *The Radical Teacher*, no. 45 (1994): 20–2.

21   On this point see Victoria Harris, 'Sex on the Margins: New Directions in
      the Historiography of Sexuality', *The Historical Journal* 53, no. 4 (2010),
      1085–1104.

22   Michel de Certeau, 'Walking the City', in *The Practice of Everyday Life*
      (University of California Press, 1984), 91–110 at 108. See also Cook ,
      'Squatting in History'.

23   Alan Sinfield pursued a related argument in relation to literature. See
      Sinfield, *Faultlines: Cultural Materialism and the Politics of Dissident
      Reading* (University of California Press, 1992).

24   Ken Lustbader, 'LGBTQ Heritage', *Change Over Time* 8, no. 2 (2018),
      136–43.

25   David Wojnarowicz, *Close to the Knives: A Memoir of Disintergration*
      (Serpent's Tail, 1992); Samuel R. Delaney, *Triton* (Grafton, 1992); Samuel R.
      Delaney and Mia Wolff, *Bread and Wine: An Erotic Tale of New York*
      (Juno Publishing, 1999). For a discussion of Delaney in these respects
      see C. Riley Snorton, '"An Ambiguous Heterotopia": On the Past of Black
      Studies' Future', *The Black Scholar* 44, no. 2 (2014), 29–36.

26   Sigmund Freud, *The Pelican Freud Library, Vol. 6: Jokes and Their Relation
      to the Unconscious*, eds James Strachey and Angela Richerds (Penguin,
      1976).

27   On this point, see Christopher S. Nealon, *Foundlings: Lesbian and Gay
      Historical Emotion before Stonewall* (Duke University Press, 2001). See
      also Amy Tooth Murphy, 'The Butch on the Ferry: The Affect and Effect of
      Butch Longing', in *Queering Desire: Lesbians, Gender and Subjectivity*, eds
      Róisín Ryan-Flood and Amy Tooth Murphy (Routledge, 2024), 272–82.

28   Lyndal Roper's 1994 study of early modern witches and witchcraft in Germany was trailblazing in this (and other) respects. Lyndal Roper, *Oedipus and the Devil: Witchcraft, Sexuality, and Religion in Early Modern Europe* (Routledge, 1994). See also James Vernon, '"For Some Queer Reason": The Trials and Tribulations of Colonel Barker's Masquerade in Interwar Britain', *Signs: Journal of Women in Culture and Society* 26, no. 1 (2000): 37-62; Seth Koven, *Slumming: Sexual and Social Politics in Victorian London* (Princeton University Press, 2004); Deborah Cohen, *Family Secrets: Living with Shame from the Victorians to the Present Day* (Viking, 2013); Matt Houlbrook, *Prince of Tricksters: The Incredible True Story of Netley Lucas, Gentleman Crook* (University of Chicago Press, 2016); Mo Moulton, 'Dogs in the Picture: Restoring the Queer History of the Irish Family', *The History of the Family* 29, no. 1 (2024): 84–108; and Julia Laite, *The Disappearance of Lydia Harvey* (Profile Books, 2021).

29   Eve Kosofsky Sedgwick, 'White Glasses', *The Yale Journal of Criticism* 5, no. 3 (1993), 193–208.

30   Silvia Posocco, 'Cool, Queer White Glasses', *The Guardian*. 15 April 2009, https://www.theguardian.com/commentisfree/2009/apr/15/sexual-identity (accessed 22 January 2025).

31   J. Laplanche and J. B. Pontalis, *The Language of Psycho-Analysis* (W. W. Norton, 1973), 205.

32   Stuart Hall, 'Introduction: Who Needs "Identity"?', in *Questions of Cultural Identity*, eds Stuart Hall and Paul du Gay (SAGE Publications, 1996), 1–17, at 3.

33   On the concept of disidentification, see José Esteban Muñoz, *Disidentifications: Queers of Color and the Performance of Politics* (University of Minnesota Press, 1999).

34   Kathryn Bond Stockton, *Beautiful Bottom, Beautiful Shame: Where 'Black' Meets 'Queer'* (Duke University Press, 2006), 27; see also Anna Clark, 'Twilight Moments', *Journal of the History of Sexuality* 14, no. 1 (2005), 139–60.

35   On the concept of orientation, see Sara Ahmed, *Queer Phenomenology: Orientations, Objects, Others* (Duke University Press, 2006).

36   Bravmann, *Queer Fictions of the Past*, 127. For an especially effective rehearsal of these processes of self-making in a different context, see Simon Marginson 'Student Self-Formation in International Education', *Journal of Studies in International Education* 18, no. 1 (2014), 6–22.

37   Judith M. Bennett deployed 'lesbian-like' in a similar vein: Bennett, '"Lesbian-Like" and the Social History of Lesbianism', *Journal of the History of Sexuality* 9, no. 1/2, (2000), 1–24.

38   On these points see Susan Stryker, Paisley Currah, and Lisa Jean Moore, 'Introduction: Trans-, Trans, or Transgender?', *Women's Studies*

Quarterly 36, no. 3/4 (2008), 11–22; Regina Kunzel, 'The Power of Queer History', *The American Historical Review* 123, no. 5 (2018), 1560–82, at 1581; Laura Doan, *Disturbing Practices: History, Sexuality and Women's Experience of Modern War* (Chicago University Press, 2013), part 1.

39   H.G. Cocks and Matt Houlbrook, 'Introduction', in *The Modern History of Sexuality*, eds Cocks and Houlbrook (Palgrave Macmillan, 2006), 1–18, at 10.

40   Clark, 'Twilight Moments'; Anna Clark, *Desire: A History of European Sexuality* (Routledge, 2008), 7.

41   They are in this sense archival, as Ann Cvetkovich argues: Ann Cvetkovich, *An Archive of Feelings: Trauma, Sexuality and Lesbian and Gay Public Cultures* (Duke University Press, 2003).

42   Joanna Bourke, 'Fear and Anxiety: Writing about Emotion in Modern History', *History Workshop Journal* 55, no. 1 (1, March 2003) 111–33.

43   Queer studies has been at the forefront of the so-called 'affective turn'. See, for example, Cvetkovich, *An Archive of Feelings*, 242–4; David M. Halperin and Valerie Traub, eds, *Gay Shame* (University of Chicago Press, 2010); Sara Ahmed, *The Cultural Politics of Emotion* (Edinburgh University Press, 2004); Heather Love, *Feeling Backward: Loss and the Politics of Queer History* (Harvard University Press, 2007); Stockton, *Beautiful Bottom, Beautiful Shame*; Marika Cifor, 'Presence, Absence, and Victoria's Hair: Examining Affect and Embodiment in Trans Archives', *TSQ: Transgender Studies Quarterly* 2, no. 4 (2015), 645–9.

44   I elaborate these points in Matt Cook, '"Archives of Feeling": The AIDS Crisis in Britain 1987', *History Workshop Journal* 83, no. 1 (2017), 51–78.

45   Seth Koven, *Slumming: Sexual and Social Politics in Victorian London* (Princeton University Press, 2004), 3.

46   Rosenwein's 'emotional communities' signal collective ways of responding emotionally. Gender historian Benno Gammerl used the connected idea of 'emotional styles' to get to the ways in which the general emotional tenor of a group, place or time did not preclude individuals feeling differently, repositioning them in relation to the emotional mainstream. Barbara H. Rosenwein, 'Worrying about Emotions in History', *The American Historical Review* 107, no. 3 (2002), 821–45; Benno Gammerl, 'Emotional Styles – Concepts and Challenges', *Rethinking History* 16, no. 2 (2012), 161–75.

47   Xine Yao, *Disaffected: The Cultural Politics of Unfeeling in Nineteenth-Century America* (Duke University Press, 2021); Cvetkovich, *Archive of Feelings*.

48   Cook, 'Archives of Feeling'.

49   David M. Halperin and Valerie Traub, 'Beyond Gay Pride', in *Gay Shame*, eds Halperin and Traub, 3–40, at 11.

50 Heather Love, *Feeling Backward: Loss and the Politics of Queer History* (Harvard University Press, 2007), 4.

51 George Chauncey, 'The Trouble with Shame', in *Gay Shame*, eds Halperin and Traub, 277–82.

52 Janice Irvine, 'Transient Feelings: Sex Panics and the Politic of Emotions', in *Moral Panics: Fear and the Fight over Sexual Rights*, ed. Gilbert Herdt (New York University Press, 2009), 234–76.

53 Anjali Arondekar, *For the Record: On Sexuality and the Colonial Archive in India* (Duke University Press, 2009), 21.

54 Ajamu X, Topher Campbell, and Mary Stevens, 'Love and Lubrication in the Archives, or rukus!: A Black Queer Archive for the United Kingdom', *Archivaria* 68 (2010), 271–94, at 272.

55 For an overview of US Black queer history, see Jennifer D. Jones, 'Finding Home: Black Queer Historical Scholarship in the United States: Parts 1 and 2', *History Compass* 17, no. 5 (2019). See also Simon Fisher, 'Challenging Dissemblance in Pauli Murray Historiography: Sketching a History of the Trans New Negro', *The Journal of African American History* 104, no. 2 (2019), 176–200; E. Patrick Johnson, *Sweet Tea: Black Gay Men of the South* (University of North Carolina Press, 2008); Jennifer Jones, *Ambivalent Affinities : A Political History of Blackness and Homosexuality after World War II* (University of North Carolina Press, 2023); Kwame Holmes, 'What's the Tea: Gossip and the Production of Black Gay Social History', *Radical History Review* 122 (2015), 55–69; Kevin Mumford, *Not Straight, Not White: Black Gay Men from the March on Washington to the AIDS Crisis* (University of North Carolina Press, 2016); Kent W. Peacock, 'Race, the Homosexual, and the Mattachine Society of Washington, 1961–1970', *Journal of the History of Sexuality* 25, no. 2 (2016), 267–296; C. Riley Snorton, *Black on Both Sides: A Racial History of Trans Identity* (University of Minnesota Press, 2017).

56 On this point, see Arondekar, *For the Record*; Ronald Hyam, *Empire and Sexuality: The British Experience* (Manchester University Press, 1990); Durba Mitra, *Indian Sex Life* (Princeton University Press, 2000); Rao, *Out of Time*; Ann Laura Stoler, *Race and the Education of Desire: Foucault's History of Sexuality and the Colonial Order of Things* (Duke University Press, 1995).

57 On racialization as a historical process, see especially Michael Banton, 'Historical and Contemporary Modes of Racialization', in *Racialization: Studies in Theory and Practice*, eds Karim Murji and John Solomos (Oxford University Press, 2005); Shu-Mei Shih, 'Comparative Racialization: An Introduction', *Publications of the Modern Language Association of America (PMLA)* 123, no. 5 (2008), 1347–62; and Avtar

Brah, 'Difference, Diversity, Differentiation: Processes of Racialisation and Gender', in *Theories of Race and Racism*, eds Les Black and John Solomos (Routledge, 2009), 503–18.

58   See, for example, Caroline Bressey and Gemma Romain, 'Tracing Queer Black Spaces in Interwar Britain', in *Locating Queer History: Places and Traces across the UK*, eds Justin Bengry, Matt Cook, and Alison Oram (Bloomsbury, 2022), 101–18; Jason Okundaye, *Revolutionary Acts: Love and Brotherhood in Black Gay Britain* (Faber and Faber, 2024); West, 'Race, Pleasure and Ruin'. On the meeting of queer and postcolonial theory see John C. Hawley. *Postcolonial, Queer: Theoretical Intersections* (State University of New York, 2001).

59   On this, see Nwanda Achebe, 'The Day I "Met" Ahebi Ugbabe, Female King of Enugu-Ezike, Nigeria', *Journal of Women's History* 21, no. 4 (2009), 134–7.

60   Edward Said, *Orientalism: Western Conceptions of the Orient* (1978; Penguin, 1995); Homi K. Bhabha, *The Location of Culture* (Routledge, 1994); Paul Gilroy, *After Empire: Melancholia or Convivial Culture?* (Routledge, 2004); Hall and du Gay, *Questions of Cultural Identity*.

61   Paul Gilroy, *Postcolonial Melancholia* (Columbia University Press, 2005), xi.

62   See, for example, Matt Cook and Alison Oram, *Queer Beyond London* (Manchester University Press, 2022), 92.

63   Said, *Orientalism*. See also Joseph Allen Boone, *The Homoerotics of Orientalism* (Columbia University Press, 2014); Joseph Andoni Massad, *Desiring Arabs* (University of Chicago Press, 2007); Mrinalini Sinha, *Colonial Masculinity: The 'Manly Englishman' and the 'Effeminate Bengali' in the Late Nineteenth Century* (Manchester University Press, 1995); Amy Sueyoshi, *Discriminating Sex: White Leisure and the Making of the American "Oriental"* (University of Illinois Press, 2018).

64   Rudi Bleys, *The Geography of Perversion: Male-to-Male Sexual Behaviour Outside the West and the Ethnographic Imagination, 1750–1918* (New York University Press, 1995). See also Siobhan Somerville, 'Scientific Racism and the Emergence of the Homosexual Body', *Journal of the History of Sexuality* 5, no. 2 (1994), 243–66.

65   John Tosh, *A Man's Place: Masculinity and the Middle-Class Home in Victorian England* (Yale University Press, 1999); Hyam, *Empire and Sexuality*; Paul Deslandes, *Oxbridge Men: British Masculinity and the Undergraduate Experience* (Indiana University Press, 2005).

66   Matt Cook, *Queer Domesticities: Homosexuality and Home Life in Twentieth Century London* (Palgrave Macmillan, 2014), chapter 1.

67   On this point see Chris Bongie, *Exotic Memories: Literature, Colonialism, and the Fin de Siècle* (Stanford University Press, 1991); Bleys, *Geography of*

Perversion; Stoler, *Race and the Education of Desire*; Hyam, *Empire and Sexuality*; Dennis Altman, 'Global Gaze/Global Gays', *GLQ: A Journal of Lesbian and Gay Studies* 3 (1997), 417–36; Mary E. John and Janaki Nair, eds, *A Question of Silence? The Sexual Economies of Modern India* (Bloomsbury, 2000); Massad, *Desiring Arabs*.

68 See, for example, Emily Channell-Justice, ed., *Decolonizing Queer Experience: LGBT+ Narratives from Eastern Europe and Eurasia* (Lexington Books, 2020); Jennifer Ung Loh and Daniel Luther, eds, *'Queer' Asia: Decolonising and Reimagining Sexuality and Gender* (Zed Books, 2019); Haley McEwen and Tommaso M. Milani, 'Introduction: Queer & Trans Art-Iculations: Decolonising Gender and Sexualities in the Global South', *Agenda: Empowering Women for Gender Equity* 28, no. 4 (102) (2014), 3–8.

69 Robyn Wiegman, 'The Anatomy of Lynching', *Journal of the History of Sexuality* 3, no. 3 (1993), 445–67.

70 Snorton, *Black on Both Sides*, 63–5.

71 Emily Skidmore, 'Recovering a Gender-Transgressive Past: A Transgender Historiography', in *A Companion to American Women's History*, eds Nancy A. Hewitt and Anne M. Valk (John Wiley, 2021), 209–22, at 216.

72 Jamey Jesperson, 'Trans Misogyny in the Colonial Archive: Re-Membering Trans Feminine Life and Death in New Spain, 1604–1821', *Gender & History* 36, no. 1 (2023), 91–111.

73 Ruth Mazo Karras, 'The Regulation of "Sodomy" in the Latin East and West', *Speculum* 95, no. 4 (2020), 969–86.

74 Deborah A. Miranda, 'Extermination of the Joyas: Gendercide in Spanish California', *GLQ: A Journal of Lesbian and Gay Studies* 16, no. 1/2 (2010), 253–84, at 267.

75 Miranda, 'Extermination of the Joyas'.

76 Abvel Sierra Madero, 'Sexing the Nation's Body during the Cuban Republican Era', in *The Sexual History of the Global South: Sexual Politics in Africa, Asia, and Latin America*, eds Saskia Wieringa and Horacio Federico Sívori (Zed Books, 2013), 65–82, at 80.

77 Sinha, *Colonial Masculinity*.

78 Basile Ndjio, 'Sexuality and Nationalist Ideologies in Post-Colonial Cameroon', in Wieringa and Sívori, *Sexual History of the Global South*, 120–43. Rahul Rao analyses related moves in the memorialization of Uganda's foundational moment. Rao, *Out of Time*.

79 On this point see Nicholas M. Creary, 'Times of Lamentation: Rethinking Periodisation in African History', *Atenea* 30, no.1/2 (2010), 107–17; R. W. Connell, 'Globalization, Imperialism, and Masculinities', in *Handbook of Studies on Men and Masculinities*, eds Jeff Hearn, Michael Kimmel and R. W. Connell (Sage, 2005), 71–89.

80   Bhabha, *Location of Culture*. See also Hall and Du Gay, eds, *Questions of Cultural Identity*; John and Nair, eds, *A Question of Silence*.

81   Pete Sigal, 'The Politicization of Pederasty among the Colonial Yucatecan Maya', *Journal of the History of Sexuality* 8, no. 1 (1997), 1–24; Sigal, *From Moon Goddesses to Virgins: The Colonization of Yucatecan Maya Sexual Desire* (University of Texas Press, 2000).

82   Marc Epprecht, '"Good God Almighty, What's This!": Homosexual "Crime" in Early Colonial Zimbabwe', in *Boy-Wives and Female Husbands: Studies in African Homosexuality*, eds Marc Epprecht, Will Roscoe, and Stephen O. Murray (State University of New York Press, 1998), 193–220; Marc Epprecht, *Heterosexual Africa? The History of an Idea from the Age of AIDS* (University of KwaZulu-Natal Press, 2008).

83   Rudolf Pell Gaudio, *Allah Made Us: Sexual Outlaws in an Islamic African City* (Wiley, 2011); Achebe, 'The Day I "Met" Ahebi Ugbabe'; Massad, *Desiring Arabs*. See also: Rao, *Out of Time*; Sylvia Tamale, *Decolonisation and Afro-Feminism* (Daraja Press, 2022).

84   Ruth Vanita, *Love Rites: Same-sex Marriage in India and the West* (Palgrave Macmillan, 2005). For other accounts of the endurance and refashioning of thought and practice in the Indian context see also: Mitra Durba, *Indian Sex Life: Sexuality and the Colonial Origins of Modern Social Thought* (Princeton University Press, 2020); and Jyoti Puri, *Woman, Body, Desire in Post-colonial India* (Routledge, 1999).

85   Gayatri Chakravorty Spivak, 'The Rani of Sirmur: An Essay in Reading the Archives', *History and Theory* 24, no. 3 (1985), 247–72. See also Abram J. Lewis, 'I Am 64 and Paul McCartney Doesn't Care: The Haunting of the Transgender Archive and the Challenges of Queer History', *Radical History Review*, no. 120 (2014), 13–34.

86   On this point, see Lewis, 'I am 64'.

87   María Elena Martinez, 'Archives, Bodies, and Imagination: The Case of Juana Aguilar and Queer Approaches to History, Sexuality, and Politics', *Radical History Review* 120 (2014), 159–82.

88   Martinez, 'Archives, Bodies, and Imagination'; see also Martha Few, 'The Monster of Nature": Gender, Sexuality and the Medicalisation of a Hermaphrodite in late Colonial Guatamala', *Ethnohistory* 54, no. 1 (2007), 159–76.

89   Arondekar, *For the Record*; Anjali Arondekar, *Abundance: Sexuality's History* (Duke University press, 2023). On these points see also Zeb Tortorici, *Sins Against Nature: Sex and Archives in Colonial New Spain* (Duke University Press, 2018), 17; Barry Reay, *Sex in the Archives: Writing American Sexual Histories* (Manchester University Press, 2018), intro. I return to these issues in Chapter 5.

90   Laurie Marhoefer, *Racism and The Making of Gay Rights: A Sexologist, His Student, and the Empire of Queer Love* (University of Toronto Press, 2022); Somerville, 'Scientific Racism'; Somerville, *Queering the Color Line: Race and the Invention of Homosexuality in American Culture* (Duke University Press, 2000); Jennifer Terry, *An American Obsession: Science, Medicine, and Homosexuality in Modern Society* (University of Chicago Press, 1999).

91   See Saskia Wieringa and Horacio Sívori, 'Sexual Discourse in the Global South: Framing the Discourse', in *Sexual History of the Global South*, eds Wieringa and Sívori, 1–21, at 6; Miller 'In Search Of Lost Time'.

92   Martin F. Manalansan, *Global Divas: Filipino Gay Men in the Diaspora* (Duke University Press, 2003).

93   Iman Al-Ghafari, 'The "Lesbian" Existence in Arab Cultures: Historical and Sociological Perspectives', in Wieringa and Sívori, eds, *Sexual History of the Global South*, 144–67.

94   See Dipesh Chakrabarty, *Provincialising Europe: Postcolonial Thought and Historical Difference* (Princeton University Press, 2000). For further discussion see chapter 3, section 3.

95   James H. Sweet, 'Male Homosexuality and Spiritualism in the African Diaspora: The Legacies of a Link', *Journal of the History of Sexuality* 7, no. 2 (1996), 184–202. See also Murray, Roscoe, and Epprecht, eds, *Boy Wives and Female Husbands*; Rajyashree Pandey, *Perfumed Sleeves and Tangled Hair: Body, Woman, and Desire in Medieval Japanese Narratives* (University of Hawaii Press, 2017).

96   Keguro Macharia, *Frottage: Frictions of Intimacy across the Black Diaspora* (New York University Press, 2019). See also Omise'eke Natasha Tinsley, 'Black Atlantic, Queer Atlantic: Queer Imaginings of the Middle Passage', *GLQ: A Journal of Lesbian and Gay Studies* 14, no. 2/3 (2008), 191–215. Macharia's method resonates with Saidiya V. Hartman's. See Hartman, *Wayward Lives, Beautiful Experiments: Intimate Histories of Riotous Black Girls, Troublesome Women, and Queer Radicals* (W.W.Norton, 2019).

97   See, for example, Kwame Holmes, 'What's the Tea'; Serdar Yalcin, *Selves Engraved on Stone: Seals and Identity in the Ancient Near East, ca.1415–1050 BCE* (Brill, 2022).

98   See for example, Michelle Caswell, *Archiving the Unspeakable: Silence, Memory, and the Photographic Record in Cambodia* (University of Wisconsin Press, 2014); Marisa Fuentes, *Dispossessed Lives: Enslaved Women, Violence, and the Archive* (University of Pennsylvania Press, 2016); Ann Stoler, *Along the Archival Grain: Epistemic Anxieties and Colonial Common Sense* (Princeton University Press, 2008); Michael-Rolph Trouillot, *Silencing the Past: Power and the Production of History* (Beacon Press, 1995).

99   Rao, *Out of Time*, 45.

100 On queer migration, see B Camminga, *Transgender Refugees and the Imagined South Africa: Bodies Over Borders and Borders Over Bodies* (Palgrave Macmillan, 2019); Lawrence La Fountain-Stokes, *Queer Ricans: Cultures and Sexualities in the Diaspora* (University of Minnesota Press, 2009); Eithne Luibhéid and Lionel Cantú, eds, *Queer Migrations: Sexuality, U.S. Citizenship, and Border Crossings* (University of Minnesota Press, 2005); Luibhéid, 'Queer/Migration: An Unruly Body of Scholarship', *GLQ: A Journal of Lesbian and Gay Studies* 14, no. 2/3 (2008), 169–90. With thanks to Mori Reithmayr.

101 Wieringa and Sívori, 'Sexual Discourse'.

102 On these points see Jasbir K. Puar, *Terrorist Assemblages: Homonationalism in Queer Times* (Duke University Press, 2007); Fatima El-Tayeb, '"Gays Who Cannot Properly Be Gay": Queer Muslims in the Neoliberal European City', *European Journal of Women's Studies* 1, no. 19 (2012), 79–95; Lisa Duggan, 'The New Homonormativity: The Sexual Politics of Neoliberalism', in *Materializing Democracy: Toward a Revitalized Cultural Politics*, eds Russ Castronovo and Dana D. Nelson (Duke University Press, 2002), 175–94; Snorton, *Black on Both Sides*; Anjali Arondekar, 'Without a Trace: Sexuality and the Colonial Archive', *Journal of the History of Sexuality* 14, no. 1/2 (2005), 10–27, at 16.

103 See especially R. W. Connell, *Gender and Power: Society, the Person, and Sexual Politics* (Allen and Unwin, 1987); Connell and James W. Messerschmidt, 'Hegemonic Masculinity: Rethinking the Concept', *Gender & Society* 19, no. 6 (2005), 829–59.

104 Hortense J Spillers, 'Mama's Baby, Papa's Maybe: An American Grammar book' *Diacritics* 17, no. 2 (1987); 65–81. On the controversy surrounding Spiller's argument about degendering see Hortense Spiller, Saidiya Hartman, Farah Jasmine Griffin, Shelly Eversley and Jennifer L. Morgan. '" Whatcha gonna do?": Revisiting" Mama's Baby, Papa's maybe: An American grammar book', *Women's Studies Quarterly* 35, no. 1/2 (2007): 299–309; Amaris Brown, Thadious M. Davis, Alexis Pauline Gumbs, Sharon P. Holland, Ra Malika Imhotep, Deborah E. McDowell, Fred Moten et al., *The Flesh of the Matter: A Critical Forum on Hortense Spillers* (Vanderbilt University Press, 2024).

105 See Spillers, 'Mama's Baby, Papa's Maybe'; Thavolia Glymph, *The Women's Fight: The Civil War's Battles for Home, Freedom, and Nation* (University of North Carolina Press, 2020); Stephanie E. Jones-Rogers, *They Were Her Property: White Women as Slave Owners in the American South* (Yale University Press, 2019).

106 Annette F. Timm, *Gender, Sex and the Shaping of Modern Europe: A History from the French Revolution to the Present Day* (Bloomsbury, 2016), 4.

107 Kathleen Canning, 'The Body as Method? Reflections on the Place of the Body in Gender History', *Gender & History* 11, no. 3 (1999), 499–513;

C. McClive, 'Masculinity on Trial: Penises, Hermaphrodites and the Uncertain Male Body in Early Modern France', *History Workshop Journal* 68, no. 1 (2009), 45–68; Karen Harvey, *Reading Sex in the Eighteenth Century: Bodies and Gender in English Erotic Culture, vol. 3* (Cambridge University Press, 2005).

108 See essays in James I. Porter, *Constructions of the Classical Body* (University of Michigan Press, 1999).

109 Craig A. Williams, *Roman Homosexuality: Ideologies of Masculinity in Classical Antiquity* (Oxford University Press, 1999), 179–181.

110 Classicists have argued that same-sex activity has been oversimplified, with, for example, ideas of Platonic reciprocity important alongside the more often recognized meanings assigned to active / passive roles. See Thomas K. Hubbard, *Homosexuality in Greece and Rome: A Sourcebook of Basic Documents* (Oxford University Press, 2003); James Davidson, *The Greeks and Greek Love: A Radical Reappraisal of Homosexuality in Ancient Greece* (Phoenix, 2008).

111 Leah DeVun, *The Shape of Sex: Nonbinary Gender from Genesis to the Renaissance* (Columbia University Press, 2021), 11.

112 Pandey, *Perfumed Sleeves*. For theoretical and literary, filmic and cultural studies work on the relationship of queer to more-than-human worlds, see *GLQ: A Journal of Lesbian and Gay Studies* special issue 21, no. 2 (2015), and especially Dana Luciano and Mel Y. Chen, 'Introduction: Has the queer ever been human?." *GLQ: A Journal of lesbian and Gay Studies* 21, no. 2 (2015): iv–207 See also Stacy Holman Jones and Anne M. Harris, *The Queer Life of Things: Performance, Affect, and the More-than-human* (Rowman & Littlefield, 2019); Heike Bauer, "In the Canine Archives of Sex: Radclyffe Hall, Una Troubridge and their dogs', *Gender & History* 35, no. 3 (2023): 994-1011; Onni Gust, 'Of Mermaids and Monsters: Transgender history and the boundaries of the human in 18th and early 19th century Britain', *Gender and History* 31, no.1 (2024), 112–129; Mo Moulton, 'Our Mushroom Moment? On the Trans Possibilities of a New History of Communal Life', inaugural lecture, University of Birmingham, 23 October 2024.

113 Thomas Laqueur, *Making Sex Body and Gender from the Greeks to Freud* (Harvard University Press, 1992).

114 See Karma Lochrie, Susan Stryker and Aren Z. Aizura, 'Selections from "Before the Tribade: Medieval Anatomies of Female Masculinity and Pleasure"', in *The Transgender Studies Reader 2* (Routledge, 2013); Valerie Traub, *The Renaissance of Lesbianism in Early Modern England* (Cambridge University Press, 2002).

115 Will Tosh, *Straight Acting: The Many Queer Lives of William Shakespeare* (Sceptre, 2024), 21–3.

116 On these points, see also Randolph Trumbach, 'Sex, Gender, and Sexual Identity in Modern Culture: Male Sodomy and Female Prostitution in Enlightenment London', *Journal of the History of Sexuality* 2, no. 2 (1991), 186–203; Faramerz Dabhoiwala, *The Origins of Sex: A History of the First Sexual Revolution* (Oxford University Press, 2012).

117 Laura Gowing, *Common Bodies: Women, Touch and Power in Seventeenth-Century England* (Yale University Press, 2003); Karen Harvey, 'The Substance of Sexual Difference: Change and Persistence in Representations of the Body in Eighteenth-Century England', *Gender & History* 14 (2002) 202–23.

118 Traub, *Renaissance of Lesbianism,* 8.

119 Lillian Faderman, *Surpassing the Love of Men: Romantic Friendship and Love between Women Form the Renaissance to the Present* (Morrow, 1981).

120 Tonje Skjoldhammer, 'Romantic Friendships and Intercourse Against Nature – Intimate Relationships Between Women in Norway in the early 1800s', paper delivered at the Queerdom Symposium, Mansfield College, University of Oxford, 20 June 2024.

121 Trumbach, 'Sex, Gender, and Sexual Identity'; Trumbach, *Sex and the Gender Revolution, Volume 1: Heterosexuality and the Third Gender in Enlightenment London* (University of Chicago Press, 1998); Michael J. Sweet and Leonard Zwilling, 'The First Medicalization: The Taxonomy and Etiology of Queerness in Classical Indian Medicine', *Journal of the History of Sexuality* 3, no. 4 (1993), 590–607; Gilbert H. Herdt, ed., *Third Sex, Third Gender: Beyond Sexual Dimorphism in Culture and History* (Zone Books 1996).

122 Randolph Trumbach, 'Sodomitical Subcultures, Sodomitical Roles, and the Gender Revolution of the Eighteenth Century: The Recent Historiography', in *'Tis Nature's Fault: Unauthorized Sexuality during the Enlightenment,* ed. Robert Purks Maccubbin (Cambridge University Press, 2010), 109–21, at 119.

123 Matt Houlbrook, 'Soldier Heroes and Rent Boys: Homosex, Masculinities, and Britishness in the Brigade of Guards, circa 1900–1960', *Journal of British Studies* 42, no. 3 (2003), 351–88; Helen Smith, *Masculinity, Class and Same-Sex Desire in Industrial England, 1895–1957* (Palgrave Macmillan, 2015).

124 Kit Heyam, *Before We Were Trans: A New History of Gender* (Basic Books, 2022), 130-131.

125 Norton, *Mother Clap's Molly House: Gay Subscribe in England 1700–1830* (GMP, 1992).

126 Norton, *Mother Clap's*; see also Ricard Davenport-Hines, *Sex, Death and Punishment: Attitudes to sex and Sexuality in Britain since the Renaissance* (Collins, 1990). Anthony Delaney, *Queer Georgians, A Hidden History of Lovers, Lawbreakers and Homemakers* (Penguin, 2025).

127 See Lucy Bland and Laura Doan, eds, *Sexology in Culture: Labelling Bodies and Desires* (Polity Press, 1998), Introduction; Kate Davison, 'Cold War Pavlov: Homosexual Aversion Therapy in the 1960s', *History of the Human Sciences* 34, no. 1 (2021), 89–119; Tommy Dickinson, *'Curing Queers': Mental Nurses and Their Patients, 1935–1974* (Manchester University Press, 2015).

128 Dickinson, *'Curing Queers'*.

129 Shannon Smith and Justin Han, 'FRO-03 The Trans-formation of Gender Confirming Surgery: A Brief History', *Journal of Urology* 201, no. 4 (2019), e244. For more on intersex history see: Elizabeth, Reis *Bodies in Doubt: An American History of Intersex* (Johns Hopkins University Press, 2021); David Griffiths, 'Georgina Somerset, British Intersex history, and the I in LGBTQI', *Journal of Homosexuality* 71, no. 5 (2024): 1177–1200; Sharon E. Preves, *Intersex and identity: The contested self* (Rutgers University Press, 2003).

130 Joanna Bourke, *The Story of Pain: From Prayer to Painkillers* (Oxford University Press, 2017); Gowing, *Common Bodies*.

131 Robert A. Nye, *Masculinity and Male Codes of Honor in Modern France* (Oxford University Press, 1993). Relatedly, Victoria Powell explores how poise and comportment matter to Victorian Actor Henry Irving's social mobility in Victoria Powell, 'The Knight from Nowhere: A Biographical Case Study of Social Mobility in Victorian Britain' (PhD diss., Birkbeck, University of London, 2017). See also Rebecca Haidt, *Embodying Enlightenment: Knowing the Body in Eighteenth-Century Spanish Literature and Culture* (Macmillan, 1998).

132 Tosh, *Straight Acting*, 24, 28, and more broadly part 1; Eve Kosofsky Sedgwick, *Between Men: English Literature and Male Homosocial Desire* (1984; Columbia University Press, 2015); Sinfield, *The Wilde Century*.

133 Judith Butler, *Gender Trouble: Feminism and the Subversion of Identity* (Routledge, 1990).

134 Eve Kosofsky Sedgwick, *Touching Feeling: Affect, Pedagogy, Performativity* (Duke University Press, 2003), 28. On the history of camp see Paul Baker, *Camp!: The Amazing Attitude that Conquered the World* (Footnote Press, 2023).

135 On this point, see Mo Moulton, '"Both Your Sexes": A Non-Binary Approach to Gender History, Trans Studies and the Making of the Self in Modern Britain', *History Workshop Journal* 95, no. 1 (2023), 75–100.

136 Robert Hill, 'Before Transgender: Transvestia's Spectrum of Gender Variance, 1960–1980', *The Transgender Studies Reader 2*, eds Susan Stryker and Aren Aizura (London: Taylor & Francis, 2006), 364–79, at 366. See also Leslie Fienberg, *Transgender Warriors: Making History from Joan of Arc to Dennis Rodman* (Beacon Press, 1996); and David Valentine, 'Imagining Transgender: An Ethnography of a Category' (Duke University Press, 2007).

137 See, for example, Neil Bartlett, *Who Was That Man: A Present for Mr Oscar Wilde* (Serpent's Tail, 1988); Morris B. Kaplan, '"Men in Petticoats": Border Crossings in the Queer Case of Mr Boulton and Mr Park', in *Imagined Londons*, ed. Pamela K. Gibert (State University of New York Press, 2002), 45–68; Neil McKenna, *Fanny and Stella: The Young Men Who Shocked Victorian England* (Faber & Faber, 2013); Simon Joyce, 'Two Women Walk into a Theatre Bathroom: The Fanny and Stella Trials as Trans Narrative', *Victorian Review* 44, no. 1 (2018), 83–98.

138 See Christopher Oldstone-Moore, 'The Beard Movement in Victorian Britain', *Victorian Studies* 48, no. 1 (2005); 7–34.

139 Bartlett, *Who Was That Man*, 142; Sinfield, *The Wilde Century*, 8.

140 Harry Cocks, *Nameless Offences: Homosexual Desire in the Nineteenth Century* (I.B. Tauris, 2003), 179.

141 On this, see especially Jen Manion, *Female Husbands: A Trans History* (Cambridge University Press, 2020); Alison Oram, *Her Husband Was a Woman! Women's Gender-Crossing in Modern British Popular Culture* (London: Routledge, 2007).

142 Joyce, 'Two Women Walk into a Theatre Bathroom'; Joyce, *LGBT Victorians: Sexuality and Gender in the Nineteenth-Century Archives* (Oxford University Press, 2022).

143 Moulton, 'Both Your Sexes', 95.

144 Moulton, 'Both Your Sexes'. See also Doan, *Disturbing Practices*; Manion, *Female Husbands*; Oram, *Her Husband Was a Woman!*

145 Moulton, 'Both Your Sexes', 96.

146 Manion, *Female Husbands*, 9.

147 On Rubin and Sedgwick, see chapter 1; on this point of conjunction see: David Valentine, 'The Categories Themselves', *GLQ: A Journal of Lesbian and Gay Studies*, 10, no. 2 (2004), 215.

148 Judith Butler, *Bodies that Matter: On the Discursive Limits of 'Sex'* (Routledge, 1993).

149 See Nadja Durbach, *Spectacle of Deformity: Freak Shows and Modern British Culture* (University of California Press, 2009).

150 Jame. I. Porter *Constructions of the Classical Body* (University of Michigan Press, 1999); Yalcin, *Selves Engraved on Stone*.

151 On this point see Martha Vicinus, 'The History of Lesbian History', *Feminist Studies* 38, no. 3 (2012), 566–96, at 573–4.

152 Timm, *Gender, Sex and the Shaping of Modern Europe*, 9; Laura Lee Downs, *Writing Gender History* (Bloomsbury, 2010).

153 On this differential impact and its implications for periodization, see Maxine Berg, 'Women's Work and the Industrial Revolution', in *New Directions in Economic and Social History: Volume II*, eds Anne Digby, Charles Feinstein and David Jenkins (Macmillan 1992), 23–36; Alexandra

Shepard and Garthine Walker, 'Gender, Change and Periodisation', *Gender and History* 20, no. 3 (2008), 453–62.

154 Heyam, *Before We Were Trans,* introduction and 60.

155 On these points, see also Marjorie B. Garber, *Vested Interests: Cross-Dressing and Cultural Anxiety* (Routledge, 1997); Oram, *Her Husband Was a Woman!*

156 Linda Garber, 'Where in the World Are the Lesbians?', *Journal of the History of Sexuality* 14, no. 1/2 (2005), 28–50; Garber, *Identity Poetics: Race, Class, and the Lesbian-Feminist Roots of Queer Theory* (Columbia University Press, 2001).

157 Rebecca Jennings, *Lesbian Intimacies and Family Life: Desire, Domesticity and Kinship in Britain and Australia, 1945-2000* (Bloomsbury, 2024).

158 Lauren Jae Gutterman, *Her Neighbor's Wife: A History of Lesbian Desire Within Marriage* (University of Pennsylvania Press, 2019). See also Alison Oram, 'Love "Off the Rails" or "Over the Teacups"? Lesbian Desire and Female Sexualities in the 1950s British Popular Press', in *Queer 1950s: Rethinking Sexuality in the Postwar Years,* eds Heike Bauer and Matt Cook (Palgrave Macmillan, 2012), 41–57.

159 Terry Castle, *Noel Coward and Radclyffe Hall: Kindred Spirits* (Columbia University Press, 1996), 40.

160 Esther Newton, *Cherry Grove, Fire Island: Sixty Years in America's First Gay and Lesbian Town* (Beacon Press, 1993).

161 Newton, *Cherry Grove, Fire Island,* 203. On this point, see also Bravmann, *Queer Fictions of the Past,* 40.

162 Gay history pioneers Jeffrey Weeks and Jonathan Ned Katz both wrote about men and women in their early (and subsequent) work, in a reflection of their social and activist lives. Weeks, *Coming Out: Homosexual Politics in Britain from the Nineteenth Century to the Present* (Quartet Books, 1977); Katz, *Gay American History: Lesbians and Gay Men in the U.S.A.: A Documentary* (Crowell, 1976).

163 The case studies in Diarmuid Hester's *Nothing Ever Just Disappears* give a sense of this range. Hester, *Nothing Ever Just Disappears: Seven Hidden Histories* (Allen Lane, 2023). See also Steven Angelides, *A History of Bisexuality* (University of Chicago Press, 2001); Lachlan MacDowall, 'Historicising Contemporary Bisexuality', *Journal of Bisexuality* 9, no. 1 (2009), 3–15; Julia Shaw, *Bi: The Hidden Culture, History, and Science of Bisexuality* (Canongate, 2022); Martha Robinson Rhodes, 'Bisexuality, Multiple-Gender-Attraction, and Gay Liberation Politics in the 1970s', *Twentieth Century British History* 32, no. 1 (2021), 119–42.

164 This was core to my argument in *Queer Domesticities* (2014), influenced especially by Sharon Marcus, *Between Women: Friendship, Desire, and Marriage in Victorian England* (Princeton University Press, 2007); Cohen,

Family Secrets; and Jeffrey Weeks, Brian Heaphy and Catherine Donovan, *Same-Sex Intimacies: Families of Choice and Other Life Experiments* (Routledge, 2001).

165 See, for example, Umphrey, 'The Trouble with Harry Thaw'; Houlbrook, 'Soldier Heroes and Rent Boys'; Cook, *Queer Domesticities*.

166 On these points see Hester, *Nothing Ever Just Disappears*; Cook and Oram, *Queer Beyond London*, Epilogue.

167 Norton, *Mother Clap's*; Elizabeth Lapovsky Kennedy and Madeline D. Davis, *Boots of Leather, Slippers of Gold: The History of a Lesbian Community* (Routledge, 1993); Jill Gardiner, *From the Closet to the Screen: Women and the Gateways Club, 1945–1985* (Pandora, 2003).

168 On these points, see Bleys, *Geography of Perversion*; Dollimore, *Sexual Dissidence*; Jonathan Dollimore, 'Orton's Black Camp', in *Joe Orton: A Casebook*, ed. Francesca Coppa (Routledge, 2003), 95–8.

169 Sinfield, *The Wilde Century*, 44–7.

170 Matt Houlbrook, 'Soldier Heroes and Rent Boys'.

171 Leila J. Rupp, *Sapphistries: A Global History of Love Between Women* (New York University Press, 2011), 221, 230.

172 Timm, *Gender, Sex and the Shaping of Modern Europe*.

173 This enlarged earlier tendencies, identified by Faderman in *Surpassing the Love of Men* (1981) and more recently by Tone Hellesund, who found a pronounced egalitarianism between independent new women in late nineteenth- and early twentieth-century Norway – an egalitarianism which, she suggests, altered the way sex and intimacy felt. Lillian Faderman, *Surpassing the Love of Men* (1981; Harper Collins, 1998); Tone Hellesund, 'Better than Orgasm: Sex, Authenticity and Intimacy in the New Women's Movement in Norway', *Gender & History* 33, no. 1 (2021), 209–26.

174 Karla Jay and Allen Young, eds, *Out of the Closets: The Voices of Gay Liberation* (New York University Press, 1992).

175 Mary Weismantel, 'A Queer Rampage Through Prehistory', in Stryker and Aizura, eds, *Transgender Studies Reader 2*, 319–34, at 324.

176 Weismantel, 'A Queer Rampage', 330.

177 Heyam, *Before We Were Trans*, 28; Jesperson, 'Trans Misogyny in the Colonial Archive'.

178 Shraddha Chatterjee, 'Transgender Shifts: Notes on Resignification of Gender and Sexuality in India', *TSQ: Transgender Studies Quarterly* 5, no. 3 (2018), 311–20. See also Jessica Hinchy, *Governing Gender and Sexuality in Colonial India: The Hijra, c.1850–1900* (Cambridge University Press, 2019).

179 Chattergee, 'Transgender Shifts'; Heyam, *Before We Were Trans*; Snorton, *Black on Both Sides*. See also Moulton, 'Both Your Sexes'; Leah DeVun and

Zeb Tortorici, 'Trans, Time, and History', *TSQ: Transgender Studies Quarterly* 5, no. 4 (2018), 518–39; Miriam J. Abelson, *Men in Place: Trans Masculinity, Race, and Sexuality in America* (University of Minnesota Press, 2019).

180 See DeVun, *The Shape of Sex*, 10; Jesperson, 'Trans Misogyny'.

181 Jack Halberstam, *In a Queer Time and Place: Transgender Bodies, Subcultural Lives* (New York University Press, 2005), 52.

182 Jay Prosser, *Second Skins: The Body Narratives of Transsexuality* (Columbia University Press, 1998), introduction.

183 Emily Skidmore, *True Sex: The Lives of Trans Men at the Turn of the Twentieth Century* (New York University Press, 2017), 69.

184 Downs, *Writing Gender History*, 170, 193.

185 See Chapter 1.

186 See Ryan Lee Cartwright, 'Out of Sorts: A Queer Crip in the Archive', *Feminist Review* 125, no. 1 (2020), 62–9; Cartwright, *Peculiar Places: A Queer Crip History of White Rural Nonconformity* (University of Chicago Press, 2021); Eli Clare, *Exile and Pride: Disability, Queerness, and Liberation* (1999; Duke University Press, 2015); Regina Kunzel, *In the Shadow of Diagnosis: Psychiatric Power and Queer Life* (University of Chicago Press, 2024); Kunzel, 'The Rise of Gay Rights and the Disavowal of Disability', in *The Oxford Handbook of Disability History*, eds Michael A. Rembis, Catherine J. Kudlick and Kim Nielsen (Oxford University Press, 2018), 459–76.

187 On transmisogyny, see Julia Serano, *Whipping Girl: A Transsexual Woman on Sexism and the Scapegoating of Femininity* (Seal Press, 2007); Jules Gill-Peterson, *A Short History of Trans Misogyny* (Verso Books, 2024).

188 Jo Brydon, 'Percy Grainger and Trans Identity in Edwardian London' (PhD diss., Birkbeck, University of London, March 2025).

189 William Jones, '"So Then … He Raped Me": Male Experiences of Sexual(ized) Violence in the Nazi Concentration Camps (DPhil diss., University of Oxford, 2024), 78, 88. See also Laurie Marhoefer, *Sex and the Weimar Republic: German Homosexual Emancipation and the Rise of the Nazis* (University of Toronto Press, 2015).

190 See Wiegman, 'The Anatomy of Lynching'.

191 Anjali Arondekar, Ann Cvetkovich, Christina B. Hanhardt, Regina Kunzel, Tavia Nyong'o, Juana María Rodríguez, Susan Stryker, Daniel Marshall, Kevin P. Murphy and Zeb Tortorici, 'Queering Archives: A Roundtable Discussion', *Radical History Review* 2015, no. 122 (2015), 211–31, at 230.

192 Arondekar et al., 'Queering Archives', 230. See also Regina G. Kunzel, *Criminal Intimacy: Prison and the Uneven History of Modern American Sexuality* (University of Chicago Press, 2022); Kunzel, *In the Shadows*.

193 Dennis Altman, 'Legitimation through Disaster: AIDS and the gay movement', *American Political Science Association* (1987).

194 See Jeffrey Weeks, *The World We Have Won: The Remaking of Erotic and Intimate Life* (Routledge, 2007); Jennings, *Lesbian Intimacies*; Cook, *Queer Domesticities*, part II. Weeks, *Same-Sex Intimacies*.

195 See also Carlo Ginzburg, 'Microhistory: Two or Three Things That I Know about It', *Critical Inquiry* 20, no. 1 (1993), 10–35, at 33.

196 Ahmed, *Queer Phenomenology*.

197 Andrea Long Chu and Emmet Harsin Drager 'After Trans Studies', *TSQ: Transgender Studies Quarterly*, 6, 1 (2019) 103–115, at 108.

Chapter 3: Space and Time

1 See Matt Cook, 'London, AIDS and the 1980s', in Simon Avery and Kate Graham, eds, *Sex, Time and Place: Queer Histories of London* (Bloomsbury, 2015), 49–64. Cook, '"Archives of Feeling": the AIDS Crisis in Britain 1987', *History Workshop Journal*, 83, 1 (Spring 2017), 51–78.

2 'Female, b.1934, Publisher, South East England', 1987 AIDS directive, Mass Observation collection, The Keep Archive Centre, Brighton.

3 AIDS is not over; there is not yet an 'after', as Sarah Schulman reminds us. Sarah Schulman, *The Gentrification of the Mind: Witness to a Lost Imagination* (University of California Press, 2012).

4 Matt Cook, 'Revisiting AIDS in the Era of Covid', *History Workshop* (online), https://www.historyworkshop.org.uk/queer-history/its-a-sin-revisiting-aids-in-the-era-of-covid/ (accessed 6 February 2021).

5 See Christopher Castiglia and Christopher Reed, *If Memory Serves: Gay Men, AIDS, and the Promise of the Queer Past* (University of Minnesota Press, 2012). Memory studies, developing from the 1980s, provided an important platform for their intervention. See especially Richard Terdiman, *Present Past: Modernity and the Memory Crisis* (Cornell University Press, 1993); Anna Green, 'Individual Remembering and "Collective Memory": Theoretical Presuppositions and Contemporary Debates', *Oral History* 32, no. 2 (2004), 35–44; Ann Cvetkovich, *An Archive of Feelings: Trauma, Sexuality, and Lesbian Public Cultures* (Duke University Press, 2003).

6 Castiglia and Reed, *If Memory Serves*, 3.

7 Stephen Kern, *The Culture of Time and Space, 1880–1918* (Weidenfeld & Nicolson, 1983).

8 Doreen Massey, 'A Global Sense of Place', in *Marxism Today* 38 (1991), 24–9; Edward Soja, 'The Spatiality of Social Life: towards a transformative

retheorisation', in *Social Relations and Spatial Structures*, eds Derek Gregory and Johny Urry (Macmillan: 1985), 90–127; Pierre Bordieu, *Outline of a Theory of Practice* (Cambridge University Press, 1977); Massey, *Space, Place, and Gender* (University of Minnesota Press, 1994) p. 2. See also Henri Lefebvre, 'The Everyday and Everydayness', *Yale French Studies*, 3 (1987), 7–11; Ed Soja, *Postmodern Geographies: The Reassertion of Space in Critical Social Theory* (Verso, 1989). For a summary of the geographical debate in the 1980s and early 1990s on place and locality (as distinct from broader categorizations of space), see John Agnew, 'Space and Place', in *Sage Handbook of Geographical Knowledge*, eds John Agnew and David Livingstone (Sage, 2011), 316–31.

9   Michel de Certeau, 'Walking the City', in *The Practice of Everyday Life* (University of California Press, 1984), 91–110.

10 Michel Foucault developed a thesis on the shaping power of the built environment – literally and as a metaphor for wider social control – in his *Discipline and Punish: The Birth of the Prison*, trans. Alan Sheridan (1975; Vintage Books, 1995). Michel de Certeau critiqued this vision because, he said, it failed to account for the way 'hauntings' from the past determined behaviour in spaces of the present. de Certeau, 'Walking the City'. For discussion see Chapter 2 of this book.

11 Matt Houlbrook, *Queer London: Pleasures and Perils in the Sexual Metropolis, 1918–1957* (University of Chicago Press, 2005), 65. See also Mark W. Turner, *Backward Glances: Cruising the Queer Streets of New York and London* (Reaktion, 2003).

12 Leif Jerram underscores the significance of the material in a piece in which he worries about the analytical emphasis on 'symbolic and imagined space' at the expense of the physical environment. Leif Jerram, 'Space: A Useless Category for Historical Analysis?', *History and Theory* 52 (2013), 400–19. See also Ralph Kingston, 'Mind Over Matter? History and the Spatial Turn', *Cultural and Social History* 7, no. 1 (2010), 111–21, at 112.

13 Johan Andersson, 'Vauxhall's Post-industrial Pleasure Gardens: "Death-wish" and Hedonism', *Urban Studies* 48, no. 1 (2011), 85–100; David Bell and Gill Valentine, eds, *Mapping Desire: Geographies of Sexualities* (Routledge, 1995); John Binnie, 'Quartering Sexualities: Gay Villages and Sexual Citizenship', in *City of Quarters: Urban Villages in the Contemporary City*, eds David Bell and Mark Jayne (Ashgate, 2004), 163–72; Gavin Brown, and Kath Browne, eds, *The Routledge Research Companion to Geographies of Sex and Sexualities* (Routledge, 2016); Gavin Brown, 'Urban (Homo) Sexualities: Ordinary Cities and Ordinary Sexualities', *Geography Compass* 2, no. 4 (2008), 1215–31; Japonica Brown-Saracino, *How Places*

Make Us: Novel LBQ Identities in Four Small Cities (University of Chicago Press, 2017); Lawrence Knopp, 'Sexuality and Urban Space: Gay Male Identity Politics in the United States, the United Kingdom, and Australia', in *Cities of Difference,* eds Ruth Fincher and Jane Jacobs (Guildford Press, 1998), 149–76.

14   On liminality and the equivocal queer meanings of public space, see Gill Valentine, '(Hetero)Sexing Space: Lesbian Perceptions and Experiences of Everyday Spaces', *Environment and Planning D: Society and Space* 11, no. 4 (1993), 395–413; Bell and Valentine, eds, *Mapping Desire*; David Bell, 'Pleasure and Danger: The Paradoxical Spaces of Sexual Citizenship', *Political Geography* 14, no. 2 (1995), 139–53; William L. Leap, ed., *Public Sex/Gay Space* (Columbia University Press, 1999); Gordon Brent Ingram, ed., *Queers in Space: Communities, Public Places, Sites of Resistance* (Bay Press, 1997); George Chauncey, 'Privacy Could Only Be Had in Public: Gay Uses of the Streets', in *Stud: Architectures of Masculinity,* ed. J. Sanders (Princeton Architectural Press, 1996), 224–67.

15   On this see Anna Clark, 'Twilight Moments', *Journal of the History of Sexuality* 14, no. 1 (2005), 139–60.

16   Michel Foucault, 'Of Other Spaces', *Diacritics* 16, no. 1 (1986), 22–7. For an applied example of Foucault's theory see Alison Oram, 'Sexuality in Heterotopia: Time, Space and Love between Women in the Historic House', *Women's History Review* 21, no. 4 (2012), 533–51.

17   Raka Shome, 'Space Matters: The Power and Practice of Space', *Communication Theory* 13, no. 1 (2003), 39–56.

18   See Julia Kristeva, Alice Jardine and Harry Blake, 'Women's Time', *Signs* 7, no. 1 (1981), 13–35; Matt Cook, *Queer Domesticities: Homosexuality and Home Life in Twentieth Century London* (Palgrave Macmillan, 2014), Introduction.

19   On these dynamics, see Rahul Rao, *Out of Time: The Queer Politics of Postcoloniality* (Oxford University Press, 2020).

20   Siobhan Somerville, 'Scientific Racism and the Emergence of the Homosexual Body', *Journal of the History of Sexuality* 5, no. 2 (1994), 243–66.

21   Johannes Fabian, *Time and the Other: How Anthropology Makes Its Object* (1983; Columbia University Press, 2014), 35, cited in Leah DeVun and Zeb Tortorici, 'Trans, Time, and History', *TSQ: Transgender Studies Quarterly* 5, no. 4 (2018), 518–39, at 522.

22   See, for example, Carolyn Dinshaw, *Getting Medieval: Sexualities and Communities, Pre- and Postmodern* (Duke University Press, 1999); Carolyn Dinshaw and Judith Halberstam, 'Theorising Queer Temporalities: A Roundtable Discussion', *GLQ: A Journal of Lesbian and Gay Studies* 13, no. 2/3 (2007), 177–95; José Esteban Muñoz, *Cruising Utopia: The*

Then and There of Queer Futurity (New York University Press, 2009); Jack Halberstam, *In a Queer Time and Place: Transgender Bodies, Subcultural Lives* (New York University Press, 2005). For more recent reflections see DeVun and Tortorici, 'Trans, Time, and History'; Rao, *Out of Time*; John Whittier Treat, 'Telling Queer Time in a Straight Empire', in *Queer Korea*, ed. Todd A. Henry (Duke University Press, 2020), 90–116.

23   Elizabeth Freeman, *Time Binds: Queer Temporalities, Queer Histories* (Duke University Press: 2010), 3–4. On alternate temporalities see Halberstam, *In a Queer Time and Place*; Matt Cook, 'Gay Times: Identity, Locality, Memory and the Brixton Squats', *Journal of Twentieth Century British History* 24, no. 1 (2013), 84–109; George Townsend, 'A Queer History of Parson's Pleasure, Oxford', in *Locating Queer History: Places and Traces across the UK*, eds Justin Bengry, Matt Cook and Alison Oram (Bloomsbury, 2022), 83–100.

24   Lee Edelman, *No Future: Queer Theory and the Death Drive* (Duke University Press, 2004). See also Jack Halberstam, *The Queer Art of Failure* (Duke University Press, 2011).

25   Katherine Bond Stockton, *The Queer Child, or Growing Sideways in the Twentieth Century* (Duke University Press, 2009).

26   Elizabeth Freeman, 'Time Binds, or, Erotohistoriography', *Social Text* 23, no. 3–4 (2005), 57–68, at 66.

27   Dinshaw, *Getting Medieval*, 36, 40, 39.

28   On this, see especially Muñoz, *Cruising Utopia*.

29   Halberstam, *In a Queer Time and Place*.

30   Jason Okundaye, *Revolutionary Acts: Love and Brotherhood in Black Gay Britain* (Faber and Faber, 2024), 109; Mathias Klitgård, 'Family Time Gone Awry: Vogue Houses and Queer Repro-Generationality at the Intersection(s) of Race and Sexuality', *Debate Feminista* 57 (2019), 108–33; Matt Cook and Alison Oram, *Queer Beyond London* (Manchester University Press, 2022), 95.

31   *Out of Time* is the apposite title of Rahul Rao's 2020 book. On these points, see also Halberstam, *In a Queer Time and Place*; Ben Cranfield, 'Performing Gestures Towards the Archive: Queer Fragments and other Ways of Mattering', in *The Materiality of the Archive: Creative Practice in Context*, eds Sue Breakell and Wendy Russell (Routledge, 2024), 245–58; and Thomas F. DeFrantz, 'Queer Social Dance, Political Leadership, and Black Popular Culture', in *The Oxford Handbook of Dance and Politics*, eds Rebekah Kowal, Gerald Siegmund and Randy Martin (Oxford University Press, 2017).

32   See Stefano Evangelista, 'Decadence and Aestheticism', in Dennis Denisoff and Talia Schaffer, eds, *The Routledge Companion to Victorian Literature*

(Routledge, 2019), 106–15; Timothy D'Arch Smith, *Love in Earnest: Some Notes on the Lives and Writing of the Uranian Poets, 1889–1930* (Routledge, 1970).

33   Their ideas had disproportionate cultural purchase, however, because of the actual and cultural capital of these men. For more on these movements and tendencies, see Matt Cook, *London and the Culture of Homosexuality, 1885–1914* (Cambridge University Press, 2003), ch. 5; Sarah Waters, "The Most Famous Fairy in History": Antinous and Homosexual Fantasy', in *Journal of the History of Sexuality,* 6, no. 2 (1995): 194–230; Linda Dowling, *Hellenism and Homosexuality in Victorian Oxford* (Cornell University Press, 1994).

34   See, for example, Brighton Ourstory Project, *Daring Hearts: Lesbian and Gay Lives of 50s and 60s Brighton* (QueenSpark, 1992); Alan Butler, 'Performing LGBT Pride in Plymouth 1950–2012' (PhD diss., Plymouth University, 2016); Jill Gardiner, *From the Closet to the Screen: Women and the Gateways Club, 1945–1985* (Pandora, 2003); Cook and Oram, *Queer Beyond London*, chs 1–4. See also: Richard Dyer, 'In Defence of Disco', *Gay Left* 8 (1979), 20–3; Tim Lawrence, 'Disco and the Queering of the Dance Floor', *Cultural Studies* 25, no. 2 (2011), 230–43.

35   On these different bar cultures, see Gardiner, *From the Closet to the Screen.* Randy Jones and Mark Bego, *Macho Man: The Disco Era and Gay America's Coming Out* (Bloomsbury Publishing USA, 2008); Tim Lawrence, '"I Want to See All My Friends at Once": Arthur Russell and the Queering of Gay Disco', in *Electronica, Dance and Club Music,* ed. Mark J. Butler (Routledge, 2017), 141–63; Tim Dean, *Unlimited Intimacy: Reflections on the Subculture of Barebacking* (University of Chicago Press, 2009); Mark Pendleton, 'And I Dance with Somebody: Queer History in a Japanese Nightclub', *History Workshop Journal* 90 (2020), 297–310; John D'Emilio, *Sexual Politics, Sexual Communities* (University of Chicago Press, 1983); Jeremy Atherton Lin, *Gay Bar: Why We Went Out* (Hachette UK, 2021); Amin Ghaziani, *Long Live Queer Nightlife: How the Closing of Gay Bar Sparked a Revolution* (Princetown University Press, 2024).

36   Mori Reithmayr, 'The Invention of Gay Community in San Francisco, 1960–1970', *The Historical Journal* (2025), 1–21.

37   On these points, see especially Clark, 'Twilight Moments'; Muñoz, *Cruising Utopia*; Andersson, 'Vauxhall's Post-industrial Pleasure Gardens'; Treat, 'Telling Queer Time'.

38   On the felt exclusions relating to class and race, see Matt Cook and Alison Oram, *Queer Beyond London* (Manchester University Press, 2023), 43, 95, 151. Okundaye, *Revolutionary Acts*; Klitgård, 'Family Time Gone Awry'; DeFrantz, 'Queer Social Dance'; Khalil R. West, 'Dark Matter: Sociality, Space,

and the Haptics of Queer (Il)legibility in "Black Liverpool", 1967–1997'
(PhD diss., European University Institute, July 2025); Christina B. Hanhardt,
Safe Space: Gay Neighbourhood History and the Politics of Violence (Duke
University Press, 2020).

39   On bookshops, see Leila Kassir and Richard Espley, eds, *Queer Between the
Covers: Histories of Queer Publishing and Queer Voices* (University of
London Press, 2021); on charities, see Myrl Beam, *Gay, Inc.: The
Nonprofitization of Queer Politics* (University of Minnesota Press, 2018);
on political groups, see D'Emilio, *Sexual Politics, Sexual Communities*;
Marcia M. Gallo, *Different Daughters: A History of the Daughters of Bilitis
and the Rise of the Lesbian Rights Movement* (Seal Press, 2007); Neil Young,
Coming Out As Republican: A History of the Gay Right (University of
Chicago Press, 2024); James Sears, *Behind the Mask of the Mattachine: The
Hal Call Chronicles and the Early Movement for Homosexual Emancipation*
(Harrington Park Press, 2006); on archival and library spaces, see Rachel
Corbman, 'A Genealogy of the Lesbian Herstory Archives, 1974–2014',
Journal of Contemporary Archival Studies 1, no. 1 (2014), 1–16; Kate
Eichhorn, 'Queer Archives', in *The Routledge History of Queer America*, ed.
Don Romesburg (Routledge, 2018), 123–34; on male-oriented video
stores, bathhouses, saunas and sex joints, see Allan Bérubé, 'The History
of Gay Bathhouses', *Journal of Homosexuality* 44, no. 3/4, 33–53; on
female-oriented sexual spaces, see the depiction of the weekly club night
Chain Reaction in London's Vauxhall in the 1980s and 1990s in the
documentary *Rebel Dykes* (Siân A. Williams and Harri Shanahan, dir.,
2021); Corie Hammers, 'An Examination of Lesbian/Queer Bathhouse
Culture and the Social Organization of (Im)Personal Sex', *Journal of
Contemporary Ethnography* 38, no. 3 (2009), 308–35. With thanks to
Mori Reithmayr.

40   West, 'Dark Matter'.

41   Superpositionality is a term West adapts from quantum physics to signify
the elision of two or more quantum states. He deploys it to envision the
infusion of heterosexual encounters and desires with the homoerotic and
vice versa, suggesting that describing these things as 'queer' would risk
losing the nuance of what was happening and imply subject positions his
'conversants' (interviewees; on the distinction see chapter 5, note 130) did
not own. West, 'Dark Matter', 61.

42   West, 'Dark Matter', 196.

43   On this point, see Victoria Harris, 'Sex on the Margins: New Directions in
the Historiography of Sexuality', *The Historical Journal* 53, no. 4 (2010),
1085–04, at 1099.

44   Tommy Dickinson, *'Curing Queers': Mental Nurses and Their Patients,
1935–1974* (Manchester University Press, 2015).

45   Regina G. Kunzel, *Criminal Intimacy: Prison and the Uneven History of Modern American Sexuality* (University of Chicago Press, 2022). See also Hugh Ryan, *The Women's House of Detention: A Queer History of a Forgotten Prison* (Bold Type Books, 2022).

46   On workhouses, see Seth Koven, *Slumming: Sexual and Social Politics in Victorian London* (Princeton University Press, 2004), chapter 1; on barracks: Matt Houlbrook, 'Soldier Heroes and Rent Boys: Homosex, Masculinities, and Britishness in the Brigade of Guards, circa 1900–1960', *Journal of British Studies* 42, no. 3 (2003), 351–88; on prisons: Kunzel, *Criminal Intimacy*.

47   See, for example, William Jones, '"So Then … He Raped Me": Male Experiences of Sexual(ized) Violence in the Nazi Concentration Camps (DPhil diss., University of Oxford, 2024); Kunzel, *Criminal Intimacy*, 152–159.

48   Arthur Clech, 'Between the Labour Camp and the Clinic: Tema or the Shared Forms of Late Soviet Homosexual Subjectivities', in *Soviet and Post-Soviet Sexualities,* ed. Richard Mole (Routledge, 2019), 32–55.

49   Jo Stanley and Paul Baker, *Hello Sailor! The Hidden History of Gay Life at Sea* (Routledge, 2015). See also Allan Bérubé, 'No Race-Baiting, Red-Baiting, or Queer-Baiting! The Marine Cooks and Stewards Union from the Depression to the Cold War', in *My Desire for History: Essays in Gay, Community, and Labor History,* eds John D'Emilio and Estelle Freedman (University of North Carolina Press, 2011), 294–320.

50   Tomasz Mossakowski, '"The Sailors Dearly Love to Make Up": Cross-Dressing and Blackface during Polar Exploration' (PhD diss., King's College London, 2015).

51   Alan Sinfield, *Out on Stage: Lesbian and Gay Theatre in the Twentieth Century* (Yale University Press, 1999); Tirza Latimer, 'Balletomania: A Sexual Disorder?', *GLQ: A Journal of Lesbian and Gay Studies* 5, no. 2 (1999), 173–97; Laurence Senelick, *The Changing Room: Sex, Drag and Theatre* (Routledge, 2000); Jean E. Howard, 'Crossdressing, The Theatre, and Gender Struggle in Early Modern England', *Shakespeare Quarterly* 39, no. 4 (1988), 418–40; Will Tosh, *Straight Acting: The Many Queer Lives of William Shakespeare* (Sceptre, 2024); Sos Eltis, 'Is She A Woman? Alternative Critical Frameworks for Understanding Cross-Dressing and Cross-Gender Casting on the Victorian Stage', *Nineteenth Century Theatre and Film* 50, no. 1 (2023), 3–20.

52   On this point, see Matt Cook, 'Warm Homes in a Cold Climate: the "Evidence of Experience"', in *Queer 1950s: Rethinking Sexuality in the Postwar Years*, eds Matt Cook and Heike Bauer (Palgrave, 2012), 115–30.

53 Sharon Marcus, *Between Women: Friendship, Desire, and Marriage in Victorian England* (Princeton University Press, 2007); Cook, *Queer Domesticities*; Stephen Vider, *The Queerness of Home: Gender, Sexuality, and the Politics of Domesticity after World War II* (University of Chicago Press, 2022); Rebecka Taves Sheffield, 'The Bedside Table Archives: Archive Intervention and Lesbian Intimate Domestic Culture', *Radical History Review* 120 (2014), 108–20; Rebecca Jennings, *Lesbian Intimacies and Family Life: Desire, Domesticity and Kinship in Britain and Australia, 1945–2000* (Bloomsbury, 2023).

54 See Eileen Cleere, *Avuncularism: Capitalism, Patriarchy, and Nineteenth-Century English Culture* (Stanford University Press, 2004). On the 'asexuality' and 'implicit heterosexuality' of the child, see Steven Bruhm and Natasha Hurley, 'Curiouser: On the Queerness of Children', in *Curiouser: On the Queerness of Children*, eds Steven Bruhm and Natasha Hurley (University of Minnesota Press, 2004), ix–xxxviii, at xi. With thanks to Hannah Stovin.

55 Matt Cook, 'The Nursery', in *Queering the Interior*, eds Andrew Gorman-Murray and Matt Cook (Routledge, 2020), 145–57.

56 Peter Stallybrass and Allon White, *The Politics and Poetics of Transgression* (Methuen, 1986).

57 Alan Hunt, 'The Great Masturbation Panic and the Discourses of Moral Regulation in Nineteenth- and Early Twentieth-Century Britain', *Journal of the History of Sexuality* 8, no. 4 (1998), 575–615; Lesley Hall, 'Forbidden by God, Despised by Men: Masturbation, Medical Warnings, Moral Panic, and Manhood in Great Britain, 1850-1950', *Journal of the History of Sexuality* 2, no. 3 (1992), 365–87.

58 Anthony S. Wohl, 'Sex and the Single Room: Incest among the Victorian Working Classes', in *The Victorian Family: Structures and Stresses*, ed. Anthony Wohl (Croom Helm, 1978), 197–216; Seth Koven, *Slumming*; Scott Herring, *Queering the Underworld: Slumming, Literature, and the Undoing of Lesbian and Gay History* (Chicago University Press, 2007).

59 John Tosh, *A Man's Place: Masculinity and the Middle-Class Home in Victorian England* (Yale University Press, 1999).

60 Brent Pilkey, 'LGBT Homemaking in London, UK: The Embodiment of Mobile Homemaking Imaginaries', *Geographical Research* 51, no. 2 (2013), 159–65; Cook, *Queer Domesticities*; Matt Cook, 'A Bend in the River: Queer Home and Heritage in a House in Hammersmith', in *Sexuality and Gender at Home*, eds Brent Pilkey, Rachel Scicluna, Ben Campkin and Barbara Penner (Routledge, 2017), 121–34; Vider, *The Queerness of Home*.

61 Emily Skidmore, *True Sex: The Lives of Trans Men at the Turn of the Twentieth Century* (New York University Press, 2017); Lauren Jae Gutterman, *Her Neighbor's Wife: A History of Lesbian Desire Within*

Marriage (University of Pennsylvania Press, 2019); Alison Oram, 'Love "Off the Rails" or "Over the Teacups"? Lesbian Desire and Female Sexualities in the 1950s British Popular Press', in *Queer 1950s,* eds Bauer and Cook, 41–57.

62   Nadia Ellis, 'Black Migrants, White Queers and the Archive of Inclusion in Post War London', *International Journal of Postcolonial Studies* 17, no. 6 (2015), 893–915, at 913.

63   Jennings, *Lesbian Intimacies*; Amy Tooth Murphy, AHRC project 2020–2022, 'Historicising Butch: Narrating Butch Lesbian Identity and Experience from 1950 to present'. On the significance of the workplace in queer formations, see Margot Canaday, *Queer Career: Sexuality and Work in Modern America* (Princeton University Press, 2023); Alan Bérubé, '"Queer Work" and Labor History', in John D'Emilio and Estelle B. Freedman, eds, *My Desire for History: Essays in Gay, Community and Labor History* (University of North Carolina Press, 2003); Phil Tiemeyer, *Plane Queer: Labor, Sexuality, and AIDS in the History of Male Flight Attendants* (University of California Press, 2013).

64   This section draws on Matt Cook, 'Cities, Suburbs and Countryside', in *Oxford Handbook of LGBT History*, eds Dominic Janes and Howard Chiang (Oxford University Press, 2026).

65   George Chauncey, *Gay New York: Gender, Urban Culture, and the Making of the Gay Male World, 1890–1940* (Basic Books, 1994); Chauncey, 'Privacy could only be had in Public'.

66   Chauncey, *Gay New York*; Henning Bech, *When Men Meet: Homosexuality and Modernity* (Chicago University Press, 1997); John D'Emilio, 'Capitalism and Gay Identity', in *Powers of Desire: The Politics of Sexuality*, eds Ann Snitow, Christine Stansell and Sharon Thompson (Monthly Review Press, 1983), 100–13.

67   For an overview of the early US urban studies, see Marc Stein, 'Theoretical Politics, Local Communities: The Making of U.S. LGBT Historiography', *GLQ: A Journal of Lesbian and Gay Studies* 11, no. 4 (2005), 605–25. US studies include: Nan Boyd, *Wide-Open Town: A History of Queer San Francisco to 1965* (University of California Press, 2003); Timothy Stewart-Winter, *Queer Clout: Chicago and the Rise of Gay Politics* (University of Pennsylvania Press, 2016); Lillian Faderman and Stuart Timmons, *Gay LA: A History of Sexual Outlaws, Power Politics and Lipstick Lesbians* (University of California Press, 2009); Joseph Plaster, *Kids on the Street: Queer Kinship and Religion in San Francisco's Tenderloin* (Duke University Press, 2023); Julio Capó Jr., *Welcome to Fairyland: Queer Miami before 1940* (University of North Carolina Pres, 2017). For studies outside the United States, see Garry Wotherspoon, *City of the Plain: History of Gay Subculture* (Hale & Iremonger, 1991); Florence Tamagne, *A History of*

Homosexuality in Europe: Berlin, London, Paris, 1919–1939 (Algora, 2004); Matt Cook, *London and the Culture of Homosexuality, 1885–1914* (Cambridge University Press, 2003); Matt Houlbrook, *Queer London: Perils and Pleasures in the Sexual Metropolis, 1918–1957* (University of Chicago Press, 2005); David Higgs, *Queer Sites: Gay Urban Histories Since 1600* (Routledge, 1999); Matt Cook and Jennifer Evans, *Queer Cities, Queer Cultures: Europe since 1945* (Bloomsbury, 2014); Moises Fendandez-Cano, 'Unveiling Madrid: Queer Intimacies under Franco' (PhD diss., European University Institute, Florence, 2024).

68 Histories of technology, travel and telecommunication are an important part of the queer story, and especially in relation to shifting and interrelated experiences of time, space and selfhood. See Lena Wånggren, '"The Freedom Machine": The New Woman and the Bicycle', in *Transport in British Fiction: Technologies of Movement, 1840–1940*, eds Adrienne Gavin and Andrew F. Humphries (Palgrave Macmillan, 2015), 123–35; Kern, *Culture of Time and Space*; Katie Hindmarch-Watson, *Serving a Wired World: London's Telecommunications Workers and the Making of an Information Capital* (University of California Press, 2000); Simeon Koole, 'How We Came to Mind the Gap: Time, Tactility, and the Tube', *Twentieth Century British History* 27, no. 4 (2016), 524–54.

69 Cook, *London*, chapter 2; Daniel Pick, *Faces of Degeneration: A European Disorder, c.1848–c.1918* (Cambridge University Press, 1989).

70 See Silvia Antosa, 'Cannibal London: racial discourses, pornography and male-male desire in late-Victorian Britain", in Simon Avery and Katherine M. Graham, eds, *Sex, Time and Place: Queer Histories of London, c. 1850 to the present* (Bloomsbury, 2016) 149–65. On the intensification and 'concretization' of imperial power dynamics in London, see especially Tariq Jazeel, *Postcolonialism* (Routledge, 2019).

71 Cook and Evans, *Queer Cities*.

72 Kate Flint, 'The "Hour of the Pink Twilight": Lesbian poetics and queer encounters in the *fin de siècle* street', *Victorian Studies* 51, no.9 (2009), 687–712. For more on the opportunities urban life afford to women, see Elizabeth Wilson, *The Sphinx in the City: Urban Life, the Control of Disorder, and Women* (Virago, 1991); Sally Ledger, *The New Woman: Fiction and Feminism at the Fin de Siècle* (Manchester University Press, 1997). On female same-sex love in public spaces, see Jen Jack Gieseking, 'Useful In/Stability: The Dialectical Production of the Social and Spatial Lesbian Herstory Archives', *Radical History Review* 122 (2015), 25–37.

73 Higgs, *Queer Sites*; Cook and Evans, *Queer Cities*; Kate Chedgzoy, Emma Francis and Murray Pratt, eds, *In a Queer Place: Sexuality and Belonging in British and European Contexts* (Ashgate, 2002); Robert Gillett, ed., *Queer in Europe: Contemporary Case Studies* (Routledge, 2016).

74 David Caron, *My Father and I: The Marais and the Queerness of Community* (Cornell University Press, 2010).

75 See Frank Mort, *Capital Affairs: London and the Making of the Permissive Society* (Yale University Press, 2010); Houlbrook, *Queer London*; Cook, *London*; Morris B. Kaplan, *Sodom on the Thames: Sex, Love, and Scandal in Wilde Times* (Cornell University Press, 2005); Judith R. Walkowitz, *Nights Out: Life in Cosmopolitan London* (Yale University Press, 2012).

76 See Kath Weston, 'Get Thee to a Big City: Sexual Imaginary and the Great Gay Migration', *GLQ: A Journal of Lesbian and Gay Studies* 2, no. 3 (1996), 253–77.

77 See John Howard, *Men Like That: A Southern Queer History* (University of Chicago Press, 1999); Chris Brickell, *Mates and Lovers: A History of Gay New Zealand* (Godwit, 2008); Martin Dines, *Gay Suburban Narratives in American and British Culture: Homecoming Queens* (Palgrave, 2009).

78 Julie Podmore and Alison Bain, 'Whither Queer Suburbanisms? Beyond Heterosuburbia and Queer Metronormativities', *Progress in Human Geography* 45, no. 5 (2021), 1254–77, at 1254; Scott Herring, *Another Country: Queer Anti-Urbanism* (New York University Press, 2010); Colin R. Johnson, *Just Queer Folks: Gender and Sexuality in Rural America* (Temple University Press, 2013); Mary L. Gray, Colin R. Johnson and Brian J. Gilley, eds, *Queering the Countryside: New Frontiers in Rural Queer Studies* (New York University Press, 2016).

79 Oram, 'Love "Off the Rails"', 54; Oram, *Her Husband was a Woman* (Routledge, 2007). See also Gutterman, *Her Neighbor's Wife*.

80 Podmore and Bain, 'Whither Queer Suburbanisms?', 1254.

81 Joanna Smith and Matthew Whitfield, *England's Suburbs, 1820–2020* (Liverpool University Press, 2025), Introduction; see also: Joanna Smith and Matthew Whitfield, 'Understanding Suburban Heritage', Historic England online feature, at: https://historicengland.org.uk/research/current/discover-and-understand/urban-public-realm/suburbs/ (accessed 8 April 2025).

82 Sara Ahmed, *The Cultural Politics of Emotion* (Edinburgh University Press, 2004), 11, 101–21.

83 Tom Allen, *No Shame: A Queer Life in Suburbia* (Hodder and Stoughton, 2020).

84 Butler, 'Performing LGBT Pride'; Cook and Oram, *Queer Beyond London*, chapter 4.

85 Or 'tearooms' in the United States. For the classic sociological text see Laud Humphries, *Tearoom Trade: Impersonal Sex in Public Places* (1970; Routledge, 2017).

86 See, for example, Oscar Moore, *A Matter of Life and Sex* (Penguin, 1992).

87 See Dines, *Gay Suburban Narratives*; Alison Bain and Julie Podmore, 'Relocating Queer: Comparing Suburban LGBTQ2S Activisms on Vancouver's Periphery', *Urban Studies* 58, no. 7 (2021), 1500–19; S. Hodge,

'No Fags out There: Gay Men, Identity and Suburbia', *Journal of Interdisciplinary Gender Studies* 1, no. 1 (1995), 41–8; Jonathan Botes, 'The Pink Inner-City: Creating Queer Spaces in Hillbrow, Johannesburg, during Apartheid', *Revue d'Histoire Contemporaine de l'Afrique* 2 (2021), 113–29.

88   Weston, 'Get Thee to a Big City'.

89   Cook, *London*, 122–33.

90   Lucas Crawford, 'A Good Ol'Country Time: Does Queer Rural Temporality Exist?', *Sexualities* 20, no. 8 (2017), 904–20; Townsend, 'Queer History of Parson's Pleasure'; Jason Goldman, '"The Golden Age of Gay Porn": Nostalgia and the Photography of Wilhelm von Gloeden', *GLQ: A Journal of Lesbian and Gay Studies* 12, no. 2 (2006), 237–58.

91   E. Patrick Johnson, *Sweet Tea: Black Gay Men of the South* (University of North Carolina Press, 2008); Johnson, *Black. Queer. Southern. Women* (University of North Carolina Press, 2018); Johnson, *Honeypot: Black Southern Women who love Women* (Duke University Press, 2019). See also Howard, *Men Like That*; Johnson, *Just Queer Folks*.

92   Caroline Bressey and Gemma Romain, 'Tracing Queer Black Spaces in Interwar Britain', in *Locating Queer History*, eds Bengry, Cook and Oram, 101–18.

93   On the landscape differences, see Michael Bunce, *The Countryside Ideal: Anglo-American Images of Landscape* (Routledge, 2005).

94   These lands were not 'virgin': they were inhabited indigenously and marked by settler incursions and the slaughter and deaths of Indigenous peoples. For a critique of a 1970s US gay male separatist project perpetuating dynamics of indigenous land theft and disenfranchisement, see Emily Hobson, *Lavender and Red: Liberation and Solidarity in the Gay and Lesbian Left* (University of California Press, 2016), 34–9.

95   On these specific ideas of escape see Catherine B. Kleiner, 'Doin' It for Themselves: Lesbian Land Communities in Southern Oregon, 1970–1995' (PhD diss., The University of New Mexico, 2003); Emily Kazyak, 'Midwest or Lesbian? Gender, Rurality, and Sexuality', *Gender & Society* 26, no. 6 (2012), 825–48. On rural Wales and England, see Darren P. Smith and Louise Holt, '"Lesbian Migrants in the Gentrified Valley" and 'other' geographies of rural gentrification', *Journal of Rural Studies* 21, no. 3 (2005), 313–22; Kip Jones, Lee-Ann Fenge, Rosie Read and Marilyn Cash, 'Collecting Older Lesbians' and Gay Men's Stories of Rural Life in South West England and Wales: "we were obviously gay girls . . . (so) he removed his cow from our field"', *Qualitative Social Research* 14, no. 2 (2013); Gavin Brown, 'Rethinking the Origins of Homonormativity: The diverse economies of rural gay life in England and Wales in the 1970s and 1980s', *Transactions of the Institute of British Geographers* 40, no. (2015), 549–61; Yvette Taylor, 'Not all Bright Lights, Big City? Classed intersections in urban and rural sexual geographies', *Reshaping Gender and Class in Rural Spaces* (Routledge, 2016), 179–98.

96 See Brickell, *Mates and Lovers*; Howard, *Men Like That*; Kazyak, 'Midwest or Lesbian?'; Valerie J. Korinek, *Prairie Fairies: A History of Queer Communities and People in Western Canada, 1930–1985* (University of Toronto Press, 2018); Jerry Watkins III, *Queering the Redneck Riviera: Sexuality and the rise of Florida Tourism* (University Press of Florida, 2021).

97 Howard, *Men Like That*.

98 This emerges in Jeffrey Weeks' memoir and is captured in its title: Weeks, *Between Worlds: A Queer Boy from the Valleys* (Partheon Press, 2021). See also Martin F. Manalansan, *Global Divas: Filipino Gay Men in the Diaspora* (Duke University Press, 2003).

99 Joanne Meyerowitz, 'Transnational Sex and U.S. History', *The American Historical Review* 114, no. 5 (2009), 1273–86; Elizabeth A. Povinelli and George Chauncey, 'Thinking Sexuality Transnationally: An Introduction', *GLQ: A Journal of Lesbian and Gay Studies* 5, no. 4 (1999), 439–49; Inderpal Grewal and Caren Kaplan, 'Global Identities: Theorizing Transnational Studies of Sexuality', *GLQ: A Journal of Lesbian and Gay Studies* 7, no. 4 (2001), 663–79. See also Rana M. Jaleel and Evren Savcı, 'Transnational Queer Materialism', *South Atlantic Quarterly* 123, no. 1 (2024), 1–31.

100 George Mosse, *Nationalism and Sexuality: Respectability and Abnormal Sexuality in Modern Europe* (H.Fertig, 1985). On the queer dynamics of port cities see: Chauncey, *Gay New York*; on Cardiff: Daryl Leeworthy, *A Little Gay History of Wales* (University of Wales Press, 2019); on Bergen: Gry Bang-Anderen and Bård Gram Økland, *Queer at Sea* (Bergen Maritime Museum, 2023); on Liverpool: West, 'Dark Matter', 202.

101 For incisive commentary, see Fatima El-Tayeb, '"Gays Who Cannot Properly Be Gay": Queer Muslims in the Neoliberal European City', *European Journal of Women's Studies* 1, no. 19 (2012), 79–95; Jennifer V. Evans, *The Queer Art of History* (Duke University Press, 2023), 187; Eithne Luibhéid, 'Queer/Migration: An Unruly Body of Scholarship', *GLQ: A Journal of Lesbian and Gay Studies* 14, no. 2 (2008), 169–90. On state institutions, see Kunzel, *Criminal Intimacy*; Margot Canaday, *The Straight State: Sexuality and Citizenship in Twentieth-Century America* (Princeton University Press, 2009).

102 André Fernandez, 'The Repression of Sexual Behaviour by the Aragonese Inquisition between 1560 and 1700', *Journal of the History of Sexuality* 7, no. 4 (1997), 469–501, at 500. For further discussion see chapter 2, section 2.

103 Jens Rydström, '"Sodomitical Sins Are Threefold": Typologies of Bestiality, Masturbation, and Homosexuality in Sweden, 1880–1950', *Journal of the History of Sexuality* 9, no. 3 (2000), 240–76.

104 Julian Jackson, *Living in Arcadia: Homosexuality, Politics, and Morality in France from the Liberation to AIDS* (University of Chicago Press, 2009);

Caron, *My Father and I*; Dagmar Herzog, ed., *Brutality and Desire: War and Sexuality in Europe's Twentieth Century* (Palgrave Macmillan, 2009); Francis John Mikus, 'The Road to an Integrated Homosexuality? A Comparative History of Same-Sex Marriage in France and the United Kingdom' (PhD diss., Queen Mary University of London, 2021).

105 Charlotte Ross, *Eccentricity and Sameness: Discourses on Lesbianism and Desire Between Women in Italy, 1860s–1930s* (Peter Lang, 2015).

106 Rebecca Jennings, *A Lesbian History of Britain: Love and Sex Between Women since 1500* (Greenwood, 2007); Tamara Chaplin, *Becoming Lesbian: A Queer History of Modern France* (University of Chicago Press, 2024).

107 Matt Cook, H. G. Cocks, Robert Mills and Randolph Trumbach, *A Gay History of Britain: Love and Sex Between Men since the Middle Ages* (Greenwood, 2007).

108 Meek, *Queer Voices*, 43.

109 See Sean Brady, 'Sectarianism and Queer Lives in Northern Ireland since the 1970s', in *Locating Queer History*, eds Bengry, Cook and Oram, 49–62; Tom Hulme, 'Queer Belfast during the First World War: Masculinity and Same-Sex Desire in the Irish City', *Irish Historical Studies* 45, no. 168 (2021), 239–61; Rachel Wallace, 'Gay Life and Liberation, a Photographic Record of 1970s Belfast: Exhibiting Private Photographs and Oral Histories', *The Public Historian* 41, no. 2 (2019), 144–62.

110 See Mole, ed., *Soviet and Post-Soviet Sexualities*; Saskia Wieringa and Horacio Sívori, eds, *The Sexual History of the Global South: Sexual Politics in Africa, Asia and Latin America* (Bloomsbury Publishing, 2013); Jennifer Ung Loh and J. Daniel Luther, eds, *'Queer' Asia: Decolonising and Reimagining Sexuality and Gender* (Zed Books, 2019); Emily Channell-Justice, ed., *Decolonizing Queer Experience: LGBT+ Narratives from Eastern Europe and Eurasia* (Lexington Books, 2020); Daniel Balderston and Donna Guy, eds, *Sex and Sexuality in Latin America: An Interdisciplinary Reader* (New York University Press, 1997).

111 Povinelli and Chauncey, 'Thinking Sexuality Transnationally'; Grewal and Kaplan, 'Global Identities'.

112 Leila J. Rupp, *Sapphistries: A Global History of Love Between Women* (New York University Press, 2011); Robert Aldrich, ed., *Gay Life and Culture: A World History* (Thames & Hudson, 2010).

113 Heike Bauer, *The Hirschfeld Archives: Violence, Death, and Modern Queer Culture* (Philadelphia: Temple University Press, 2017). See also Laurie Marhoefer, *Racism and The Making of Gay Rights: A Sexologist, His Student, and the Empire of Queer Love* (University of Toronto Press, 2022).

114 Jorge Salessi, 'The Argentine Dissemination of Homosexuality, 1890–1914', *Journal of the History of Sexuality* 4, no. 3 (1994), 337–68.

115 Gregory Woods, *Homintern: How Gay Culture Liberated the Modern World* (Yale University Press, 2016); see also David Johnson, *The Lavender Scare: The Cold War Persecution of Gays and Lesbians in the Federal Government* (University of Chicago Press, 2004).

116 See Yener Bayramoğlu, Łukasz Szulc and Radhika Gajjala, 'Transnational Queer Cultures and Digital Media: an introduction', *Communication, Culture & Critique* 17, no. 3 (2024): 147–51; S. Nair, 'Hey Good Lookin'!: Popular Culture, Femininity, and Lesbian Representation in Transnational Regimes', *Journal of Lesbian Studies* 12, no. 4 (2008), 407–22. For transnational dimensions of UK and USA queer popular culture see also essays in: Paul Burston and Colin Richardson, eds, *A Queer Romance: Lesbians, Gay Men and Popular Culture* (Routledge, 2005); and Thomas Peele, ed., *Queer Popular Culture: Literature, Media, Film, and Television* (Palgrave MacMillan, 2007).

117 Hongwei Bao, '"Queer Comrades": Transnational Popular Culture, Queer Sociality, and Socialist Legacy', *English Language Notes* 49, no. 1 (2011), 131–7. See also Fran Martin, 'Queer Pop Culture in the Sinophone Mediasphere', in *Routledge Handbook of East Asian Popular Culture*, eds Iwabuchi Koichi, Eva Tsai and Chris Berry (Routledge, 2016), 205–15.

118 On Stonewall's mythologization in the US context, see Elizabeth A. Armstrong and Suzanna M. Crage, 'Movements and Memory: The Making of the Stonewall Myth', *American Sociological Review* 71, no. 5 (2006), 724–51.

119 Andrew D. J. Shield, 'The Legacies of the Stonewall Riots in Denmark and the Netherlands', *History Workshop Journal* 89 (2020), 193–206; Dan Callwood, 'Re-Evaluating the French Gay Liberation Moment 1968–1983' (PhD diss., Queen Mary University of London, 2017); Jackson, *Living in Arcadia*; Rydström, 'Sodomitical Sins Are Threefold'.

120 Povinelli and Chauncey, 'Thinking Sexuality Transnationally', 439; see also Eithne Luibhéid and Lionel Cantú, eds, *Queer Migrations: Sexuality, U.S. Citizenship, and Border Crossings* (University of Minnesota Press, 2005).

121 On this point, see Bruce Baskerville, '"Could Not Even be Named": Sodomites Transported to Western Australia between 1851 and 1863', *Studies in Western Australian History* 34 (2020), 123–46.

122 Laurie Marhoefer, *Sex and the Weimar Republic: German Homosexual Emancipation and the Rise of the Nazis* (University of Toronto Press, 2015).

123 Jonathan Dollimore, *Sexual Dissidence: Augustine to Wilde, Freud to Foucault* (Oxford: Clarendon, 1991), chapters 4 and 20; Goldman, 'Golden Age of Gay Porn'; Jan-Henrik Friedrichs, 'Transnational Networks of Child Sexual Abuse and Consumerism: Edward Brongersma and the Pedophilia Debate of the 1970s and 1980s', *Journal of the History of Sexuality* 31, no. 2 (2022), 169–91.

124   Stanley and Baker, *Hello Sailor*; Tiemeyer, *Plane Queer*; Benjamin
      Bateman, 'Train(ing) Modernism: Virginia Woolf, E.M. Forster, and the
      moving locations of queerness', in *Transport in British Fiction:
      Technologies of Movement, 1840–1940*, eds Adrienne Gavin and Andrew
      Humphries (Palgrave Macmillan UK, 2015), 185–98.

125   See Manalansan, *Global Divas*; Manalansan, 'The "Stuff" of Archives:
      Mess, migration, and queer lives'. *Radical History Review* 2014, no. 120
      (2014), 94–107; Katherine Fobear, 'Nesting Bodies: Exploration of the
      body and embodiment in LGBT refugee oral history and participatory
      photography', *Social Alternatives* 35, no. 3 (2016), 33–43.

126   Rebecca Jennings, '"It Was a Hot Climate and It Was a Hot Time":
      Lesbian Migration and Transnational Networks in the Mid-Twentieth
      Century', *Australian Feminist Studies* 25, no. 63 (2010), 31–45; Bob Cant,
      Invented Identities? Lesbians and Gays Talk About Migration (Cassell,
      1997); Melissa Autumn White, 'Archives of Intimacy and Trauma: Queer
      Migration Documents as Technologies of Affect', *Radical History Review*
      120 (2014), 75–93.

127   Manalansan, *Global Divas*; Chauncey, *Gay New York*.

128   On the latter see Victor Román Mendoza, *Metroimperial Intimacies:
      Fantasy, Racial-Sexual Governance, and the Philippines in US Imperialism*
      (Duke University Press, 2015), 27.

129   Others who use a transnational lens in local, urban contexts include
      Chauncey, *Gay New York* and Capó, *Welcome to Fairyland*.

130   See, for example, Lyons, 'Mapping an Atlantic Sexual Culture'; Chauncey,
      Gay New York; Manalansan, *Global Divas*; Herzog, ed., *Brutality and Desire*.

131   For a revealing case study of these dynamics as exhibited in 1980s
      US-Nicaraguan gay and lesbian solidarity efforts, see Hobson, *Lavender
      and Red,* 120–54.

132   Jasbir Puar, *Terrorist Assemblages: Homonationalism in Queer Times*
      (Duke University Press, 2007).

133   See, for example, Evans, *The Queer Art of History*.

134   Dipesh Chakrabarty, *Provincializing Europe: Postcolonial Thought and
      Historical Difference* (Princeton University Press, 2000). Rahul Rao
      provides an especially lucid account of the queer significance of
      Chakrabarty's argument in Rao, *Out of Time*, 21–2.

135   Scott Bravmann, *Queer Fictions of the Past: History, Culture, and
      Difference* (Cambridge University Press, 1997), 95; Kunzel, *Criminal
      Intimacy*, 5–6; Rao, *Out of Time*.

136   A technique elaborated in Joe Moran, 'The Death of an Irishman: A
      Speculative Biography', *History Workshop Journal*, 98 (Autumn 2024),
      209–33.

137 On this see Laura Doan, *Disturbing Practices: History, Sexuality, and Women's Experience of Modern War* (Chicago: University of Chicago Press, 2013), especially chapter 2.

138 Carlo Ginzburg, 'Microhistory: Two or Three Things That I Know about It', *Critical Inquiry* 20, no. 1 (1993), 10–35, at 26.

139 Valerie Traub, *Thinking Sex with the Early Moderns* (University of Pennsylvania Press, 2016), 84–6.

140 Leah DeVun, *The Shape of Sex: Nonbinary Gender from Genesis to the Renaissance* (Columbia University Press, 2021), 203, 207.

141 On the development of these ideas through Foucault's work, see Michel Foucault, 'Nietzsche, Genealogy, History' (1971), in *Language, Counter Memory, Practice: Selected Essays and Interviews by Michel Foucault*, ed. Donal F. Bouchard (Cornell University Press, 1980); Foucualt, *Discipline and Punish*; and Foucault, *History of Sexuality Volume 1: An Introduction* (Allen Lane, 1979).

142 On this point, see Valerie Traub, 'The New Unhistoricism in Queer Studies', *PMLA* 128, no. 1 (2013), 21–39, at 25.

143 Mary Poovey, *Uneven Developments: The Ideological Work of Gender in Mid-Victorian England* (University of Chicago Press, 1988).

144 Elizabeth Freeman, 'Packing History, Count(er)ing Generations', *New Literary History* 31, no. 4 (2000), 727–44, at 728.

145 Halperin, *How to Do the History of Homosexuality*, 104–37. Anthropologist Stephen Murray offered another partially overlapping set of categories: of juvenile homosexuality, age-structured homosexuality, egalitarian homosexuality, and transgendered homosexuality. Stephen O'Murray, *Homosexualities* (University of Chicago Press, 2000).

146 Love, *Feeling Backward*.

147 Doan, *Disturbing Practices*, 35.

148 Chris Waters, 'Havelock Ellis, Sigmund Freud and the State: Discourses of Homosexual Identity in Interwar Britain', in *Sexology in Culture: Labelling Bodies and Desires*, eds Lucy Bland and Laura Doan (Polity, 1998), 165–79; Waters, 'The Homosexual as a Social Being in Britain, 1945–1968', *The Journal of British Studies* 51, no. 3 (2007), 685–710.

149 See essays in Joseph Bristow, ed., *Oscar Wilde and Modern Culture: The Making of a Legend* (Ohio University Press, 2008) – including my own 'Wilde Lives: Derek Jarman and the Queer Eighties', 285–304.

150 On which see Michael Roper, 'Between Manliness and Masculinity: the "war generation" and the psychology of fear in Britain, 1914–1950', *Journal of British Studies* 44, no. 2 (2005), 343–62; Santanu Das, '"Kiss Me, Hardy": Intimacy, Gender, and Gesture in First World War Trench Literature', *Modernism/Modernity* 9, no. 1 (2002): 51–74.

151 Charles Upchurch, *'Beyond the Law': The Politics Ending the Death Penalty for Sodomy in Britain* (Temple University Press, 2021).

152 Mort, *Capital Affairs*; Houlbrook, *Queer London*; Bauer and Cook, *Queer 1950s*.

153 Bravmann, *Queer Fictions*, 49.

154 For a meditation on the meanings accruing to essentially meaningless units of time – like the decade – see: Sally Ledger and Scott McCracken, eds, *Cultural Politics at the fin de siècle* (Cambridge University Press, 1995); Walter Loqueur, 'Fin-de-siècle: Once more with feeling', *Journal of Contemporary History* 31, no. 1 (1996), 5–47; David Geiringer, 'The Nineties in 1990s Britain: long-sighted temporalities at the turn of the millennium', *Historical Research* 98, no. 279 (2025), 124–44.

155 Evans, *The Queer Art of History*, 23; Halberstam, *The Queer Art of Failure*.

156 On this point see Alexandra Shepard and Garthine Walker, 'Gender, Change and Periodisation', *Gender and History* 20, no. 3 (2008), 453–62.

157 Madhavi Menon, 'Period Cramps', in *Queer Renaissance Historiography: Backward Gaze*, eds Vincent Joseph Nardizzi, Stephen Guy-Bray and Will Stockton (Ashgate, 2009), 229–38.

158 Traub, 'New Unhistoricism', 29, 32.

159 On queer pleasures in the supposedly dour 1950s, see Bauer and Cook, *Queer 1950s*; Houlbrook, *Queer London*; Mort, *Capital Affairs*.

160 See Susan Stryker, *Transgender History: The Roots of Today's Revolution*, 2nd edn (Seal Press, 2017), and her film *Screaming Queens: The Riot at Compton's Cafeteria* (2005); see also Mark Gevisser, *The Pink Line: The World's Queer Frontiers* (Profile Books, 2020); Stuart Timmons, *The Trouble with Harry Hay: Founder of the Modern Gay Movement* (Alyson, 1990); Eric Cervini, *The Deviant's War: The Homosexual vs. the United States of America* (Farrar, Straus and Giroux, 2020). On the radical dimensions of pre-Stonewall activism, see David Minto, 'Mr Grey Goes to Washington: The Homophile Internationalism of Britain's Homosexual Law Reform Society', in Brian Lewis, ed., *British Queer History: New Approaches and Perspectives* (Manchester University Press, 2013), 219–43; Jackson, *Living in Arcadia*; Martin Meeker, 'Behind the Mask of Respectability: Reconsidering the Mattachine Society and Male Homophile Practice, 1950s and 1960s', *Journal of the History of Sexuality* 10, no. 1 (2001), 78–116; Reithmayr, 'The Invention of Gay Community'; Mori Reithmayr, 'Community Before Liberation: Theorizing Gay Community in San Francisco, 1953–1969' (PhD diss., University of Oxford, 2023).

161 On this point, see Tomás Almaguer, 'Chicano Men: A Cartography of Homosexual Identity and Behavior', in *Lesbian, Gay, Bisexual, and Transgender History: Critical Readings, Volume 4: The Contemporary Period*, ed. Michael Bronski (Bloomsbury Academic, 2020), 258–78; Cook and Oram, Queer Beyond London.

162 Chakrabarty, *Provincialising Europe*, 16. Rao cites this neat summation too in his discussion of Chakrabarty – see Rao, *Out of Time*, 21.

163 On this theme see Jeremy Chow and Bradi Bushman, 'Hydro-eroticism', in *English Language Notes* 57, no.1 (2009), 960–114; Christopher Brown and Paul Hirsch, 'Introduction: The Erotics of the Swimming Pool', in eds Brown and Hirsch, *The Cinema of the Swimming Pool* (Peter Lang, 2014), 1–20.

164 Turner, *Backward Glances*.

165 Cook and Oram, *Queer Beyond London*, 122–3.

Chapter 4: Queer History/Public History

1 The roster of events included 'Rebel Failures: Art, Sex, Politics and the Rebel Dykes', Nottingham Contemporary, 24 September 2023; 'Northern Dykes Consultation', Islington Mill, Salford, 27 October 2024; Butch Revival Club Night, 'Inspired by Chain Reaction and the Hacienda', Manchester, 22 February 2025.

2 For more on the Rebel Dykes History Project, see https://www.rebeldykeshistoryproject.com (accessed 12 December 2024).

3 *Rebel Dykes* (dir. Siân A. Williams and Harri Shanahan, 2021).

4 For further discussion detail see Cook and Oram, *Queer Beyond London*, 208.

5 Correspondence with Siobhan Fahey, 17–23 January 2025.

6 National Council on Public History, https://ncph.org/what-is-public-history/about-the-field/ (accessed 30 November 2024).

7 Raphael Samuel, *Theatres of Memory, Volume 1: Past and Present in Contemporary Culture* (Verso, 1994), 8, 18. For an overview of different strands of public history practice, see especially Hilda Kean and Paul Ashton, 'Introduction: People and their Pasts and Public History Today', in *Public History Today*, eds Hilda Kean and Paul Ashton (Palgrave Macmillan, 2009), 1–20.

8 On this point see Ludmilla Jordanova, *History in Practice* (Hodder Arnold, 2000), 156.

9 Jack Halberstam, 'What's That Smell? Queer Temporalities and Subcultural Lives', *International Journal of Cultural Studies* 6, no. 3 (2003), 313–33, at 318.

10 On this, see Robert Archibald, *A Place to Remember: Using History to Build Community* (AltaMira Press, 1999); David Glassberg, 'Public History and the Study of Memory', *The Public Historian* 18, no. 2 (1996), 11.

11   Gareth Maeer, 'A People-Centred Approach to Heritage: The Experience of the Heritage Lottery Fund 1994–2014', *Journal of Community Archaeology & Heritage* 4, no. 1 (2017), 38–52.

12   Samuel, *Theatres of Memory*.

13   Mark Pendleton, 'And I Dance with Somebody: Queer History in a Japanese Nightclub', *History Workshop Journal* 90 (2020), 297–310.

14   See, for example, the successful campaign to achieve listed (protected) status for the Royal Vauxhall Tavern in London's Vauxhall in 2015, the same year the iconic George and Dragon pub in Shoreditch closed due to rent increases. The latter had earlier been recreated at London's Institute of Contemporary Arts. See Ben Walters, 'Supporting Statement to Have the Royal Vauxhall Tavern Added to the National Heritage List for England' (2015), http://www.rvt.community/wp-content/uploads/2015/09/Initial-RVT-listing-application-January-2015.pdf (accessed 16 December 2024).

15   Carolyn Dinshaw, *Getting Medieval: Sexualities and Communities, Pre- and Postmodern* (Duke University Press, 1999), 36, 40.

16   On liminality, heterotopia, and the equivocal queer meanings of public space, see Chapter 2, section 1.

17   See Robert Mills, 'Theorizing the Queer Museum', *Museums & Social Issues* 3, no. 1 (2008), 41–52; Anne Rensma, Daniel Neugebauer and Olle Lundin, '"A Museum Can Never Be Queer Enough": The Van Abbemuseum as a Testing Ground for Institutional Queering', in *Museums, Sexuality, and Gender Activism*, eds Joshua G. Adair and Amy K. Levin (Routledge, 2020), 278–87; Erica Robenalt, *The Queer Museum: Radical Inclusion and Western Museology* (Taylor and Francis, 2024).

18   On these points see Douglas Crimp, *On the Museum's Ruins* (MIT press, 1993), 18–19; Mills, 'Theorizing the Queer Museum'; Rensma, Neugebauer and Lundin, 'A Museum Can Never Be Queer Enough'; Robenalt, *The Queer Museum*; Juana María Rodríguez, *Sexual Futures, Queer Gestures, and Other Latina Longings* (New York University Press, 2014); Kwame Holmes, 'What's the Tea: Gossip and the Production of Black Gay Social History', *Radical History Review* 122 (2015), 55–69; José Esteban Muñoz, *Disidentifications: Queers of Color and the Performance of Politics* (University of Minnesota Press, 1999); Ajamu X, Topher Campbell and Mary Stevens, 'Love and Lubrication in the Archives, or rukus!: A Black Queer Archive for the United Kingdom', *Archivaria* 68 (2010), 271–94, at 272.

19   Timothy D'Arch Smith, *Love in Earnest: Some Notes on the Lives and Writing of the Uranian Poets, 1889–1930* (Routledge, 1970); Matt Cook, *London and the Culture of Homosexuality, 1885–1914* (Cambridge University Press, 2003), chapter 5.

20   On these points see Sarah Waters, 'The Most Famous Fairy in History: Antinous and Homosexual Fantasy', *Journal of the History of Sexuality* 6,

no. 2 (1995), 194–230; Cook, *London and the Culture of Homosexuality*, chapter 5.

21   See Cook, *London*, 34.

22   On this point, see Alison Oram, 'Going on an Outing: The Historic House and Queer Public History', *Rethinking History* 15, no. 2 (2011), 189–207.

23   Clare Barlow, *Queer British Art 1861–1967* (Tate Britain, 2017); Robenalt, *Queer Museum*, 34–54.

24   On 'Beyond the Binary', see Beth Asbury, 'Out in Oxford and Beyond the Binary: LGBTQ+ Stories in the Pitt Rivers Museum', *The Archaeologist* 110 (2020), 14–15. On such queer reflexivity more broadly, see Robenalt, *Queer Museum*.

25   See 'Pride of Place' at https://historicengland.org.uk/research/inclusive-heritage/lgbtq-heritage-project/ (accessed 16 December 2024); and also Justin Bengry, Robert Bevan and Richard Morrice, *Pride of Place: A Guide to Understanding and Protecting Lesbian, Gay, Bisexual, Transgender and Queer (LGBTQ) Heritage* (Historic England, 2016) at https://research.gold.ac.uk/id/eprint/22253/ (accessed 16 December 2024).

26   Jennifer Evans, *The Queer Art of History* (Duke University Press, 2023), 62. See also Michael Thomas Taylor, 'Magnus Hirschfeld's Institute for Sexual Science as Archive, Museum and Exhibition', in *Not Straight from Germany: Sexual Publics and Sexual Citizenship since Magnus Hirschfeld*, eds Michael Thomas Taylor, Annette Timm and Rainer Herrn (University of Michigan Press, 2017).

27   Katie Sutton, 'Sexology's Photographic Turn: Visualizing Trans Identity in Interwar Germany', *Journal of the History of Sexuality* 27, no. 3 (2018), 442–79.

28   The Wellcome Collection in London, for example, has its roots in Henry Wellcome's ethnographic and sexological collecting, including of erotica, as revealed in their 2014 exhibition 'The Institute of Sexology'. See *Institute of Sexology* (Wellcome Collection, 2014).

29   See Laurie Marhoefer, *Sex and the Weimar Republic: German Homosexual Emancipation and the Rise of the Nazis* (University of Toronto Press, 2015).

30   Jennifer V. Evans, 'Harmless Kisses and Infinite Loops: Making Space for Queer Place in 21st Century Berlin', in *Queer Cities, Queer Cultures: Europe Since 1945*, eds Matt Cook and Jennifer V. Evans (Bloomsbury, 2014), 75–94; Evans, *Queer Art of History*, chapters 4 and 5, especially 128.

31   Evans, *Queer Art of History*, 4.

32   Evans, *Queer Art of History*, 163.

33   See Marhoefer, *Sex and the Weimar Republic*.

34 Robert Weyeneth suggests something similar in relation to the American built environment between 1880 and 1960 which embedded racial segregation but has only been used unevenly since to bring it to public consciousness. Robert Weyeneth, 'What I've learned Along the Way: A Public Historian's Intellectual Odyssey', *The Public Historian* 36, no. 2 (2014), 9–25.

35 Evans, *Queer Art of History*, 112, 120–1.

36 Susan Ferentinos, 'Ways of Interpreting Queer Pasts', *The Public Historian* 41, no. 2 (2019), 19–43.

37 See: https://www.schwulesmuseum.de/presseaktuell/a-stroll-with-sex-workers-through-schoeneberg/?lang=en (accessed 16 December 2024).

38 Ann Cvetkovich, *An Archive of Feelings: trauma, forgetting and lesbian public cultures* (Duke University Press, 2003).

39 Ashkan Sepahvand, *Odarodle* (Schwules Museum, 2017), 22–3.

40 Robenalt, *Queer Museum*, chapter 6; Birgit Bosold, E.-J. Scott and Renaud Chantraine, 'Queer Tactics, Handwritten Stories: Disrupting the Field of Museum Practices', *Museum International* 72, no. 3/4 (2020), 212–25.

41 Opening panel, 'Our Vast Queer Past' exhibition (2011–14), GLBT Historical Society Museum.

42 Don Romesburg, 'Going Viral with Brick-and-Mortar Queer History: Opening the GLBT History Museum', talk presented as part of a panel titled 'The Pleasures and Perils of LGBTQ Public History', American Historical Association Annual Meeting, Chicago, 8 January 2012, cited in Gerard Koskovich, 'Displaying the Queer Past: Purposes, Publics, and Possibilities at the GLBT History Museum', *QED: A Journal in GLBTQ Worldmaking* 1, no. 2 (2014), 61–78, at 70. See also Gerard Koskovich, Don Romesburg and Amy Sueyoshi, 'Curators in Conversation: Conceiving the Queer Past at the GLBT Historical Society Museum', *Museum International* 72, no. 3/4 (2020), 66–79. With thanks to Gerard Koskovich.

43 Jennifer Tyburczy, *Sex Museums: The Politics and Performance of Display* (University of Chicago Press, 2016), 121.

44 Tyburczy, *Sex Museums*, 121–4.

45 On the erotics of such spaces, see Barry Reay, *Sex in the Archives: Writing American Sexual Histories* (Manchester University Press, 2018), 229; Zeb Tortorici, 'Queer Museum Studies: Sex, Archives, and Exhibitions', *GLQ: A Journal of Lesbian and Gay Studies* 24, no. 1 (2018), 162–4; Jill Austin, Jennifer Brier, Jessica Herczeg-Konecny and Anne Parsons, 'When the Erotic Becomes Illicit: Struggles Over Displaying Queer History at a Mainstream Museum', *Radical History Review*, 113 (2012), 187–97.

46 Nan Alamilla Boyd, *Wide-Open Town: A History of Queer San Francisco to 1965* (University of California Press, 2003); Susan Stryker and Jim Van Buskirk, *Gay by the Bay: A History of Queer Culture in the San Francisco Bay Area* (San Francisco, 1996).

47 Koskovich, 'Displaying the Queer Past'.

48 See Don Romesburg and Amy Sueyoshi, 'Passionate Struggle: Dynamics of San Francisco's GLBT History', *Fabulas: The Journal of the Gay, Lesbian, Bisexual, Transgender Historical Society* (2008), 1–17.

49 Koskovich, 'Displaying the Queer Past'. For a list of temporary exhibitions at the museum see https://www.glbthistory.org/past-exhibitions (accessed 23 January 2025).

50 The honor walk includes doctor and activist Marie Equi (1872–1952), singer and actress Josephine Baker (1906–75); artist Frida Kahlo (1907–54), early recipient of gender reassignment surgery and trans advocate Christine Jorgensen (1926–89); Iranian actor, poet and activist Fereydoun Farrokhzad (1938–92), and many others. See http://rainbowhonorwalk.org/ (accessed 28 January 2025).

51 Koskovich, Romesburg and Sueyoshi, 'Curators in Conversation', 71.

52 Another temporary exhibition by the GLBT Historical Society, 'Two-Spirit Voices: Returning to the Circle' (2019), celebrated the twentieth anniversary of Bay Area American Indian Two Spirits (BAAITS), 'an organization committed to activism and service for the Two-Spirit and ally communities of the San Francisco Bay Area', https://www.glbthistory.org/two-spirit-voices (accessed 28 January 2025).

53 Susan Stryker, 'At the Crossroads of Turk and Taylor', *Places Journal* (2021), https://placesjournal.org/article/transgender-resistance-and-prison-abolitionism-san-francisco-tenderloin/?cn-reloaded=1 (accessed 15 August 2024); Madison Levesque, 'National Register Nomination for Compton's Cafeteria' (Sacramento, California State University, 2022).

54 For details of the march see https://www.glbthistory.org/labor-of-love-info (accessed 21 January 21 2025). On the Glide Memorial Church, see David Holly, 'Coming Out Under Jesus: Glide Memorial and the Struggle for Gay Civil Rights in San Francisco', *Clio's Scroll* 14, no. 2 (2013), 49–72; and Heather White, *Reforming Sodom: Protestants and the Rise of Gay Rights* (University of North Carolina Press, 2015), 71–107.

55 Thomas R. Dunn, *Queerly Remembered: Rhetorics for Representing the GLBTQ Past* (University of South Carolina Press, 2016).

56 See https://en.uit.no/tmu/utstillinger/utstilling?p_document_id=789153 (accessed 12 December 2024).

57 Vidar Fagerheim Kalsås, 'Skeive Sjøfolk, Bergen's Sjøfartsmuseum (28. oktober 2022 – haust 2024)', *Norsk Museumstidsskirft* 9, no. 1/2 (2023), 70–6.

58 Cited at https://museoq.org (accessed 12 August 2024).

59 Cited at https://museoq.org (accessed 12 August 2024). Instagram @museoq

60   Rita Paqvalén, 'Beyond Toma and Tove: Queering Finnish Museums from an Intersectional Perspective', *Journal for Queer Studies in Finland* 14, no. 1/2 (2020), 62–77; Visa Aleksis Immonen, 'What Is Queer Heritage? Queercache and the Epistemology of the Closet', *Lambda Nordica: Tidskrift Om Homosexualitet* 27, no. 2 (2022), 41–68.

61   See https://www.helsinginkaupunginmuseo.fi/en/events/launch-art-project-queercache/ (accessed 12 July 2025).

62   Immonen, 'What Is Queer Heritage?'. On the use of intimate, handwritten stories, see Bosold, Scott and Chantraine, 'Queer Tactics, Handwritten Stories'.

63   See Chapter 3, section 2.

64   See Alex Bakker, Rainer Hern, Michael Thomas Taylor and Annette Timm, 'Others of My Kind: Transatlantic Transgender Histories' (Calgary University Press, 2020); and https://www.schwulesmuseum.de/ausstellung/transtrans-transatlantic-transgender-histories/?lang=en (accessed 15 October 2024).

65   *Legend of the Underground* (dir. Nneka Onuora and Giselle Bailey, 2021).

66   Projects have included 'Queer in Brighton' (2012) and 'Brighton Trans*formed' (2014); Brighton Museum exhibitions have included 'Museum of Transology' (from 2014), 'Queer Looks' (from 2018), and 'Queer the Pier'(from 2020). See *Brighton Trans*formed* (QueenSpark Books, 2014); Anthony Luvera and Maria Jastrzębska, eds, *Queer in Brighton* (New Writing South, 2014).

67   Nina Simon, *The Participatory Museum* (Museum 2.0, 2010); Bosold, Scott and Chantraine, 'Queer Tactics, Handwritten Stories'.

68   See Will Fellows, *A Passion to Preserve: Gay Men as Keepers of Culture* (University of Wisconsin Press, 2004).

69   See Richard L. Florida, *The Rise of the Creative Class* (Basic Books, 2002); John Potvin, *Bachelors of a Different Sort: Queer Aesthetics, Material Culture and the Modern Interior in Britain* (Manchester University Press, 2014); Potvin, 'Collecting Intimacy One Object at a Time: Material Culture, Aestheticism, and the Spaces of Aesthetic Companionship', in *Material Cultures, 1740–1920: The Meanings and Pleasures of Collecting*, eds Potvin and Alla Myzelev (Ashgate, 2009), 191–208; Jason Edwards, 'The Lessons of Leighton House: Aesthetics, Politics, Erotics', in *Rethinking the Interior, c.1867–1896*, eds Jason Edwards and Imogen Hart (Ashgate, 2010), 85–110; Matt Cook and Alison Oram, *Prejudice and Pride: Celebrating LGBT Heritage* (National Trust, 2017); Matt Cook, 'Domestic Passions: Unpacking the Homes of Charles Shannon and Charles Ricketts', *Journal of British Studies* 51, no. 3 (2012), 618–40.

70   Matt Cook, *Queer Domesticities: Homosexuality and Home Life in Twentieth Century London* (London: Palgrave Macmillan, 2014), 85.

71   Ibid.

72   For more on this and the genesis of the ArQuives and the ONE Archive see Rebecka Taves Sheffield, *Documenting Rebellions: A Study of Four Lesbian and Gay Archives in Queer Times* (Sacramento: Litwin Books, 2020). On the Australian Queer Archive see: Daniel Marshall, 'The Queer Archive: Teaching and Learning Sexuality in Australia', *Transformations*, 21, no. 2 (2010), 36.

73   Queer Indonesian Archive: https://qiarchive.org/en/; Acervo Bajubá: https://acervobajuba.com.br/sobre/ (both accessed 11 January 2025).

74   Rachel Orbman, 'A Genealogy of the Lesbian Herstory Archives, 1974–2014', *Journal of Contemporary Archival Studies* 1, no. 1 (2014), 1.

75   Joan Nestle, 'The Will to Remember: The Lesbian Herstory Archives of New York', *Feminist Review* 34, no. 1 (1990), 86–94; Nestle, 'Who Were We to Do Such a Thing? Grassroots Necessities, Grassroots Dreaming: The LHA in Its Early Years', *Radical History Review* 122 (2015), 233–42.

76   Jen Jack Gieseking, 'Useful In/Stability: The Dialectical Production of the Social and Spatial Lesbian Herstory Archives', *Radical History Review* 122 (2015), 25–37, at 33.

77   On these issues in relation to the admission policies of the Feminist Archive North in the United Kingdom, see Jeska Rees, '"Are you a Lesbian?" Challenges in Recording and Analysing the Women's Liberation Movement in England', *History Workshop Journal* 69, no. 1 (2010), 177–87.

78   K. J. Rawson, 'Archival Justice: An Interview with Ben Power Alwin', *Radical History Review* 122 (2015), 177–87, at 179, 187.

79   Ajamu X in interview at: https://www.frieze.com/article/ajamu-pleasures-darkroom (accessed 10 December 2024).

80   Ajamu X, Campbell, and Stevens, 'Love and Lubrication'; Daniel Marshall, Kevin P. Murphy and Zeb Tortorici, 'Editors' Introduction: Queering Archives: Intimate Tracings', *Radical History Review* 122 (2015), 1–10, at 6.

81   Anthony Manion and Ruth Morgan, 'The Gay and Lesbian Archives: Documenting Same-Sexuality in an African Context', *Agenda: Empowering Women for Gender Equity* 67 (2006), 29–35.

82   Nestle, 'Who Were We to Do Such a Thing?'; K. J. Rawson, 'Archival Justice'.

83   I am grateful to Runar Jordåen and Ben Miller for their tours of the Skievt and Schwules archives respectively.

84   See, for example, the trans-led Digital Transgender Archive which has involved wide ranging collaboration with trans and LGBTQ+ collections, including ArQuives, GLBT Historical Society, Leather Archives and Museum, Transgender Oral History Project, and ONE National Gay and Lesbian Archives. See: https://www.digitaltransgenderarchive.net (accessed 23 June 2025).

85   The Transgender Archive was founded at the University of Ulster in 1986
     by academic Richard Ekins in collaboration with the British Self-help
     Association of Transexuals (SHAFT); it transferred to Canada in 2013.

86   Manion and Morgan, 'The Gay and Lesbian Archives'.

87   Malcolm Corrigall and Jenny Marsden, '"District Six Is Really My Gay
     Vicinity": The Kewpie Photographic Collection', *African Arts* 53, no. 2
     (2020), 10–27; Ruth Ramsden-Karelse, 'Moving and Moved: Reading
     Kewpie's District Six', *GLQ: A Journal of Lesbian and Gay Studies* 26, no. 3
     (2020), 405–38.

88   Manion and Morgan, 'The Gay and Lesbian Archives'.

89   On queer martrys - and their iconic status - see Brett Krutzsch, *Dying to
     Be Normal: Gay Martyrs and the Transformation of American Sexual
     Politics* (Oxford University Press, 2019); Jordy Jones, 'A Martyr in the
     Archive: The Life and Afterlife of Harvey Milk's Suit', *Somatechnics* 1, no. 2
     (2011), 372–87; Dominic Janes, *Visions of Queer Martyrdom from John
     Henry Newman to Derek Jarman* (University of Chicago Press, 2015). See
     also James Marion Holbrook IV, *Performing Queer History: Creating
     Community and Identity through Biographical Theatre* (The Catholic
     University of America, 2020);

90   On this point, see Matt Cook, 'Wilde Lives: Derek Jarman and the Queer
     Eighties', in *Oscar Wilde and Modern Culture: The Making of a Legend*,
     ed. Joseph Bristow (Ohio University Press, 2009), 368–89.

91   Simon Joyce, *LGBT Victorians: Sexuality and Gender in the Nineteenth-
     Century Archives* (Oxford University Press, 2022), coda.

92   Laura Doan, 'Queer History / Queer Memory: The Case of Alan Turing',
     GLQ: A Journal of Lesbian and Gay Studies 23, no. 1 (2017), 113–36.

93   On Turing, see especially Doan, 'Queer History / Queer Memory'.

94   Jon Wargo and J. J. Coleman, 'Pinkwashing Picturebooks: Reading
     Homonational Heroes Through Contemporary US LGBTQ + Biographies',
     Children's Literature in Education 55 (2024), 37–59, at 37.

95   See Charles Upchurch, 'Following Anne Lister: Continuity and queer
     history before and after the late nineteenth century', *Journal of Lesbian
     Studies* 26, no. 4 (2022), 400–14.

96   On this point, see Anna Clark, 'Anne Lister's Construction of Lesbian
     Identity', *Journal of the History of Sexuality* 7, no. 1 (1996), 23–50; see also
     Jill Liddington, 'Anne Lister of Shibden Hall, Halifax (1791–1840): Her
     Diaries and the Historians', *History Workshop* 35 (1993), 45–77.

97   Caroline Eisner, 'Shifting the Focus: Anne Lister as Pillar of
     Conservatism', *a/b: Auto/Biography Studies* 17, no. 1 (2001), 28–42.

98   Liddington, 'Anne Lister', 52.

99   Ibid.

100 Ibid., 55; Clark, 'Anne Lister's Construction of Lesbian Identity', 27.

101 On this point, see Martha Vicinus, 'The History of Lesbian History',
      Feminist Studies 38, no. 3 (2012), 566–96.

102 Chris Roulston, 'The Revolting Anne Lister: The UK's First Modern
      Lesbian', *Journal of Lesbian Studies* 17, no. 3/4 (2013), 267–78.

103 'Revealing Anne Lister', BBC 2 (dir. Matthew Hill, broadcast on 9 June
      2010); 'The Secret Diaries of Miss Anne Lister', BBC Radio HD (broadcast
      on 31 May 31 2010).

104 https://unesco.org.uk/our-sites/memory-of-the-world/diaries-of-anne-
      lister (accessed 28 January 2025).

105 Jennifer Reed, 'From Anne Lister to Gentleman Jack to Anne Lister',
      Memory Studies 16, no. 1 (2023), 154–60.

106 https://english.northwestern.edu/about/anne-lister-society/als-fourth-
      meeting-2025.html (accessed 28 January 2025).

107 Papers from the first meeting were published in the *Journal of Lesbian
      Studies* 26 (2022).

108 On this cross-over, see especially Jill Liddington, *As Good as a Marriage:
      The Anne Lister Diaries 1836–38* (Manchester University Press, 2023);
      Caroline Gonda and Chris Roulston, eds, *Decoding Anne Lister: From the
      Archives to 'Gentleman Jack'* (Cambridge University Press, 2023).

109 Simon Joyce, 'The Perverse Presentism of Rainbow Plaques: Memorializing
      Anne Lister', *Nineteenth Century Contexts* 41, no. 5 (2019), 601–10.

110 https://www.bbc.co.uk/news/uk-england-york-north-yorkshire-47404525
      (accessed 28 January 28 2025). For broader discussion of lesbian erasure
      in such contexts see Thomas R. Dunn, 'Whence the lesbian in queer
      monumentality? Intersections of gender and sexuality in public memory',
      Southern Communication Journal 82, no. 4 (2017), 203–15.

111 Jessica Campbell, 'Can We Call Anne Lister a Lesbian?', *Journal of Lesbian
      Studies* 26, no. 4 (2022), 354–66.

112 Kit Heyam, *Before We Were Trans: A New History of Gender* (Basic Books,
      2022), 84–9; Joyce, *LGBT Victorians*, chapters 1 and 6. Joyce develops
      this argument by bringing Lister into conversation and comparison with
      four of her contemporaries (Scottish school teachers Jane Pirie and
      Marianne Woods, and Vermont couple Charity Bryant and Sylvia Drake).
      See also Jack Halberstam, *Female Masculinity* (Duke University Press,
      1998), 72.

113 Liddington, 'Anne Lister', 56; Jill Liddington, 'Beating the Inheritance
      Bounds: Anne Lister (1791–1840) and Her Dynastic Identity', *Gender &
      History* 7, no. 2 (1995), 260–74; Liddington, 'Anne Lister 1806–32: Diarist
      and Heiress', in *Female Fortune: The Anne Lister Diaries, 1833–36: Land,
      Gender and Authority* (Manchester University Press, 2022), 15–26;
      Liddington, 'Anne Lister and Emily Brontë, 1838–39: Landscape with
      Figures', *Brontë Society Transactions* 26, no. 1 (2001), 46–67; Liddington,
      'The Listers of Shibden Hall', in *Female Fortune*, 3–14.

114 Saidiya Hartman, 'Venus in Two Acts', *Small Axe 12*, no. 2 (2008), 1–14, at 1; Hartman, 'Intimate History, Radical Narrative', *The Journal of African American History* 106, no. 1 (2021), 127–35; Hartman, *Wayward Lives, Beautiful Experiments: Riotous Black Girls, Troublesome Women, and Queer Radicals* (WW Norton & Company, 2019).

115 David Dean, 'Theatre: A Neglected Site of Public History?', *The Public Historian* 34, no. 3 (2012), 21–39, at 37. For examples of what performance can reveal historically see Karl Toepfer, 'Nudity and Modernity in German Dance, 1910–30', *Journal of the History of Sexuality* 3, no. 1 (1992), 58–108; Laurence Senelick, 'The Homosexual as Villain and Victim in Fin-de-Siècle Drama', *Journal of the History of Sexuality* 4, no. 2 (1993), 201–29.

116 Dean, 'Theatre'. On performance and gestures as sources of historical knowledge, see also Joseph Roach, *Cities of the Dead: Circum-Atlantic Performance* (Columbia University Press, 1996), Rebecca Schneider, 'Archives: Performance Remains', *Performance Research* 6, no. 2 (2001), 100–8; Holbrook, *Performing Queer History*.

117 Peter Bailey, 'Conspiracies of Meaning: Music Hall and the Knowingness of Popular Culture', *Past & Present* 144, no. 1 (1994), 138–70, at 169.

118 On this point, see especially Simon Dodi, 'Camp Affections: Experiential Insights into British Camp Performance' (PhD diss., The Royal Central School of Speech and Drama, 2022); Dodi, 'Camp Can Be Such a Drag: Approaches to Understanding Camp and Drag', in *Drag Histories, Herstories and Hairstories: Drag in a Changing Scene, vol. 2*, eds Mark Edward and Stephen Farrier (Methuen Drama, 2021), 83–96.

119 Ajamu X, Frieze interview.

120 João Florêncio and Ben Miller, 'Sexing the Archive: Gay Porn and Subcultural Histories', *Radical History Review* 142 (2022), 133–41.

121 Heike Bauer, 'Literature and Biography as Sources for LGBTQ Lived Experience', in eds Dominic Janes and Howard Chiang, *The Oxford Handbook of LGBTQ History* (Oxford University Press, 2026).

122 Mary Renault, *The Charioteer* (Longman, 1953); *Oscar Wilde* (dir. Gregory Ratoff, 1960); *The Trials of Oscar Wilde* (dir. Ken Hughes, 1960).

123 See, for example, the film *Victim* (dir. Basil Dearden, 1961) and Rodney Garland, *The Heart in Exile* (1953; Milliveres, 1995). For discussion, see Cook, *Queer Domesticities*, part 3; Richard Hornsey, *The Spiv and the Architect: Unruly Life in Postwar London* (University of Minnesota Press, 2010).

124 Matt Cook, 'Words Written Without Any Stopping', in Roger Wollen and James Cary Parkes et al., *Derek Jarman: A Portrait* (Thames & Hudson, 1996), 105–11; Janes, *Visions of Queer*; Karl Fugelso, Chris Jones and Robert Mills, eds, *Derek Jarman's Medieval Modern* (Boydell & Brewer, 2018).

125 Neil Bartlett, *Who Was That Man: A Present for Mr Oscar Wilde* (Serpent's Tail, 1988), back cover.

126 Patrick Gale, *A Place Called Winter* (Tinder Press, 2015); Sarah Waters, *Tipping the Velvet* (Virago, 1998); Tom Crew, *The New Life* (Chatto & Windus, 2023).

127 There is now a long list of countries with an LGBTQ+ History Month, including Hungary (from 2013), Germany (2014), Canada, Finland (both 2018) and Italy and Cuba (both 2022).

128 See John Vincent, *LGBT People and the UK Cultural Sector: The Response of Libraries, Museums, Archives and Heritage since 1950* (Routledge, 2016). See also the special issue on collecting, interpreting and displaying LGBTQ history in *Social History of Museums* 41 (2017).

129 Matt Houlbrook, *Queer London: Perils and Pleasures in the Sexual Metropolis, 1918–1957* (Chicago University Press, 2005).

130 https://www.theguardian.com/world/2017/sep/18/william-john-bankes-forced-into-exile-after-gay-liaison-celebrated-by-national-trust (accessed 28 January 2025).

131 Surveys of LGBTQ+ people in the United Kngdom have signalled relatively higher levels of homelessness, drug misuse, and mental health issues (including higher rates of self-harm and attempted suicide), as well as continuing feelings of stigma and shame associated with HIV status. Avowed homophobia has endured, albeit at significantly lower levels than in the 1980s; transphobia meanwhile has burgeoned. On homelessness see https://www.crisis.org.uk/ending-homelessness/about-homelessness/about-lgbtqplus-homelessness/ (accessed 10 April 2025); on mental health see: David Batty, 'Suicide and self-harm risk twice as high in LGB+ adults in England and Wales', *The Guardian* (9 April 2025); on HIV stigma see: https://www.stigmaindex.org (accessed 10 April 2025); on broader attitudes to homosexuality see: https://natcen.ac.uk/sites/default/files/2023-09/BSA.pdf (accessed 10 April 2025); on growing transphobia see Michael Goodier, 'Hate crime against transgender people hit record high in England and Wales', *The Guardian* (5 October 2023).

132 Leah DeVun and Zeb Tortorici, 'Interview with Maya Mikdashi and Carlos Motta on Deseos / رغبات', *TSQ: Transgender Studies Quarterly* 5, no. 4 (2018), 648–57.

133 Leah DeVun and Zeb Tortorici, 'Trans, Time, and History', *TSQ: Transgender Studies Quarterly* 5, no. 4 (2018), 518–39, at 520.

134 Macarena Gómez-Barris, 'How to Block the Extractive View', *GLQ: A Journal of Lesbian and Gay Studies* 24, no. 4 (2018), 527–32; Gómez-Barris, *Beyond the Pink Tide: Art and Political Undercurrents in the Americas* (University of California Press, 2018).

135 See Holbrook IV, *Performing Queer History*; Dean, 'Theatre'.

136 The last two ALMS conferences were held in London (2016) and Berlin (2019). Recent examples of university-based queer conferences incude:

The Stonewall 50 conference in New York (2017); the Bienniel Moving
Trans History Forward conferences since 2014; and the two international
queer history conferences in 2023, 'Queer History' in San Francisco and
'What is Queer History?' in Bergen, which involved active involvement of
local queer archives and museums.

137 Alison Oram and Matt Cook, *Prejudice and Pride: Celebrating LGBT
Heritage* (National Trust, 2017). For more on this conundrum see Matt
Cook, 'Queer Cities, Suburbs and Countryside', in Janes and Chiang, *The
Oxford Handbook*, conclusion. For more on the Birmingham back-to-
backs, see Matt Cook, 'Back-to-back in the Gay Village', Queer Beyond
London blog, https://queerbeyondlondon.com/sources/back-to-back-in-
the-gay-village/ (accessed June 20 2023).

138 Matt Cook, 'A Bend in the River: Queer home and heritage in a house in
Hammersmith', in *Sexuality and Gender at Home*, eds Brent Pilkey, Rachael
Scicluna, Ben Campkin, and Barbara Penner (Bloomsbury, 2017), 121–134;
'A Most Queer House', Sunday Feature, BBC Radio 3, June 16, 2024.

Chapter 5: Archives and Sources

1 J. W. Scott, 'The Evidence of Experience', *Critical Inquiry* 17, no. 4 (1991),
773–97.

2 Jacques Derrida, *Archive Fever: A Freudian Impression*, trans. Eric
Prenowitz (University of Chicago Press, 1998).

3 Anjali Arondekar, Ann Cvetkovich, Christina B. Hanhardt, Regina
Kunzel, Tavia Nyong'o, Juana María Rodríguez, Susan Stryker, Daniel
Marshall, Kevin P. Murphy and Zeb Tortorici, 'Queering Archives: A
Roundtable Discussion', *Radical History Review* 122 (2015), 211–31, at
212; see also Robb Hernández, 'Drawn from the Scraps: The Finding
AIDS of Mundo Meza', *Radical History Review* 122 (2015), 70–88; Francis
X. Blouin Jr. and William G. Rosenberg, *Processing the Past: Contesting
Authorities in History and the Archives* (Oxford University Press, 2011).

4 Zeb Tortorici, *Sins Against Nature: Sex and Archives in Colonial New Spain*
(Duke University Press, 2018), 17; see also Deborah A. Miranda,
'Extermination of the Joyas: Genocide in Spanish California', in *The
Transgender Studies Reader Remix*, eds Susan Stryker and Dylan
Macarthy Blackstone (Routledge, 2023), 157–69.

5 For a flavour of the debate see especially the two issues of *Radical History
Review* focused on queer archives, *Radical History Review* 120 (2014) and
122 (2015); and *Transgender Studies Quarterly (TSQ)* 2, no. 4 (2015). On
the 'abundance' of the archive see: Anjali Arondekar, *Abundance:
Sexuality's History* (Duke University Press: 2023).

6   Daniel Marshall, Kevin P. Murphy and Zeb Tortorici, 'Editors' Introduction: Queering Archives: Historical Unravellings', *Radical History Review* 120 (2014), 1–11, at 5. See also Abram J. Lewis, 'I Am 64 and Paul McCartney Doesn't Care: The Haunting of the Transgender Archive and the Challenges of Queer History', *Radical History Review* 120 (2014), 13–34, at 27.

7   On literal and metaphorical archival dust see Barry Reay, *Sex in the Archives: Writing American Sexual Histories* (Manchester University Press, 2018), 1; Carolyn Steedman, *Dust* (Manchester University Press, 2001).

8   Reay, *Sex in the Archives*, 1–2.

9   Steven Paige, 'Cruising the Archive: discovering a queer methodology', *Art and the Public Sphere* 12, no.2 (2023), 209–224. See also note 15.

10   On approaches to Mass Observation, see Nick Hubble, *Mass Observation and Everyday Life: Culture, History, Theory* (Palgrave Macmillan, 2005); Anabella Pollen, 'Research Methodology in Mass Observation Past and Present: "Scientifically about as Useful as a Chimpanzee's Tea Party at the Zoo"', *History Workshop Journal* 75, no. 1 (2013), 213–35; Matt Cook, 'AIDS, Mass Observation, and the Fate of the Permissive Turn', *Journal of the History of Sexuality* 26, no. 2 (2017), 239–72. For an early use of MO in the history of sexuality, see P. Gurney, '"Intersex" and "Dirty Girls": Mass-Observation and Working-Class Sexuality in England in the 1930s', *Journal of the History of Sexuality* 8, no. 3 (1997), 256–90.

11   'Trump is Emancipating Unbridled Hatred', Judith Butler interview with Rina Soloveitchik, *Zeit Online* (28 October 2016), http://www.zeit.de/kultur/2016–10/judith-butler-donald-trump-populism-interview, (accessed 11 November 2016).

12   See William M. Reddy, *The Navigation of Feeling: A Framework for the History of Emotions* (Cambridge University Press, 2001); Janice Irvine, 'Transient Feelings: Sex Panics and the Politic of Emotions', in *Moral Panics: Fear and the Fight over Sexual Rights,* ed. Gilbert Herdt (New York University Press, 2009), 234–76; Monique Scheer, 'Are Emotions a Kind of Practice (and Is That What Makes Them Have a History)? A Bourdieuian Approach to Understanding Emotion', *History and Theory* 51, no. 2 (2012), 193–220.

13   See Estelle Freedman, '"The Burning of Letters Continues": elusive identities and the historical construction of sexuality', *Journal of Women's History* 9, no. 4 (1998), 181–200; Daniel Eisenberg, 'Lorca and Censorship: The Gay Artist Made Heterosexual' (1992) at https://www.academia.edu/26025777/Lorca_and_Censorship_The_Gay_Artist_Made_Heterosexual, (accessed 12 August 2024).

14   For more on this see Matt Cook, 'Orton in the Archives', *History Workshop Journal* 66 (2008), 163–79; Steven Maynard, 'Police/Archives', *Archivaria* 68 (2009), 159–82.

15   Arondekar et al., 'Queering Archives', 229. On scavenger and feral methodologies, archival cruising, ephemera and anecdote, see Jack Halberstam, *The Queer Art of Failure* (Duke University Press, 2011); José E. Muñoz, 'Ephemera as Evidence: Introductory Notes to Queer Acts', *Women & Performance: A Journal of Feminist Theory* 8, no. 2 (1996), 5–18; Melissa Adler, *Cruising the Library: Perversities in the Organization of Knowledge* (Fordham University Press, 2017); Jane Gallop, *Anecdotal Theory* (Duke University Press, 2003).

16   Lesley Woods, 'Queer in Brighton: Conference Keynote', Brighton and Sussex Sexualities Network (2013), http://www.queerinbrighton.co.uk/wp-content/uploads/2013/09/BSSN-Conference-Keynote.pdf (accessed 17 April 2019).

17   Marthe Glad Munch Møller, 'Researching Early Norwegian Trans History', paper, Queerdom symposium, Mansfield College, University of Oxford, 20 June 2024.

18   See Charles Upchurch, 'Full-Text Databases and Historical Research: Cautionary Results from a Ten-Year Study', *Journal of Social History* 46, no. 1 (2012), 89–105.

19   On this point and for an incisive discussion of small and digital history more broadly, see Julia Laite, .'The Emmet's Inch: Small history in a digital age." *Journal of Social History* 53, no. 4 (2020): 963–989.

20   Laite, 'Emmet's Inch', 970.

21   Upchurch, 'Full-Text Databases'.

22   Laite, 'Emmet's Inch', 975. See also Ben Cowan, '"A Passive Homosexual Element": Digitized Archives and the Policing of Homosex in Cold War Brazil', *Radical History Review* 120 (2014), 183–203.

23   See E. Chenier, 'Privacy Anxieties: Ethics versus Activism in Archiving Lesbian Oral History Online', *Radical History Review* 122 (2015), 129–41; Laite, 'Emmet's Inch', 976.

24   See McKinney, 'Body, Sex, Interface: Reckoning with Images at the Lesbian Herstory Archives', *Radical History Review* 122 (2015), 115–28.

25   Joan Nestle, 'About the Archives', *Lesbian Herstory Archives News* 5 (1979), 3.

26   John Howard, *Men Like That: A Southern Queer History* (University of Chicago Press, 1999), xvi.

27   Madison Moore, 'Dark Room: Sleaze and the Queer Archive', *Contemporary Theatre Review* 31, no. 1/2 (2021), 191–6. See also Martin F. Manalansan, 'The "Stuff" of Archives: Mess, Migration, and Queer Lives', *Radical History Review* 120 (2014), 94–107.

28   Moore, 'Dark Room'.

29   Anjali Arondekar, 'Without a Trace: Sexuality and the Colonial Archive', *Journal of the History of Sexuality* 14, no. 1/2 (2005), 10–27, at 16.

30   Rebecca Jennings, 'Ethics and Queer Histories of the Recent Past: What if the letters weren't burned?', *History Workshop Journal* (forthcoming). See also Julia Laite, *The Disappearance of Lydia Harvey* (Profile, 2021).

31   On this point, see Dominic Janes, *Picturing the Closet: Male Secrecy and Homosexual Visibility in Britain* (Oxford University Press, 2015); Harry Cocks, *Nameless Offences: Homosexual Desire in the Nineteenth Century* (I.B. Tauris, 2003).

32   Eve Kosofsky Sedgwick, *Epistemology of the Closet* (Harvester Wheatsheaf, 1991), 45.

33   Halberstam, *The Queer Art of Failure*.

34   Arondekar et al., 'Queering Archives', 230.

35   See Hera Cook, 'Demography', in H. G. Cocks and Matt Houlbrook, eds, *The Modern History of Sexuality* (Palgrave Macmillan, 2006), 19–40.

36   See, for example, Judith Walkowitz, *City of Dreadful Delight: Narratives of Sexual Danger in Late-Victorian London* (University of Chicago Press, 1992); Ed Cohen, *Talk on the Wilde Side Towards a Genealogy of the Discourse on Male Homosexuality* (Stanford University, 1988). On the significance of literacy now and in the past, see E. D. Pritchard, '"Like Signposts on the Road": The Function of Literacy in Constructing Black Queer Ancestors', *Literacy in Composition Studies* 2, no. 1 (2014), 29–56.

37   As in Tiger Bay in Cardiff. See Daryl Leeworthy, *A Little Gay History of Wales* (University of Wales Press, 2019), 28–31, 69.

38   The Great Britain Historical GIS project. Data at www.visionofbritain.org.uk (accessed 29 January 2025).

39   André Fernandez, 'The Repression of Sexual Behavior by the Aragonese Inquisition between 1560 and 1700', *Journal of the History of Sexuality* 7, no. 4 (1997), 469–501; Helmut Puff, 'Localizing Sodomy: The "Priest and Sodomite" in Pre-Reformation Germany and Switzerland', *Journal of the History of Sexuality* 8, no. 2 (1997), 165–95.

40   See Anna Lvovsky, *Vice Patrol: Cops, Courts, and the Struggle over Urban Gay Life before Stonewall* (University of Chicago Press, 2021); Matt Houlbrook, *Queer London: Pleasures and Perils of the Sexual Metropolis, 1918–1957* (Chicago University Press, 2005).

41   On this point, see Robertson, 'What's Law got to do with it? Legal Records and Sexual Histories', *Journal of the History of Sexuality* 14, no. 1 (2005), 161–85.

42   See Cocks, *Nameless Offences*; Helen Smith, *Masculinity, Class and Same-Sex Desire in Industrial England, 1895–1957* (Palgrave Macmillan, 2015); Smith, 'Working Class Ideas and Experiences of Sexuality in Twentieth Century Britain: Regionalism as a Category of Analysis', *Twentieth Century British History* 29, no. 1 (2018), 58–78.

43   Michael Rocke, *Forbidden Friendships: Homosexuality and Male Culture in Renaissance Florence* (Oxford University Press, 1996).

44 For a striking recent example, see Averill Earls, *Love in the Lav: a social biography of same-sex desire in Ireland, 1922–1972* (Temple University Press, 2025).

45 Cook, *London*; Matt Cook, 'Law', in *History of Sexuality*, eds Cocks and Houlbrook, 64–86; Susanne Davies, 'Sexuality, Performance, and Spectatorship in Law: The Case of Gordon Lawrence, Melbourne, 1888', *Journal of the History of Sexuality* 7, no. 3 (1997), 389–408.

46 Alan Bray, *Homosexuality in Renaissance England* (Columbia University Press, 1995), 41.

47 George Robb and Nancy Erber, *Disorder in the Court: Trials and Sexual Conflict at the Turn of the Century* (Macmillan, 1999), 74.

48 See Caroline Derry, *Lesbianism and the Criminal Law: Three centuries of legal regulation in England and Wales* (Palgrave Macmillan, 2020); Martha Vicinus, 'Lesbian Perversity and Victorian Marriage: The 1864 Codrington Divorce Trial', *Journal of British Studies* 36, no. 1 (1997), 70–98; Lillian Faderman, *Scotch Verdict: Miss Pirie and Miss Woods v. Dame Cumming Gordon* (Morrow, 1983); Theo van der Meer, 'Tribades on Trial: Female Same-Sex Offenders in Late Eighteenth-Century Amsterdam', *Journal of the History of Sexuality* 1, no. 3 (1991), 424–45.

49 Simon Joyce, 'Two Women Walk into a Theatre Bathroom: The Fanny and Stella Trials as Trans Narrative', *Victorian Review* 44, no. 1 (2018), 83–98; Morris B. Kaplan, '"Men in Petticoats": Border Crossings in the Queer Case of Mr Boulton and Mr Park', in *Imagined Londons*, ed. Pamela Gilbert (SUNY Press, 2002), 45–68.

50 Steven Maynard, 'Through a Hole in the Lavatory Wall: Homosexual Subcultures, Police Surveillance, and the Dialectics of Discovery, Toronto, 1890–1930', *Journal of the History of Sexuality* 5, no. 2 (1994), 207–42.

51 Stephen Robertson, 'What's law got to do with it? Legal records and sexual histories', *Journal of the History of Sexuality* 14, no. 1 (2005), 161–85; see also Lvovsky, *Vice Patrol*.

52 See, for example, F. B. Smith, 'Labouchere's Amendment to the Criminal Law Amendment Bill', *Historical Studies* 17, no. 67 (1976), 165–73.

53 Derry, *Lesbianism and the Criminal Law*.

54 Alison Oram and Annmarie Turnbull, *The Lesbian History Sourcebook: Love and Sex between Women in Britain from 1780 to 1970* (Routledge, 2001), 155; Cook, 'Law'; Derry, *Lesbianism and the Criminal Law*.

55 Alison Oram, 'Love "Off the Rails" or "Over the Teacups"? Lesbian Desire and Female Sexualities in the 1950s British Popular Press', in *Queer 1950s: Rethinking Sexuality in the Postwar Years*, eds Heike Bauer and Matt Cook (Palgrave Macmillan UK, 2012), 41–57; Alison Oram, *Her Husband Was a Woman! Women's Gender-Crossing in Modern British Popular Culture* (Routledge, 2007).

56   Laurel Brake, 'The Old Journalism and the New: Forms of Cultural Production in London in the 1880s', in *Papers for the Millions: The New Journalism in Britain, 1850–1914*, ed. Joel Wiener (Greenwood, 1988), 1–24.

57   Justin Bengry, 'Films and Filming: The Making of a Queer Marketplace in Pre-Decriminalisation Britain', in *British Queer History: New Approaches and Perspectives,* ed. Brian Lewis (Manchester University Press, 2015), 244–66; Bengry, 'Courting the Pink Pound: Men Only and the Queer Consumer 1935–9', *History Workshop Journal* 68, no. 1 (2009), 122–48.

58   Justin Bengry and H. G. Cocks show how 'lonely hearts' columns in twentieth-century newspapers and magazines are a rich vein for understanding the queer euphemism, language and dynamics. Bengry, 'Films and Filming'; H. G. Cocks, *Classified: The Secret History of the Personal Column* (Random House, 2009).

59   John D'Emilio, *Sexual Politics, Sexual Communities* (1983; University of Chicago Press, 1998); Marcia Gallo, *Different Daughters: A History of the Daughters of Bilitis and the Rise of the Lesbian Rights Movement* (Seal Press, 2007); Martin Meeker, 'Behind the Mask of Respectability: Reconsidering the Mattachine Society and Male Homophile Practice, 1950s and 1960s', *Journal of the History of Sexuality* 10, no. 1 (2001), 78–116; Craig Loftin, *Letters to ONE: Gay and Lesbian Voices from the 1950s and 1960s* (SUNY Press, 2012); Ben Serby, '"Not to Produce Newspapers, but Committed Radicals": The Underground Press, the new Left, and the Gay liberation Counterpublic in the United States, 1965–1976', *Journal of the History of Sexuality* 32, no. 1 (2023), 1–26; Kwame Holmes, 'What's the Tea: Gossip and the Production of Black Gay Social History', *Radical History Review* 122 (2015), 55–69.

60   Bengry, 'Courting the Pink Pound'; David Johnson, *Buying Gay: How Physique Entrepreneurs Sparked a Movement* (Columbia University Press, 2019).

61   See Alison Oram, 'Feminism, Androgyny and Love between Women in Urania, 1916–1940', *Media History* 7, no. 1 (2001), 57–70; Amy Austin, 'Transing the Narrative: Transgender Identities in Britain, 1870–1940s' (PhD diss., Reading University, 2023), chapter 7.

62   Marc Stein, 'Canonizing Homophile Sexual Respectability: Archives, History, and Memory', *Radical History Review* 120 (2014), 53–73, especially 53–62.

63   On this point see Laura Doan, *Disturbing Practices: History, Sexuality, and Women's Experience of Modern War* (University of Chicago Press, 2013); Chris Waters, 'Havelock Ellis, Sigmund Freud and the State: Discourses of Homosexual Identity in Interwar Britain', in *Sexology in Culture: Labelling Bodies and Desires,* eds Lucy Bland and Laura L. Doan (Polity, 1998), 165–79; Heike Bauer, *English Literary Sexology: Translations of Inversion, 1860–1930* (Palgrave, 2009).

64 Jules Gill-Peterson, 'Trans of Color Critique before Transsexuality', *TSQ: Transgender Studies Quarterly* 5, no. 4 (2018), 606–20, at 607.

65 See Jeffrey Meek, *Queer Voices in Post-War Scotland: Male Homosexuality, Religion and Society* (Palgrave Macmillan, 2015); Paul Johnson and Robert Vanderbeck, *Law, Religion and Homosexuality* (Routledge, 2014); Anthony Petro, *After the Wrath of God: AIDS, Sexuality, and American Religion* (Oxford University Press, 2015), Oman Karsmari, *Queer Companions: Religion, Public Intimacy and Saintly Affects in Pakistan* (Duke University Press, 2022); Leah DeVun, *The Shape of Sex: Nonbinary Gender from Genesis to the Renaissance* (Columbia University Press, 2021); Dominic Janes, *Visions of Queer Martyrdom from John Henry Newman to Derek Jarman* (University of Chicago Press, 2015); Scott Larson, 'Histrionics of the Pulpit: Trans Tonalities of Religious Enthusiasm', *Transgender Studies Quarterly* 6, no. 3 (2019), 315–37; Heather White, *Reforming Sodom: Protestants and the Rise of Gay Rights* (University of North Carolina Press, 2015).

66 See Chapter 1, section 2.

67 Heike Bauer, 'Literature and Biography as Sources for LGBTQ Lived Experience', in *The Oxford Handbook of LGBTQ History*, eds Dominic Janes and Howard Chiang (Oxford University Press, 2026).

68 See, for example, Dan Callwood, 'Anxiety and Desire in France's Gay Pornographic Film Boom 1974–1983', *Journal of the History of Sexuality* 26, no. 1 (2017), 26–52; J. Engelberg and G. Needham, 'Purging the Queer Archive: Tumblr's Counterhegemonic Pornographies', *Porn Studies* 6, no. 3 (2019), 350–4; Jason Goldman, '"The Golden Age of Gay Porn": Nostalgia and the Photography of Wilhelm von Gloeden', *GLQ: A Journal of Lesbian and Gay Studies* 12, no. 2 (2006), 237–58; Jo Brydon, 'Percy Grainger and Trans Identity in Edwardian London' (PhD diss., Birkbeck, University of London, 2025).

69 Diana Lewis Burgin, 'Mother Nature versus the Amazons: Marina Tsvetaeva and Female Same-Sex Love', *Journal of the History of Sexuality* 6, no. 1 (1995), 62–88; Jessica Seidel, 'Trans Times: Que(e)rying Normative Logic of Temporality, Gender and Sexuality in Virginia Woolf's *Orlando*', *Intersectional Perspectives: Identity, Culture and Society* 3 (2024), 1–31.

70 An approach I used in Cook, 'The Nursery', in *Queering the Interior*, eds Andrew Gorman Murray and Matt Cook (Bloomsbury, 2017), 145–57.

71 Aaron Betsky, *Queer Space: Architecture and Same-Sex Desire* (William Morrow, 1997). See also essays in Hilde Heynen and Gulsum Baydar, eds, *Negotiating Domesticity: Spatial Productions of Gender in Modern Architecture* (Routledge, 2005).

72 On this see Jack Halberstam's latest work on 'anarchitecture', including Jack Halberstam, *The Wild Beyond: Music, Architecture and Anarchy* (forthcoming).

73   Cook, *Queer Domesticities*, chapter 2.

74   See, for example, Robert Mills, *Seeing Sodomy in the Middle Ages* (University of Chicago Press, 2015); DeVun, *The Shape of Sex*; Janes, *Visions of Queer Martyrdom*; Rachel Wall, '"Saint Sebastian in the Renaissance": The Classicization and Homoeroticization of a Saint', *Art Journal* 1 (2012), 11–23; Richard A. Kaye, 'Losing His Religion: Saint Sebastian as Contemporary Gay Martyr', in *Outlooks: Lesbian and Gay Sexualities and Visual Cultures*, eds Peter Horne and Reina Lewis (Routledge, 1996), 86–105.

75   Clare Barlow, *Queer British Art 1861–1967* (Tate Publishing, 2017).

76   Julia Hirsch, *Family Photographs: Content, Meaning and Effects* (Oxford University Press, 1981); 'Queering the Trans* Family Album: Elspeth H. Brown and Sara Davidmann in Conversation', *Radical History Review* 122 (2015), 188–200; Paul Julian Smith, *Vision Machines: Cinema, Literature and Sexuality in Spain and Cuba, 1983–93* (Verso, 1996); Lisa Daniel, *The Bent Lens: A World Guide to Gay & Lesbian Film* (Roundhouse, 2003).

77   See, for example, Mori Reithmayr, 'Homosexuality Inverted: José Sarria's Performance Archive and the Making of Nelly Queens, 1958–1963', *The Historical Journal* (2025), (1–2); Ruth Ramsden-Karelse, 'Moving and Moved: Reading Kewpie's District Six', *GLQ: A Journal of Lesbian and Gay Studies* 26, no. 3 (2020), 405–38; Treva Ellison, 'The Labor of Werqing It: The Performance and Protest Strategies of Sir Lady Java', in *Trap Door: Trans Cultural Production and the Politics of Visibility*, eds Tourmaline, Eric Stanley and Johanna Burton (MIT Press, 2017), 1–22.

78   On queer image analysis, see Jennifer V. Evans, *The Queer Art of History* (Duke University Press, 2023), 51–123; Evans, 'Seeing Subjectivity: Erotic Photography and the Optics of Desire', *The American Historical Review* 118, no. 2 (2013), 430–62.

79   On the relationship between amnesia and the archive, see Derrida, *Archive Fever*, 12.

80   *Uncle Denis?* (dir. Adrian Goycoolea, 2010).

81   On the queer significance of such figures, see Eileen Cleere, *Avuncularism: Capitalism, Patriarchy, and Nineteenth-Century English Culture* (Stanford University Press, 2004); Eve Sedgwick, *Tendencies* (Routledge, 1994).

82   Mo Moulton, 'Dogs in the Picture: Restoring the Queer History of the Irish Family', *The History of the Family* 29, no. 1 (2024), 84–108.

83   Evans, *The Queer Art of History*, 63; Dan Healey, 'Active, Passive, and Russian: The National Idea in Gay Men's Pornography', *The Russian Review* 69, 2 (2010), 210–230.

84   See Callwood, 'Anxiety and Desire'; J. Engelberg and G. Needham, 'Purging the Queer Archive'; Goldman, 'The Golden Age of Gay Porn'; R. Meyer,

'Mapplethorpe's Living Room: Photography and the Furnishing of Desire', *Art History* 24, no. 2 (2001), 292–311.

85   Evans, *The Queer Art of History*, 75. See also Kyle Frackman, 'Homemade Pornography and the Proliferation of Queer Pleasure in East Germany', *Radical History Review* 142 (2022), 93–109; João Florêncio and Ben Miller, 'Sexing the Archive: Gay Porn and Subcultural Histories', *Radical History Review* 142 (2022), 133–41.

86   The project, led by João Florêncio (Linkoping University/Exeter University), John Mercer (Birmingham City University) and Jana Funke (Exeter University), is a collaboration between Exeter University, Birmingham City University, Bishopsgate Institute and Schwules Museum.

87   In her documentary *Circus of Books* (2019), director Rachel Mason unfolds a story of the gay porn bookstore which became a key hub of support and sex positivity in the eighties. See also Johnson, *Buying Gay*.

88   See Reay, *Sex in the Archives*; Goldman, 'Golden Age of Gay Porn'; Simon Watney, *Policing Desire: Pornography, AIDS and the Media* (Comedia, 1986); Callwood, 'Anxiety and Desire'.

89   See Evans, *Queer Art of History*, 107; Fernández Galeano, 'Running Mascara: The Hermeneutics of Trans Visual Archives in Late Franco-Era Spain', *Radical History Review* 142 (2022), 72–92; T. Benjamin Singer, 'From the Medical Gaze to Sublime Mutations: The Ethics of (Re)Viewing Non-Normative Body Images', in *The Transgender Studies Reader*, eds Susan Stryker and Stephen Whittle (Routledge, 2006), 601–20. See also Haley McEwen and Tommaso M. Milani, 'Queer & Trans Art-Iculations: Decolonising Gender and Sexualities in the Global South', *Agenda: Empowering Women for Gender Equity* 28, no. 4 (102) (2014), 3–8.

90   On this and the relationship between democracy, mass culture and the visual, see Susan Buck-Morss, *Dialectics of Seeing: Walter Benjamin and the Arcades Project* (MIT Press, 1991).

91   A foundational text in this area is Igor Kopytoff, 'The Cultural Biography of Things: Commoditization as Process' in *The Social Life of Things: Commodities in Cultural Perspective*, ed. Arjun Appadurai (Cambridge University Press, 1988), 64–92.

92   Lauren Fried, 'A Material History of Trans Identity in UK Performance (1967–1990)' (PhD diss., Royal College of Art, 2019); Shaun Cole and Reina Lewis, 'Seeing, Recording and Discussing LGBTQ Fashion and Style', *Fashion, Style, & Popular Culture* 3, no. 2 (2016), 149–56. See also Jordy Jones, 'A Martyr in the Archive: The Life and Afterlife of Harvey Milk's Suit', *Somatechnics* 1, no. 2 (2011), 372–87.

93   Jane Bennett, *Vibrant Matter: A Political Ecology of Things* (Duke University Press, 2010), 10, 6.

94 Matt Houlbrook, '"The Man with the Powder Puff" in Interwar London', *The Historical Journal* 50, no. 1 (2007), 145–71.

95 Chris Brickell and Judith Collard, 'The Queerness of Objects', *in Queer Objects,* eds Collard and Brickell (Otago University Press, 2019), 11–21, at 18.

96 Matt Cook, 'The Rotary Dial Telephone', and Simon Clay, 'Queer Smartphones', in *Queer Objects,* eds Brickell and Collard, 223–30 and 387–93.

97 Arondekar et al., 'Queering Archives', 213.

98 Muñoz, 'Ephemera as Evidence'; Hernández, 'Drawn from the Scraps', 75.

99 Rebecka Taves Sheffield, 'The Bedside Table Archives: Archive Intervention and Lesbian Intimate Domestic Culture', *Radical History Review* 120 (2014), 108–20; Cook, *Queer Domesticities*, 81–5; Muñoz, 'Ephemera as Evidence', 10.

100 On this point, see Charles Henry Rowell, '"Words Don't Go There": An Interview with Fred Moten', *Callaloo* 27, no. 4 (2004), 955–66. See also Niels Van Doorn, 'The Fabric of Our Memories: Leather, Kinship, and Queer Material History', *Memory Studies* 9, no. 1 (2016), 85–98; Herring Scott, 'Material Deviance: Theorizing Queer Objecthood', *Postmodern Culture* 21, no. 2 (2011); Jane Bennett, 'The Force of Things: Steps Toward an Ecology of Matter', *Political Theory* 32, no. 3 (2004), 347–72.

101 Anna Clark, 'Twilight Moments', *Journal of the History of Sexuality* 14, no. 1 (2005), 139–60.

102 Hernández, 'Drawn from the Scraps'.

103 Marshall, Murphy and Tortorici, 'Editors' Introduction', 2.

104 Scott, 'The Evidence of Experience'; Nan Alamilla Boyd, 'Who is the Subject? Queer Theory Meets Oral History', *Journal of the History of Sexuality* 17, no. 2 (2008), 177–89, at 180.

105 Boyd, 'Who is the Subject?'

106 Laura Doan, *Disturbing Practices*, 140.

107 Elizabeth Lapovsky Kennedy, 'Telling Tales: Oral History and the Construction of Pre-Stonewall Lesbian History', *Radical History Review* 62 (1995), 59–79, at 59.

108 Lisa Duggan, 'The Discipline Problem: Queer Theory Meets Lesbian and Gay History', *GLQ: A Journal of Lesbian and Gay Studies* 2, no. 3 (1995), 179–91, at 188, 187.

109 On this point, see also Jeffrey Escoffier, *American Homo: Community and Perversity* (Verso, 2018).

110 Gayle Rubin forcefully counters the 'dismissive attitude towards empirical work'. 'It is a big mistake', she says, 'to decide that since data are imperfect, it is better to avoid the challenges of dealing with data altogether.' Gayle Rubin with Judith Butler, 'Sexual Traffic: Interview', in *Feminism Meets*

Queer Theory, eds Elizabeth Weed and Naomi Schor (Indiana University Press, 1997), 68–108.

111 Carolyn Steedman, *Master and Servant: Love and Labour in the English Industrial Age* (Cambridge University Press, 2007), 1.

112 On this point, see Laite, 'Emmet's Inch'.

113 A. Revathi, *Truth About Me: A Hijra Life Story* (2015); Laxmi Narayan Tripathi, *Me Hijra, Me Laxmi* (Oxford University Press, 2015). For analysis and wider context, see Rovel Sequeira, 'Show and Tell: Life History and Hijra Activism in India', *Signs: Journal of Women in Culture and Society* 47, no. 2 (2022), 451–74; Shalini Jayaprakash, 'Re-writing the Subject and the Self: A Study of Hijra Life Writings', in *Transgender India: Understanding Third Gender Identities and Experiences*, Douglas Vakoch, ed. (Springer, 2022), 19–35; Jessica Hinchy, *Governing Gender and Sexuality in Colonial India: The Hijra, c.1850–1900* (Cambridge University Press, 2019).

114 Cook, *London*, 25–6; *Roger Casement's Diaries: 1910: The Black and the White*, ed. Roger Sawyer (Pimlico, 1997).

115 Barry Reay, 'Sex in the Archives', *Radical History Review* 122 (2015), 103–13, at 111; Cook, 'Orton in the Archives'.

116 Entry of Tuesday, 11 May 1993 in Derek Jarman, *Smiling in Slow Motion* (Century, 2000), 342.

117 This emerges strongly in the interviews conducted by Khalil West in 'Dark Matter: Sociality, Space, and the Haptics of Queer (Il)legibility in "Black Liverpool", 1967–1997' (PhD diss., July 2025, European University Institute).

118 On these dimensions of Mass Observation, see note 11.

119 William Jones, '"So Then … He Raped Me": Male Experiences of Sexual(ized) Violence in the Nazi Concentration Camps' (DPhil diss., University of Oxford, 2024), 245.

120 On this point, see Nan Alamilla Boyd and Horacio N. Roque Ramírez, 'Introduction: Close Encounters: The Body and Knowledge in Queer Oral History', in *Bodies of Evidence: The Practice of Queer Oral History*, eds Boyd and Roque Ramírez (Oxford University Press, 2012), 1–22; Clare Summerskill, Amy Tooth Murphy and Emma Vickers, 'Introduction', in *New Directions in Queer Oral History: Archives of Disruption*, eds Summerskill, Tooth Murphy and Vickers (Routledge, 2022), 1–18, at 8.

121 Summerskill et al., *New Directions*, 7.

122 Elizabeth Lapovsky Kennedy and Madeline D. Davis, *Boots of Leather, Slippers of Gold: The History of a Lesbian Community* (1993; Routledge, 2024), 23.

123 For example, Brighton Ourstory Project, *Daring Hearts: Lesbian and Gay Lives of 50s and 60s Brighton* (QueenSpark, 1992); Esther Newton, *Cherry Grove, Fire Island: Sixty Years in America's First Gay and Lesbian Town*

(Beacon Press, 1993); Lisa Power, *No Bath but Plenty of Bubbles: An Oral History of the Gay Liberation Front, 1970–1973* (Cassell, 1995); Kennedy and Davis, *Boots of Leather.*

124 Afsaneh Najmabadi, 'Reading Transsexuality in "Gay" Tehran (Around 1979)', in *Transgender Studies Reader Remix,* eds Stryker and McCarthy Blackston (Routledge, 2022), 414–25, at 415.

125 Boyd, 'Who is the Subject?', 186.

126 Matt Cook and Alison Oram, *Queer Beyond London* (Manchester University Press, 2022), 121–2.

127 Christopher Reid and Christopher Castiglia, *If Memory Serves: Gay Men, AIDS, and the Promise of the Queer Past* (University of Minnesota Press, 2012), 105.

128 Anna Green, 'Individual Remembering and "Collective Memory": Theoretical Presuppositions and Contemporary Debates', *Oral History* 32, no. 2 (2004), 35–44, at 35; Penny Summerfield, *Histories of the Self: Personal Narratives and Historical Practice* (Routledge, 2018). See also Martha Rose Beard, 'Re-Thinking Oral History: A Study of Narrative Performance', *Rethinking History* 21, no. 4 (2017), 529–48, at 530.

129 Matt Cook, '"Gay Times": Identity, Locality, Memory, and the Brixton Squats in 1970s London', *Modern British History* 24, no. 1 (2013), 84–109; Cook, 'Squatting in History: Queer Pasts and the Cultural Turn' in *Social Research After the Cultural Turn,* eds Sasha Roseneil and Stephen Frosh (Palgrave, 2012), 93–109. My discussion here draws on the latter especially.

130 Khalil West accounts for such dynamics by referring to his 'conversants' rather than interviewees – a gesture which disarms the implicit interview hierarchy. West, 'Dark Matters'.

131 Bryant Alexander, *Performing Black Masculinity: Race, Culture and Queer Identity* (Altamira Press, 2006), xx.

132 Writing good history, US historian Lawrence Levine reminds us, means 'never assuming that one's subjects were incapable of recognising the same "hegemonising forces" subsequently identified by professional intellectuals'. Levine, cited by James W. Cook and Lawrence B. Glickman in their introduction to *The Cultural Turn in U.S. History: Past, Present, and Future* (University of Chicago Press, 2008), 25.

133 See, for example, Amy Tooth Murphy, 'Listening in, Listening out: Intersubjectivity and the Impact of Insider and Outsider Status in Oral History Interviews', *Oral History* 48, no. 1 (2020), 35–44; Nan Alamilla Boyd, 'Talking about Sex: Cheryl Gonzales and Rikki Streicher Tell Their Stories', in *Bodies of Evidence,* eds Boyd and Roque Ramírez, 95–112, at 102–3.

134 Esther Newton, 'My Best Informant's Dress: The Erotic Equation in Fieldwork', *Cultural Anthropology* 8, no. 1 (1993), 3–23, at 10–11. See also Boyd and Roque Ramírez, 'Introduction', 9–10.

135 Matt Cook, '"Archives of Feeling": The AIDS Crisis in Britain 1987', *History Workshop Journal* 83, no. 1 (2017), 51–78.

136 British National HIV Story Trust at https://www.nhst.org.uk, (accessed 12 December 2024).

137 See: Ann Cvetkovich, *An Archive of Feelings: Trauma, Sexuality, and Lesbian Public Cultures* (Duke University Press, 2003).

138 Harrison Apple, '"I Want to Come Out Looking Glamorous One More Time": The Pittsburgh Queer History Project', paper, 'Queering Memory' ALMS Conference (Berlin, 2019). See also Harrison Apple, 'A Social Member in Good Standing: Pittsburgh's Gay After-Hours Social Clubs, 1960–1990' (PhD diss., University of Arizona, 2021).

139 'Queer Beyond London Workshop, Leeds', 2017. For discussion see Cook and Oram, *Queer Beyond London.*

140 Jocelyn Viterna, *Women in War: The Micro-Processes of Mobilization in El Salvador* (Oxford University Press, 2013), 40–1. Thanks to Matthew Littleford.

141 'Queer Beyond London Workshop', Plymouth, 2017.

142 Boyd and Roque Ramírez, 'Introduction', 1.

143 Arondekar, *Abundance*

144 See Saidiya Hartman, 'Venus in Two Acts', *Small Axe 12*, no. 2 (2008), 1–14, at 11; Hartman, 'Intimate History, Radical Narrative', *The Journal of African American History* 106, no. 1 (2021), 127–35.

145 Carolyn Dinshaw, *Getting Medieval: Sexualities and Communities, Pre- and Postmodern* (Duke University Press, 1999), Heather Love, *Feeling Backward: Loss and the Politics of Queer History* (Harvard University Press, 2007).

146 Reay, *Sex in the Archives*, 13.

Epilogue

1 Joe Moran, 'The Death of an Irishman: A Speculative Biography', *History Workshop Journal* 98 (2024), 209–33, at 210.

2 On 'queer detritus' see: Robb Hernández, 'Drawn from the scraps: the finding AIDS of Mundo Meza', *Radical History Review* 122 (2015), 70–88, at 71.

3 See Matt Cook, 'The Rotary Dial Telephone', in *Queer Objects*, Judith Collard and Chris Brickell eds (Otago University Press, 2019).

4 Sara Ahmed, *The Cultural Politics of Emotion* (Edinburgh University Press, 2004), 6–8.

5 For conundrums in using these methodologies, see especially Julia Laite, host, *History Workshop Podcast*, 'Difficult Stories and Ethical Dilemmas

in Family History', https://www.historyworkshop.org.uk/podcast/
difficult-stories-and-ethical-dilemmas-in-family-history/ (accessed 19
August 2024).

6   Cook, 'Archives of Feeling'; Cook, 'AIDS, Mass Observation, and the Fate
of the Permissive Turn'.

7   Penny Summerfield, *Histories of the Self: Personal Narratives and
Historical Practice* (Routledge, 2019), 2.

Selected Bibliography

Adair, Joshua G. and Amy K. Levin, eds. *Museums, Sexuality, and Gender Activism*. Routledge, 2020.

Adler, Melissa. *Cruising the Library: Perversities in the Organization of Knowledge*. Fordham University Press, 2017.

Ahmed, Sara., *Queer Phenomenology: Orientations, Objects, Others*. Duke University Press, 2006.

Ahmed, Sara. *The Feminist Killjoy Handbook*. Random House, 2023.

Aldrich, Robert, ed. *Gay Life and Culture: A World History*. Thames & Hudson, 2010.

Apple, Harrison. 'A Social Member in Good Standing: Pittsburgh's Gay After-Hours Social Clubs, 1960–1990'. PhD diss., University of Arizona, 2021.

Armstrong, Elizabeth A., and Suzanna M. Crage. 'Movements and Memory: The Making of the Stonewall Myth'. *American Sociological Review* 71, no. 5 (2006), 724–51.

Arondekar, Anjali. *For the Record: On Sexuality and the Colonial Archive in India*. Duke University Press, 2009.

Arondekar, Anjali. *Abundance: Sexuality's History*. Duke University Press, 2023.

Arondekar, Anjali, Ann Cvetkovixh, Christina B. Hanhardt, Regina Kunzel, Tavia Nyong'o, Juana María Rodríguez, Susan Stryker, Daniel Marshall, Kevin P. Murphy and Zeb Tortorici. 'Queering Archives: A Roundtable Discussion'. *Radical History Review* 122 (2015), 211–31.

Auchmuty, Rosemary, Sheila Jeffreys and Elaine Miller. 'Lesbian History and Gay Studies: Keeping a Feminist Perspective'. *Women's History Review* 1, no. 1 (1982), 89–108.

Austin, Amy. 'Transing the Narrative: Transgender Identities in Britain, 1870–1940s'. PhD diss., Reading University, 2023.

Avery, Simon, and Kate Graham, eds. *Sex, Time and Place: Queer Histories of London*. Bloomsbury, 2015.

Balderston, Daniel, and Donna Guy, eds. *Sex and Sexuality in Latin America: An Interdisciplinary Reader*. New York University Press, 1997.

Baker, Paul. *Outragious: The Story of Section 28 and Britain's Battle for LGBT Education*. Reaktion: 2022.

Baker, Paul. *Camp! The Story of the Attitude that Conquered the World*. Footnote: 2023.

Barlow, Clare. *Queer British Art 1861–1967*. Tate Britain, 2017.

Bartlett, Neil. *Who Was That Man: A Present for Mr Oscar Wilde*. Serpent's Tail, 1988.

Bauer, Heike. *The Hirschfeld Archives: Violence, Death, and Modern Queer Culture*. Temple University Press, 2017.

Bauer, Heike. 'In the Canine Archives of Sex: Radclyffe Hall, Una Troubridge and their dogs', *Gender & History* 35, no. 3 (2023), 994–1011.

Bauer, Heike, and Matt Cook, eds. *Queer 1950s: Rethinking Sexuality in the Postwar Years*. Palgrave Macmillan UK, 2012.

Bell, David, and Gill Valentine, eds. *Mapping Desire: Geographies of Sexualities*. Routledge, 1995.

Bengry, Justin. 'Courting the Pink Pound: Men Only and the Queer Consumer 1935–9'. *History Workshop Journal* 68, no. 1 (2009), 122–48.

Bengry, Justin, Matt Cook and Alison Oram, eds. *Locating Queer Histories: Places and Traces across the UK*. Bloomsbury, 2023.

Bennett, Judith. 'Lesbian-like and the Social History of Lesbianisms'. *Journal of the History of Sexuality* 9, no. 1/2 (2000), 1–24.

Bérubé, Allan. *Coming Out Under Fire: The History of Gay Men and Women in World War II*. Free Press, 1990.

Betsky, Aaron. *Queer Space: Architecture and Same-Sex Desire*. William Morrow, 1997.

Bland, Lucy and Laura L. Doan, eds. *Sexology in Culture: Labelling Bodies and Desires*. Polity, 1998.

Bleys, Rudi. *The Geography of Perversion: Male-to-Male Sexual Behaviour Outside the West and the Ethnographic Imagination, 1750 – 1918*. New York University Press, 1995.

Bond Stockton, Kathryn. *Beautiful Bottom, Beautiful Shame: Where 'Black' Meets 'Queer'*. Duke University Press, 2006.

Boone, Joseph Allen. *The Homoerotics of Orientalism*. Columbia University Press, 2014.

Bosia, Michael J., Sandra McEvoy and Momin Rahman, eds. *The Oxford Handbook of Global LGBT and Sexual Diversity Politics*. Oxford University Press, 2020.

Boswell, John. *Christianity, Social Tolerance, and Homosexuality: Gay People in Western Europe from the Beginning of the Christian Era to the Fourteenth Century*. University of Chicago Press, 1980.

Boyd, Nan Alamilla. *Wide-Open Town: A History of Queer San Francisco to 1965*. University of California Press, 2003.

Boyd, Nan Alamilla. 'Who is the Subject? Queer Theory Meets Oral History'. *Journal of the History of Sexuality* 17, no. 2 (2008), 177–89.

Boyd, Nan Alamilla, and Horacio Roque Ramirez. *Bodies of Evidence: The Practice of Queer Oral History*. Oxford University Press, 2012.

Bravmann, Scott. *Queer Fictions of the Past: History, Culture, and Difference.* Cambridge University Press, 1997.

Bray, Alan. *Homosexuality in Renaissance England.* Columbia University Press, 1995.

Bray, Alan. *The Friend.* University of Chicago Press, 2003.

Brickell, Chris. *Mates and Lovers: A History of Gay New Zealand.* Godwit, 2008.

Brickell, Chris, and Judith Collard, eds. *Queer Objects.* Otago University Press, 2019.

Brighton Ourstory Project. *Daring Hearts: Lesbian and Gay Lives of 50s and 60s Brighton.* QueenSpark, 1992.

Bristow, Joseph, ed. *Oscar Wilde and Modern Culture: The Making of a Legend.* Ohio University Press, 2008.

Bronski, Michael. *A Queer History of the United States.* Beacon Press, 2011.

Brydon, Jo. 'Percy Grainger and Trans Identity in Edwardian London'. PhD diss., Birkbeck, University of London, March 2025.

Butler, Alan. 'Performing LGBT Pride in Plymouth 1950–2012'. PhD diss., Plymouth University, 2016.

Callwood, Dan. 'Re-Evaluating the French Gay Liberation Movement 1968– 1983'. PhD diss., Queen Mary University of London, 2017.

Callwood, Dan. 'Anxiety and Desire in France's Gay Pornographic Film Boom 1974–1983'. *Journal of the History of Sexuality* 26, no. 1 (2017), 26–52.

Canaday, Margot. *The Straight State: Sexuality and Citizenship in Twentieth-Century America.* Princeton University Press, 2009.

Canaday, Margot. *Queer Career: Sexuality and Work in Modern America.* Princeton University Press, 2023.

Capó Jr., Julio. *Welcome to Fairyland: Queer Miami before 1940.* University of North Carolina Press, 2017.

Caron, David. *My Father and I: The Marais and the Queerness of Community.* Cornell University Press, 2010.

Cartwright, Ryan Lee. *Peculiar Places: A Queer Crip History of White Rural Nonconformity.* University of Chicago Press, 2021.

Cashman, Holly, and Marilyn Martin-Jones. *Queer, Latinx, and Bilingual: Narrative Resources in the Negotiation of Identities.* Routledge, 2017.

Castiglia, Christopher, and Christopher Reed. *If Memory Serves: Gay Men, AIDS, and the Promise of the Queer Past.* University of Minnesota Press, 2012.

Castle, Terry. *The Apparitional Lesbian: Female Homosexuality and Modern Culture.* Columbia University Press, 1993.

Cervini, Eric. *The Deviant's War: The Homosexual vs. the United States of America.* Farrar, Straus and Giroux, 2020.

Channell-Justice, Emily, ed. *Decolonizing Queer Experience: LGBT+ Narratives from Eastern Europe and Eurasia.* Lexington Books, 2020.

Chaplin, Tamara. *Becoming Lesbian: A Queer History of Modern France.* University of Chicago Press, 2024.

Chauncey, George. *Gay New York: Gender, Urban Culture, and the Making of the Gay Male World, 1890–1940.* Basic Books, 1994.

Chenier, E. 'Privacy Anxieties: Ethics versus Activism in Archiving Lesbian Oral History Online'. *Radical History Review* 122 (2015), 129–41.

Chiang, Howard. *Transtopia in the Sinophone Pacific.* Columbia University Press, 2020.

Chiang, Howard. 'Archiving Peripheral Taiwan: The Prodigy of the Human and Historical Narration'. *Radical History Review* 120 (2014), 204–25.

Chitty, Christopher. *Sexual Hegemony: Statecraft, Sodomy, and Capital in the Rise of the World System.* Duke University Press, 2020.

Clark, Anna. 'Anne Lister's Construction of Lesbian Identity'. *Journal of the History of Sexuality* 7, no. 1 (1996), 23–50.

Clark, Anna. 'Twilight Moments'. *Journal of the History of Sexuality* 14, no. 1 (2005), 139–60.

Cocks, H. G. *Nameless Offences: Homosexual Desire in the Nineteenth Century.* I.B. Tauris, 2003.

Cocks, H. G., and Matt Houlbrook, eds. *The Modern History of Sexuality.* Palgrave Macmillan, 2006.

Cohen, Cathy. 'Punks, Bulldaggers and Welfare Queens: The Radical Potential of Queer Politics'. *GLQ: A Journal of Lesbian and Gay Studies* 3, no. 4 (1997), 437–65.

Cohen, Cathy. *The Boundaries of Blackness: AIDS and the Breakdown of Black Politics.* University of Chicago Press, 1999.

Cohen, Deborah. *Family Secrets: Living with Shame from the Victorians to the Present Day.* Viking, 2013.

Cohen, Ed. *Talk on the Wilde Side Towards a Genealogy of the Discourse on Male Homosexuality.* Stanford University Press, 1988.

The Combahee River Collective Statement. April 1977.

Cook, Matt. *London and the Culture of Homosexuality, 1885–1914.* Cambridge University Press, 2003.

Cook, Matt. 'Sex Lives and Diary Writing: The Journals of George Ives'. In *Life Writing and Victorian Culture,* edited by David Amigoni. Ashgate, 2006, 195–214.

Cook, Matt. 'Squatting in History: Queer Pasts and the Cultural Turn'. In *Social Research After the Cultural Turn,* edited by Sasha Roseneil and Stephen Frosh. Palgrave, 2012, 93–109.

Cook, Matt. *Queer Domesticities: Homosexuality and Home Life in Twentieth Century London.* Palgrave Macmillan, 2014.

Cook, Matt. 'AIDS, Mass Observation, and the Fate of the Permissive Turn'. *Journal of the History of Sexuality* 26, no. 2 (2017), 239–72.

Cook, Matt. '"Archives of Feeling": The AIDS Crisis in Britain 1987'. *History Workshop Journal* 83, no. 1 (2017), 51–78.

Cook, Matt, and Jennifer Evans. *Queer Cities, Queer Cultures: Europe since 1945*. Bloomsbury, 2014.

Cook, Matt, and Alison Oram. *Queer Beyond London*. Manchester University Press, 2022.

Crenshaw, Kimberlé. 'Mapping the Margins: Intersectionality, Identity Politics, and Violence against Women of Color'. *Stanford Law Review* 43, no. 6 (1991), 1241–99.

Crimp, Douglas. *On the Museum's Ruins*. MIT Press, 1993.

Cvetkovich, Ann. *An Archive of Feelings: Trauma, Sexuality, and Lesbian Public Cultures*. Duke University Press, 2003.

D'Emilio, John. 'Capitalism and Gay Identity'. In *Powers of Desire: The Politics of Sexuality*, edited by Ann Snitow, Christine Stansell and Sharon Thompson. Monthly Review Press, 1983, 100–14.

D'Emilio, John. *Sexual Politics, Sexual Communities: The Making of a Homosexual Minority in the United States, 1940–1970*. 2nd edn 1983; Chicago University Press, 1998.

Dabhoiwala, Faramerz. *The Origins of Sex: A History of the First Sexual Revolution*. Oxford University Press, 2012.

Davenport-Hines, Richard. *Sex, Death and Punishment: Attitudes to Sex and Sexuality in Britain since the Renaissance*. Collins, 1990.

Delaney, Anthony. *Queer Georgians: A Hidden History of Lovers, Lawbreakers and Homemakers*. Penguin: 2025.

Derry, Caroline. *Lesbianism and the Criminal Law: Three Centuries of Legal Regulation in England and Wales*. Palgrave Macmillan, 2020.

DeVun, Leah. *The Shape of Sex: Nonbinary Gender from Genesis to the Renaissance*. Columbia University Press, 2021.

DeVun, Leah, and Zeb Tortorici. 'Trans, Time, and History'. *TSQ: Transgender Studies Quarterly* 5, no. 4 (2018), 518–39.

Dickinson, Tommy. *'Curing Queers': Mental Nurses and Their Patients, 1935–1974*. Manchester University Press, 2015.

Dines, Martin. *Gay Suburban Narratives in American and British Culture: Homecoming Queens*. Palgrave, 2009.

Dinshaw, Carolyn. *Getting Medieval: Sexualities and Communities, Pre- and Postmodern*. Duke University Press, 1999.

Dinshaw, Carolyn, and Judith Halberstam. 'Theorising Queer Temporalities: A Roundtable Discussion'. *GLQ: A Journal of Lesbian and Gay Studies* 13, no. 2/3 (2007), 177–95.

Doan, Laura. *Disturbing Practices: History, Sexuality and Women's Experience of Modern War*. Chicago University Press, 2013.

Doan, Laura. 'Queer History / Queer Memory: The Case of Alan Turing'. *GLQ: A Journal of Lesbian and Gay Studies* 23, no. 1 (2017), 113–36.

Dodi, Simon. 'Camp Affections: Experiential Insights into British Camp Performance'. PhD diss., The Royal Central School of Speech and Drama, 2022.

Dollimore, Jonathan. *Sexual Dissidence: Augustine to Wilde, Freud to Foucault.* Clarendon, 1991.

Dover, Kenneth. *Greek Homosexuality.* 1978; Bloomsbury, 2016.

Duggan, Lisa. 'The Discipline Problem: Queer Theory Meets Lesbian and Gay History'. *GLQ: A Journal of Lesbian and Gay Studies* 2, no. 3 (1995), 179–91.

Duggan, Lisa. 'The New Homonormativity: The Sexual Politics of Neoliberalism'. In *Materializing Democracy: Toward a Revitalized Cultural Politics,* edited by Russ Castronovo and Dana D. Nelson. Duke University Press, 2002, 175–94.

Duberman, Martin, George Chauncey and Martha Vicinus. *Hidden from History: Reclaiming the Gay and Lesbian Past.* Meridian Books, 1990.

Dunn, Thomas R. *Queerly Remembered: Rhetorics for Representing the GLBTQ Past.* University of South Carolina Press, 2016.

Earls, Averill. *Love in the Lav: a social biography of same-sex desire in Ireland, 1922–1972.* Temple University Press, 2025.

Edelman, Lee. *No Future: Queer Theory and the Death Drive.* Duke University Press, 2004.

El-Tayeb, Fatima. '"Gays Who Cannot Properly Be Gay": Queer Muslims in the Neoliberal European City'. *European Journal of Women's Studies* 1, no. 19 (2012), 79–95.

Epprecht, Marc, Will Roscoe and Stephen O. Murray, eds. *Boy-Wives and Female Husbands: Studies in African Homosexuality.* State University of New York Press, 1998.

Escoffier, Jeffrey. *American Homo: Community and Perversity.* University of California Press, 1998.

Evans, Jennifer V. *The Queer Art of History.* Duke University Press, 2023.

Faderman, Lillian. *Surpassing the Love of Men.* 1981; Harper Collins, 1998.

Faderman, Lillian. *Scotch Verdict: Miss Pirie and Miss Woods v. Dame Cumming Gordon.* Morrow, 1983.

Faderman, Lillian, and Stuart Timmons. *Gay LA: A History of Sexual Outlaws, Power Politics and Lipstick Lesbians.* University of California Press, 2009.

Fellows, Will. *A Passion to Preserve: Gay Men as Keepers of Culture.* University of Wisconsin Press, 2004.

Fendandez-Cano, Moises. 'Unveiling Madrid: Queer Intimacies under Franco'. PhD diss., European University Institute, Florence, 2024.

Fernandez, André. 'The Repression of Sexual Behaviour by the Aragonese Inquisition between 1560 and 1700'. *Journal of the History of Sexuality* 7, no. 4 (1997), 469–501.

Fienberg, Leslie. *Transgender Warriors: Making History from Joan of Arc to Dennis Rodman*. Beacon Press, 1996.

Florêncio, João, and Ben Miller. 'Sexing the Archive: Gay Porn and Subcultural Histories'. *Radical History Review* 142 (2022), 133–41.

Foster, Jeannette. *Sex Variant Women in Literature: A Historical and Quantitative Study*. 1952; Naiad Press, 1985.

Frackman, Kyle. 'Homemade Pornography and the Proliferation of Queer Pleasure in East Germany'. *Radical History Review* 142 (2022), 93–109.

Freeman, Elizabeth. *Time Binds: Queer Temporalities, Queer Histories*. Duke University Press, 2010.

Fried, Lauren. 'A Material History of Trans Identity in UK Performance (1967–1990)'. PhD diss., Royal College of Art, 2019.

Foucault, Michel. *History of Sexuality, Volume 1: An Introduction*. Translated by Robert Hurley. Allen Lane, 1979.

La Fountain-Stokes, Lawrence *Queer Ricans: Cultures and Sexualities in the Diaspora*. University of Minnesota Press, 2009.

Gagnon, John H. and William Simon. *Sexual Conduct: The Social Sources of Human Sexuality*. Routledge, 1973.

Gallo, Marcia M. *Different Daughters: A History of the Daughters of Bilitis and the Rise of the Lesbian Rights Movement*. Seal Press, 2007.

Garber, Linda. 'Where in the World Are the Lesbians?' *Journal of the History of Sexuality* 14, no. 1/2 (2005), 28–50.

Garber, Marjorie B. *Vested Interests: Cross-Dressing & Cultural Anxiety*. Routledge, 1997.

Gardiner, Jill. *From the Closet to the Screen: Women and the Gateways Club, 1945–1985*. Pandora, 2003.

Gaudio, Rudolf Pell. *Allah Made Us: Sexual Outlaws in an Islamic African City*. Wiley, 2011.

Gelfand, Rachel. 'Between Archives: Yerushe, Intergenerational Collaboration, and Aging in Queer Family'. *Radical History Review* 139 (2021), 200–10.

Ghaziani, Amin. *Long Live Queer Nightlife: How the Closing of Gay Bar Sparked a Revolution*. Princeton University Press, 2024.

Gieseking, Jen Jack. 'Useful In/Stability: The Dialectical Production of the Social and Spatial Lesbian Herstory Archives'. *Radical History Review* 122 (2015), 25–37.

Gluckman, Amy and Betsy Reed, eds. *Homo Economics: Capitalism, Community, and Lesbian and Gay Life*. Routledge, 2012.

Gonda, Caroline, and Chris Roulston, eds. *Decoding Anne Lister: From the Archives to 'Gentleman Jack'*. Cambridge University Press, 2023.

Gorman-Murray, Andrew, and Matt Cook, eds. *Queering the Interior*. Routledge, 2020.

Gray, Mary L., Colin R. Johnson and Brian J. Gilley, eds. *Queering the Countryside: New Frontiers in Rural Queer Studies*. New York University Press, 2016.

Grosskurth, Phyllis. *John Addington Symonds: A Biography*. Longmans, Green and Co, 1964.

Gutterman, Lauren Jae. *Her Neighbor's Wife: A History of Lesbian Desire Within Marriage*. University of Pennsylvania Press, 2019.

Halberstam, Jack. 'Transgender Butch: Butch/FTM Border Wars and the Masculine Continuum'. *GLQ: A Journal of Lesbian and Gay Studies* 4, no. 2 (1998), 287–310.

Halberstam, Jack. *In a Queer Time and Place: Transgender Bodies, Subcultural Lives*. New York University Press, 2005.

Halperin, David. *Saint Foucault: Towards a Gay Hagiography*. Oxford University Press, 1997.

Halperin, David. *How to Do the History of Homosexuality*. University of Chicago Press, 2004.

Halperin, David, and John J. Winkler. *Before Sexuality: The Construction of Erotic Experience in the Ancient Greek World*. Princeton University Press, 1990.

Halperin, David, and Valerie Traub, eds. *Gay Shame*. University of Chicago Press, 2010.

Hanhardt, Christina B. *Safe Space: Gay Neighbourhood History and the Politics of Violence*. Duke University Press, 2020.

Harris, Victoria. 'Sex on the Margins: New Directions in the Historiography of Sexuality'. *The Historical Journal* 53, no. 4 (2010), 1085–1104.

Hartman, Saidiya V. *Wayward Lives, Beautiful Experiments: Intimate Histories of Riotous Black Girls, Troublesome Women, and Queer Radicals*. W. W. Norton, 2019.

Hawley, John C. *Postcolonial, Queer: Theoretical Intersections*. State University of New York Press, 2001.

Healey, Dan. *Russian Homophobia from Stalin to Sochi*. Bloomsbury, 2017.

Healey, Dan. 'Active, Passive, and Russian: The National Idea in Gay Men's Pornography'. *The Russian Review* 69, 2 (2010), 210–230.

Hellesund, Tone. 'Better than Orgasm: Sex, Authenticity and Intimacy in the New Women's Movement in Norway'. *Gender & History* 33, no. 1 (2021), 209–26.

Hester, Diarmaid. *Nothing Ever Just Disappears: Seven Hidden Histories*. Penguin, 2024.

Heyam, Kit. *Before We Were Trans: A New History of Gender*. Basic Books, 2022.

Higgs, David. *Queer Sites: Gay Urban Histories Since 1600*. Routledge, 1999.

Hinchy, Jessica. *Governing Gender and Sexuality in Colonial India: The Hijra, c.1850–1900*. Cambridge University Press, 2019.

Hinsch, Bret. *Passions of the Cut Sleeve: The Male Homosexual Tradition in China*. University of California Press, 1990.

Hobson, Emily. *Lavender and Red: Liberation and Solidarity in the Gay and Lesbian Left*. University of California Press, 2016.

Holmes, Kwame. 'What's the Tea: Gossip and the Production of Black Gay Social History'. *Radical History Review* 122 (2015), 55–69.

Houlbrook, Matt. 'Soldier Heroes and Rent Boys: Homosex, Masculinities, and Britishness in the Brigade of Guards, circa 1900–1960'. *Journal of British Studies* 42, no. 3 (2003), 351–88.

Houlbrook, Matt. *Queer London: Perils and Pleasures in the Sexual Metropolis, 1918–1957*. University of Chicago Press, 2005.

Howard, John. *Men Like That: A Southern Queer History*. University of Chicago Press, 1999.

Hulme, Tom. 'Queer Belfast During the First World War: Masculinity and Same-Sex Desire in the Irish City'. *Irish Historical Studies* 45, no. 168 (2021), 239–61.

Hyam, Ronald. *Empire and Sexuality: The British Experience*. Manchester University Press, 1990.

Hyde, H. Montgomery. *The Other Love. An Historical and Contemporary Survey of Homosexuality in Britain*. Heinemann, 1970.

Hyde, H. Montgomery. *The Trials of Oscar Wilde*. Dover, 1973.

Hyde, H. Montgomery. *The Cleveland Street Scandal*. W. H. Allen, 1976.

Jackson, Julian. *Living in Arcadia: Homosexuality, Politics, and Morality in France from the Liberation to AIDS*. University of Chicago Press, 2009.

Jagose, Annamarie. *Queer Theory*. Melbourne University Press, 1997.

Janes, Dominic. *Picturing the Closet: Male Secrecy and Homosexual Visibility in Britain*. Oxford University Press, 2015.

Janes, Dominic. *Visions of Queer Martyrdom from John Henry Newman to Derek Jarman*. University of Chicago Press, 2015.

Janes, Dominic, and Howard Chiang. *The Oxford Handbook of LGBTQ History*. Oxford University Press, 2026.

Jennings, Rebecca. *A Lesbian History of Britain: Love and Sex between Women since 1500*. Greenwood, 2007.

Jennings, Rebecca. '"It Was a Hot Climate and It Was a Hot Time": Lesbian Migration and Transnational Networks in the Mid-Twentieth Century'. *Australian Feminist Studies* 25, no. 63 (2010), 31–45.

Jennings, Rebecca. *Lesbian Intimacies and Family Life: Desire, Domesticity, and Kinship in Britain and Australia, 1945–2000*. Bloomsbury, 2024.

Jesperson, Jamey. 'Trans Misogyny in the Colonial Archive: Re-Membering Trans Feminine Life and Death in New Spain, 1604–1821'. *Gender & History* 36, no. 1 (2023), 91–111.

Johnson, Colin R. *Just Queer Folks: Gender and Sexuality in Rural America*. Temple University Press, 2013.

Johnson, E. Patrick. *Sweet Tea: Black Gay Men of the South*. University of North Carolina Press, 2008.

Johnson, E. Patrick. *Black. Queer. Southern. Women.* University of North Carolina Press, 2018.

Jones, Jennifer Dominique. 'Finding Home: Black Queer Historical Scholarship in the United States: Parts 1 and 2'. *History Compass* 17, no. 5 (2019).

Jones, Jennifer Dominique. *Ambivalent Affinities: A Political History of Blackness and Homosexuality after World War II.* University of North Carolina Press, 2023.

Joyce, Simon. 'Two Women Walk into a Theatre Bathroom: The Fanny and Stella Trials as Trans Narrative'. *Victorian Review* 44, no. 1 (2018), 83–98.

Joyce, Simon. *LGBTQ+ Victorians: Sexuality and Gender in the Nineteenth-Century Archives.* Oxford University Press, 2022.

Kadji, Amin. 'Taxonomically Queer? Sexology and New Queer, Trans, and Asexual Identities'. *GLQ: A Journal of Lesbian and Gay Studies* 29, no. 1 (2023), 91–107.

Kaplan, Morris B. 'Who's Afraid of John Saul? Urban Culture and the Politics of Desire in Late Victorian London'. *GLQ: A Journal of Lesbian and Gay Studies* 5, no. 3 (1999), 267–314.

Kaplan, Morris B. *Sodom on the Thames: Sex, Love, and Scandal in Wilde Times.* Cornell University Press, 2005.

Karras, Ruth Mazo. 'The Regulation of "Sodomy" in the Latin East and West'. *Speculum* 95, no. 4 (2020), 969–86.

Katz, Jonathan. *Gay American History: Lesbians and Gay Men in the U.S.A.: A Documentary.* Crowell, 1976.

Katz, Jonathan. *The Invention of Heterosexuality.* 1995; University of Chicago Press, 2007.

Kennedy, Elizabeth Lapovsky. 'Telling Tales: Oral History and the Construction of Pre-Stonewall Lesbian History'. *Radical History Review* 62 (1995), 59–79.

Kleiner, Catherine B. 'Doin' It for Themselves: Lesbian Land Communities in Southern Oregon, 1970–1995'. PhD diss., The University of New Mexico, 2003.

Korinek, Valerie J. *Prairie Fairies: A History of Queer Communities and People in Western Canada, 1930–1985.* University of Toronto Press, 2018.

Koskovich, Gerard. 'Displaying the Queer Past: Purposes, Publics, and Possibilities at the GLBT History Museum'. *QED: A Journal in GLBTQ Worldmaking* 1, no. 2 (2014), 61–78.

Koskovich, Gerard. 'The History of Queer History: One Hundred Years of the Search for Shared Heritage'. In *Preservation and Place: Historic Preservation by and of LGBTQ Communities in the United States,* edited by Katherine Crawford-Lackey and Megan E. Springate. Berghahn, 2019, 30–84.

Kosofsky Sedgwick, Eve. *Epistemology of the Closet.* Harvester Wheatsheaf, 1991.

Kosofsky Sedgwick, Eve. *Tendencies.* Routledge, 1994.

Kosofsky Sedgwick, Eve. *Between Men: English Literature and Male Homosocial Desire.* 1984; Columbia University Press, 2015.

Koven, Seth. *Slumming: Sexual and Social Politics in Victorian London.* Princeton University Press, 2004.

Kunzel, Regina. 'The Power of Queer History'. *The American Historical Review* 123, no. 5 (2018), 1560–82.

Kunzel, Regina. 'The Rise of Gay Rights and the Disavowal of Disability'. In *The Oxford Handbook of Disability History*, edited by Michael A. Rembis, Catherine J. Kudlick and Kim Nielsen. Oxford University Press, 2018, 459–76.

Kunzel, Regina. *Criminal Intimacy: Prison and the Uneven History of Modern American Sexuality.* University of Chicago Press, 2022.

Kunzel, Regina. *In the Shadow of Diagnosis: Psychiatric Power and Queer Life.* University of Chicago Press, 2024.

Lapovsky Kennedy, Elizabeth, and Madeline Davis. *Boots of Leather, Slippers of Gold: The History of a Lesbian Community.* Routledge, 1993.

Laqueur, Thomas. *Making Sex Body and Gender from the Greeks to Freud.* Harvard University Press, 1992.

Leeworthy, Daryl. *A Little Gay History of Wales.* University of Wales Press, 2019.

Lemmey, Huw, and Ben Miller. *Bad Gays: A Homosexual History.* Verso Books, 2022.

Lesbian History Group, ed. *Not a Passing Phase.* Women's Press, 1989.

Lewis, Abram J. 'I Am 64 and Paul McCartney Doesn't Care: The Haunting of the Transgender Archive and the Challenges of Queer History'. *Radical History Review* 120 (2014), 13–34.

Lewis, Brian, ed. *British Queer History: New Approaches and Perspectives.* Manchester University Press, 2013.

Liddington, Jill. 'Anne Lister of Shibden Hall, Halifax (1791–1840): Her Diaries and the Historians', *History Workshop* 35 (1993), 45–77.

Liddington, Jill. *As Good as a Marriage: The Anne Lister Diaries 1836–38.* Manchester University Press, 2023.

Long Chu, Andrea and Emmet Harsin Drager. 'After Trans Studies'. *TSQ: Transgender Studies Quarterly* 6, no. 1 (2019), 103–15.

Love, Heather. *Feeling Backward: Loss and the Politics of Queer History.* Harvard University Press, 2007.

Lvovsky, Anna. *Vice Patrol: Cops, Courts, and the Struggle over Urban Gay Life before Stonewall.* University of Chicago Press, 2021.

Macharia, Keguro. *Frottage: Frictions of Intimacy across the Black Diaspora.* New York University Press, 2019.

Manalánsan, Martin F. *Global Divas: Filipino Gay Men in the Diaspora.* Duke University Press, 2003.

Manion, Jen. *Female Husbands: A Trans History*. Cambridge University Press, 2020.

Marhoefer, Laurie. *Sex and the Weimar Republic: German Homosexual Emancipation and the Rise of the Nazis*. University of Toronto Press, 2015.

Marhoefer, Laurie. 'Was the Homosexual Made White? Race, Empire, and Analogy in Gay and Trans Thought in Twentieth-Century Germany'. *Gender & History* 31, no. 1 (2019), 91–114.

Marhoefer, Laurie. *Racism and The Making of Gay Rights: A Sexologist, His Student, and the Empire of Queer Love*. University of Toronto Press, 2022.

Martinez, María Elena. 'Archives, Bodies, and Imagination: The Case of Juana Aguilar and Queer Approaches to History, Sexuality, and Politics'. *Radical History Review* 120 (2014), 159–82.

Massad, Joseph Adoni. *Desiring Arabs*. University of Chicago Press, 2007.

Maynard, Steven. 'Through a Hole in the Lavatory Wall: Homosexual Subcultures, Police Surveillance, and the Dialectics of Discovery, Toronto, 1890–1930'. *Journal of the History of Sexuality* 5, no. 2 (1994), 207–42.

Maynard, Steven. 'Police/Archives'. *Archivaria* 68 (2009), 159–82.

McClive, C. 'Masculinity on Trial: Penises, Hermaphrodites and the Uncertain Male Body in Early Modern France'. *History Workshop Journal* 68, no. 1 (2009), 45–68.

McIntosh, Mary. 'The Homosexual Role'. *Social Problems* 16, no. 2 (1968), 182–92.

McKenna, Neil. *Fanny and Stella: The Young Men Who Shocked Victorian England*. Faber & Faber, 2013.

McKinney, Cait. 'Body, Sex, Interface: Reckoning with Images at the Lesbian Herstory Archives', *Radical History Review* 122 (2015), 115–28.

Meek, Jeffrey. *Queer Voices in Post-War Scotland: Male Homosexuality, Religion and Society*. Palgrave Macmillan, 2015.

Mikus, Francis John. 'The Road to an Integrated Homosexuality? A Comparative History of Same-Sex Marriage in France and the United Kingdom'. PhD diss., Queen Mary University of London, 2021.

Miller, Ben. 'In Search of Lost Time: Primitivist Homomythopoetics and the Self-Invention of the White Gay Man'. PhD diss., Freie Universität Berlin, 2024.

Mills, Robert. 'Theorizing the Queer Museum'. *Museums & Social Issues* 3, no. 1 (2008), 41–52.

Mills, Robert. *Seeing Sodomy in the Middle Ages*. University of Chicago Press, 2015.

Miranda, Deborah A. 'Extermination of the Joyas: Gendercide in Spanish California'. *GLQ: A Journal of Lesbian and Gay Studies* 16, no. 1/2 (2010), 253–84.

Mole, Richard, ed. *Soviet and Post-Soviet Sexualities* Routledge, 2019.

Mort, Frank. *Capital Affairs: London and the Making of the Permissive Society.* Yale University Press, 2010.

Mosse, George. *Nationalism and Sexuality: Respectability and Abnormal Sexuality in Modern Europe.* H.Fertig, 1985.

Mossakowski, Tomasz. '"The Sailors Dearly Love to Make Up": Cross-Dressing and Blackface during Polar Exploration'. PhD diss., King's College, London, 2015.

Moulton, Mo. '"Both Your Sexes': A Non-Binary Approach to Gender History, Trans Studies and the Making of the Self in Modern Britain". *History Workshop Journal* 95, no. 1 (2023), 75–100.

Moulton, Mo. 'Dogs in the Picture: Restoring the Queer History of the Irish Family'. *The History of the Family* 29, no. 1 (2024), 84–108.

Mumford, Kevin. *Not Straight, Not White: Black Gay Men from the March on Washington to the AIDS Crisis.* University of North Carolina Press, 2016.

Muñoz, José Esteban. *Disidentifications: Queers of Color and the Performance of Politics.* University of Minnesota Press, 1999.

Muñoz, José Esteban. *Cruising Utopia: The Then and There of Queer Futurity.* New York University Press, 2009.

Najmabadi, A. 'Beyond the Americas: Are Gender and Sexuality Useful Categories of Analysis?' *Journal of Women's History* 18, no. 1 (2006), 11–21.

Nardizzi, Vincent Joseph, Stephen Guy-Bray and Will Stockton, eds. *Queer Renaissance Historiography: Backward Gaze.* Ashgate, 2009.

Nestle, Joan. 'The Will to Remember: The Lesbian Herstory Archives of New York'. *Feminist Review* 34, no. 1 (1990), 86–94.

Newton, Esther. *Cherry Grove, Fire Island: Sixty Years in America's First Gay and Lesbian Town.* Beacon Press, 1993.

Norton, Rictor. *Mother Clap's Molly House: Gay Subculture in England 1700–1830.* GMP, 1992.

Okundaye, Jason. *Revolutionary Acts: Love and Brotherhood in Black Gay Britain.* Faber and Faber, 2024.

Oram, Alison. '"Embittered. Sexless or Homosexual": Attacks on Spinster Teachers'. In *Not a Passing Phase*, edited by Lesbian History Group. Women's Press, 1989, 99–118.

Oram, Alison. *Her Husband Was a Woman! Women's Gender-Crossing in Modern British Popular Culture.* Routledge, 2007.

Alison Oram and Matt Cook. *Prejudice and Pride: Celebrating LGBT Heritage.* National Trust, 2017.

Penn, Donna. 'Queer: Theorizing Politics and History'. *Radical History Review* 62 (1995), 24–43.

Pierce, Joseph M., María Amelia Viteri, Diego Falconí Trávez, Salvador Vidal-Ortiz and Lourdes Martínez-Echazábal. 'Introduction: *Cuir*/Queer

Américas: Translation, Decoloniality, and the Incommensurable'. *GLQ: A Journal of Gay and Lesbian Studies* 27, no. 3 (2021), 321–7.

Plaster, Joseph. *Kids on the Street: Queer Kinship and Religion in San Francisco's Tenderloin*. Duke University Press, 2023.

Porter, Roy, and Lesley Hall. *The Fact of Life: The Creation of Sexual Knowledge in Britain, 1650–1950*. Yale University Press, 1995.

Powell, Victoria. 'The Knight from Nowhere: A Biographical Case Study of Social Mobility in Victorian Britain'. PhD diss., Birkbeck, University of London, 2017.

Power, Lisa. *No Bath but Plenty of Bubbles: An Oral History of the Gay Liberation Front, 1970–1973*. Cassell, 1995.

Povinelli, Elizabeth A., and George Chauncey. 'Thinking Sexuality Transnationally: An Introduction'. *GLQ: A Journal of Lesbian and Gay Studies* 5, no. 4 (1999), 439–49.

Puar, Jasbir. *Terrorist Assemblages: Homonationalism in Queer Times*. Duke University Press, 2007.

Rao, Rahul. *Out of Time: The Queer Politics of Postcoloniality*. Oxford University Press, 2020.

Reade, Brian, ed. *Sexual Heretics: Male Homosexuality in English Literature from 1850 to 1900*. Routledge & Kegan Paul, 1970.

Reay, Barry. *Sex in the Archives: Writing American Sexual Histories*. Manchester University Press, 2018.

Reid-Pharr, Robert. *Black Gay Man: Essays*. New York University Press, 2001.

Reithmayr, Mori. 'Community before Liberation: Theorizing Gay Resistance in San Francisco, 1953–1969'. PhD diss., Oxford University, 2022.

Reithmayr, Mori. 'The Invention of Gay Community in San Francisco, 1960–1970', *The Historical Journal* (2025), 1–21.

Rich, Adrienne. 'Compulsory Heterosexuality and Lesbian Existence'. *Signs* 5, no. 4 (1980), 631–60.

Robenalt, Erica. *The Queer Museum: Radical Inclusion and Western Museology*. Taylor & Francis, 2024.

Robertson, Stephen. 'What's Law got to do with it? Legal Records and Sexual Histories'. *Journal of the History of Sexuality* 14, no. 1 (2005), 161–85.

Robinson, Lucy. 'Three Revolutionary Years: The Impact of the Counter Culture on the Development of the Gay Liberation Movement in Britain'. *Cultural and Social History* 3, no. 4 (2006), 445–71.

Robinson Rhodes, Martha. 'Bisexuality, Multiple-Gender-Attraction, and Gay Liberation Politics in the 1970s'. *Twentieth Century British History* 32, no. 1 (2021), 119–42.

Rocke, Michael. *Forbidden Friendships: Homosexuality and Male Culture in Renaissance Florence*. Oxford University Press, 1996.

Roper, Lyndal. *Oedipus and the Devil: Witchcraft, Sexuality, and Religion in Early Modern Europe*. Routledge, 1994.

Rosenfeld, Sophia *Common Sense: A Political History*. Harvard University Press, 2011.

Rossiter, Hannah. 'She's Always a Woman: Butch Lesbian Trans Women in the Lesbian Community'. *Journal of Lesbian Studies* 20, no. 1 (2016), 87–96.

Rowse, A. L. *Homosexuals in History: A Study of Ambivalence in Society, Literature and the Arts*. Weidenfeld and Nicolson, 1977.

Rubin, Gayle, with Judith Butler. 'Sexual Traffic: Interview'. In *Feminism Meets Queer Theory*, edited by Elizabeth Weed and Naomi Schor. Indiana University Press, 1997, 68–108, at 100–1.

Rubin, Gayle S. 'Thinking Sex: Notes for a Radical Theory of the Politics of Sexuality'. In *Culture, Society and Sexuality*, edited by Peter Aggleton and Richard Parker. Taylor & Francis, 1999, 143–78.

Rupp, Leila J. *Sapphistries: A Global History of Love Between Women*. New York University Press, 2011.

Ryan-Flood, Róisín, and Amy Tooth Murphy, eds. *Queering Desire: Lesbians, Gender and Subjectivity*. Routledge, 2024.

Rydström, Jens. '"Sodomitical Sins Are Threefold": Typologies of Bestiality, Masturbation, and Homosexuality in Sweden, 1880–1950'. *Journal of the History of Sexuality* 9, no. 3 (2000), 240–76.

Rydström, Jens, and Kati Mustola, *Criminally Queer: Homosexuality and Criminal Law in Scandinavia 1842–1999*. Aksant Academic Publishers, 2007.

Sandell, Richard, Rachael Lennon, Matt Smith and Anna Lincoln. *Prejudice and Pride: LGBTQ Heritage and its Contemporary Implications*. University of Leicester, 2018.

Schulman, Sarah. *Let the Record Show: A Political History of ACT UP New York, 1987–1993*. Farrar, Straus and Giroux, 2021.

Sears, Claire, *Arresting Dress: Cross-Dressing, Law, and Fascination in Nineteenth-Century San Francisco*. Duke University Press, 2015.

Sears, James. *Behind the Mask of the Mattachine: The Hal Call Chronicles and the Early Movement for Homosexual Emancipation*. Harrington Park Press, 2006.

Sedgwick, Eve Kosofsky. *Epistemology of the Closet*. Harvester Wheatsheaf, 1991.

Sedgwick, Eve Kosofsy. *Tendencies*. Routledge, 1994.

Sedgwick, Eve Kosofsky. *Between Men: English Literature and Male Homosocial Desire*. 1984; Columbia University Press, 2015.

Segal, Lynne. *Slow Motion: Changing Masculinities, Changing Men*. Virago, 1997.

Sequeira, Rovel. 'Show and Tell: Life History and Hijra Activism in India'. *Signs: Journal of Women in Culture and Society* 47, no. 2 (2022), 451–74.

Severs, George. *Radical ACTS: HIV/AIDS Activism in the Late Twentieth Century*. Bloomsbury, 2024.

Shaw, Julia. *Bi: The Hidden Culture, History, and Science of Bisexuality*. Canongate, 2022.

Sheffield, Rebecka Taves. 'The Bedside Table Archives: Archive Intervention and Lesbian Intimate Domestic Culture'. *Radical History Review* 120 (2014), 108–20.

Showalter, Elaine. *Sexual Anarchy: Gender and Culture at the Fin de Siècle*. Viking, 1990.

Sigal, Pete. *From Moon Goddesses to Virgins: The Colonization of Yucatecan Maya Sexual Desire*. University of Texas Press, 2000.

Sinfield, Alan. *Faultlines: Cultural Materialism and the Politics of Dissident Reading*. University of California Press, 1992.

Sinfield, Alan. *The Wilde Century: Effeminacy, Oscar Wilde and the Queer Moment*. Cassell, 1994.

Sinfield, Alan. *Shakespeare, Authority, Sexuality: Unfinished Business in Cultural Materialism*. Routledge: 2006.

Sinha, Mrinalini. *Colonial Masculinity: The 'Manly Englishman' and the 'Effeminate Bengali' in the Late Nineteenth Century*. Manchester University Press, 1995.

Skidmore, Emily. *True Sex: The Lives of Trans Men at the Turn of the Twentieth Century*. New York University Press, 2017.

Skidmore, Emily. 'Recovering a Gender-Transgressive Past: A Transgender Historiography'. In *A Companion to American Women's History*, edited by Nancy A. Hewitt and Anne M. Valk. 2nd edition. John Wiley & Sons, 2021, 209–22.

Smith, Helen. *Masculinity, Class and Same-Sex Desire in Industrial England, 1895–1957*. Palgrave Macmillan, 2015.

Smith, T. A. *Love in Earnest: Some Notes on the Lives and Writings of English 'Uranian' Poets from 1889 to 1930*. Routledge & Kegan Paul, 1970.

Smith-Rosenberg, Carroll. 'The Female World of Love and Ritual: Relations between Women in Nineteenth Century America'. *Signs* 1, no. 1 (1975), 1–29.

Snorton, C. Riley. *Black on Both Sides: A Racial History of Trans Identity*. University of Minnesota Press, 2017.

Somerville, Siobhan. 'Scientific Racism and the Emergence of the Homosexual Body'. *Journal of the History of Sexuality* 5, no. 2 (1994), 243–66.

Somerville, Siobhan. *Queering the Color Line: Race and the Invention of Homosexuality in American Culture*. Duke University Press, 2000.

Stanley, Jo, and Paul Baker, *Hello Sailor! The Hidden History of Gay Life at Sea*. Routledge, 2015.

Stein, Edward, ed. *Forms of Desire: Sexual Orientation and the Social Constructionist Controversy*. Routledge, 1992.

Stein, Marc. 'Theoretical Politics, Local Communities: The Making of U.S. LGBT Historiography'. *GLQ: A Journal of Lesbian and Gay Studies* 11, no. 4 (2005), 605–25.

Stein, Marc. 'Canonizing Homophile Sexual Respectability: Archives, History, and Memory'. *Radical History Review* 120 (2014), 53–73.

Stein, Marc. *Queer Public History: Essays on Scholarly Activism*. University of California Press, 2022.

Stewart-Winter, Timothy. *Queer Clout: Chicago and the Rise of Gay Politics*. University of Pennsylvania Press, 2016.

Stoler, Ann Laura. *Race and the Education of Desire: Foucault's History of Sexuality and the Colonial Order of Things*. Duke University Press, 1995.

Stryker, Susan. *Transgender History: The Roots of Today's Revolution*. 2nd edition. Seal Press, 2017.

Stryker, Susan, and Aren Aizura, eds. *The Transgender Studies Reader 2*. Taylor & Francis, 2006.

Stryker, Susan, and Dylan Macarthy, eds. *The Transgender Studies Reader Remix*. Routledge, 2023.

Stryker, Susan, Paisley Currah and Lisa Jean Moore. 'Introduction: Trans-, Trans, or Transgender?' *Women's Studies Quarterly* 36, no. 3/4 (2008), 11–22.

Sweet, James H. 'Male Homosexuality and Spiritualism in the African Diaspora: The Legacies of a Link'. *Journal of the History of Sexuality* 7, no. 2 (1996), 184–202.

Tamagne, Florence. *A History of Homosexuality in Europe: Berlin, London, Paris, 1919–1939*. Algora, 2004.

Terry, Jennifer. *An American Obsession: Science, Medicine, and Homosexuality in Modern Society*. University of Chicago Press, 1999.

Tiemeyer, Phil. *Plane Queer: Labor, Sexuality, and AIDS in the History of Male Flight Attendants*. University of California Press, 2013.

Timm, Annette F. *Gender, Sex and the Shaping of Modern Europe: A History from the French Revolution to the Present Day*. Bloomsbury, 2016.

Timmons, Stuart. *The Trouble with Harry Hay: Founder of the Modern Gay Movement*. Alyson, 1990.

Tinsley, Omise'eke Natasha. 'Black Atlantic, Queer Atlantic: Queer Imaginings of the Middle Passage'. *GLQ: A Journal of Lesbian and Gay Studies* 14, no. 2/3 (2008), 191–215.

Tortorici, Zeb. *Sins Against Nature: Sex and Archives in Colonial New Spain*. Duke University Press, 2018.

Tosh, Will. *Straight Acting: The Many Queer Lives of William Shakespeare*. Sceptre, 2024.

Traub, Valerie. *The Renaissance of Lesbianism in Early Modern England*. Cambridge University Press, 2002.

Traub, Valerie. 'The New Unhistoricism in Queer Studies'. *PMLA* 128, no. 1 (2013), 21–39.

Traub, Valerie. *Thinking Sex with the Early Moderns*. University of Pennsylvania Press, 2016.

Trumbach, Randolph. 'Sex, Gender, and Sexual Identity in Modern Culture: Male Sodomy and Female Prostitution in Enlightenment London'. *Journal of the History of Sexuality* 2, no. 2 (1991), 186–203.

Trumbach, Randolph. *Sex and the Gender Revolution, Volume 1: Heterosexuality and the Third Gender in Enlightenment London*. University of Chicago Press, 1998.

Turner, Mark W. *Backward Glances: Cruising the Queer Streets of New York and London*. Reaktion, 2003.

Tyburczy, Jennifer. *Sex Museums: The Politics and Performance of Display*. University of Chicago Press, 2016.

Umphrey, M. 'The Trouble with Harry Thaw'. *Radical History Review* 62 (1995), 9–23.

Ung Loh, Jennifer, and J. Daniel Luther, eds. *'Queer' Asia: Decolonising and Reimagining Sexuality and Gender*. Zed Books, 2019.

Upchurch, Charles. *Before Wilde: Sex Between Men in Britain's Age of Reform*. University of California Press, 2009.

Upchurch, Charles. *'Beyond the Law': The Politics Ending the Death Penalty for Sodomy in Britain*. Temple University Press, 2021.

Upchurch, Charles. 'Following Anne Lister: Continuity and Queer History Before and After the Late Nineteenth Century'. *Journal of Lesbian Studies* 26, no. 4 (2022), 400–414.

Vakoch, Douglas, ed. *Transgender India: Understanding Third Gender Identities and Experiences*. Springer, 2022.

van der Meer, Theo. 'Tribades on Trial: Female Same-Sex Offenders in Late Eighteenth-Century Amsterdam'. *Journal of the History of Sexuality* 1, no. 3 (1991), 424–45.

Van Doorn, Niels. 'The Fabric of Our Memories: Leather, Kinship, and Queer Material History'. *Memory Studies* 9, no. 1 (2016), 85–98.

Vanita, Ruth. *Love Rites: Same-sex Marriage in India and the West*. Palgrave Macmillan, 2005.

Vicinus, Martha. 'Distance and Desire: English Boarding-School Friendships'. *Signs* 9, no. 4 (1984), 600–22.

Vicinus, Martha. '"They Wonder to Which Sex I Belong": The Historical Roots of the Modern Lesbian Identity'. *Feminist Studies* 18, no. 3 (1992), 467–97.

Vicinus, Martha. *Intimate Friends: Women Who Loved Women, 1798–1928*. Chicago University Press, 2006.

Vicinus, Martha. 'The History of Lesbian History'. *Feminist Studies* 38, no. 3 (2012), 566–96.

Vider, Stephen. *The Queerness of Home: Gender, Sexuality, and the Politics of Domesticity after World War II*. University of Chicago Press, 2022.

Vincent, John. *LGBT People and the UK Cultural Sector: The Response of Libraries, Museums, Archives and Heritage since 1950*. Routledge, 2016.

Warner, Michael. *Fear of a Queer Planet: Queer Politics and Social Theory*. University of Minnesota Press, 1993.

Waters, Chris. 'Havelock Ellis, Sigmund Freud and the State: Discourses of Homosexual Identity in Interwar Britain'. In *Sexology in Culture: Labelling Bodies and Desires*, edited by Lucy Bland and Laura L. Doan. Polity, 1998, 165–79.

Weeks, Jeffrey. *Coming Out: Homosexual Politics in Britain from the Nineteenth Century to the Present*. Quartet Books, 1977.

Weeks, Jeffrey. *The World We Have Won: The Remaking of Erotic and Intimate Life*. Routledge, 2007.

Weeks, Jeffrey. 'Queer(y)Ing the "Modern Homosexual"'. *Journal of British Studies* 51, no. 3 (2012), 523–39.

Weeks, Jeffrey. *Sex, Politics and Society: The Regulations of Sexuality since 1800*. 3rd edition. Longman, 2012.

Weeks, Jeffrey. *What Is Sexual History?* John Wiley, 2016.

Weeks, Jeffrey. *Sexuality and its Discontents: Meanings, Myths, and Modern Sexualities*. Taylor & Francis, 2022.

West, Khalil. 'Race, Pleasure and Ruin: Transatlantic Oral Histories of Black Queer Men Who Do Sex Work'. *The Black Scholar: Journal of Black Studies and Research* 53, no. 3/4 (2023), 19–28.

West, Khalil. 'Dark Matter: Sociality, Space, and the Haptics of Queer (Il)legibility in 'Black Liverpool', 1967–1997'. PhD diss., European University Institute, Florence, 2025.

White, Heather. *Reforming Sodom: Protestants and the Rise of Gay Rights*. University of North Carolina Press, 2015.

White, Melissa Autumn. 'Archives of Intimacy and Trauma: Queer Migration Documents as Technologies of Affect'. *Radical History Review* 120 (2014), 75–93.

Wiegman, Robyn. 'The Anatomy of Lynching'. *Journal of the History of Sexuality* 3, no. 3 (1993), 445–67.

Wieringa, Saskia, and Horacio Federico Sívori, eds. *The Sexual History of the Global South: Sexual Politics in Africa, Asia, and Latin America*. Zed Books, 2013.

Williams, Craig A. *Roman Homosexuality: Ideologies of Masculinity in Classical Antiquity*. Oxford University Press, 1999.

Woods, Gregory. *Homintern: How Gay Culture Liberated the Modern World*. Yale University Press, 2016.

Wotherspoon, Garry. *City of the Plain: History of Gay Subculture*. Hale & Iremonger, 1991.

X, Ajamu, Topher Campbell and Mary Stevens. 'Love and Lubrication in the Archives, or rukus!: A Black Queer Archive for the United Kingdom'. *Archivaria* 68 (2010), 271–94.

Yao, Xine. *Disaffected: The Cultural Politics of Unfeeling in Nineteenth-Century America*. Duke University Press, 2021.

Young, Neil J. *Coming Out Republican: A History of the Gay Right*. University of Chicago Press, 2024.

Index

Note: this index includes selected scholars and historical figures discussed in the book but does not include all names mentioned.